A Guide to
Econometric
Methods for the
Energy-Growth Nexus

A Guide to Econometric Methods for the Energy-Growth Nexus

Angeliki Menegaki

*Agricultural University of Athens, Athens (Campus of Amfissa),
Greece*

ELSEVIER

ACADEMIC PRESS
An imprint of Elsevier

Academic Press is an imprint of Elsevier
125 London Wall, London EC2Y 5AS, United Kingdom
525 B Street, Suite 1650, San Diego, CA 92101, United States
50 Hampshire Street, 5th Floor, Cambridge, MA 02139, United States
The Boulevard, Langford Lane, Kidlington, Oxford OX5 1GB, United Kingdom

Notices
Knowledge and best practice in this field are constantly changing. As new research and experience
broaden our understanding, changes in research methods, professional practices, or medical treatment
may become necessary.

Practitioners and researchers must always rely on their own experience and knowledge in evaluating
and using any information, methods, compounds, or experiments described herein. In using such
information or methods they should be mindful of their own safety and the safety of others, including
parties for whom they have a professional responsibility.

To the fullest extent of the law, neither the Publisher nor the authors, contributors, or editors, assume
any liability for any injury and/or damage to persons or property as a matter of products liability,
negligence or otherwise, or from any use or operation of any methods, products, instructions, or ideas
contained in the material herein.

Library of Congress Cataloging-in-Publication Data
A catalog record for this book is available from the Library of Congress

British Library Cataloguing-in-Publication Data
A catalogue record for this book is available from the British Library

ISBN 978-0-12-819039-5

For information on all Academic Press publications
visit our website at https://www.elsevier.com/books-and-journals

Publisher: Brian Romer
Editorial Project Manager: Andrea Dulberger
Production Project Manager: Selvaraj Raviraj
Cover Designer: Alan Studholme

Typeset by SPi Global, India

Working together
to grow libraries in
developing countries

www.elsevier.com • www.bookaid.org

This book is dedicated to my Pantelis and Foteini for keeping me happy and motivated!

Contents

Preface

This is a reference and advice book for junior energy-growth researchers. It summarizes key knowledge and applications with case studies that can serve as a quick reminder of the methodologies and tools used in the energy-growth nexus. Having additional aid at the beginning can save one valuable time to speed up later. Keep this book at your work station.

An editorial and an introduction to the economics of the energy-growth nexus: Current challenges for applied and theoretical research

1 Introduction

Since 1972, the report of the Club of Rome has made clear the fact that resources will not last forever and has paved the road for a more environmental friendly way of treatment of the natural and energy resources to leave behind the amount of resources that our offspring are also entitled to. Much later the financial crisis of 2007 endorsed these findings and has morally and psychologically obliged every citizen of this earth to consider a sustainable way of life as a priority and a movement away from consumption and materialism. The latter will also reduce energy consumption together with greenhouse gas emissions. As additional developing countries have embarked on the road of industrialization and a new middle class has been shaped and is still being shaped in many countries, the demand for energy is bound to increase, particularly at a moment that still a considerable number of world population live below the line of poverty and on top of that energy poverty.

According to Kramer et al. (2015), while the daily energy needs per person are about 50–100 Gigajoules, this amount goes up to 175 Gigajoules in Japan, which is a quite energy-efficient country. Conversely the United States appears to be a consumerist and squandering country with 300 Gigajoules per person, and this shows the energy inequality across the world and the unequal participation in the production of greenhouse emissions. This has a negative impact on our common environment. The same authors estimate that for everybody on earth to live a decent life, we are going to need a double quantity of energy from the one we use today.

The need for more energy goes together with the need for less carbon emissions and the need to combat climate change. The Kyoto Protocol in 1997, the Montreal protocol for the elimination of ozone-depleting chlorofluorocarbons and hydro chlorofluorocarbons in 1989, and the Copenhagen Agreement in 2009 all of them manifested a need for global decision power and coordination in the curtailment of the emissions problem with a view to combat climate change.

A Guide to Econometric Methods for the Energy-Growth Nexus. https://doi.org/10.1016/B978-0-12-819039-5.00016-1

It is important to make countries think and plan long term instead of short term for their immediate political interests. The replacement of fossil fuels with renewable energies is not a straightforward solution. It gives countries independence, but new dependences are born, since significant raw material is required for their infrastructure to be built and to cope with energy security as a whole. The latter cannot let fossil fuel energy go away soon, due to geopolitical risks; there must always be some percentage of energy supply in the fossil fuel form for the sake of diversification.

A great deal of coordination between different countries and even among different people and households within the same society will be necessary so that the maximum is achieved for individual and social utility. With increased opportunities to go-off grid and each household to become the producer of its own energy, this means that a large number of players must be coordinated. Foremost, today's choice to decarbonize entails the implementation of long-to-build infrastructure, sometimes longer than the duration of a typical political cycle. To overcome political myopia, countries must establish statutory targets bound by a solid legal framework that will guarantee the full implementation of relevant projects, irrespective of which new government will be elected each time. Energy conservation and the adoption of a low-carbon economy may involve a period of creative destruction, which entails that the structure of the economy must be renewed before the economy can move forward.

After this brief introduction (Section 1), the rest of the chapter is structured as follows: Section 2 discusses trends and scenarios for global energy, Section 3 presents policies for decarbonization, Section 4 offers renewable energy and energy efficiency opportunities, Section 5 provides the fundamentals of oil production and the natural gas economics, Section 5 discusses nuclear energy challenges, Section 6 comments on energy security, and Section 7 provides a separate overview of energy and social injustice and development. Section 8 offers some concluding remarks.

2 Trends and scenarios in global energy

Nowadays, we have to face a dual challenging reality: the rising energy demand and the requirement for reduction of greenhouse emissions. The energy sector is characterized by a major transition in any perceived direction, namely, political, economic, and technological. There are many scenarios circulating in literature, and each one makes its own predictions based on different starting assumptions. Next, we summarize the essentials of three energy scenarios globally.

2.1 The Statkraft scenario

Statkraft (2018) predicts further adoption of renewable energies with a subsequent reduction in its cost. This will guarantee a low-carbon electricity provision for all sectors of an economy: industry, households, transport, buildings etc. This scenario predicts a reduction of 2°C in the global temperature by 2040, which will be a consequence of lower carbon emissions, due to the increased adoption of renewable. If policy makers solve the problem of intermittency in renewables, the way toward a completely renewable electricity generation is paved with less difficulty.

The most important points of the 2040 scenario setup by Statkraft (2018) is that the power sector will reach a renewable energy participation of about 70%, of which 30% will be solar and 20% will be wind. As a consequence of the lower emissions by 30% than today's level, the 2°C reduction in temperature will be feasible. Countries with a great share of solar power will require a greater level of short-term flexibility, due to their high share of intermittent generation. India is expected to have a quite large share of this flexibility, which will be up to 80%. Countries with a high share of wind energy such as Germany and the United Kingdom will require a higher level of long-term flexibility, lasting about 2 weeks. Flexibility refers to being able to make swift changes in production and consumption at any time so that there is balance in the power system.

Global power plant retirements exceeded 25GW in 2017, and investments in renewable energy generation plants will continue to outnumber the fossil fuel ones. The transition toward renewables will affect global trade terms and energy dependence relations. Since a nontrivial percentage of global population remains with no access to electricity, the increasing living standards will lead to an energy demand increase by 2.4% annually, until the benchmark year of this scenario study, namely, 2040. However, the progress in energy efficiency that is expected to occur will make this energy demand less intense. In the transport sector the demand of electric cars will increase exponentially, and this will be strengthened by the lower cost of batteries and their technology progress that will be materialized through time. In the industry sector the velocity of change depends on the type of industry. For example, for industry sectors that require high-temperature thermal processes, the most possible solution will probably be hydrogen from electrolysis of natural gas with carbon capture and storage.

Flexibility will give markets the signals to adapt their demand and supply, since a differential price scheme will be applicable in any case to encourage market clearing. Furthermore, different climatic conditions applicable in different countries and different starting points present in the progress of renewable energies will require that each country utilizes a different plan to make its flexibility plan to work. Next, we discuss two other scenarios, one by BP and Shell.

2.2 The BP scenario

The BP highlights the correlation of economic development and energy consumption, and this largely justifies the requirement for additional energy-growth nexus research to take place in the future. According to the United Nations, the Human Development Index increases up to 100 Gigajoules per head. This translates into a very important conclusion. When consumption per head goes beyond that point, it does not contribute to growth, and policy making should concentrate on policy measures that boost energy efficiency, so that this threshold is not crossed.

The BP states that it builds its scenarios around the concept of the evolving transition (BP, 2019). Countries that thrived as fossil energy producers will have to adapt to a new reality, while the natural gas is a new actor in the energy scene. Foremost, energy consumption is monitored more efficiently and smartly through new digital technologies, which will favor the dissemination of information through more competitive markets.

First of all, with respect to the 2040 horizon, BP predicts that GDP will have doubled. Energy demand will also increase, and this increase will be driven by one-third by the newly developed Asian countries such as India and China. However, BP predicts that even after this rise in income and energy demand, still a significant proportion of global population will remain deprived of energy. Industry and the building sector will remain major players who will absorb about 70% of the energy increase. On the other hand the transport sector will be more reserved in its consumption, due to the gains from vehicle energy efficiency caused by new technologies of hybrid cars and the new trend for increased usage of mass transportation. BP also predicts that renewables will account for about half of energy supplies by 2040.

Since it does not grow fast enough though, the demand for coal energy will also increase. Despite the huge replacement of fossil fuels with renewable energies, carbon emissions will keep increasing, and this increase will be about 10% by 2040. The BP scenario also highlights the ban of single use plastics and the start of their complete elimination from 2040 onward. BP also predicts that the increased prosperity and the autonomous vehicles will contribute to the increase of traffic congestion phenomena. As a result of increased efficiency, however, the emissions from the transport sector are reduced.

According to this scenario, depending on the rate of technology evolution and the rate of retirement of power plants, there are four possible future outcomes with respect to the employed share of renewables and the carbon emissions in the power sector. Thus as far as technology is concerned, the rate of adoption for renewable energies ranges from 29% to 36% (fast technology adoption). Depending on the rate of power plant retirement, the adoption of renewable energies ranges from 29% to 34% (this is the fastest rate of retirement). In the case of the fastest retirement of power plants, depending on the technology progress, carbon emissions reduction range from 12.1 to 9.9 Gt. In the case of the fastest technology progress, carbon emission reduction ranges from 11.9 to 9.9 Gt. Overall the growth of renewables will be favored by fast technology and fast retirement of power plants. The former depends on the amount of effort and means placed on R&D, while the latter depends on the age of the plant and of the assets, which cannot be scrapped unless they are not productive anymore. Also, there is an estimation of the future carbon price to escalate to about $200/t by 2040. The share of coal will thus decline from today's 40%–5% by 2040, but it will remain a popular fossil fuel for India, which will be growing rapidly until 2040.

The position of energy producing countries is worth investigating because it affects international trade and alters the terms of trade. According to BP, Russia will remain the largest exporter of gas and oil, but its energy production declines. The first position is also facilitated, because Russia is a slow growth consumer. On the other hand the United States has been the largest energy producer until 2020, but this will not continue so until 2040, because the production of tight oil stabilizes and declines. China will be the leader in energy production, driven particularly by renewable energy and nuclear energy, despite its adjustment for a more sustainable rate of economic growth. The position of Middle East remains pivotal, and this is aided by gas production in Qatar. If Middle East economies reform their economies and reduce their dependence on oil production, then, as there will be less pressure on oil demand, the supply will be delivered at cheaper prices and in more competitive markets. BP also describes a rapid transition scenario, which will be dictated by greater efficiency, fuel switching, and the use of carbon capture and utilization. For example, in this rapid transition scenario, the carbon capture and utilization are used mostly in the power sector and the industry and will capture almost 4.5 Gt of CO_2 emissions by 2040. Renewables will account for 30% of primary energy and oil and gas together for 50% of the primary energy.

While carbon emissions will be inevitable to produce, the challenge may lie in focusing in the reduction of those emissions that are the hardest to abate. For example, it is easier to electrify cars in the transport sector, but much harder to electrify aviation. Difficulty in abatement relies either in the necessity of high temperatures or the fact that in some processes, carbon emission is inherent. The latter applies for iron and steel, cement and chemical production processes, etc. Overall, to further reduce energy consumption, there must be an appropriate blending among initiatives in resource efficiency, the employment of low-carbon energy sources and the carbon storage and removal.

Each of these actions can be implemented again with another mixture of strategies. For example, the resource efficiency can be implemented with recycling and reusing through the principles of circular economy, the adoption of energy efficiency technologies and the digitalization technologies, and other support material that will reconcile energy demand and supply with higher accuracy. And the lower carbon energy sources initiative can be implemented through the increased decarbonization of the power sector, hydrogen and bioenergy usage increase, the larger penetration of renewable with a supporting technology on grid interconnections, the demand side management accuracy, and energy storage capabilities.

The continuing consumption of gas, coal, and oil should be accompanied with carbon capture utilization initiatives. Before closing this short presentation of the BP scenario for future energy trends, it is worthy reporting what the self-evaluation and self-judgement BP does for its own scenario. This scenario falls within the range of other external anticipations about energy demand. Thus, while this range of anticipated demands lies between 0.9% and 1.3% yearly, the BP scenario makes a forecast of 1.2%, namely, quite close to the upper end. The BP scenario also forecast an oil demand growth equal to 0.3% yearly, which is more conservative than other external forecasts, while at the same time makes a more optimistic forecast for natural gas. BP finally comments that making predictions about renewable energies or nuclear energy encloses in itself high uncertainty due to the difficulty in predicting policy support and the evolution of technology, which will favor the development of renewables and/or safe nuclear energy with a higher speed. However, they assign top optimistic prospects for renewable and the lowest for nuclear energy (Table 1).

2.3 The shell energy scenario

The shell energy scenario is centered on the pillars of population, economic growth, environmental pressures, technology, resource availability, and people's choices with totally 75 different specific scenario-based inputs from them. The produced scenarios are evaluated based on historic and current trends, existent plans, and projections by experts.

Shell recognized income and prices as the two most important factors that determine energy demand.

Table 1 Key figures based on the evolving transition BP energy scenario.

	% Yearly change	
Basic macroenergy economics figures	**1995–2017**	**2017–40**
GDP (trillion US$ PPP)	3.7	3.2
Population (billion)	1.2	0.9
GDP per capita (thousand US$)	2.4	2.3
Energy intensity (toe per US$m)	−1.5	−1.9
Net CO_2 emissions (Gt of CO_2)	1.9	0.3
Primary energy (by fuel)		
Oil	1.3	0.3
Gas	2.5	1.7
Coal	2.4	−0.1
Nuclear	0.6	1.1
Hydro	2.2	1.3
Renewable energies	12.3	7.1
Primary energy (by end-use sector)		
Transport	2.3	1.0
Industry	2.0	1.1
Noncombusted	2.4	1.7
Buildings	2.0	1.5
Of which: inputs to power	2.6	2.0

Adapted from BP, 2019. BP Energy Outlook, 2019 Edition, Available from: https://www.bp.com/content/dam/bp/business-sites/en/global/corporate/pdfs/energy-economics/energy-outlook/bp-energy-outlook-2019.pdf, Accessed 29/02/2020.

The so-called energy ladder refers to the situation when, as people become richer, they consume more energy. The energy ladder may sometimes be explained by the effective prices, and hence, this is one of the reasons that energy ladders are country specific. To begin with, total primary energy is defined as the total quantity of the consumed energy sources in a country. However, the end-users such as households or other do not directly buy these sources, but they rather buy their carriers such as electricity or liquid fuels. Thus total final consumption is defined as the demand for energy carriers by end-users. The energy ladder is supposed to have an S-curve with inflection points at 4000 USD per capita and 15,0000 USD per capita, meaning that when people reach the former level of income, they start increasing their consumption and when they reach the latter level, they somehow stabilize their consumption due to saturation effects.

End-user choices for energy carriers constitute a very interesting topic both for energy producing companies and for the policy makers. According to Shell International BV (2017), the end users pay attention and weigh a series of factors such as prices, energy security, and relevant policies. Shell makes predictions on the usage of certain fuels and their consumption trend by several countries, which will be significant consumers up to the horizons of 2040 and 2060 because of their significant economic growth. These numbers are not reported here in detail for space consideration reasons, and the interested reader could refer directly to the source (Shell International BV, 2017). The following part presents and discusses policies for decarbonization.

3 Policies for decarbonization

Paris Agreement requires the increase in global average temperature to be well below 2°C above preindustrial levels. Decarbonization can take place either through low or no carbon emitting technologies in energy production or by foregoing consumption. Since 2008, levies to electricity have increased to contribute to their cost being recovered through markets. However, this fiscal treatment makes renewables less competitive in comparison with fossil fuels. Robinson et al. (2017) recommend that to successfully implement decarbonization and also to favor all alternatives equally, the policies must be better aligned to this target. Since, for example, transport and buildings account for 60% of greenhouse gas emissions in Europe, it is natural to require that the focus in Europe is prioritized to these most difficult directions. They are regarded as difficult because they have to do with decisions from the household and the individual, but at the same time, they imply huge expenditures on new infrastructure. According to Bataille et al. (2018), efforts to limit the temperature increase to 1.5°C require global greenhouse gas emissions to reach net-zero and probably negative increases by 2055–80.

Tagliapetra (2018) describes and discusses the consequences of decarbonization in economies whose GDP relies much on fossil fuel production, such as Middle East counties or the broader MENA region. This percentage is about 40% of the GDP, and even the nonoil produced GDP is somehow and indirectly related to oil production. According to Meinshausen et al. (2009), they report that the cumulative amount of carbon emissions that need to be curtailed between 2011 and 2050 is about 1100 Gigatones and this reduction corresponds to a 50% chance of keeping the global temperature below 2°C. Furthermore, according to McGlade and Ekins (2015), 50% of gas reserves and about 80% of coal reserves currently must remain unused to reach the target of temperature reduction by 2°C. With this figures, it can be clearly understood that economies, which rely so heavily on fossil fuel production and export, need a radical restructuring and a new sociopolitical contract to comply with this targets.

Regarding the policies that are used for decarbonization, these broadly include carbon pricing, subsidies, support for green R&D, and green technology deployment. Not all measures have been successful at all times, and each country has its own story in their development. After all, there is a wider range of instruments that can be applied such as research support, subsidies, tax rebates, loan guarantees, and direct mandates for renewables. According to Meckling et al. (2017), these measures, to produce the best possible outcome, should also come at a certain sequence. This sequence will lead to a progressive tightening of environmental regulation without the risk of being opposed from the stakeholders. The policy that should come first is the green technology support. This entails early high subsidies that can easily be pulled back when the situation becomes mature and the technology has been widely accepted. Withdrawal is not easy with other measures, because they become deeper rooted from an institutional and legal point of view. On the other hand, feed-in tariffs and clean energy support schemes do not guarantee emission cuts. Carbon pricing is the second stage in the sequence and was introduced by countries that had already established high fuel taxes and could basically serve as a backstop measure to avoid sliding back to unsustainable practices. The third instrument is the deployment of green technology. Thus it is advisable that the available decarbonization policies are connected, in a proper sequence, in a way that it has been shown empirically to be fruitful. Thus tying green subsidies to revenues from a carbon tax or auctions in cap-and-trade systems gives low-carbon energy firms direct incentives to support a tightening of carbon prices (Meckling et al., 2017). Afterward, establishing the gradual increase in the tax rate could end in a ratcheting up effect, and the 5-year review periods required by Paris agreement in decentralized international climate architecture will lead to no dead ends or "lock in" of valuable social resources. Moreover, they must be cost-effective and not excessive rent seeking. Last, countries should derive best examples from successful entities such as the EU and California. Their success was much relied on the fact that they first supplied benefits to clean energy contingencies before imposing costs on polluters.

The promotion of decarbonization measures is not always an easy task, because there are still many people who do not have access to electricity or they cannot afford energy and this imposes a life in energy deprivation. Some governments regard the implementation of affordability as a priority that should be implemented before any decarbonization takes place. For example, in Australia, decarbonization measures have come to a dead end, despite the government's understanding to curtail emissions. East Australia has suffered the worst wildfires due to persistent droughts, which have been the worst in the past 60 years and are largely attributed to climate change. The fact that energy affordability must be set as a priority in front of emissions cuts has been confirmed though the revision of the government energy guarantee package from which the government removed the requirements that the carbon emissions produced from the power section should be reduced by 26% (based on 2005 levels) until the year 2030 (EnergyPress, 2018).

Europe is the third largest emitter, but it has the most ambitious carbon emission scheme (to cut emissions by 40% by 2030 compared with 1990 levels). There are about 11,000 power plants in Europe, and they are obliged to buy a permit for every tone of carbon they produce. The system has not been a success because of the large surplus of the permits and their low price due to the financial crisis in Europe. A solution that has been suggested for the improvement of the inefficiencies of the system is the annual reduction of the emission allowances that are auctioned through the granting of pollution permits (European Parliament, 2018).

3.1.1 Decarbonization as direct air capture (DAC)

This new method suggests a sustainable way of decarbonization, but research is required to decide about its economic feasibility. The idea involves capturing carbon, concentrate it, and store it in pressurized from (Okesola et al., 2018). It is not the business as usual (BAU) process, where carbon dioxide is selected at the point of production such as an industry or a power plant or other producer. It is ideal for cleaning of various smaller producers (distributed sources of production), such as cars with their exhaust fumes or other fossil fuelled energy equipment. Capturing carbon occurs through a chemical or a biological process. The cost of direct air capture reported in literature is in the range of $100/tC and $500/tC ($27/tCO$_2$–$136/tCO$_2$) as stated in Ranjan (2010).

4 Renewable energies and energy efficiency opportunities

Quite as early as in 1896, a Swedish scientist named Svante Arrhenius had warned about the fossil fuels causing global warming (Renewable Resources Co, 2016). However, the intensive pursuit of clean energies started much later, in 1979 after the first oil crisis (CRES.gr, 2020), and nowadays the most important forms of them are the wind energy, the solar energy, hydraulic energy, biomass energy, geothermal energy, ocean energy from tides and waves, the osmosis energy (from mixing the fresh with sea water), etc.

Renewable energies are bound to increase, and fossil fuels will be reduced in energy production. Thus the impact on the global warming will be reduced, and public health will also be improved because the reduction of greenhouse emissions will not lessen its part in the contribution of respiratory and other problems due to air pollution in big cities. Foremost, both wind and solar energy (active systems, passive systems, and bioclimatic architecture and solar panel systems) do not contaminate water resources, something that fossil fuel extraction does. The latter occurs because for instance, both coal extraction and natural gas pipeline establishment run the possibility of water resource contamination.

Furthermore, hydroelectricity with carbon combustion and natural gas may require the usage of water for their freezing processes. However, power stations that work with geothermal energy and biomass may also require huge amounts of water resources, and this may harm the water balance in the area of operation. Last, hydrogen is going to be an important renewable energy type in the future, since it constitutes 90% of the universe. Since one of the most important drawbacks of renewable energies is the mismatch between production and demand and how the surplus renewable energy can be stored to be used at a different time, the solution of batteries has emerged as one solution.

However, a more recent solution is hydrogen storage. The production of hydrogen occurs through electrolysis, and its cost will be competitive to batteries (Maggio et al., 2019). Besides their renewable and nonpolluting nature, other benefits of renewable energies are their local nature, which supports the energy security of each country and does not require a high burden of the infrastructure and transport cost. Most of the times, their cost is low and does not depend of the fluctuations of the international prices of fossil fuels. The investment on renewables also creates a significant number of new jobs and work positions and can also boost local development of poor areas.

4.1 Intermittency and system integration

The intermittency of certain types of renewable energies is a problem that can be managed appropriately though and thus overcome the barriers of adopting them. Predictions about wind and solar energy are possible, and the more reliable that prediction is, the higher the value of renewable energies. This prediction becomes safer, the closer the time of renewable energy supply to a central system. Some countries impose a balancing charge when there is a deviation of the prediction from the actual quantity that is produced. If there is high penetration of the intermittent renewables in the electricity production of a country, this pattern can be strengthened by a support system, which will include a dependence premium on the price of electricity of immediate delivery. This rectifies the risk of the electricity system being deprived of the necessary energy to work.

Access and integration of the renewables into a central electricity system is also very important for the success of this venture. The electricity network and infrastructure was mainly built at an era when the electricity sector belonged mainly to the public sector and was such positioned to enable large power stations to be close to mines and rivers or major consumption centers such as cities (European Commission, 2005). However, renewable energy generation units are not to be found at the same places as conventional power stations and they also have a different size from them. European member states have established legislation, which guarantees that the companies already connected to the electricity network will guarantee the transportation and transmission of the energy produced from renewable energies injected into the main system. Supporting mechanisms that can fully integrate renewables into the main system will lower the financial burden for consumers.

4.2 Energy efficiency in buildings

A lot is said nowadays about energy efficiency and countries set up incentives for its pursuit. Energy productivity can increase when energy efficiency increases. Low energy productivity refers to high energy intensity. The wide availability of public transportation and the regulation for building insulation can boost energy efficiency. Household buildings and tertiary sector buildings are responsible for a significant percentage of total energy production. Energy efficiency in buildings occurs through wall, ceiling and window frames insulation, the replacement of lights, and heating and cooling systems with ones of higher energy performance.

European countries have a long-run target for buildings. The European building supply should become energy efficient and have a zero carbon footprint by 2050. Energy refurbishment should take place taking into account technical and economic feasibility, comfort, and human health. Moreover, buildings should be smart and connected to the energy system (EPBD, 2016). Table 2 provides an overview of the policies implemented in the European Union with respect to energy efficiency in buildings. Their number and persistent issuance reveals the importance that governments nowadays place on them.

With respect to Table 2, the first European Directive 89/106 aims at making sure that the manufacturing materials for the construction of buildings in Europe, which should comply with mechanical stability and balance, fire safety, hygiene, health and environment, usage security, noise protection, energy saving, and heat insulation. Second, European Directive 92/42 defines the performance requirement on hot water boilers fueled with liquid or solid fuels nominal capacity equal or larger than 4 KW. Directive 2000/55 is quite technical and it will not be referred to in here. Third, Directive 2002/91 aims at improving energy efficiency of buildings in the member states, taking into account climatological and local conditions and cost. The performance of the building is related to the surface of the building, its age, its position, and other technological parameters. This directive dictates the prerequisites for the issuance of an energy performance certificate. Fourth, Directive 2004/8 aims at increasing energy performance through the cogeneration of thermal power and electricity. Sixth, Directive 2005/32 is about the products that consume energy. They must have complied with eco-design criteria and bear a relevant quality certification (about the consumption of resources necessary for their production, produced emissions, recycling opportunities in their production, etc.). Seventh, Directive 2006/32 deals with the revocation of the hindrances of every type, for example, institutional, financial, and legal that hinder the effective use of energy. Eighth the Directive 2009/72 aims at setting common rules for the production, transport, distribution, and procurement of electricity as well as the obligations and rights of consumers and the obligations of

Table 2 Selective representation of European Legislation on energy efficient buildings.

Directive	Summary content/topic
89/106	The approximation of laws, regulations, and administrative provisions of the member states relating to construction products
92/42	Efficiency requirements for new hot-water boilers fired with liquid or gaseous fuels
96/57	Energy efficiency requirements for household electric refrigerators, freezers, and combinations thereof
2000/55	Energy efficiency requirements for ballasts for fluorescent lighting
2002/91	Energy performance of buildings
2004/8	The promotion of cogeneration based on a useful heat demand in the internal energy market
2005/32	Establishing a framework for the setting of eco-design requirements for energy-using products
2006/32	Energy end-use efficiency and energy services
2009/72	Common rules for the internal market for electricity
2014/25	Public procurement guidelines (energy, water, transport, and postal services)
2019/944	Common rules for the internal market for electricity (amending a previous Directive 2012/27 and abolishes 2009/72)

Modified from Ageridis, G., Tzanaki, E., 2008. Energy Efficiency in Construction and Products: The European Vision and Its Application, Available from: http:/uest.ntua.gr/archive/suscon/sinedrio_18_9/ enotita_3/ageridis_kape_suscon.pdf, Accessed 10/03/2020.

competition. Ninth the Directive 2014/25 sets the rules for procurement by water and energy utilities, transport, and postal services. These sectors are very important for the economy, and thus they need special attention. Last the Directive 2019/944 abolishes Directive 2009/72 by updating its content. It clarifies and strengthens consumer rights, provides pricing guidelines, updates access rules to energy data, and describes the energy communities among consumers and various other points about electric cars and energy transportation. Overall, there are barriers for the energy efficiency measures to be adopted, and these are as follows (Fig. 1):

4.3 Energy efficiency in transportation

Since 2007 the transport sector has started making essential progress steps in energy efficiency, with a 60% improvement that can be attributed to passenger vehicles, although the economic crisis cannot be overseen for its contribution in traffic reduction and thus in a reduction in traffic emissions. From 2000, energy efficiency of transport has increased by a yearly 1.2% in EU. Greater progress in energy efficiency has been implemented from cars and airplanes and less from trucks and light goods vehicles. The last is due to the so-called empty running, which is a result of the

The Market

1) Market organization and price distortion prevent consumers from appreciating the importance and value of Energy Efficiency

2) Transaction costs are high
3) Split incentive problems are created when investors cannot reap the benefits of improved energy efficiency

Financial

4) High Upfront costs and dispersed benefits discourage investors from getting involved in energy efficiency investments
5) There is a widespread perception that Energy Efficiency Investments are risky and complicated
6) Financial Institutions lack the awareness of Energy Efficiency Financial benefits

Information and Awareness

7) Lack of information and understanding from consumers. This prevents them from making rational choices
8) Incentive structures encourage energy providers to sell energy rather than invest in cost-effective energy efficiency
9) There is institutional bias towards supply side investments

Technical

10) Lack of affordable Energy efficiency technologies suitable to local conditions
11) Insufficient capacity to identify, develop, implement and maintain energy efficiency investments

FIG. 1

Barriers for the adoption of energy efficiency measures.
Adapted from OECD/IEA, 2010. Energy Efficiency Governance—Handbook, second ed., France.

economic crisis and the reduced aggregate demand characterizing European economies on average. The share of public transport as a percentage of passenger traffic has remained almost stable, about 20%. Alternative fuels in transport are about 5% of their total consumption. Most of that comes from biofuels and less from natural gas, with Sweden being a leader.

The largest part of policy measures in transport (about 70%) is concerns passenger mode and the private vehicle, and they have induced the adoption of more energy efficient solutions and practices in this sector. There is still more space for additional positive records in this sector. Policy making is centered around three pillars: (i) energy consumption and emission standards for new cars, (ii) renewal of old cars, and (iii) traffic management (Odyssee-Mure, 2015). Policy making at EU level is far less (20%) compared with regional and local level policy making. Therefore countries are still responsible for the largest part of this policy making.

A new path in the transport sector is the usage of hydrogen and electricity as carriers. Since the latter are not energy sources, it is vital to produce them from clean energies. Thus hydrogen and electricity can improve the situation but cannot solve it. They can be used to help reconciling the intermittent nature of demand and supply of renewable, but not to basically produce energy. Nowadays, there is an unprecedented momentum for hydrogen to make a unique contribution to clean energy transition. However, according to Birol (2019), the demand for hydrogen absorbs 6% of natural gas and 2% of global coal. Therefore it is responsible for the production of about 800 m tons of CO_2 per annum, which is equivalent to the emissions size of the United Kingdom and Indonesia together. Hydrogen is produced from fossil fuels, biomass, or water. Thus its cost is determined to a large extend by the price of the aforementioned resources. In transport the success of hydrogen fuel cells will be determined by the cost of the fuels and the establishment of fuel stations (IEA, 2020). For more progress on the establishment of hydrogen, policy makers should devote efforts to eliminate barriers and smooth risks for the newcomers in this market and set up the deadlines and terms for its markets.

The global stock of electric cars has reached 2 million in 2016, mostly led by China, Japan, the United States, and major European countries. There are two types of electric cars. One is the battery electric vehicle (BEV), and the other is the plug-in hybrid electric vehicle (PHEV). The former is relied on a battery to store energy, and the battery needs to be recharged. The latter includes both a battery and a liquid fuel storage. Electric vehicles are not free of upstream pollutant emissions, so they should not be regarded as panacea. For them to establish their presence and usage in current networks and societies, the following prerequisites must apply the following: (i) decarbonization of electricity generation, (ii) the establishment of charging points, and (iii) further electrification of cars and their grid integration.

4.4 World RES consumption

Progress has been made in the consumption and production of world renewables, but still a lot of road has to be covered until the stipulated targets in Paris agreement have been reached. In fact the efforts have to be intensified and scaled at least six times faster (Pek, 2020). Particularly the most challenging sector for renewable energy is the industry, which contains energy intensive industries with high emission products. This transformation will require a more holistic approach with a life cycle considerations.

According to the IEA (2019c), wind and solar PV are found on a continuous expansion, and this entails that renewables will overtake coal in the power generation mix in the mid-2020s. Furthermore, by 2040, low-carbon sources will provide more than half of total electricity generation. Hydropower together with the nuclear power retains significant shares in electricity production. These are 15% and 8% of total generation in 2040, respectively. The position of future renewables' consumption will seriously depend on the cost of batteries. The increased importance of offshore wind power will be seen with the increased investment that will take place until the next time benchmark, namely, 2040.

Despite the ongoing progress in renewables' production and consumption (Fig. 2), one cannot ignore the so-called locked-in carbon emissions, which refer to the fact that some power plants, which still have a long useful life in front of them, are major emitters and this cannot change in the short term. Needless to say that the subsidies still granted for fossil fuels are a major hindrance to the further adoption of renewable energies (Roberts, 2019). These subsidies are direct and are applicable in about 75 countries worldwide equal to more than USD 100 million each. This support is double the level of support provided for renewable energies (at a global level). This reveals the need for a deeper and radical change for which policy making is not ready yet due to immature circumstances. To reach the targets set for 2040 or 2050 by different countries, it seems there is a long way to be covered in a short time, but one should not oversee the fact that with renewable energy consumption, also energy efficiency will be increased and thus less energy will be required for anything to be done. Moreover the power of correct subsidies is so strong that the subsidies for renewable energy can disappear completely, if carbon gas emissions are correctly priced (Pek, 2020). European Union countries are obliged to abide by the Directive 2009/28/EC. With this the use of energy from renewable sources was promoted, and

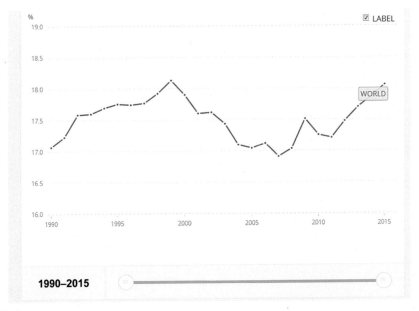

FIG. 2

Renewable energy consumption as percentage of total energy consumption.
From World Bank, 2020. World Development Indicators, Renewable Energy Consumption as Percentage of Total Energy Consumption, Available form: https:/data.worldbank.org/indicator/eg.fec.rnew.zs, Accessed 03/04/2020.

relevant countries had been asked to achieve a 20% share of renewable energy sources (RES) in their gross final energy consumption by 2020 and a 10% share of renewable energy in transport energy consumption (European Environmental Agency, 2018).

China has been the largest investor in renewable energies in 2018. Solar energy investments are quite labor intensive with wind energy creating the least jobs among all types of renewable energy. Renewables are doing well in electricity production, but still they have won only a small part in cooling, heating, and transportation. The latter is only a meager 3.3% compared with the 26% that has reached in global electricity production (Roberts, 2019). The consumption of renewable energies is gathered mostly in cities rather than in villages and the countryside. At least 100 cities around the world have managed to consume 90%–100% of global renewable energy electricity, and they have also set goals for complete reliance on renewable energies for some particular sectors (Energy Cities, 2020). Fig. 3 shows the renewable energy consumption as percentage of total energy consumption in Europe.

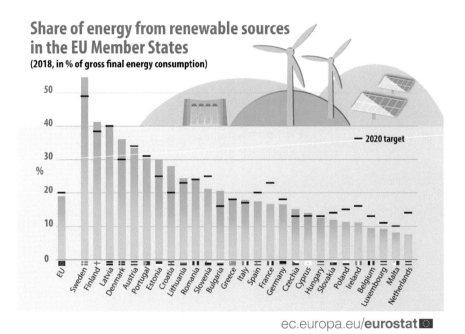

FIG. 3

Renewable energy consumption as percentage of total energy consumption in Europe.
From Eurostat, 2020. Renewable Energy Consumption as Percentage of Total Energy Consumption in Europe Member States, Available from: https://ec.europa.eu/eurostat/statistics-explained/index.php/Renewable_energy_statistics, Accessed 03/04/2020.

5 Oil production and reserves: Emerging solutions from natural gas production

With oil reserves, we refer to the proven existence of crude oil in a certain area. When oil is located at depths where they cannot be exploited with available technology, they cannot be included as reserves. According to BP estimates, there are 1.73 trillion barrels of oil reserves that can satisfy global needs at 2018 levels (BP, 2020). To refer only to the top 10 countries with the largest reserves, the largest quantity of oil reserves is found in Venezuela (300.0 billion barrels), Saudi Arabia (297.3 billion barrels), Canada (167.8 billion barrels), Iran (155.6 billion barrels), Iraq (147.2 billion barrels), Russia (106.2 billion barrels), Kuwait (101.5 billion barrels), Arab Emirates (97.6 billion barrels), USA (61.2 billion barrels), and Libya (48.4 billion barrels). OPEC countries govern about 80% of world reserves and include eight out the aforementioned countries (Chen and Barnier, 2020).

Oil consists mainly of carbon by 87% and nitrogen by 13% (Sunshine, 2019). Oil is classified based on its origin, its physical characteristics, and chemical synthesis. Depending on its density, it can be termed as light or heavy while depending on its content of sulfur content, it can be termed as sweet or sour (high sulfur content). Furthermore, the processing level gives different names to the resulted oil product (e.g., asphalt and gasoline). Oil is classified based on toxicity and harmfulness. For example, light oil can permeate the environment in an easier way. And oil fuels are classified based on their viscosity (ability to flow) and their volatility (ability to evaporate). High viscosity refers to slow flow.

Fossil fuel formation is an old and slow process. They were formed from the remains of dead marine organisms (plankton) over the passage of a very long time lasting for millions of years (300–400 millions of years) through a process of heat and pressure. On the other hand, coal has been formed from dead trees and plant organisms. Fossil fuels are regarded as nonrenewable, because liquid fuels are consumed at a much quicker pace than they can be replaced (BBC, 2020). Moreover, fuels can be categorized as liquid, gaseous, and solid. Liquid fuels can be easily transferred and are easy to handle. The most widely used liquid fuel is gasoline, diesel, kerosene, and liquefied petroleum gas (LPG).

The exploitation of oil is accompanied by negative ecological side effects. Air pollution, sea pollution through oil spills, fires, and damages in land are produced by oil industry. Upstream oil industry is the exploration and production sectors while the downstream is the refinement and distribution. The effects caused by production can broadly be the following: (i) land-use changes; (ii) sociocultural changes in the areas where production takes place; (iii) atmospheric impacts due to flaring, fugitive gases from loading operation airborne particulates from soil disturbance, and particulates from burning processes; (iv) aquatic impacts through drilling fluids, wash and drainage water, sewerage, leakages, etc.; (v) ecosystem impacts through their negative effects on habitats, food and nutrient supplies, migration routes of animals, changes in grazing patterns, etc. (UNEP, 2020).

According to OPEC, oil demand will continue to rise until 2040s and will most likely start declining at the end of that decade (Little, 2019). Some producers such as BP is more conservative, and estimates that the point of difference will occur earlier, namely, within 2030s. Of course, it is not easy to predict when decarbonization will be completed. There are many parameters that must be included such as technology developments, the penetration of electric vehicles, the cost of renewable energy resources and their price differential from oil prices, and political decisions; all participate in the final cadre and inject much uncertainty in the estimation of the time change (Eberhart, 2018).

Given the ongoing discussion about decarbonization, this poses a clear existential question about the oil companies. For a start, oil companies could direct themselves to the production of oils that are lower in their content of greenhouse gases that will complement renewable. They can develop and support oil decarbonization technologies, carbon capture and storage, and hydrogen technologies, and enhance methane efficiency. Of course, they have costly investments in place with much useful life to spend, and these must be carefully examined as well their social marketing messages so that the companies become aligned with Paris climate goals and they become accepted by public in their new role.

Oil companies in the past have earned themselves a bad reputation due to environmental accidents, incidences of corruption, and problematic cases of resource exploitation. Therefore oil companies must contribute to the electricity supply chain, support the hydrogen economy, and invest in gas projects, which as low-carbon emitting entities. Gas will play a significant role in the transition to a lower emission footprint economy and will give a new role to oil companies. Oil companies can engage into renewable energy technology venture investments and focus on technology startups such as microgrid, electric vehicles, and batteries. Also, given that that have the deepwater expertise, they could involve themselves in offshore wind energy production, which has major barriers to entry because of the financial and operational complexities of such projects, which is possessed by oil companies and cannot be easily achieves from smaller companies, which deal with solar power production, which is one of the saturated sectors of renewable energy production (Johnston et al., 2020).

Shale production is a new source of production referring to hydraulic fracturing and horizontal drilling, which has enabled the United States to increase oil and gas production from tight oil formations (The University of Texas and Austin, 2020). Shale oil is a substitute of crude oil, which is produced in a costlier and more environmental damaging process. Oil shales should not be confused with oil-bearing shales, which are shale deposits that contain tight oil. Oil shale is defined as an organic-rich, fine-grained sedimentary rock containing kerosene from which liquid oil can be produced (Wikipedia, 2020a).

5.1 Natural gas economics

This is a hydrocarbon gas form, consisting mainly of methane, also a small percentage of carbon dioxide, hydrogen, nitrogen, and other chemical elements (Wikipedia, 2020b). Natural gas is nonrenewable; it is used mainly for heating, cooking and electricity generation. It is less environmentally damaging than coal, which it usually supplements. Natural gas is produced in a biogenic and a thermogenic way. The first refers to an underground rock formation created by methanogenic organisms in the ground. The second way refers to its production within the petroleum production process.

Based on data from the global energy statistical yearbook (2019), production of natural gas takes place throughout the world, with the United States being the highest yearly producer (864 bcm) producing almost 45% of total production, Russia (741 bcm), Iran (232 bcm), Canada (188 bcm), Qatar (168 bcm), China (160 bcm), Norway (127 bcm), Australia (125 bcm), Saudi Arabia (98 bcm), Algeria (96 bcm), Turkmenistan (85 bvm), and Indonesia (75 bcm). Production has also increased in China, and this is due to the substitution of coal with gas in the electricity sector, which is a basic movement toward more sustainability.

Natural gas is transported through pipelines on land and in ships by sea. However, most of it is transported globally with the former means. With the priorities on climate change worldwide, natural gas is regarded more as a bridge fuel toward the replacement of fossil fuels with renewable. This is so because the main element of natural gas is methane, which is a greenhouse gas. Also the transportation of natural gas bears environmental risks because of potential leakages (Gerasimchuk, 2020).

Nowadays, unconventional US shale gas has become available in large quantities, and this has led other countries in Europe and Asia to follow the same route and paradigm. This largely contributes to changing the geopolitics of the natural gas market. According to Jaffe and O'Sullivan (2012), shale gas production will most highly quadruple in the next two decades, with 50% of that being US production by 2030. The former Soviet Union countries will be the largest supplier by 2040, both for conventional and conconventional gas production. Qatar and Australia will remain together (at 40%) as the largest LNG exporters until 2040. The Asian demand driven basically from India and China will set the natural demand growth. Depending on the degree of liberalization and the success of unconventional gas, Jaffe and O'Sullivan (2012) have proposed four scenarios under which the industry will evolve. These are shown in Table 3.

Depending on the coal bans and the electricity prices applicable for household and industries, the evolution of renewables' cost, and the development of new transportation routes, pressure will be exercised for gas markets to develop rapidly or less rapidly. In each country and geographical region, different manifestations of the aforementioned happen and shape new gas geopolitical trends.

The relationship with the suppliers of Russia will change toward and in favor of Europe and China. Russia possesses gas fields both in Western and Eastern Siberia. The trade terms will depend on where the pipelines will be built. For example, nowadays, Russia has favored a pipeline in East Siberia to facilitate trade with China. As gas demand will grow, it will become more similar to the oil market and will become as flexible as that and less sensitive to geopolitical games. More countries are becoming producers and exporters gradually (Table 4).

Table 3 The four gas market scenarios.

Liberalization	Success of unconventional gas		
		High	Low
	High	High global gas supply High liberalization and market integration	Limited development of market Gas markets remain segregated
	Low	High global gas supply Liberalization continues but at a lower rate	Resources are comprehensively developed Little liberalization

Adapted from Jaffe, A.M., O'Sullivan, M.G., 2012. The Geopolitics of Natural Gas, Report of Scenarios workshop of Harvard's University's Belfer Center and Rice University's Baker Institute Energy Forum, Available from: https:/www.belfercenter.org/sites/default/files/files/publication/The%20Geopolitics% 20of%20Natural%20Gas.pdf, Accessed 07/05/2020.

Table 4 Top 10 countries in gas reserves, production and consumption.

World's top 10 reserves holder countries	Quantity	World's Top 10 producer countries	Quantity	World's top 10 producer countries	World's top 10 producer countries
Russia	49.896	USA	718,85	USA	746,67
Iran	34,020	Russia	630,77	Russia	450,03
Qatar	24,531	Iran	170,08	China	181,60
USA	9960	Qatar	169,81	Iran	173,64
Turkmenistan	9904	Canada	161,39	Japan	128,63
Saudi Arabia	8489	China	129,91	Canada	104,03
United Arab Emirates	6091	Norway	113,30	Saudi Arabia	81,04
Venezuela	5617	Turkmenistan	84,42	Germany	76,47
Nigeria	5111	Saudi Arabia	81,68	Mexico	73,71
Algeria	4504	Algeria	80,87	UK	71,25
Sum of 10 top countries	158,123	Sum of 10 top countries	2341.09	Sum of 10 top countries	2087.06
Rest of the World	43,648	Rest of the World	1133.37	Rest of the World	1356.80

Adapted from World Oil and Gas Review, 2015. Natural Gas Reserves, Production, Reserves/Production Ratio, Consumption, Per Capita Consumption, Production/Consumption Ratio, Exports, Imports, Traded Gas, LNG-Liquefaction and Ragasification Capacity etc, Available from: https:/www.eni.com/ assets/documents/02-Sezione-Natural-Gas.pdf, Accessed 07/05/2020. Data year is 2014.

One of the latest technologies in gas production is the floating liquefied natural gas vessels (FLNG). A sea floating vessel enables unlocking reserves, which in the past had been difficult to extract. By 2020 there are estimated to be about 22 FLNG vessels in place. After the extraction of gas, it is liquefied to reduce its volume by 600 times. Then, it is loaded onto ships for transfer to the markets. The extracted gas is stored on the FLNG, and this makes the process more environmentally friendly and less costly.

Regarding major natural gas pipelines, some of them are as follows: the four west-east gas pipeline that run between east and west of China (From Lunnan to Shanghai). Three of the pipelines entered into operation in 2005, 2012, and 2014. One is still pending. Another major pipeline is the 4107 km long Yamal-Europe pipeline that runs across Russia (that part is owned by Gazprom), Belarus, Poland, and Germany. It started in 1993. A third gas pipeline is the Rockies Express of 2755 km length. With this pipeline, gas is transferred from the production point being the Rocky Mountain and Appalachian Basin toward the Midwest and Eastern parts of the United States (NS Energy, 2019).

Natural gas has been adopted in transportation as a cheaper (about 30% from diesel and 50% from petroleum) and a cleaner fuel. It reduces greenhouse gas emissions by 30 as compared with petrol. Also, it is a safer means of energy because it is less inflammable (IGU, 2017), and in cases of car crash, it evaporated into the air instead of forming a pool, which can go on fire due to crash. As the hindrances for the buy of gas powered vehicles are gradually eliminated, their fleet will become increasingly higher. The obstacles are the high initial cost and the automobile performance characteristics.

6 Nuclear energy challenges

This type of energy originates from the core of the nucleus of an atom. The energy is produced from the bonds that hold the atom together. This energy can be released in two ways: (i) the nuclear fission and (ii) nuclear fusion. The former is implemented by dividing the atom into smaller atoms. At this stage the energy is released. The second way refers to the atoms joining together to form a larger atom. Uranium is used in nuclear plants since its atoms can be divided more easily. Nuclear power plants use the heat from the fission to turn water into steam, which powers turbines to produce electricity (AZO, 2008).

Nuclear energy used to be considered as a smart energy solution in the 1960s when the first oil crises became evident and renewable and were still away from development and adoption. It was considered to be a very cheap energy source. Nuclear energy contributes to the enhancement of energy security, because the supplies that are used in operation and production processes are produced worldwide and hence it is highly unlikely that they will be in shortage. Moreover, this type of energy is less costly and more reliable. It is unlikely that its production will be affected by carbon emissions restrictions that are placed by governments and international agreements (Nuclear Energy Agency, 2010). Overall, nuclear energy reduces energy dependence from other countries and increases/diversifies the energy mix.

Currently, there are around 450 commercial power plants in the world with a production of about 400 Gigawatts of clean electricity. The production capacity is shown in Fig. 4. More than 100 power reactors with a total capacity of 120,000 MW have been ordered or planned. Most of them are in Asia, with fast-growing economies and consequent electricity demand (World Nuclear Energy Association, 2020). From the 47 planned until 2026, 12 of them will be in China and 7 of them in India.

Nuclear energy production facilities are more expensive than conventional ones, because of the protective measures that have to be taken against radiation (Touran, 2020). However, after many years of experimentation and research, there are factors that must be taken into account, so that the cost is kept at a low level (e.g., through capturing of economies of scale, improved design and construction methods, improved procurement, and other organizational issues). Fig. 4 reveals the total capacity of nuclear power in different world regions.

Based on Luciani, (2012), the long-run marginal cost for 1 MWh of nuclear energy is $66, and w can observe the variations of this base case cost with respect to six factors: the overnight cost, the cost of capital, the capacity factor, the construction time, the fuel cost, and the economic lifetime. The parameter that appears to have the highest impact is the overnight cost, and the rest of parameters have been ranked according to their variation range, from highest to the lowest. The overnight cost refers to the imaginary situation that the nuclear plant is built in one night so that

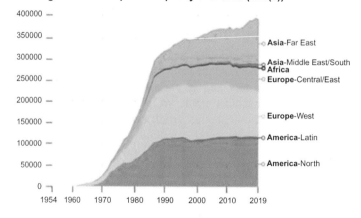

FIG. 4

Total capacity of nuclear power in different world regions.

From International Atomic Energy Agency, IAEA, 2019. Power Reactor Information Systems, Available from: https:/www.iaea.org/resources/databases/power-reactor-information-system-pris, Accessed 09/05/2020.

no cost of money has to be taken into account. Thus the cost of the plant would be $3500 per KW. The cost of capital depends on whether a private company finances (in this case it is the more expensive) the plant or a public authority. The higher capacity at which the factory works, the lower the long run marginal cost will be. The same will be achieved if the construction time is shrinking. Overall, if the aforementioned factors are managed properly, this can render nuclear energy production much cheaper. It is now better understandable that there is a large variety of factors that can make a project costly or cheap, and this cost increase or decrease is then transferred to the price of nuclear energy.

In March 2010 there was an earthquake of magnitude much greater than the conditions that could keep the nuclear plant in Fukushima unaffected. To make matters worse, after the earthquake a tsunami followed. After the Fukishima accident in 2010, the world has become again skeptical about the benefits and costs of nuclear energy and the Democratic Party of Japan embarked on a new energy policy aiming at abandoning nuclear energy by 2030, something to which the opposing Liberal Democratic Party does not agree (Suzuki, 2019). Before the accident the share of nuclear energy production in Japan was 25%, while after the accident, it was reduced to a meager 1.7% in 2016. Compared with Chernobyl accident the Fukushima accident was 10 times less serious in results and impact (Corradini, 2020).

Apart from the aforementioned risks occurring by natural disasters and other accident circumstances, there is also the common fear that nuclear energy projects will be used for military purposes and the production of nuclear weapons. This can occur at the point of enrichment and reprocessing of nuclear fuel and the production of fissile material used for weapons. For example, uranium must be converted in another form before it is used for weapon production. It must be enriched to increase the concentration of uranium. Also, some forms of spent fuel reprocessing allow for the extraction of plutonium, which can be used in the production of nuclear weapons (Center for Arms Control and Non-Proliferation, 2020). There are few ways to supervise this malpractice and, to some degree, to deter it. The International Atomic Energy Agency (IAEA) is an international organization responsible for the latter. States that form part of the IAEA are required to sign a nonnuclear weapon agreement.

Another major issue about nuclear energy concerns safety and the ways this can be done without polluting the environment or putting people's health at risk. The waste has radioactivity, which decays with time, and this makes necessary the prolonged storage of the waste before it is finally disposed of. Storage can take place under water or in a dry environment. Geological disposal in deep and stable geological formations takes place at the end as more long-term means of disposal (World Nuclear Energy Association, 2020). Waste disposal is a challenging issue that contributes to the nuclear energy being regarded as risky option for energy production. Therefore the development of the nuclear energy-growth nexus field has much less work to show which is in accordance with the consumers' skepticism and acceptance as a safe energy.

7 Energy security

In the wake of the oil crisis in 1973, energy security is at the forefront of all country energy policies. Energy security entails that a supply system can meet maximum demand in the event of failure, disruption, or loss of the most important supply unit (may that be a supplier or a route of supply). Different levels of energy security require different levels of cost and willingness to pay about them. Security cannot be guaranteed 100% because it is highly formed by probabilities. Through smart metering, in the future, we will be able to decide how much energy security we wish. For example, we will be able to have continuous information on prices, and this knowledge will enable our direct decisions on whether we consume electricity at a favorable moment and price or not. This will be particularly favored with the increase continuous penetration of renewable energies into the grid. When wind or sunshine are abundant, this will increase the produced energy injected into the grid and will be offered to consumers at rather low prices. This will make consumers change their attitude from passive price takers to more responsible consumers monitoring the price range to find the most favorable one.

As the market grows and becomes more liberalized with more producers in place, consumers will be able to choose producer and change from one to the other if they are not satisfied. Security expands to the existence of a stable relationship between the consumer and the producer, and this stability will be viable only if both parts are satisfied and interdependent.

For countries to safeguard their energy security that comes from oil, which is very vulnerable to geopolitical unrest, accidents, and disasters, nowadays, countries are obliged to keep emergency oil stocks capable to last for 90 days of net oil imports (IEA, 2019a, b). This obligation is part of an International agreement signed by countries under the auspices of the International Energy Association. Of course, these reserves are destined only for short-term alleviation from oil supply disruptions. Long-term solution can be materialized only through fuel diversification, the adoption of alternative forms of energy such as renewables, and the reduction of fuels import reliance. In extreme circumstances of prolonged oil supply disruption, the countries under IEA can assume collective action. Such circumstances have appeared three times so far: in 1991, 2005, and 2011. The events were the Gulf War, the Hurricanes Katrina and Rita, and the Libyan War, respectively (IEA, 2019a, b).

Energy security is earning in significance, as more pressure is exercised for decarbonization. To cope with this transition, countries must cooperate and integrate their power systems across borders. Such initiatives are easier under regimes of already established economic cooperation across coalitions such as the European Union. The word "borders" is a bit tricky because it refers not only to national borders but also to technical and jurisdictional ones. Particularly for Europe, countries must anyway conform to common European Directives permeating all economic sectors, not lest energy. Thus much of the cooperation required for energy and electricity security for European countries is pertinent to the wider treaty relationship of the member states (Wittenstein et al., 2016).

Electricity security is a multifaceted issue that needs to confront both external threats and internal policies. The way of confrontation requires some general, basic, and urgent solutions and some more specific ones. As external threats one can consider the fuel security, the resilience of the system and the cybersecurity parameter. In the internal policies fall the capacity adequacy and the system security, the grid integration of renewable, and the smart grids and distribution systems (Wittenstein, 2016).

Energy security is not the only attribute we would wish for an ideal energy system. We also need an energy system that is equitable (which will bring us to the discussion of the next topic in this chapter) and environmentally friendly. Therefore policy makers are faced with a trilemma regarding how much of each of this attributes is feasible and affordable and at what price. To provide a benchmark for comparison, the World Energy Council has developed an index called the energy trilemma index and ranks 125 countries based on the achievement of their energy system with respect to each of the aforementioned three parameters: security, equity, and environmental sustainability (Wyman, 2019). Top 10 performing countries are: Switzerland, Sweden, Denmark, the United Kingdom, Finland, France, Austria, Luxembourg, Germany, and New Zealand. Apparently, nine out of the top 10 performing countries are European (World Energy Council, 2019).

8 Energy, social justice and development

Albeit energy production grows, so does the demand, and these two aspects are not always reconciled with each other. More than 1.2 million people worldwide did not have access to electricity in 2011. Most of them live in developing countries with sub-Saharan Africa being the worst afflicted area (Toreco, 2015). Energy alone does not solve underdevelopment and poverty, but it affects the provision of health services, education, environmental protection, and income generation through work (Kanagawa and Nakata, 2008).

Energy is destined to contribute to growth and development. After all, this is a major question that is investigated in the energy-growth nexus for which plentiful of research has been launched and thousands of research papers have been written. Energy enables the improvement of technology and productivity, and this in turn leads to economic growth and development. The energy transition is not only a technological issue but also a social and political one. Unless everybody is convinced that they are going to win from the energy transition, there will be opposition and resistance.

Pricing are very important policy tools. They convey important signals for consumers. Sometimes, energy prices are kept below their economic price and below full cost, and this bears some side effects. The paid price is thus impossible to pay for new capital. Therefore utilities cannot finance their demand expansion or the new transition grids. Poor countries have a lot of unconnected places, and this makes people move to big cities and contribute to urbanization. Moreover, low prices create energy squandering and do not give any motive for controlling consumption and pay any attention to environmental problems such as climate change through global warming. Therefore many utilities nowadays charge their customers for carbon emissions and renewable infrastructure.

Many countries impose carbon taxes on transportation fuels to collect money for the energy transition. Overall high energy prices are damaging collective affordability but at the same time will contribute to the increase of accessibility by enabling utilities to renew and expand their infrastructure. It is difficult to make the trade off, and all stakeholders should be taken into consideration in this venture. On the other hand, greater emphasis should be placed in putting taxes on emissions and not the consumption of energy per se. To enhance social justice in the energy transition, not the same consumers should carry the burden all the time. The idea is to make everybody gain something in order to minimize opposition.

Access to energy is considered as a human right to be able to establish the minimum living condition for oneself. In fact, it is considered as one of the global sustainability goals. This is facilitating through a building block tariff, whereby consumption is divided in blocks and for each block applies a different tariff. As consumption increases from the low block toward the higher blocks, a different tariff is applicable. Things are worse for poor countries with low energy reserves, which rely on energy imports to meet demand. Foremost the environmental considerations and goals each country has sometimes require additional energy consumption for their implementation. Such an example is the setup of carbon storage and sequestration. This will increase costs and price but will decrease the net energy supply available to end consumers. Furthermore, through decarbonization, economies become more capital intensive and less labor intensive, and this affects negatively income distribution. It is vital to keep and foster only the good sides of the energy transition and protect the poor social groups with carefully planned subsidies.

9 Instead of a conclusion

This introductory chapter provides an overview of the current picture in energy economics. This update informs new energy-growth researchers of the new challenges that need to be addressed in future energy-growth research. While the book focuses on energy-growth econometrics tips and implementation, this chapter offers crucial background dimensions on current energy economics. For the rest of the chapters, I focus on specific aspects of energy-growth econometrics on which new researchers would find useful to have summarized reference knowledge.

References

AZO, 2008. Nuclear Energy—An introduction to Nuclear Energy. Available from: https://www.azocleantech.com/article.aspx?ArticleID=60. (Accessed 8 May 2020).

Bataille, C., Åhman, M., Neuhoff, K., Nilsson, L.J., Fischedick, M., Lechtenböhmer, S., Solano-Rodriquez, B., Denis-Ryan, A., Stiebert, S., Waisman, H., Sartor, O., Rahbar, S., 2018. A review of technology and policy deep decarbonization pathway options for making energy-intensive industry production consistent with the Paris Agreement. J. Clean. Prod. 187, 960–973.

BBC, 2020. Fossil Fuels. Available from: https://www.bbc.co.uk/bitesize/guides/z27thyc/revision/1. (Accessed 7 April 2020).

Birol, F., 2019. The future of hydrogen. IEA Report. Available from: https://www.iea.org/reports/the-future-of-hydrogen. (Accessed 21 August 2020).

BP, 2019. BP Energy Outlook, 2019 Edition. Available from: https://www.bp.com/content/dam/bp/business-sites/en/global/corporate/pdfs/energy-economics/energy-outlook/bp-energy-outlook-2019.pdf. (Accessed 29 February 2020).

BP, 2020. Oil. Available from: https://www.bp.com/en/global/corporate/energy-economics/statistical-review-of-world-energy/oil.html. (Accessed 7 April 2020).

Center for Arms Control and Non-Proliferation, 2020. Nuclear Proliferation Risks in Nuclear Energy Programs. Available from: https://armscontrolcenter.org/nuclear-proliferation-risks-in-nuclear-energy-programs/. (Accessed 9 May 2020).

Chen, J., Barnier, B., 2020. Organization of the Petroleum Exporting Countries (OPEC). Available from: https://www.investopedia.com/terms/o/opec.asp. (Accessed 7 April 2020).

Corradini, M., 2020. The Future of Nuclear Power After Fukushima. University of Wisconsin Energy Institute Chair. http://www.energy.wisc.edu. Available from: https://ans.org/about/officers/docs/FutureOfNuclearPowerAfterFukushima.pdf. (Accessed 9 May 2020).

CRES.gr, 2020. Renewable Energy Sources. Available from: http://www.cres.gr. (Accessed 10 March 2020).

Eberhart, D., 2018. Forecasts of Peal Oil Demand Overstated. Available form: https://www.forbes.com/sites/daneberhart/2018/09/18/forecasts-of-peak-oil-demand-overstated. (Accessed 7 April 2020).

Energy Cities, 2020. Cities Heading Towards 100% Renewable Energy by Controlling Their Consumption. Available from: https://energy-cities.eu/publication/cities-heading-towards-100-renewable-energy-by-controlling-their-consumption. (Accessed 3 July 2020).

EnergyPress, 2018. Australia: The Carbon Emissions Have Come to a Dead-End, Published in Naftemporiki. Available from: https://energypress.gr/news/aystralia-vrikan-toiho-oi-politikes-meiosis-ton-ekpompon-anthraka. (Accessed 8 March 2020).

EPBD, Energy Performance of Buildings Directive, 2016. Implementing the EPBD-Featuring Country Reports. Available from: www.buildup.eu/en/practices/publications/2016. (Accessed 10 March 2020).

European Commission, 2005. Announcement: Support of Electricity Production From Renewable Energies. Available from: http://eur-lex.europa.eu/legal-content/EL. (Accessed 10 March 2020).

European Environmental Agency, 2018. Estimated Effects of Increased RES Consumption Since 2005 on Fossil Fuels and GHG Emissions. Available from: https://www.eea.europa.eu/data-and-maps/data/estimated-effects-of-increased-res-2. (Accessed 3 April 2020).

European Parliament, 2018. The EU Emissions Trading Scheme and Its Reform in Brief. Available from: https://www.europarl.europa.eu/news/en/headlines/society/20170213STO62208/the-eu-emissions-trading-scheme-ets-and-its-reform-in-brief. (Accessed 8 March 2020).

Gerasimchuk, 2020. Natural Gas Transport, Student Energy. Available from: https://www.studentenergy.org/topics/natural-gas-transport. (Accessed 9 April 2020).

IEA, 2019a. The Future of Hydrogen, Technology Report June 2019. Available from: http://www.iea.org/reports/the-future-of-hydrogen. (Accessed 13 March 2020).

IEA, 2019b. Oil Security, The Global Oil Market Remains Vulnerable to a Wide Range of Risk Factors. Available at: https://www.iea.org/areas-of-work/ensuring-energy-security/oil-security. (Accessed 9 May 2020).

IEA, 2019c. World Energy Outlook. Available from: https://www.iea.org/reports/world-energy-outlook-2019. (Accessed 3 April 2020).

IEA, 2020. Hydrogen. IEA Report. Available from: https://www.iea.org/reports/hydrogen (Accessed 21 August 2020).

IGU, International Gas Union, 2017. Natural Gas Fuels Transportation. Available from: https://www.igu.org/natural-gas-fuels-transportation. (Accessed 8 May 2020).

Jaffe, A.M., O'Sullivan, M.G., 2012. The Geopolitics of Natural Gas, Report of Scenarios workshop of Harvard's University's Belfer Center and Rice University's Baker Institute Energy Forum. Available from: https://www.belfercenter.org/sites/default/files/files/publication/The%20Geopolitics%20of%20Natural%20Gas.pdf. (Accessed 7 May 2020).

Johnston, R.J., Blakemore, R., Bell, R., 2020. The Role of Oil and Gas Companies in the Energy Transition. Available from: https://www.atlanticcouncil.org/wp-content/uploads/2020/01/OGT-final-web-version.pdf. (Accessed 8 April 2020).

Kanagawa, M., Nakata, T., 2008. Assessment of access to electricity and the socio-economic impacts in rural areas of developing countries. Energy Policy 36, 2016–2029.

Kramer, G.J., Laurens, C., Bentham, J., Vermeer, B., 2015. Energy, sustainability and progress, introduction. In: Kramer, G.J., Vermeer, B. (Eds.), The Colors of Energy, Essays on the Future of Energy in Society. Shell International BV, Amsterdam.

Little, B., 2019. Are We in Peal Oil Demand? Available from: https://insideevs.com/features/387794/peak-oil-demand. (Accessed 7 April 2020).

Luciani, G., 2012. The rationale for nuclear energy in the Persian Gulf countries. Secur. Index: Russ. J. Int. Secur. 18 (4), 7–14.

Maggio, G., Nicita, A., Squadrito, G., 2019. How the hydrogen production from RES could change energy and fuel markets: a review of recent literature. Int. J. Hydrog. Energy 23, 11371–11384.

McGlade, C., Ekins, P., 2015. The geographical distribution of fossil fuels unused when limiting global warming to 2°C. Nature 517, 187–190.

Meckling, J., Sterner, T., Wagner, G., 2017. Policy sequencing toward decarbonization. Nat. Energy 3, 243.

Meinshausen, M., Meinshausen, N., Hare, W., Raper, S.C.B., Frieler, K., Knutti, R., Frame, D.J., Allen, M.R., 2009. Greenhouse-gas emission targets for limiting global warming to 2°C. Nature 458, 1158–1162.

NS Energy, 2019. Profiling the World's Major Oil and Gas Pipeline Projects. Available from: https://www.nsenergybusiness.com/features/worlds-major-oil-and-gas-pipelines. (Accessed 7 May 2020).

Nuclear Energy Agency, 2010. Energy Supply and the Contribution of Nuclear Energy, Executive Summary. Available from: https://www.oecd-nea.org/pub/security-energy-exec-summary.pdf. (Accessed 8 May 2020).

Odyssee-Mure, 2015. Energy Efficiency Trends and Policies in Transport. Available from: https://www.odyssee-mure.eu/publications/archives/energy-efficiency-in-transport.html. (Accessed 13 March 2020).

Okesola, A.A., Oyedeji, A.A., Abdulhamid, A.F., Olowo, J., Ayodele, B.E., Alabi, T.W., 2018. Direct Air Capture: a review of carbon dioxide capture from the air. IOP Conf. Ser., Mater. Sci. Eng. 413, 012077. pp. 3.

Pek, A., 2020. The Global Renewable Energy Share Can Exceed 30% by 2030 at No Extra Cost—IRENA Report. Global Wind Energy Council. Available from: https://gwec.net/the-global-renewable-energy-share-can-exceed-30-per-cent-2030-extra-cost-irena-report/. (Accessed 3 April 2020).

Ranjan, M., 2010. Feasibility of Air Capture. Master Thesis, Massachusetts Institute of Technology. Available from: https://sequestration.mit.edu/pdf/ManyaRanjan_Thesis_June2010.pdf. (Accessed 9 March 2020).

Renewable Resources Co, 2016. 11 Different Sources of Alternative Energy. Available from: https://www.renewableresourcescoalition.org/alternative-energy-sources. (Accessed 9 March 2020).

Roberts, D., 2019. The Global Transition to Clean Energy, Explained in 12 Charts. Available from: https://www.vox.com/energy-and-environment/2019/6/18/18681591/renewable-energy-china-solar-pv-jobs. (Accessed 3 April 2020).

Robinson, D., Keay, M., Hammes, K., 2017. Fiscal Policy for Decarbonisation of Energy in Europe, OIES PAPER: EL 22. The Oxford Institute for Energy Studies. Available from: https://www.oxfordenergy.org/wpcms/wp-content/uploads/2017/09/Fiscal-policy-for-decarbonization-of-energy-in-Europe-EL-25.pdf?v=f214a7d42e0d. (Accessed 3 March 2020).

Shell International BV, 2017. Shell World Energy Model, A View to 2100. Available from: https://www.shell.com/energy-and-innovation/the-energy-future/scenarios/shell-scenarios-energy-models/world-energy-model/_jcr_content/par/textimage.stream/1510344160326/2ee82a9c68cd84e572c9db09cc43d7ec3e3fafe7/shell-world-energy-model.pdf. (Accessed 1 March 2020).

Statkraft, 2018. Global Energy Trends. Available from: https://www.statkraft.com/globalassets/explained/statkrafts-low-emissions-scenario-report-2018.pdf. (Accessed 25 February 2020).

Sunshine, W.L., 2019. The Basics of Crude Oil Classification. Available from: https://www.thebalance.com/the-basics-of-crude-oil-classification-1182570. (Accessed 7 April 2020).

Suzuki, T., 2019. Nuclear Energy Policy After the Fukushima Nuclear Accident: An Analysis of Polarized Debate in Japan. Available from: https://www.intechopen.com/online-first/nuclear-energy-policy-after-the-fukushima-nuclear-accident-an-analysis-of-polarized-debate-in-japan. (Accessed 9 May 2020).

Tagliapetra, S., 2018. The Impact of Global Decarbonization Policies and Technological Improvements on Oil and Gas Producing Countries in the Middle East and North Africa. IEMed.

The University of Texas and Austin, 2020. The U.S. Shale Revolution. Available from: https://www.strausscenter.org/energy-and-security/the-u-s-shale-revolution.html. (Accessed 8 April 2020).

Toreco, M., 2015. The impact of rural electrification: challenges and ways forward. Rev. Econ. Dev. 23, 49–75. Available from: https://www.cairn.info/revue-d-economie-du-developpement-2015-HS-page-49.html. (Accessed 9 May 2020).

Touran, N., 2020. Why Are Nuclear Reactors Expensive? Available from: https://whatisnuclear.com/economics.html. (Accessed 9 May 2020).

UNEP, 2020. Environmental Management in Oil and Gas Exploration and Production. Available from: https://wedocs.unep.org/bitstream/handle/20.500.11822/8275/-Environmental

%20Management%20in%20Oil%20%26%20Gas%20Exploration%20%26%20Produc
tion-19972123.pdf?sequence=2%26isAllowed=y. (Accessed 7 April 2020).

Wikipedia, 2020a. Oil Shale. Available from: https://en.wikipedia.org/wiki/Oil_shale.
(Accessed 8 April 2020).

Wikipedia, 2020b. Natural Gas. Available from: https://en.wikipedia.org/wiki/Natural_gas.
(Accessed 9 April 2020).

Wittenstein, M., 2016. Electricity Security System Framework, Extending the Framework
Beyond Borders, ESAP Workshop VII. Available from: https://www.ceer.eu/docu
ments/104400/-/-/afd316dd-f203-bfe0-e4da-b6c46012a40d. (Accessed 9 May 2020).

Wittenstein, M., Scott, J., Razali, N.M.M., 2016. Electricity security across borders. In: Case
Studies on Cross—Border Electricity Security in Europe. International Energy Agency.
Insights Series 2016, Available from: https://euagenda.eu/upload/publications/untitled-
69930-ea.pdf. (Accessed 9 May 2020).

World Energy Council, 2019. World Energy Trilemma Index/2019. Available from: https://
trilemma.worldenergy.org/reports/main/2019/2019%20Energy%20Trilemma%20Index.
pdf. (Accessed 9 May 2020).

World Nuclear Energy Association, 2020. Plans For New Reactors Worldwide. Available
from: https://www.world-nuclear.org/information-library/current-and-future-generation/
plans-for-new-reactors-worldwide.aspx. (Accessed 9 May 2020).

Wyman, O., 2019. World Energy Trilemma Index. Available from: https://www.worldenergy.
org/transition-toolkit/world-energy-trilemma-index. (Accessed 9 May 2020).

Further reading

Enerdata, 2019. Natural Gas Production. Available from: https://yearbook.enerdata.net/natu
ral-gas/world-natural-gas-production-statistics.html. (Accessed 9 April 2020).

FIRCROFT50, 2020. Everything You Need to Know About FLNG. Available from: https://
www.fircroft.com/blogs/everything-you-need-to-know-about-flng-82911813351.
(Accessed 7 May 2020).

IEMed, 2018. Mediterranean Yearbook 2018. Available from: https://bruegel.org/wp-content/
uploads/2018/10/Global_Decarbonization_Simone_Tagliapietra_Medyearbook2018-1.
pdf. (Accessed 3 March 2020).

International Energy Agency—IEA, 2010. Transport Energy Efficiency—Implementation of
the IEA Recommendations Since 2009 and Next Steps. France.

Kramer, G.J., Vermeer, B. (Eds.), 2015. The Colors of Energy, Essays on the Future of Energy
in Society. Shell International BV, Amsterdam. Available from: https://www.shell.com/
shared/energy-and-innovation/_jcr_content/par/textimage_599045333.stream/
1461569264888/2c4d2cef2e60098f0c636e82c76ae38a2cd19297/the-colours-of-energy.
pdf. (Accessed 2 March 2020).

Stationarity and an alphabetical directory of unit roots often used in the energy-growth nexus

1 Introduction

The increased use of panel data in a macrofield such as the energy-growth nexus has brought up issues such as the homogeneity of panels, their cross-sectional dependence, and the issue of breaks. All these make the conventional unit root tests doubtable and the work for energy-growth researchers much challenging. When researchers are not aware of the existence of the previous issues in their data, they become compelled to use the so-called and referred to in many papers as such "battery of unit root tests" in an attempt to captivate as much information as possible about the peculiarities, the anomalies, and the interconnections among their energy-growth series and the respective covariates. Cointegration and cross-sectional dependence are discussed in different chapters of this book. Thus, I will not spend time discussing these concepts in this chapter.

It is common knowledge that when the series with unit roots are not sufficiently and correctly identified, there is the risk of spurious regressions (high R-squared and a low Durbin Watson statistic indicating autocorrelation in residuals being some of the side effects), which means that the information received from the series makes no sense for policy making. Foremost, in the energy-growth nexus field, the focus of the research is on energy consumption and the answer focuses on whether energy conservation can occur without hindering economic growth. This means that policy makers would wish that energy conservation does not cause a chaotic degrowth situation with no stability, but they care that it leads to energy-efficient economies, which will be achieving more output with less energy consumption. Hence, analysts care about equilibria (a stable mean for each variable, around which the observations fluctuate) and stability. In a different case, one cannot say with a degree of certainty which of the four major hypotheses (growth, conservation, feedback, and neutrality) apply in each country or group of countries.

There are various ways to divide the unit root tests into groups and categories depending on their characteristics and attributes, depending on which is the zero hypothesis they investigate or their chronological order of publication. This chapter provides them alphabetically because it is part of a guide of first aid reference for energy-growth nexus researchers. The explosion of energy-growth studies and

A Guide to Econometric Methods for the Energy-Growth Nexus. https://doi.org/10.1016/B978-0-12-819039-5.00002-1

the fact that many countries embark on international energy conservation, agreements make it compulsory for researchers to study countries in groups of various sizes. Unavoidably, this translates into having to use large sets of entities with shorter time spans. This places researchers in a different asymptotic analysis cadre from that used in time-series analysis in which the time span was long and the studies series few. The early panel unit root tests have been constructed as extensions of their univariate counterparts with the caveat of employing the t-test from a pooled Dickey-Fuller test and under the restrictive assumption of homogeneity across panels.

After this brief introduction (Section 1) that motivates the chapter, the rest of the chapter is structured as follows: Section 2 provides a concise technical background on the concept of the unit roots and stationarity and the two generations' tests. Section 3 hosts an alphabetical directory of unit roots employed in the energy-growth nexus, and Section 4 concludes the chapter.

2 The concepts of unit root and stationarity: Broadly two generations of unit root tests

Nonstationarity describes a series with a nonstationary covariance. One would expect that most of the typical components in a production function-oriented energy-growth relationship would be characterized by stationarity. For example, capital formation shows less fluctuation than financial variables. To study a series and reach results that are not spurious, the series must be stationary, namely, its mean, variance, and autocorrelation must be constant over time. A unit root describes a stochastic process, which prevents a series from being stationary, because it has a trend. The name of unit root stems from the mathematics behind this process. Each unit root can at least be described as a monomial, which has a root (solution). If one of these solutions (roots) is unity, this makes the unit root (Statistics How to, 2019). When the solution is unity, this means that the series does not recover to its initial value. If a unit root is not present, the series is stationary. Stationarity means that a series has mean reversion, and there is a long run mean around which it fluctuates. The opposite occurs with nonstationarity when the series does not return to a long-run mean path. Thus, when a series has a unit root, it follows a random walk, and it cannot be used for forecasting.

Let's take, for example, the following stationary series, which has a constant and grows at a constant rate b and an error term. Therefore the variable y_t is trend stationary because it has a stationary fluctuation around the expression $a + bt$, which is the trend. Please see Eq. (1).

$$y_t = a + bt + e_t \qquad (1)$$

If one removes the trend, one gets the detrended version of the series. This can be done by regressing y on t. Next, let's see a model, which is not stationary. In this case y grows on a rate based on its previous value with an error term.

$$y_t = y_0 + a_t + \sum_{i=1}^{t} e_i \qquad (2)$$

If we take first differences of this model (Eq. 2), it becomes difference stationary, and the first difference is $a + bt$. This model can be called random walk with a drift, and the path of this series is given by the addition of disturbances. The error term affects the current period together with the future periods. This model stands for the unit root hypothesis, because the coefficient on $y_t - 1$ is one. The two series, the trend stationary and the difference stationary, have different implications; therefore many tests examine both versions of the models.

Unit root testing is the first stage in the energy-growth nexus research that is always undertaken before any other modeling procedures take place. There are many ways to test for unit roots. The tests have evolved in time, and they are divided into first-generation unit roots and second-generation unit roots (Table 1). The former assumes the existence of cross-sectional independence, while the second generation of tests rejects this hypothesis. For example, oil shocks are common and affect a large number of worldwide countries. This is an example of cross-sectional dependence cause.

In the energy-growth nexus field, we are interested about unit roots, because when they are present, then a shock can cause a persistent effect to the time series. This is very crucial for the energy consumption, which is at the forefront in the

Table 1 First- and second-generation panel unit root tests as shown in Hurlin and Mignon (2007).

First generation	Cross-sectional independence
1. Nonstationarity tests	Levin and Lin (1992, 1993)
	Levin et al. (2002)
	Harris and Tzavalis (1999)
	Im et al., 1997, 2003, Im and Pesaran, 2003
	Maddala and Wu (1999)
	Choi, (1999), Choi (2001)
2. Stationarity tests	Hadri (2000)
Second generation	**_Cross-sectional dependence_**
1. Factor structure	Bai and Ng (2001), Bai and Ng, (2004)
	Moon and Perron (2004)
	Phillips and Sul (2003)
	Pesaran (2003)
	Choi (2002)
2. Other approaches	O' Connell (1998)
	Chang (2002, 2004)

From Hurlin, C., Mignon, V., 2007. Second Generation Panel Unit Root Tests, halshs-00159842, Available from: halshs.archives-ouverts.fr/halshs-00159842/document, Accessed 28/08/2019.

energy-growth nexus research. In the energy-growth nexus papers, researchers apply a variety of tests, sometimes with contradictory results. Starting with the first-generation tests (Table 1) is a good idea for researchers to get some hint on how the series behave. Moreover, it is useful to employ a cross-sectional dependence tests to find out how dependent panels are. This is why I believe that countries with heterogeneous economies and energy characteristics are tough to study and to reach reliable conclusions and they have different short run and long run dynamics.

Panel unit roots allow us to mitigate the problem of low power of unit roots in small samples. However, with panel data, arises the issue of heterogeneity. There is a general structure applicable in most unit root tests. This is shown in Eq. (3):

$$\Delta y_{it} = \rho_i y_{i,t-1} + \sum_{l=1}^{p_i} \varphi_{i,l} \Delta y_{i,t-l} + a_i d_{it} + \varepsilon_{it} \tag{3}$$

The following notation applies for Eq. (3):

> $d =$ deterministic component.
> when $\rho_i = 0$, this means that the process has a unit root for the individual i.
> when $\rho_i < 0$, this means that the process is stationary around the deterministic part.

Given that sufficiently large series are not always available in the energy-growth nexus, researchers often use panel data. Panel data unit roots can be distinguished to those assuming cross-sectional dependence and those that assume cross-sectional independence. Within the latter, tests can be divided into two categories: tests that adopt the covariance restrictions approach and the tests that assume the factor structure approach in the way shown in the succeeding text with Eqs. (4), (5):

$$Y_{i,t} = \xi_{1i} F_{1t} + E_{1,i,t} \tag{4}$$

$$X_{i,t} = \xi_{2i} F_{2t} + E_{2,i,t} \tag{5}$$

$i = 1 \ldots N$ is the panel, $t = 1, \ldots T$ is the time, F includes the common factors, and E comprises the idiosyncratic components. Belke et al. (2011) decompose each variable into two uncorrelated components, a common and an idiosyncratic component through principal component analysis. The common component in variables depends on a small number of shocks, which affect the respective variable of all the countries. Belke et al. (2011) describe in detail the steps for the identification and quantification of the common factor among variables. The interested reader should refer to that study.

Within the second generation of tests, two main approaches are distinguished (Barbieri, 2006): the covariance restrictions approach, adopted notably by Chang (2002, 2004), and the factor structure approach, such as the ones by Bai and Ng, (2004), Phillips and Sul (2003), Moon and Perron (2004), Choi (2002), and Pesaran (2003).

3 The alphabetical directory of unit roots in the energy-growth nexus

This section comprises the definition and basic description of 35 unit root tests that could possibly be applied in the energy-growth nexus studies. This directory has been compiled with the purpose to allow new researchers some quick reference.

3.1 Aparico et al. (2006) or a "range unit root"

This is a nonparametric test. Aparico et al. (2006) propose a range unit root test, which is constructed as a scaled sum of the number of changes of the observed time series range. It is worthy to note that nonparametric tests handle the outliers in a more efficient way. These researchers have thought of an innovative way to test for the type of "long-wave" patterns. They study the trend exhibited in the data, without imposing any constraint on the generating mechanism. The term "range unit root (RUR)" is used because it is constructed from running ranges of the series. The test has a lot of desirable properties such as its error-model-free asymptotic distribution, the invariance to nonlinear monotonic transformations of the series, and the robustness to the presence of level shifts and additive outliers. Last but not least, the RUR test outperforms the power of standard unit root tests on near-unit-root stationary time series. To the best of my knowledge, I have not seen an application of this unit root test in the energy-growth nexus field.

3.2 (The) Augmented Dickey-Fuller test (ADF), 1981

The general and all inclusive form of the conventional Dickey-Fuller test is provided as follows in Eqs. (6), (7):

$$y_t = a + bt + uy_{t-1} + e_t \qquad (6)$$

It is estimated by OLS as follows in Eq. (7):

$$\triangle y_t = (u-1)y_{t-1} + a + bt + e_t \qquad (7)$$

The augmented Dickey-Fuller (ADF) test consists in testing the null hypothesis that $u = 1$. If the null cannot be rejected, then we cannot reject the existence of a unit root. As aforementioned, this test has two versions, one with an intercept and another with a trend. Most unit root tests that we will examine in this chapter also have the null hypothesis of a unit root. This test is not appropriate for structural breaks. It has low power. This is the most common test one meets in the energy-growth nexus papers, and it is used in almost all studies as a benchmark. Nowadays, energy-growth papers do not stay on this test only, but it is a good starting point.

3.3 Bai and Ng (2001)

This is one of the second-generation tests where the cross-sectional dependence is specified as a common factor model (it assumes the factor structure approach) as in Eq. (8).

$$y_{i,t} = D_{it} + \lambda_i' F_t + e_{it} \tag{8}$$

D_{it}, polynomial time function of order t.
F_t, $(r,1)$ vector of common factors.
λ_i, vector of factor loadings.

Bai and Ng (2001) suggest a separate investigation of the presence of the unit root in the common and the individual component: the D_{it} and the $\lambda_i' F_t$ components. This is the so-called Panel Analysis of Nonstationarity in the Idiosyncratic and Common Components methodology (PANIC). This is one of the second-generation tests where the cross-sectional dependence is specified as a common factor model (it assumes the factor structure approach).

3.4 Breitung (2002)

This is a nonparametric approach. As such, it is more robust but a less powerful test. Breitung (2002) claims that this test has "nice" power properties within a certain local neighborhood of unit. Suppose a panel data variable y_{it}, which is generated by the process shown in Eq. (9):

$$y_{it} = \mu_i + \beta_i t + x_{it} \tag{9}$$

The unobserved error term follows the process shown in Eq. (10):

$$x_{it} = p_i x_{it-1} + \varepsilon_{it} \tag{10}$$

The test investigates the presence of a unit root in all cross-sectional units, namely, the hypothesis is set up as shown in Eq. (11):

$$H_0 : p_i = 1 \text{ for all } i \tag{11}$$

The investigation of the hypothesis is pursued through the following statistic in Eq. (12):

$$B_{nT} = \left(\frac{\hat{\sigma}^2}{nT^2} \sum_{i=1}^{n} \sum_{t=2}^{T-1} \left(y_{it-1}^* \right)^2 \right)^{-1/2} \frac{1}{\sqrt{n}} \frac{1}{T} \sum_{i=1}^{n} \sum_{t=2}^{T-1} (\Delta y_{it})^* y_{it-1}^* \tag{12}$$

3.5 Breitung and Das (2005)

This is one of the second-generation tests where the cross-sectional dependence is specified from unknown factors and imposes restrictions on the covariance matrix of residuals. Breitung and Das (2005) suggest a prewhitening of variables with the following first-differenced regression wherein the H_0 is imposed, which eliminates serial correlation without requiring the estimation of a long-term variance. Thus, under the H_0, they assume having a relationship as shown in Eq. (13):

$$\Delta y_{it} = \sum_{j=1}^{p} \varphi_j \Delta y_{it-j} + e_{it} \tag{13}$$

In terms of levels, the relationship can be written as of Eq. (14):

$$y_{it} = \sum_{s=2}^{t} \Delta y_{is} = \sum_{j=1}^{p} \varphi_j \sum_{s=2}^{t} \Delta y_{is-y} + \sum_{s=2}^{t} e_{is} = \sum_{j=1}^{p} \varphi_j y_{it-j} + y_{it}^s \tag{14}$$

with the H_0 imposed the y_{it}^s becomes a random walk with uncorrelated increments e_{it}. For more details in the implementation of the test, the interested readers could refer to Westerlund and Breitung (2009): Myths and Facts about Unit root tests, Department of Economics, Lund University, Sweden.

3.6 Breitung and Gourieroux (1997)

Nonparametric test. They provide test statistics that are computed on the ranks of the observations instead of using the actual observations. Nonparametric tests handle the outliers in a more efficient way. The test consists in replacing the first difference of observations Δy_t by their ranks in the Dickey-Fuller test statistics. With the same computations used in Fotopoulos and Ahn, (2003), the unit roots can be written as in Reisen et al. (2016):

$$T(\hat{\rho}_{BG} - 1) = T \frac{\sum_{t=2}^{T} \left(r_{T,t} - \frac{T+1}{2} \right) \left\{ \sum_{j=1}^{t-1} \left(r_{T,j} - \frac{T+1}{2} \right) \right\}}{\sum_{t=2}^{T} \left\{ \sum_{j=1}^{t-1} \left(r_{Tj} - \frac{T+1}{2} \right) \right\}^2} \tag{15}$$

$$\hat{\tau}_{BG} = \frac{\hat{\rho}_{BG} - 1}{\hat{\sigma}_{BG}} \left[\sum_{t=2}^{T} \left\{ \sum_{j=1}^{t-1} \left(r_{Tj} - \frac{T+1}{2} \right) \right\}^2 \right]^{1/2} \tag{16}$$

The limiting distribution of the BG test statistics are outlier free.

3.7 Breitung and Meyer (1994)

They adapt the asymptotic normality of the DF test for a large N and a small fixed DF. I provide this test only for historical purposes because it has already been improved for its drawbacks by Levin and Lin (1992, 1993). This approach does not allow the same dimension for time and cross section, namely, the T and N. Foremost, this approach is restrictive in that it cannot host heterogeneous residual distributions and the possible impact from individual specific effects (Barbieri, 2006).

3.8 Cavaliere and Taylor (2007, 2008)

This is a nonparametric approach, which is simulation based and resembling based. As such, it is more robust but less powerful test. They have set up a bootstrap approach unit root test that is valid in the presence of a wide class of permanent variance changes that includes single and multiple (abrupt and smooth transition) volatility change processes as special cases. They use of the so-called wild bootstrap principle, which preserves the heteroskedasticity present in the original shocks. "Wild bootstrap" refers to the bootstrap sample that is constructed without replacement such that it replicates patterns of heteroskedasticity present in the original data. In essence, they employ bootstrap variants of the GLS-detrended M-tests of Ng and Perron (2001).

3.9 Chang (2002, 2004)

He proposes nonlinear instrumental variables or bootstrap approaches to solve the cross-sectional dependence issue. This test uses the covariance restriction approach. In the first case, an instrument generated by a nonlinear function of lagged values is used, namely, $F(y_{it-1})$. The null hypothesis is that $H_0 : \rho_i = 1$, and the test has its own t-ratio statistic denoted as Z_i in Eq. (17):

$$Z_i = \frac{\hat{\rho}_i - 1}{\hat{\sigma}_{\hat{\rho}_i}} \tag{17}$$

$\hat{\rho}_i$ is the nonlinear instrumental variable estimator.

For unbalanced panels with cross-sectional dependence, one can employ the average instrumental variable t-ratio statistic defined as shown in Eq. (18):

$$S_N = \frac{1}{\sqrt{N}} \sum_{i=1}^{N} Z_i \tag{18}$$

$N^{-1/2}$ is a normalization factor.

An advantage in this test is that it does not require large samples (Barbieri, 2006). However, the test is regarded as oversized for moderate situations of cross-sectional dependence, even for small (in the N dimension) samples. As far as bootstrap approaches are concerned, since each cross section is characterized by different linear processes, these are approximated through autoregressive-integrated processes that form a system of equations. Bootstrap methodologies are applied to approximate autoregressions and obtain critical values for the panel unit root tests. This is one of the second-generation tests where the cross-sectional dependence is specified from unknown factors and imposes restrictions on the covariance matrix of residuals.

3.10 Choi (1999, 2001)

It tests the null hypothesis of a unit root. To address the restrictions of the panel unit root tests before him, such as the fact that they required an infinite number of cross sections, all the cross sections were assumed to have the same nonstochastic component type, unbalanced data were not their strong point, and the fact that the alternative hypothesis in those tests required an intermediate situation with some of the cross sections would have a unit root while others would not, also notwithstanding the sensitivity of the critical values of the new statistics required for testing. Choi uses a combination of standardized p values from the unit roots in each panel. He assumes a model of the type shown in Eqs. (19)–(21).

$$
\begin{aligned}
y_{it} &= d_{it} + x_{it} \\
d_{it} &= a_{i0} + a_{i1}t + \ldots + a_{im_i}t^{m_i} \\
x_{it} &= \rho_i x_{i(t-1)} + u_{it}
\end{aligned}
\tag{19}
$$

$$
\begin{aligned}
i &= 1,\ldots N \\
t &= 1,\ldots N
\end{aligned}
\tag{20}
$$

d_{it} is a nonstochastic process.

Thus the unit root test in this framework is formulated as shown in Eq. (21):

$$
\begin{aligned}
H_0 &: \rho_i = 1 \text{ for all } i \\
H_1 &: |\rho_i| < 1 \text{ for at least one } i \text{ for finite } N \\
H_1 &: |\rho_i| < 1 \text{ for some } i\text{'s for infinite } N
\end{aligned}
\tag{21}
$$

The Z test proposed by Choi is shown in Eq. (22):

$$
Z = \frac{1}{2\sqrt{N}} \sum\nolimits_{i=1}^{N} (-2 \ln p_i - 2)
\tag{22}
$$

If the Choi's test is destined to examine stationarity, the null hypothesis is formulated as an inequality <1, while the alternatives as equalities.

3.11 Clemente-Montanes-Reyes (1998)

Clemente et al. (1998) basically propose two tests, which allow for and test for two different events occurring in the revealed period. The first test is the CMRIO, and the second is the CMRAO test. These approaches are more suited for small samples. As far as the CMRIO model is concerned, that allows for two mean changes (breaks) that belong to the innovational outlier. On the other hand the CMRAO model allows for two mean shifts, which are presented as additive outliers. The null hypothesis is about the existence of a unit root in the examined series. An application of the Clemente-Montanes-Reyes test has been performed by Shahbaz et al. (2013) and a relevant presentation extract is in Table 2.

3.12 Elliott et al. (1996)

This is a test based on quasidifferencing of the series. They suggest a generalized least squares (GLS) detrending scheme as an alternative without losing asymptotic power. The test is based on the following regression (Eq. 23):

$$
y_t^{\bar{p}} = \mu^{\bar{p}'} Z_t^{\bar{p}} + u_t^{\bar{p}}
\tag{23}
$$

Table 2 Application of Clemente-Montanes-Reyes detrended structural break unit root test in an energy-growth nexus study.

Variable	Innovative outliers				Additive outliers			
	T-statistic	TB1	TB2	Decision	T-statistic	TB1	TB2	Decision
ln (income)	−1.105 (2)	1975	1990	Unit root exists	−5.990(2)*	1975	1989	Stationary
ln (energy)	−4.438 (3)	1984	2000	Unit root exists	−6.719(3)*	1976	1999	Stationary
ln (financial development)	−1.223 (3)	1981	1993	Unit root exists	−6.227(3)*	1978	1984	Stationary
ln (capital)	−1.798 (1)	1989	2001	Unit root exists	−6.148(3)*	1980	1988	Stationary
ln (exports)	−2.794 (1)	1976	2001	Unit root exists	−6.140(2)*	1976	1980	Stationary
ln (imports)	−3.162 (3)	1976	1998	Unit root exists	−6.413(5)*	1977	1984	Stationary
ln (trade)	−3.106 (2)	1976	1998	Unit root exists	−6.407(2)*	1976	1981	Stationary

* Significance at 5%.
From Shahbaz, M., Khan, S., Tahir, M.I., 2013. The dynamic links between energy consumption, economic growth, financial development and trade in China: fresh evidence from multivariate framework analysis. Energy Econ. 40, 8–21.

With $\bar{p} = 1 + \bar{c}/T$ is a local detrending parameter as shown in Eq. (24):

$$\left(y_0^{\bar{p}}, y_t^{\bar{p}}\right) = (y_0, (1 - \bar{p}L)y_t) \tag{24}$$

Detrended data are provided by $\tilde{y}_t = y_t - \hat{\mu}^{\bar{p}'} z_t$. The test statistic that is based on that is called ADF^{GLS}. This test has been applied in Chiou-Wei et al. (2016), but no details of the implementation and results are revealed in the paper.

3.13 Hadri (2000)

The Hadri test has a null hypothesis of stationarity. It is an extension of the Kwiatkowski et al. (1992) stationarity test (Barbieri, 2006). It is about a Lagrange multiplier (LM) test with the null hypothesis that all series in the panel are stationary, while the alternative supports the existence of at least one single root. The LM test is the average of the individual univariate KPSS stationarity test, following a normal distribution. Four model specifications are available in Eqs. (25)–(28):

$$(1)\ y_{it} = a_i + f_{it} + \delta_i D_{it} + \varepsilon_{it}, \text{ shift in level no trend} \tag{25}$$

$$(2)\ y_{it} = a_i + f_{it} + \delta_i D_{it} + \beta_{it} + \varepsilon_{it}, \text{ shift in level with trend} \tag{26}$$

$$(3)\ y_{it} = a_i + f_{it} + \gamma_i DT_{it} + \beta_{it} + \varepsilon_{it}, \text{ shift in level, constant, and trend} \tag{27}$$

$$(4)\ y_{it} = a_i + f_{it} + \delta_i D_{it} + \gamma_i DT_{it} + \beta_{it} + \varepsilon_{it}, \text{ shift in level and trend and constant} \tag{28}$$

The following nomenclature applies for Eqs. (25)–(28):

f_{it} = random walk.
ε_{it}, u_{it} are i.i.d. across i and t.
δ_i, γ_i stand for the size of break.
D_{it}, DT_{it} dummies for breaks.

The LM statistic is consistent, has an asymptotic normal distribution, and is provided by the following Eq. (29):

$$LM = \frac{1}{\hat{\sigma}_e^2} \frac{1}{NT^2} \left(\sum_{i=1}^{N} \sum_{t=1}^{T} S_{it}^2 \right) \tag{29}$$

$\hat{\sigma}_e^2$ This is a consistent estimator of the error variance under the null hypothesis.
S_{it} This is the partial sum process of the residuals.

3.14 Harris and Tzavalis (1999)

This is a panel unit root test. The null hypothesis is that the panels contain a unit root. The panels are considered to be homogeneous, and this is a drawback. These tests have significant power also when not all panels are stationary. Thus a rejection of the null hypothesis is not convincing enough that all series are stationary. For avoiding the extreme statements of the zero hypotheses such that that either support that each of the series is stationary as a panel, or that at least one of the series in the panel is generated by a stationary process, Pesaran (2011) advises toward the identification of the proportion of the sample for which the null hypothesis is rejected. The model is based on the following data generation process in Eq. (30):

$$y_{it} = a_i + u_{it} \text{ with } u_{it} = \rho u_{i,t-1} + \varepsilon_{it} \text{ and } |\rho < 1| \tag{30}$$

Also, Eq. (31) applies as follows:

$$y_{it} = y_{i,t-1} + \varepsilon_{it} \text{ with } \rho = 1 \text{ and } \varepsilon_{it} \sim N[0, \sigma^2] \tag{31}$$

Under the null hypothesis of $\rho = 1$, the least squares dummy variable estimator has a limiting normal distribution of the form shown in Eq. (32):

$$\sqrt{N}(\rho - 1 - B_2) \to N(0, C_2) \tag{32}$$

The following notation applies in Eq. (32):

$$B_2 = -3/(T+1)$$
$$C_2 = \frac{3(17T^2 - 20T + 17)}{5(T-1)(T+13)}$$

The t-test that is applicable in this situation is based on the estimated ρ, standardized by its mean and variance.

3.15 Harvey and Bates (2003)

This is one of the second-generation tests where the cross-sectional dependence is specified from unknown factors and imposes restrictions on the covariance matrix of residuals. Harvey and Bates (2003) have set up an asymptotic remedy for the problem of cross-sectional correlation.

3.16 Im, Pesaran, and Shin (1997, 2002, 2003)—IPS

It tests the null hypothesis of a unit root. The IPS test is based on Eq. (33):

$$\Delta y_{i,t} = a_i + \rho y_{i,t-1} + \sum_{z=1}^{\rho_i} \beta_{i,z} \Delta y_{i,t-z} + \varepsilon_{i,t} \tag{33}$$

This test allows heterogeneity in the value of ρ_i under the alternative hypothesis:

$$H_0 : \rho = 0$$
$$H_1 : \rho = \rho_i < 0$$

In the alternative hypothesis applies $i = 1, \dots N$ when rho < 0 and $i = N_1 + 1, \dots N$ when rho $= 0$ with $0 < N_1 \leq N$. Rejection of the null hypothesis does not imply that it is rejected at all cross sections, but that the hypothesis is rejected for $N_1 < N$ cross sections such that $N \to \infty, \frac{N_1}{N} \to \delta > 0$. Thus careful interpretation of the rejection of the null hypothesis is required particularly when no information is there for the values δ parameter takes and no suggestions as to which cross sections reject the null hypothesis.

The IPS does not entail pooling of the data, but separates usage of the test for different individuals (panels). The appropriate t-test for test examination is the t_bar statistic. The standardization of the t_bar test is denoted with the Ztbar test and the Wtbar test, which are asymptotically equivalent. However, the Wtbar performs better in small samples.

The t-bar statistic is an average of the individual ADF statistics and is shown in Eq. (34):

$$\bar{t} = \frac{1}{N} \sum_{i=1}^{N} t_{iT} \tag{34}$$

with t_{iT} being the individual ADF statistic, which has finite mean and variance. The power of the t-bar test is affected by a rise in T (time) than in N. Also, if a large enough lag order is selected for the ADF regressions, then the finite sample properties of the t-bar is better than of the LL test (Barbieri, 2006).

Im et al. (2003) are strong opposers to homogeneity. Im et al. (2003) solves LLC serial correlation problem by assuming heterogeneity between units in a dynamic panel framework. The test shows that under the null of nonstationarity, the statistic follows the standard normal distribution asymptotically (Saidi and Mbarek, 2017).

3.17 Jonsson (2005)

This is one of the second-generation tests where the cross-sectional dependence is specified from unknown factors and imposes restrictions on the covariance matrix of residuals. This test is based on an OLS Dickey-Fuller regression, and cross-sectional dependence is accounted for by application of so-called panel corrected standard errors (Beck and Katz, 1995) with robust covariance estimation.

3.18 Kapetanios et al. (2003)

Kapetanios et al. (2003) had suggested a univariate testing procedure to identify the existence of nonlinearity against the nonlinear ESTAR process. The unit root test by Kapetanios (2003) is based on an ADF type test, which is specified against ESTAR. The latter is specified in Eq. (35):

$$\Delta y_t = a y_{t-1} + \varphi y_{t-1} \left(1 - \exp\left\{ -\gamma (y_{t-1} - c)^2 \right\} \right) + \varepsilon_t, \tag{35}$$

The following applies:

$$\varepsilon_t \sim iid\left(0, \sigma^2\right)$$

γ is a smoothness parameter approaching zero, which turns the ESTAR model into Eq. (36):

$$\Delta y_t = a y_{t-1} + \varepsilon_t \tag{36}$$

This is stationary if $-2 < a < 0$.

Kapetanios et al. (2003) show that if $\alpha = 0$ and $\gamma = 0$, the ESTAR model turns into Eq. (37):

$$\Delta y_t = \varphi y_{t-1}\left(1 - \exp\left\{-\gamma(y_{t-1} - c)^2\right\}\right) + \varepsilon_t \qquad (37)$$

Given that this formation does not have a unique unit root and testing, a Taylor approximation around γ was suggested as follows in Eq. (38):

$$G(y_{t-1}; \gamma, c) = 1 - \exp\left\{-\gamma(y_{t-1} - c)^2\right\} \qquad (38)$$

Kapetanios et al. (2003) make the restriction that $c = 0$ and the Taylor approximation lead to the following auxiliary equation as in Eq. (39):

$$\Delta y_t = \beta_1 y_{t-1}^3 + u_t \qquad (39)$$

The cubic term aims to represent nonlinearity: u_t is the noise term. The Kapetanios et al. (2003) unit root test is carried out through the Dickey-Fuller type t-test, known as KSS in Eq. (40):

$$KSS = \frac{\hat{\beta}_1}{\sqrt{\hat{var}}} = \frac{\sum_{t=1}^{T} y_{t-1}^3 \Delta y_t}{\sqrt{\hat{\sigma}^2 \sum_{t=1}^{T} y_{t-1}^6}} \qquad (40)$$

The suggestion of the proportion identification reported in Pesaran (2011) is advised differently in Kapetanios (2003) and Chortareas and Kapetanios (2004, 2009) who propose a sequential panel selection method that consists of applying them, Pesaran, and Shin (2003)'s panel unit root test sequentially. Their suggested handling requires the selection of consecutive smaller fractions of the original data. The reduction is implemented with leaving out the series for which there is evidence for stationarity.

3.19 KPSS: The Kwiatkowski et al. (1992) and the newly arrived GKPSS

Before going to the newly arrived GKPSS, it is helpful to go through the old KPSS. Starting with a series y_t as shown in Eq. (41)

$$y_t = a + \beta t + d \sum_{i=1}^{t} u_i + \varepsilon_t \qquad (41)$$

u_i and ε_t are covariance stationaries with zero mean. Zero mean stationarity refers to the condition that $a = \beta = d = 0$, and mean stationarity refers to $\beta = d = 0$. Trend stationarity means that $d = 0$. If a unit root exists, namely, $d = 1$, the series contains the I(1) component. Under both the old and new framework, namely, the KPSS and the GKPSS, the tests examine the cumulative sums of the detrended or demeaned or level series of the residuals. The GKPSS version reduces size distortions of the KPSS when the series contains strong autoregressive constituents. The original KPSS uses the Bartlett kernel function for an estimation of the autocovariance, while the GKPSS is based on a quadratic spectral kernel with automatic lag selection (Sephton, 2017).

3.20 Levin and Lin (1992, 1993); Levin et al. (2002)

It tests the null hypothesis of a unit root. This is a complicated unit root test, whose alternative hypothesis is that the ρ_i are identical and negative. The fixed nature of ρ_i across panels entails that all data need to be pooled into a single regression. The Levin and Lin test is based on Eq. (42):

$$\Delta y_{i,t} = a_i + \rho y_{i,t-1} + \sum_{z=1}^{\rho_i} \beta_{i,z} \Delta y_{i,t-z} + \varepsilon_{i,t} \tag{42}$$

$i =$ the panel or individual.
$t =$ time.

The error $\varepsilon_{i,\,t}$ is independently and normally distributed across individuals and follows a stationary ARMA process for each individual. The hypothesis is tested with the Levin and Lin test:

$$\begin{aligned} H_0 &: \rho = 0 \\ H_1 &: \rho = \rho_i < 0 \end{aligned} \quad \text{for all } i = 1, \dots N \text{ and } a_i = 0 \text{ in the } H_0$$

The LL test suggests using an adjusted t-statistic whose components have been simulated by the authors. The creators of this test suggest that the most appropriate panel size (for the usage of this test) is one of moderate size with parameters, for example, $10 < N < 250$ and $25 < T < 250$ (Barbieri, 2006).

In essence, Levin and Lin (1992) extended the model to allow for fixed effects, individual deterministic trends and heterogeneous serially correlated errors. Both T and N are assumed to tend to infinity and $N/T \rightarrow 0$. This test is a generalization of the Quah's test with a higher power and has various subcases, which are all estimated as pooled OLS regression models. Thus, in the presence of individual specific fixed effects and serial correlation of the disturbances, the adjusted t-statistic used by Levin and Lin is based on the following relationship as shown in Eq. (43):

$$t_\rho^* = \frac{t_{\rho=0} - N\tilde{T}\hat{S}_N\hat{\sigma}_\varepsilon^{-2}RSE(\hat{\rho})\mu_{m\bar{T}}^*}{\sigma_{m\bar{T}}^*} \tag{43}$$

The following notation applies:

$\mu_{\bar{T}}^*$ is the mean adjustment tabulated in Levin and Lin's paper (Levin and Lin, 1992).
$\sigma_{\bar{T}}^*$ is the standard deviation adjustment tabulated in Levin and Lin's paper (Levin and Lin, 1992).

$$\hat{S}_{NT} = \frac{1}{N} \sum_{i=1}^{N} \frac{\hat{\sigma}_{yi}}{\hat{\sigma}_{ei}}$$

$\hat{\sigma}^2_{yi}$ is a kernel estimator of the long-run variance for individual i.

The major limitation of the LL test that suggests that the autoregressive parameters are equal across the cross sections is addressed and improved in the IPS test (Im et al., 1997; Im and Pesaran, 2003). Last but not least the critical values are sensitive to the selection of lag lengths in the ADF regressions. Generally, it should be borne in mind that the LL test tends to overreject the null hypothesis as N increases, independently of whether models have serially correlated errors or not. Note: The test assumes homogeneity in the dynamics of the autoregressive coefficients for all panel units (Saidi and Mbarek, 2017).

3.21 Lee and Strazicich (2001)

Lee and Strazicich, (2001) provided a correction of Lumsdaine and Papell, (1997) for the incorrect break calculation as of one period behind the true break (Solarin and Shahbaz, 2013). The strength of this test becomes undermined in the presence of more than one break. The break date is chosen over a range of possible break points, where the t-statistic testing the null of a unit root, is minimized in Eq. (44):

$$\Delta \tilde{S}_t = \Delta Z_t \delta + \varphi \tilde{S}_{t-1} + \sum_{l}^{k} c_j \Delta \tilde{S}_{t-j} + e_t \qquad (44)$$

with k being the augmented lag order, $\tilde{S}_t$ the detrended series.

3.22 Lumsdaine and Papell (1997)

This test belongs to the unit root analysis in the presence of structural breaks. Lumsdaine and Papell, (1997) introduce a procedure to capture two structural breaks and argue that unit roots tests that account for two significant structural breaks are more powerful that those that allow for a single break. Lumsdaine and Papell extend the Zivot and Andrews (1992, b) model allowing for two structural breaks under the alternative hypothesis of the unit root test and additionally allow for breaks in level and trend (Glynn et al., 2007).

3.23 Maddala and Wu (1999)

It tests the null hypothesis of a unit root. This is a test applicable in the case of cross-sectional independence. This test comes as an improvement to the drawbacks faced in the IPS or LL, also reported in this chapter. They have proposed a Fisher type test as shown in Eq. (45):

$$P = -2 \sum_{i=1}^{N} \ln p_i \qquad (45)$$

The following notation applies for Eq. (45):

pi is the *p*-value from each panel i.

P is distributed as $\chi 2$ with $2N$ d.f. as $T_i \to \infty$ for all N.

Apparently, this is a nonparametric test based on the *P*-values of the unit root tests in each cross section.

Its advantages:

(1) N can be finite or not.
(2) Each panel may have stochastic and nonstochastic components.
(3) It can host imbalanced data.
(4) H_1 allows some panels to have unit roots and other not.

Both the Maddala and Wu test and the IPS test are more powerful than the LL. When there is cross-sectional correlation, the Maddala and Wu performs better (Barbieri, 2006). They are supporters of the heterogeneity hypothesis, and they pursue the development of unit root tests for panel data that are more realistically characterized by heterogeneity. The heterogeneous tests are constructed either by averaging the statistics of the univariate unit root tests of by averaging their P values. Maddala and Wu (1999) employ nonparametric methods in conducting panel unit roots tests with the Fisher ADF and Fisher PP tests with the advantage of allowing heterogeneity across units (Saidi and Mbarek, 2017).

3.24 Moon and Perron (2004) or MP test

This is one of the second-generation tests where the cross sectional dependence is specified as a common factor model (it assumes the factor structure approach). Moon and Perron (2004) test the orthogonal projection of the data on the common factors by retaining the spirit of the original panel unit root test of Levin et al. (2002), which estimates and tests the pooled first-order autoregressive parameter (Bai and Ng, 2010).

They have slight difference from the model of Bai and Ng, (2004) because they assume that the error terms are generated by r common factors and idiosyncratic shocks in Eqs. (46)–(48) (Hurlin, 2007):

$$y_{it} = a_i + y_{it}^0 \tag{46}$$

$$y_{it}^0 = \rho_i y_{i,t-1}^0 + \mu_{it} \tag{47}$$

$$\mu_{it} = \lambda_i' F_t + e_{it} \tag{48}$$

F_t refers to a vector of common factors, and λ_i is a vector of factor loadings and e_{it} is i. i.d. across i and over t.

3.25 Ng and Perron (2001) also called NGP test

Ng and Perron (2001) have developed a new set of tests, which are superior in cases of negative moving average process. The test output is affected by the choice of the spectral density estimator. The test combines detrending with SD to set up a new test. In essence the test consists of four other tests, the MZ_a, MZ_t, MSB, and the MPT. These tests are shown in Eqs. (49)–(52):

$$MZ_a = \frac{\left(\left(T^{-1}\tilde{y}_t\right)^2 - \hat{f}(0) \right)}{2k} \tag{49}$$

$$MZ_t = MZ_a * MSB \tag{50}$$

$$MSB = \left(\frac{k}{\hat{f}(0)} \right)^{\frac{1}{2}} \tag{51}$$

$$MPT = \frac{\dfrac{\bar{c}^2 k - \bar{c}T^{-1}\left(\tilde{y}_t\right)^2}{\hat{f}(0)}}{\dfrac{\bar{c}^2 k + (1-\bar{c})T^{-1}\left(\tilde{y}_t\right)^2}{\hat{f}(0)}} \tag{52}$$

With d_t^0 as drift d_t^1 as drift and trend in the data generating process. The $\hat{f}(0)$ is the estimate of spectral density at frequency zero. An empirical example of the application of the Ng and Perron (2001) test is provided in Table 3. This test has also been used in Chiou-Wei et al. (2016) with no details about its results.

Table 3 An example of Results presentation from Ng-Perron unit root test by Islam et al. (2013).

Variables	MZ_a	MZ_t	MSB	MPT
ln (energy consumption)	−9.67	−2.15	0.22	9.61
ln (GDP)	−10.90	−2.29	0.21	8.53
ln (population)	2.36	2.03	0.85	197.86
ln (financial development)	−4.20	−1.18	0.28	19.21
Δln (energy consumption)	−20.47	−3.19	0.15	4.45
Δln (GDP)	−23.90	−3.45	0.14	3.81
Δln(population)	−21.48	−3.20	0.14.	4.66
Δln (financial development)	−40.07	−4.47	0.11	2.27

Note: One asterisk denotes rejection of the null at 1%. Two asterisks denote rejection of the null at 5%.

3.26 O' Connell (1998)

This is one of the second-generation tests where the cross-sectional dependence is specified under a covariance restriction approach. This test was the first to deal with cross-sectional dependence in the panel data. The method is valid only when N is fixed and deals with a covariance matrix similar to the one that would arise in an error component model with mutually independent random time effects and individual effects (Barbieri, 2006).

3.27 Park and Choi (1988); Park (1990)

This test is a nonparametric approach that is based on the following equation (Eq. 53):

$$y_t = \tilde{\beta}' s_t + e_t \tag{53}$$

The following applies for Eq. (53):

$s_t = (s_{1t}, \ldots, s_{mt})'$ is a simulated Gaussian random walk of dimensions $m \times 1$.

$\tilde{\beta} = \left(\tilde{\beta}_1, \ldots \tilde{\beta}_m\right)'$ is the $m \times 1$ vector of OLS estimates. The test has the following null hypothesis $H_0 : \tilde{\beta} = (0, \ldots 0)'$.

The following test is used (Eq. 54):

$$J_2(m) = T^{-1} F\left(\tilde{\beta}\right) = T^{-1} \frac{RSS_1 - RSS_2}{RSS_2} \tag{54}$$

where $RSS_1 = \sum_{t=1}^{T} y_t^2$ is the residual sum of squares for the constrained equation.

$RSS_2 = \sum_{t=1}^{T} \left(y_t - \tilde{\beta}' s_t\right)^2$ is the residual sum of squares for the unconstrained equation.

$F\left(\tilde{\beta}\right)$ is a standardized Wald statistic.

3.28 Perron (1989) unit roots with breaks

Unit root tests can be biased toward nonrejection of the unit root when there are structural breaks in the series. Perron, (1989) provides three versions of unit root investigation in a model. These are the following:

- a change in the intercept (this is the level of the series)
- a change in the slope (this is rate of growth)
- a change in both magnitudes, that is, intercept and slope

The hypothesis in this case is formulated as follows (Eqs. 55–56):

$$H_0 : a_0 + y_{t-1} + \mu_1 D_P + \mu_2 D_L + e_t \tag{55}$$

$$H_1 : a_0 + a_2 t + \mu_2 D_L + \mu_3 D_T + e_t \tag{56}$$

The following applies:

D_p: is a dummy variable, which equals 1, if $t = Tb + 1$ and zero if not.
D_L: is a dummy variable, which equals 1, if $t > Tb$ and zero if not.
D_T: is a dummy variable, which equals 1, if $DT = t - Tb$ and zero if not.
Also, for Tb applies that $1 < Tb < T$.

The breaks are exogenously determined, and this has been the point for much criticism. To solve this problem, various statistics are suggested (Libanio, 2005) such as recursive statistics (with subsamples), rolling statistics (with a subsample of fixed size, rolling through the sample), or sequential statistics (allowing for a shift sequentially at every point in the sample). The Perron, (1989) method has been challenged of exogenous determination of structural breaks because it introduces breaks in a subjective way (Solarin and Shahbaz, 2013).

3.29 Pesaran (2003, 2007)

This is one of the second-generation tests where the cross-sectional dependence is specified as a common factor model (It assumes the factor structure approach). Pesaran (2007) augments the ADF regression with the cross-sectional averages of lagged levels and first differences of the individual series (Fang and Chang, 2016). The cross-sectionally augmented Dickey-Fuller (CADF) regression is provided in Eq. (57):

$$\Delta y_{it} = a_i + \rho_i y_{i,t-1} + d_0 \bar{y}_{t-1} + \sum_{j=0}^{\rho} d_{j+1} \Delta \bar{y}_{t-j} + \sum_{k=1}^{p} c_k \Delta y_{i,t-k} + \varepsilon_{it} \qquad (57)$$

$\bar{y}_t$ is the average at time t of all N observations. After the estimation of CADF for every panel, the CIPS statistic is estimated as in Eq. (58):

$$CIPS = \frac{1}{N} \sum_{i=1}^{N} CADF_i \qquad (58)$$

3.30 Phillips and Sul (2003)

This is one of the second-generation tests where the cross-sectional dependence is specified as a common factor model (it assumes the factor structure approach). The one used in Phillips and Sul (2003) is a special case as they only allow for one factor, and the idiosyncratic errors are independently distributed across time as shown in Eq. (59):

$$X_{it} = D_{it} + \lambda_i' F_t + e_{it} \qquad (59)$$

with F_t being an $r*1$ vector of common factors that induce correlation across units, λ_i is an $r*1$ vector of factor loadings, e_{it} is an idiosyncratic error.

3.31 Phillips and Perron (1988)

It is a semiparametric approach with a serial correlation robust nonparametric variance estimator (Newey and West, 1987) that accounts for serially dependent innovations and is shown in Eq. (60):

$$s_{NW}^2 = T^{-1} \sum_{t=1}^{T} \hat{u}_t^2 + 2T^{-1} \sum_{\tau=1}^{k} w_\tau \sum_{t=r+1}^{T} u_t u_{t-r} \tag{60}$$

where $w_\tau = 1 - \tau/(k+1)$ is the weight function. Nonparametric variance estimators are used to account for serial correlation and heteroskedasticity. However, one can say they are similar to Dickey-Fuller tests in that they rely on first order autoregressions. This test is biased against rejecting the null of a unit root, when the time series is stationary around a structural break (Solarin and Shahbaz, 2013).

3.32 Ploberger and Phillips (2002)

This test is an optimal invariant panel unit root test that maximizes average local power (Moon et al., 2003). The test is so designed as to accommodate cross-sectional dependence. It is based on the following statistic shown in Eq. (61) (Trapani, 2004):

$$V_{NT}^{PP} = \frac{\sqrt{N}}{\hat{\sigma}^2} \left[\frac{1}{NT^2} tr\left(\hat{Y}\hat{Y}'\right) - \omega_T^{PP} \hat{\sigma}^2 \right] \tag{61}$$

The test rejects the null of a unit root for small values of V_{NT}^{PP}. When both N and T converge to infinity, then $V_{NT}^{PP} \rightarrow N\,(0, 1/45)$.

3.33 (The) RALS-LM (Meng et al. 2014)

This method combines both the virtues of tests identifying exogenous and endogenous breaks. This method considers a three step procedure to test for a unit root together with the identification of breaks. It adds one more step to the LM procedure of Lee et al. (2012). The first step investigates the break, and the second examines the unit root. The third step incorporates the information from nonnormal errors into the model to strengthen the LM test. The test is based on Eq. (62):

$$\Delta y_t = \delta' \Delta Z_t + \varphi \overline{S}_{t-1}^* + \sum_{j=1}^{k} d_j \Delta \overline{S}_{t-j}^* + \hat{w}_i' \gamma + u_t \tag{62}$$

Notes: The null consists in $\varphi = 0$.
Z_t is exogenous with $Z_t = [1, t, D_{1t}^*, \dots D_{Rt}^*, DT_{1t}^*, \dots, DT_{Rt}^*]'$ with $DT_{1t}^* = 1$ for $t \geq T_B + 1$ and $DT_{1t}^* = 0$ in all other cases.
$DT_{1t}^* = t - T_{Bi}$ for $t \geq T_B + 1$ and $DT_{1t}^* = 0$ in all other cases.
T_{Bi} is the location of breaks
Δ are the coefficients in the regression of Δy_t on $\Delta Z_t \widetilde{S}_t^*$.
$\widetilde{S}_t = y_t - \widetilde{\psi} - Z_t \widetilde{\delta}$ is the detrended series.

For a detailed implementation of this unit root test, the interested reader should see Farhani and Solarin, (2017).

3.34 Quah (1994)

It tests the null hypothesis of a unit root. Quah (1994) suggested a test for unit root in a panel data without fixed effects when both N and T go to infinity at the same rate such that N/T is constant. Moreover, Quah (1994) has allowed N and T to pass to infinity along a specific diagonal path in the two-dimensional array, which can be determined by a monotonically increasing functional relation of $T = T(N)$. The same has been assumed by Levin and Lin (1992). In essence, this is another unit root test whose shortcomings have been addressed by Levin and Lin (1992, 1993) whose model is a generalization of Quah's to allow for heterogeneity of individual effects (constant and linear trend) and the heterogeneous serial correlation of the error term. The way this is done is through a pooled t-statistic. More is explained under the subtitle of Levin and Lin (1992, 1993) in this chapter.

3.35 Zivot and Andrews (1992)

Zivot and Andrews method is a method of endogenous determination of structural breaks and hence remedies the criticism against the Perron, (1989) method of exogenous determination of breaks. The method was also extended by Lumsdaine and Papell, (1997) to host more than one breaks. Table 4 shows the way results are presented in one of the studies it was applied (Shahbaz et al., 2013).

Table 5 offers an indicative selection of energy-growth nexus studies containing various of the unit root tests presented in this chapter.

Table 4 Zivot-Andrews structural trended unit root test from Shahbaz et al. (2013).

Variable	At level		At first difference	
	T-statistic	**Time break**	**T-statistic**	**Time break**
ln (income)	−3.174 (1)	2002	−4.938 (0)*	1985
ln (energy)	−4.226 (1)	2001	−4.668 (2)**	1997
ln (financial development)	−3.453 (1)	1978	−5.714 (1)*	1984
ln (capital)	−3.557 (1)	1990	−4.800 (0)**	1994
ln (exports)	−3.554 (1)	1982	−5.118 (2)*	2005
ln (imports)	−3.373 (1)	1986	−5.763 (2)*	1980
ln (trade)	−4.404 (1)	1988	−5.273 (1)*	1980

Notes: Lag order is shown in parenthesis. One asterisk represents significance at 1% level; two asterisks denote significance at 10% level.

Table 5 An indicative selection of energy-growth studies containing various of the unit root tests presented in this chapter.

Study	Journal	Dataspan	Number of years	Countries	Unit root tests	Formation of the null	Result	Variables	Main method
Kahouli (2017)	Energy Economics	1995–2015	11	Six South Mediterranean countries: Algeria, Egypt, Israel, Lebanon, Morocco, Tunisia	ADF, PP with constant term (level), with constant and trend, with constant term (first difference)	They test the null of the presence of a unit root against the alternative of the absence of a unit root	Most variables are integrated of I(1) The ADF and PP tests with constant and/or trend, do not allow rejection of the null The null is rejected for series in 1st difference	GDP per capita, Financial Development, Energy consumption per capita, trade, capital, urbanization	ARDL bounds testing approach
(Saidi and Mbarek, 2017)	Progress in Nuclear Energy	1990–2013	14	Nine developed countries: Canada, France, Japan, Netherlands, Spain, Sweden, Switzerland, UK, USA	LLC, IPS W-stat, MW-ADF Fisher chi-square, MW-Fisher chi-square, Hadri Z-stat, heteroskedastic consistent Z-stat (all at level and first differences)	The null stands for a unit root, except for the Hadri Z-stat and the Heteroskedastic Consistent Z-stat	All tests reject the null when variables are used in 1st differences	Nuclear energy consumption, Renew able Energy consumption, CO_2 emissions, Labor, GDP per capita	Pedroni cointegration (within dimension: panel v-statistic, panel rho statistic, panel PP-statistic, and panel ADF statistic; Between dimension: group p-statistic, group pp-statistic, and group ADF-statistic), Kao residual cointegration, with FMOLS, and DOLS

Continued

Table 5 An indicative selection of energy-growth studies containing various of the unit root tests presented in this chapter. *Continued*

Study	Journal	Dataspan	Number of years	Countries	Unit root tests	Formation of the null	Result	Variables	Main method
Belke et al. (2011)	Energy Economics	1981–2007	27	25 OECD countries: Australia, Austria, Belgium, Canada, Czech Republic, Denmark, Finland, France, Germany, Greece, Hungary, Ireland, Italy, Japan, Slovakia, South Korea, Luxembourg, Mexico, Netherlands, Portugal, Poland, Spain, Sweden, UK, USA	They use tests that take into account cross-sectional dependence by taking into account a common factor structure	ADF (tests the null of unit root-assumes homogeneity), PP ADF (tests the null of unit root, allows heterogeneity), KPPS (tests the null of stationarity)	Random walks in the data are driven by international developments (long-run relationship may exist between the common components)	Real GDP per capita, Final energy consumption, Energy Price index	Johansen reduced rank approach, DOLS,
Shahbaz et al. (2013)	Energy Economics	1971–2011	41	China	ADF (with intercept and trend in levels and differences), PP (levels and differences) Zivot and Andrews (1992) structural break trended test Clemente et al. (1998) detrended structural break test		All series are found nonstationary at levels (in their intercept and trend versions). They become stationary at 1st difference.	Real domestic output, Energy consumption, real capital use, Labor, Financial Development, Real trade openness	ARDL bounds test approach
Fang and Chang (2016)	Energy Economics	1970–2011	42	Sixteen Asia Pacific countries (Australia, Bangladesh, China, Hong Kong, Indonesia, India, Japan, Korea, Malaysia, New Zealand, Pakistan, Philippines, Singapore, Thailand, Taiwan, Vietnam	Pesaran (2007) if cross-sectional dependence is identified or CADF		The presence of the unit root cannot be rejected for all the five variables at levels (trend or not). They are stationary at 1st difference	GDP, physical and human capital, labor, primary energy consumption	Continuously updated fully modified (Cup-FM), FMOLS

Study	Journal	Period	No.	Country	Unit root test	Null hypothesis	Stationarity result	Variables	Methodology
Islam et al. (2013)	Economic Modeling	1971–2009	39	Malaysia	Ng-Perron		Each series is non-stationary in level, but it is stationary at 1st difference	Energy consumption, economic growth (real GDP), Population, Financial Development (domestic credit to the private sector as share of GDP)	ARDL
Erdal et al. (2008)	Energy Policy	1970–2006	37	Turkey	ADF, PP	As aforementioned	1st difference of the series lead to stationarity	Primary energy Consumption, Gross National Product	Johansen cointegration test, pair wise granger causality
Shahbaz et al. (2011)	Energy Policy	1971–2009	39	Portugal	ADF, PP, generalized Dickey-Fuller (DF-GLS)		1st difference of the series lead to stationarity	Real GDP per capita, electricity consumption per capita, employment	Bounds testing approach (Pesaran et al., 2001)
Ghosh (2010)	Energy Policy	1971–2006	37	India	ADF, PP, KPSS (with constant and constant and trend versions)	ADF, PP: the null is a unit root; KPSS: the null is the series is stationary	3 out of 5 variables appear as stationary in both levels and 1st differences of the KPSS	Real GDP, real investment, employment, CO_2 emissions, total primary energy	Johansen-Juselius cointegration, bounds test cointegration
Wang et al. (2011a, b)	Energy Policy	1972–2006	35	China	ADF, PP, KPSS	ADF, PP: the null is a unit root; KPSS: the null is the series is stationary	1st difference of the series lead to stationarity	GDP, Energy Consumption, Capital, Labor	ARDL
Solarin and Shahbaz (2013)	Energy Policy	1971–2009	39	Angola	ADF, PP, LS	The null is the existence of unit root for all three tests	All tests reject the null at 1st differences.	Real GDP per capita, Electricity consumption per capita, urbanization	Gregory-Hansen structural cointegration approach, ARDL
Chiou-Wei et al. (2016)	Energy	1950–2010	46	Five ASEAN countries: China, Singapore, South Korea, Philippines, Taiwan	ADF, PP, ERS, Ng, and Perron		All variables are 1st difference trend stationary	Real GDP, real exchange rates, real oil price, energy consumption	EGARCH-M (Nelson, 1991)

Continued

Table 5 An indicative selection of energy-growth studies containing various of the unit root tests presented in this chapter. *Continued*

Study	Journal	Dataspan	Number of years	Countries	Unit root tests	Formation of the null	Result	Variables	Main method
Esso and Keho (2016)	Energy Policy	1971–2010	41	Twelve Selected Sub-Saharan countries: Benin, Cameroon, Congo, Congo DR (Democratic Republic), Ghana, Nigeria, Senegal, Cote d'Ivoire, Gabon, Ghana, Kenya, South Africa, Togo	PP (constant and trend in level and first differences)	As aforementioned	All tests reject the null at 1st differences.	Real GDP, Energy use, CO2 emissions	ARDL
Farhani and Solarin, (2017)	Energy	1973q1–2014q4	168q	USA	RALS-LM structural break Unit root tests	The null is the existence of a unit root Note that the test has three steps	Each series is I (1) with strikes located in the early 1980s	Primary energy consumption, Foreign Direct Investment, Trade, capital, Real GDP, Financial development	Bayer-Hanck cointegration approach
Wang et al. (2011a, b)	Energy Policy	1995–2007	13	China (28 provinces)	LLC, IPS, MW	The null is that there exists a unit root	All tests reject the null at first differences	CO2 emissions, energy consumption, real economic output	Pedroni (1999, 2004)
Rafindadi and Ozturk (2017)	Renewable and Sustainable Energy Reviews	1971q1–2013q4	42 yrs., 172 quarters	Germany	Ng-Perron, CMR	The null is that there exists a unit root	All tests reject the null at first differences	Renewable energy consumption, Labor, Capital, Real GDP	ARDL, Johansen cointegration, Bayer-Hanck cointegration
Faisal et al., (2017)	Procedia Economics and Finance	1990–2011	22	Russia	ADF, PP	As aforementioned	All tests reject the null at first differences	Energy consumption, Electricity Consumption, GDP	Toda-Yamamoto

Notes on the abbreviated names of tests: ADF, augmented Dickey-Fuller (1981); PP, Phillips and Perron (1988); LLC, Levin, Lin, and Chu (2002); IPS, Im, Pesaran, and Shin; Fisher ADF, Maddala and Wu (1999); Fisher PP, Maddala and Wu (1999); KPSS, Kwiatkowski et al. (1992); DOLS, dynamic ordinary least squares; LS, Lee and Strazicish (2004); ERS, Elliot, Rothenberg, and Stock; RALS, residual augmented least squares; MW, Maddala and Wu; Z-A, Zivot-Andrews (1992); CMR, Clemente-Montanes-Reyes (1998).

4 Concluding remarks

The type of the unit root test that we used in the energy-growth nexus field depends on the null hypothesis and its alternative, the decision on how to handle the small samples, and whether we assume homogeneity or heterogeneity of the sample. Unit root tests and stationary tests can be used in conjunction with each other, depending on what is the most suitable and convenient hypothesis for the available data.

This chapter includes an alphabetical directory of unit roots, time series, and panel data ones, both first and second generation, and of various other classifications. Since the aim of the whole book is to serve as a first aid reference guide of junior energy-growth researchers and students, this is the first time unit root, and stationarity tests have been collected and classified this way. Of course, many tests have been omitted because they have not been used in the energy-growth nexus so far or because more recent improvements of those tests have replaced the older versions of the tests.

References

Aparico, F., Escribano, A., Sipolis, A.E., 2006. Range unit-root (rur) tests: robust against non-linearities, error distributions, structural breaks and outliers. J. Time Ser. Anal. 27 (4), 545–576.

Bai, J., Ng, S., 2001. A PANIC Attack on Unit Roots and Cointegration. MIMEO, Boston College, Department of Economics.

Bai, J., Ng, S., 2004. A PANIC attack on unit roots and cointegration. Econometrica 72 (4), 1127–1178.

Bai, J., Ng, S., 2010. Panel unit root tests with cross section dependence: a further investigation. Econometr. Theory 26, 1088–1114.

Barbieri, L., 2006. Quaderni del dipartamento di scienze economiche e sociali, Serie Rossa: Economia-Quaderno N.43, ottobre 2006. Available from Research Gate, Accessed 11/09/2019.

Beck, N., Katz, J.N., 1995. What to do (and not to do) with time-series cross-section data. Am. Polit. Sci. Rev. 89, 634–647.

Belke, A., Dobnik, F., Dreger, C., 2011. Energy consumption and economic growth: new insights into the cointegration relationship. Energy Econ. 33, 782–789.

Breitung, J., 2002. Nonparametric tests for unit roots and cointegration. J. Econ. 108 (2), 343–363.

Breitung, J., Das, S., 2005. Panel unit root tests under cross sectional dependence. Statistica Neerlandica 59 (4), 414–433.

Breitung, J., Gourieroux, C., 1997. Rank tests for unit roots. J. Econ. 81 (1), 7–27.

Breitung, J., Meyer, W., 1994. Testing for unit roots in panel data: are wages on different bargaining levels cointegrated? Appl. Econ. 26, 353–361.

Cavaliere, G., Taylor, A.M.R., 2007. Testing for unit roots in time series with non-stationary volatility. J. Econ. 140 (2), 919–947.

Cavaliere, G., Taylor, A.M.R., 2008. Bootstrap unit root tests for time series with nonstationary volatility. Economet. Theory 24 (1), 43–71.

Chang, Y., 2002. Nonlinear IV unit root tests in panels with cross-sectional dependency. J. Econ. 120, 261–292.

Chang, Y., 2004. Bootstrap unit root tests in panels with cross-sectional dependency. J. Econ. 120, 263–293.

Chiou-Wei, S.Z., Zhu, Z., Chen, S.H., Hsueh, S.P., 2016. Controlling for relevant variables: energy consumption and economic growth nexus revisited in an EGARCH-M (Exponential GARCH-in-Mean) model. Energy 109, 391–399.

Choi, I., 1999. Asymptotic analysis of a nonstationary error component model (Manuscript). Kookmin University, Korea.

Choi, I., 2001. Unit root tests for panel data. J. Int. Money Financ. 20, 249–272.

Choi, I., 2002. Combination Unit Root Tests for Cross-Sectionally Correlated Panels. MIMEO, Hong Kong University of Science and Technology.

Chortareas, G., Kapetanios, G., 2009. Getting PPP right: identifying mean-reverting real exchange rates in panels. J. Bank. Financ. 33, 390–404.

Chortareas, G., Kapetanios, G., 2004. "The yen real exchange rate may be stationary after all" evidence from non-linear unit root tests. Oxf. Bull. Econ. Stat. 66, 113–131.

Clemente, J., Antonio, M., Marcelo, R., 1998. Testing for a unit root in variables with a double change in the mean. Econ. Lett. 59, 175–182.

Elliott, G., Rothenberg, T.J., Stock, J.H., 1996. Efficient tests for an autoregressive unit root. Econometrica 64 (4), 813–836.

Erdal, G., Erdal, H., Esengün, K., 2008. The causality between energy consumption and economic growth in Turkey. Energy Policy 36, 3838–3842.

Esso, L.J., Keho, Y., 2016. Energy consumption, economic growth and carbon emissions: cointegration and causality evidence from selected African countries. Energy 114, 492–497.

Faisal, F., Tursoy, T., Ercantan, O., 2017. The relationship between energy consumption and economic growth: evidence from non-Granger causality test. Procedia Comput. Sci. 120, 671–675.

Fang, Z., Chang, Y., 2016. Energy, human capital and economic growth in Asia Pacific countries—evidence from a panel cointegration and causality analysis. Energy Econ. 56, 177–184.

Fotopoulos, S.B., Ahn, S.K., 2003. Rank based dickey-fuller test statistics. J. Time Ser. Anal. 24 (6), 647–662.

Ghosh, S., 2010. Examining carbon emissions economic growth nexus for India: a multivariate cointegration approach. Energy Policy 38, 3008–3014.

Glynn, J., Perera, N., Verma, R., 2007. Unit root tests and structural breaks: a survey with applications. Rev. Métodos Cuant. Econ. Empresa 3 (1), 63.

Hadri, K., 2000. Testing for unit roots in heterogeneous panel data. Econ. J. 3, 148–161.

Harris, R.D.F., Tzavalis, E., 1999. Inference for unit roots in dynamic panels where time dimensions are fixed. J. Econ. 91, 201–226.

Harvey, A., Bates, D., 2003. Multivariate Unit Root Tests, Stability and Convergence. University of Cambridge. DAE Working Paper No. 301. Homogeneous panel data unit root test. Oxford Bulletin of Economics and Statistics, 67(3):369-392.

Hurlin, C., Mignon, V., 2007. Second Generation Panel Unit Root Tests, halshs-00159842. Available from: halshs.archives-ouverts.fr/halshs-00159842/document, Accessed 28/08/2019.

Hurlin, C., 2007. What Would Nelson and Plosser Find Had They Used Panel Unit Root Tests? Available from: https://www.univ-orleans.fr/deg/masters/ESA/CH/Nelson_AE.pdf.

Im, K.S., Pesaran, M.H., 2003. On the Panel Unit Root Tests Using Nonlinear Instrumental Variables. MIMEO, University of Southern California.

Im, K.S., Pesaran, M.H., Shin, Y., 1997. Testing for Unit Roots in Heterogeneous Panels. DAE Working Paper 9526, University of Cambridge.

Im, K.S., Pesaran, M.H., Shin, Y., 2003. Testing for unit roots in heterogeneous panels. J. Econ. 115 (1), 53–74.

Islam, F., Shahbaz, M., Ahmed, A.U., Alam, M.M., 2013. Financial development and energy consumption nexus in Malaysia: a multivariate time series analysis. Econ. Model. 30, 435–441.

Jonsson, K., 2005. Cross-sectional dependency and size distortion in a small sample homogeneous panel data unit root test. Oxf. Bull. Econ. Stat. 67, 369–392.

Kahouli, B., 2017. The short and long run causality relationship among economic growth, energy consumption and financial development: evidence from South Mediterranean Countries (SMCs). Energy Econ. 68, 19–30.

Kapetanios, G., 2003. Determining the Poolability Properties of Individual Series in Panel Datasets. Queen Mary, University of London. Working Paper No. 499.

Kapetanios, G., Shin, Y., Snell, A., 2003. Testing for a unit root in the nonlinear STAR framework. J. Econ. 112, 359–373.

Kwiatkowski, D., Phillips, P.C.B., Schmidt, P., Shin, Y., 1992. Testing the null hypothesis of stationarity against the alternative of a unit root. How sure are we that economic time series have a unit root? J. Econ. 54, 159–178.

Lee, J., Strazicich, M.C., 2001. Break point estimation and spurious rejections with endogenous unit root tests. Oxf. Bull. Econ. Stat. 63, 535–558.

Lee, J., Strazicish, M.C., Meng, M., 2012. Two step LM unit root tests with trend breaks. J. Stat. Econ. Methods 1, 81–107.

Levin, A., Lin, C.F., 1992. Unit Root Test in Panel Data: Asymptotic and Finite Sample Properties. University of California at San Diego. Discussion Paper 92-93.

Levin, A., Lin, C.F., 1993. Unit Root Test in Panel Data: New Results. University of California at San Diego. Discussion Paper 93-56.

Levin, A., Lin, C.F., Chu, C.S.J., 2002. Unit root test in panel data: asymptotic and finite sample properties. J. Econ. 108, 1–24.

Libanio, G.A., 2005. Unit roots in macroeconomic time series: theory, implications and evidence. Nova Econ. 15 (3), 1980–5381. Available from: www.scielo.br/scielo.php. (Accessed 4 September 2019).

Lumsdaine, R.L., Papell, D.H., 1997. Multiple trend breaks and the unit root hypothesis. Rev. Econ. Stat. 79 (2), 212–218.

Maddala, G.S., Wu, S., 1999. A comparative study on unit root tests with panel data and a new simple test. Oxf. Bull. Econ. Stat. 61, 631–652.

Meng, M., Im, K.S., Lee, J., Tieslau, M.A., 2014. More powerful LM unit root tests with nonnormal errors. In: Sickles, R.C., Horrage, W.C. (Eds.), Festschrift in Honor Peter Schmidt. Springer, New York, pp. 343–357.

Moon, H.R., Perron, B., 2004. Testing for a unit root in panels with dynamic factors. J. Econ. 122, 81–126.

Moon, H.R., Perron, B., Phillips, P.C.B., 2003. Incidental Trends and the Power of Panel Unit Root Tests. Available from: http:/dido.econ.yale.edu/korora/phillips/papers/efpunit4.pdf. (Accessed 7 April 2020).

Nelson, D.B., 1991. Conditional heteroskedasticity in asset returns: a new approach. Econometrica 59, 347–370.

Newey, W.K., West, K.D., 1987. A simple, positive semi-definite, heteroskedasticity and autocorrelation consistent covariance matrix. Econometrica 55 (3), 703–708.

Ng, S., Perron, P., 2001. Lag length selection and the construction of unit root test with good size and power. Econometrica 69, 1519–1554.

O' Connell, P., 1998. The overvaluation of purchasing power parity. J. Int. Econ. 44, 1–19.

Park, J.Y., 1990. Testing for unit roots and cointegration by variable addition. In: Fromby, T., Rhodes, F. (Eds.), Advances in Econometrics: Cointegration, Spurious Regression and Unit Roots. Jai Press, Cambridge.

Park, J.Y., Choi, B., 1988. A New Approach to Testing for a Unit Root. CAE Working Paper No. 88-23, Cornell University, Ithaca, NY.

Pedroni, P., 1999. Critical values for cointegration tests in heterogeneous panels with multiple regressors. Oxf. Bull. Econ. Stat. 61, 653–670.

Pedroni, P., 2004. Panel cointegration: asymptotic and finite sample properties of pooled time series tests with an application to the PPP hypothesis. Economet. Theory 20, 597–614.

Perron, P., 1989. The great crash, the oil price shock and the unit root hypothesis. Econometrica 57 (6), 1361–1401.

Pesaran, H.M., 2003. A Simple Panel Unit Root Test in the Presence of Cross Section Dependence. MIMEO, University of Southern California.

Pesaran, M.H., 2007. A simple panel unit root test in the presence of cross section dependence. J. Appl. Econ. 22 (2), 265–312.

Pesaran, M.H., 2011. On the Interpretation of Panel Unit Root Tests. Available from: http://www.econ.cam.ac.uk/people-files/emeritus/mhp1/wp11/Interpretation-Panel-Unit-September-2011.pdf. (Accessed 15 September 2019).

Pesaran, M.H., Shin, Y., Smith, R.J., 2001. Bounds testing approaches to the analysis of level relationships. J. Appl. Econometr. 16, 289–326.

Phillips, P.C.B., Perron, P., 1988. Testing for a unit root in time series regression. Biometrika 75 (2), 335–346.

Phillips, P.C.B., Sul, D., 2003. Dynamic panel estimation and homogeneity testing under cross section dependence. Econ. J. 6 (1), 217–259.

Ploberger, W., Phillips, P.C.B., 2002. Optimal Testing for Unit Roots in Panel Data. MIMEO.

Quah, D., 1994. Exploiting cross-section variations for unit root inference in dynamic data. Econ. Lett. 44, 9–19.

Rafindadi, A.A., Ozturk, I., 2017. Impacts of renewable energy consumption on the German economic growth: evidence from combined cointegration test. Renew. Sust. Energ. Rev. 75, 1130–1141.

Reisen, V.A., L' Evy-Leduc, C., Bourguignon, M., Boistard, H., 2016. Robust Dickey-Fuller Tests Based on Ranks for Time Series With Additive Outliers. Available from: https://www6.inrae.fr/mia-paris/content/download/4666/43730/version/1/file/REVISION-METRIKA-V3_cllV3-imprev1.pdf. (Accessed 5 July 2020).

Saidi, K., Mbarek, M.B., 2017. The impact of income, trade, urbanization, and financial development on CO_2 emissions in 19 emerging economies. Environ. Sci. Pollut. Control Ser. 24, 12748–12757.

Sephton, P., 2017. Finite sample critical values of the generalized KPSS stationarity test. Comput. Econ. 50, 161–173.

Shahbaz, M., Khan, S., Tahir, M.I., 2013. The dynamic links between energy consumption, economic growth, financial development and trade in China: fresh evidence from multivariate framework analysis. Energy Econ. 40, 8–21.

Shahbaz, M., Tang, C.F., Shahbaz Shabbir, M., 2011. Electricity consumption and economic growth nexus in Portugal using cointegration and causality approaches. Energy Policy 39, 3529–3536.

Solarin, S.A., Shahbaz, M., 2013. Trivariate causality between economic growth, urbanisation and electricity consumption in Angola: cointegration and causality analysis. Energy Policy 60, 876–884.

Statistics How to, 2019. Unit Root: Simple Definition, Unit Root Tests. Available from: www.statisticshowto.datasciencentral.com/unit-root. (Accessed 28 August 2019).

Trapani, L., 2004. Testing for Unit Roots in Heterogeneous Panels Under Cross Sectional Dependence. Faculty of Finance, Cass Business School. Available from: https:/www.cass.city.ac.uk/__data/assets/pdf_file/0007/65176/Trapani.pdf. (Accessed 7 July 2020).

Wang, S.S., Zhou, D.Q., Zhou, P., Wang, Q.W., 2011a. CO_2 emissions, energy consumption and economic growth in China: a panel data analysis. Energy Policy 39, 4870–4875.

Wang, Y., Zhou, J., Zhu, X., Lu, G., 2011b. Energy consumption and economic growth in China: a multivariate causality test. Energy Policy 39, 4399–4406.

Westerlund, J., Breitung, J., 2009. Myths and Facts About Unit Root Tests. Department of Economics, Lund University, Sweden. Available from: http:/conference.iza.org/conference_files/pada2009/breitung_j1604.pdf. (Accessed 4 July 2020).

Zivot, E., Andrews, D., 1992. Further evidence of great crash, the oil price shock and unit root hypothesis. J. Bus. Econ. Stat. 10, 251–270.

Farhani, S., Solarin, S.A., 2017. Financial development and energy demand in the United States: new evidence from combined cointegration and asymmetric causality tests. Energy 134 (C), 1029–1037.

Further reading

Breitung, J., Pesaran, H.M., 2008. Unit roots and cointegration in panels. In: Matyas, L., Sevestre, P. (Eds.), The Econometrics of Panel Data: Fundamentals and Recent Developments in Theory and Practice. Kluwer Academic Publishers, Dordrecht.

Cavaliere, G., Taylor, A.M.R., 2009. Bootstrap M unit root tests. Econ. Rev. 28 (5), 393–421.

Chen, M.-Y., 2013. Panel Unit Root and Cointegration Tests. Department of Finance, National Chung Hsing University. Available from: http:/photo.jlwu.idv.tw/~finmyc/Tim_panl_unit_p.pdf. (Accessed 15 September 2019).

Choi, I., 2006. Combination unit root tests for cross-sectionally correlated panels. In: Corbae, D., Durlauf, S., Hansen, B. (Eds.), Econometric Theory and Practice: Frontiers of Analysis and Applied Research. Cambridge University Press, New York.

Hall, B.H., Mairesse, J., 2002. Testing for Unit Roots in Panel Data: An Exploration Using Real and Simulated Data. Available from: https:/eml.berkeley.edu/~bhhall/papers/HallMairesseJan03%20unitroot.pdf. (Accessed 15 September 2019).

Jalil, A., Feridun, M., 2011. The impact of growth, energy and financial development on the environment in China: a cointegration analysis. Energy Econ. 33, 284–291.

Kruse, R., 2008. A New Unit Root Test Against ESTAR Basedon a Class of Modified Statistics. Diskussionsbeitrag, No. 398, Leibniz Universität Hannover, Wirtschaftswissenschaftliche Fakultät, Hannover.

Tursoy, F.T., Resatoglou, N.G., 2016. Energy consumption, electricity, and GDP causality: the case of Russia, 1990-2011. Procedia Econ. Finance 39, 653–659.

An A–Z guide for complete research when using the autoregressive distributed lag (ARDL) bounds test approach in the broader energy-growth nexus

1 Introduction

Up-to-date various cointegration and causality methods have been used in the energy-growth nexus and the X-variable nexus framework, with the most common having been the Engle and Granger (1987) based on residuals, the Phillips and Hansen (1990) with a modified ordinary least square procedure, Johansen (1988), and the Johansen and Juselius (1990) maximum likelihood methods. However, some years later, it was realized that these methods may not be appropriate for small samples (Narayan and Smyth, 2005). Foremost, studies before the ARDL establishment, and this was much the case for the energy-growth nexus, used much cross-sectional analysis through their panel data configuration, and this entailed that the countries included in those samples were not homogeneous enough with respect to their economic development level (Odhiambo, 2009). Unless results became country specific, they are of little use for policy making.

The autoregressive distributed lag (ARDL) method or bounds test was initiated by Pesaran and Shin, (1999) and further developed by Pesaran et al., (2001). It is regarded as one of the most flexible methods in the econometric analysis of the energy-growth nexus, particularly when the research framework is shaped by shocks and regime shifts that change the pattern of energy consumption or the evolution of other involved variables in the models. Moreover, the fact that the ARDL method may accommodate different lags in different variables renders the method very attractive and underlines its flexibility. The accommodation of sufficient lags enables best capturing of the data generating process mechanism. More specifically the method can be applied irrespective of whether the time series is $I(0)$, namely, stationary at levels, or $I(1)$, namely, stationary at first differences or frictionally integrated (Pesaran et al., 2001). Nevertheless, within the ARDL framework, the series should not be $I(2)$ because this integration order invalidates the F-statistics and all critical values established by Pesaran and have been calculated for series that are $I(0)$ and/or $I(1)$. Also the ARDL method provides unbiased estimates and valid

A Guide to Econometric Methods for the Energy-Growth Nexus. https://doi.org/10.1016/B978-0-12-819039-5.00007-0

T-statistics, even if some of the regressors may be endogenous (Harris and Sollis, 2003; Jalil and Ma, 2008). Actually, due to the appropriate lag selection, residual correlation is eliminated, and thus the endogeneity problem is also solved (Ali et al., 2017a). Moreover the short-run adjustments can be integrated with the long-run equilibrium through the error correction mechanism (ECM) through a linear transformation without sacrificing information about the long-run horizon (Ali et al., 2017a,b). Also the method allows the correction of outliers with impulse dummies (Marques et al., 2017a,b) and the approach distinguished between dependent and independent variables. Last but not least the interpretation of the ARDL approach and its implementation are easy (Rahman and Kashem, 2017), and the ARDL framework requires a single form equation (Bayer and Hanck, 2013), while other procedures require a system of equations. The ARDL approach is more reliable for small samples than Johansen and Juselius's cointegration methodology (Haug, 2002). Halicioglu (2007) also mentions two more advantages of the method. These are the simultaneous estimation of short- and long-run effects and the ability to test hypotheses on the estimated coefficients in the long run something that the Engle-Granger method did not do.

This chapter is organized as follows: After the introduction (Section 1), it follows the methodology with best practice example from various published papers. Section 3 contains a literature review with applications of the method in the energy-growth nexus and other fields; Section 4 deals with the strategies and guidelines in the ARDL framework for the energy-growth nexus, and Section 5 concludes the chapter.

2 The methodology with best practice examples from published papers

For reasons of educative simplicity, we will assume two series, the Y_t and the X_t. Of course in the energy-growth nexus, more variables are usually present in the right hand side of the production function equation. The reader can easily generalize into more variables. In a bivariate energy-growth nexus model, the Y_t stands for economic growth, and the X_t stands for energy consumption. It is also typical in the energy growth nexus to use logarithms of the variables to translate variable coefficients as elasticities. The series in the ARDL procedure is the investigation of (i) stationarity, (ii) cointegration, and then (iii) causality. Of course, there are ways to proceed to causality analysis without the first two steps, but this occurs within other methodological frameworks.

2.1 Stationarity

The first step in the ARDL analysis, after a presentation of the descriptive statistics of the series (mean, median, minimum and maximum values, skewness, kurtosis and the standard deviation, Jarque-Bera normality test, and pairwise correlation), is the unit root analysis. Since we devote a whole chapter of this book (Chapter 2) in this matter, we will not spend time repeating this analysis at this point. The unit root analysis will inform us of the degree of integration of each variable. To satisfy the bounds test assumption of the ARDL models, each variable must be I(0) or I(1). Under no circumstances, should it be I(2). De Vita (De Vita et al., 2006) also notes that the dependent variable should be I(1). However, this is not claimed in the current literature. Stationarity is examined with the augmented Dickey-Fuller (ADF) and the Kwiatkowski-Phillips-Schmidt-Shin (KPSS) in Bölük and Mert (2015). Ali et al. (2016) have used the augmented Dickey-Fuller (ADF) and the Phillips-Perron (PP) test, both in levels and differenced forms. Marques et al. (2017a,b) employ second generation tests such as the cross-sectional augmented IPS-CIPS (Pesaran, 2007). Lee and Strazicich, (2003) used a Lagrange multiplier (LM) test that is appropriate for large data sizes and structural break identification.

Flashback 1: The concept of Integration

Integration is the process with which a nonstationary series is converted into a stationary series. This is accomplished when the series is differenced, namely, we take first difference of each observation with its previous one. If the series needs to be differenced d times to become stationary, then we state that it is integrated of degree d. This is shown as $Yt \rightarrow I(d)$.

2.1.1 Determining the lag length of the variables

The lag length in the variables is decided with the help of the Schwarz Bayesian Information Criterion (SIC) or the Akaike Information Criterion (AIC). These statistics are applied on the unrestricted models of the ARDL. Namely, the lag length is decided from an unrestricted VAR model with the help of AIC and BIC statistics. The ARDL method estimates $(p+1)^k$ number of regressions to obtain the optimal lag length for each variable, with p being the maximum number of lags and k is the number of variables in the required equation.

Flashback 2: The AIC, BIC, and the HQC criteria

The Akaike Information Criterion (AIC) and the Schwarz Information Criterion (BIC) are used as statistics of good fit, and we use them for the selection of the most appropriate-best fit model from a sum of estimated ones. We select the model with the lowest AIC or BIC statistic. The mathematical formulae for these statistics are shown in Eqs. (1)–(3)

$$AIC = \ln\left(\frac{RSS}{n-k}\right) + \frac{2}{n}k \tag{1}$$

$$BIC = \ln\left(\frac{RSS}{n-k}\right) + \frac{k}{n}\ln(n) \tag{2}$$

with RSS being the residual sum of squares of the regression, n the sample size, and k the number of parameters in the model.

The Hannan-Quinn Criterion is given by the following relationship:

$$HQC = -2L_{max} + 2kln(\ln(n)) \tag{3}$$

with L_{max} being the log-likelihood, k is the number of parameters, and n is the number of observations.

After this is decided, we can proceed with the application of the ARDL bounds test, which is an *F*-type test.

Flashback 3: What do we mean by an *F*-type test?

It is any test where the test statistic follows the F-distribution under the null hypothesis. One of the most common reasons we employ an *F*-type test is to test the hypothesis that a data set in a regression analysis follows the simpler of two proposed linear models that are nested within each other. If Model 1 is "nested" within Model 2, Model 1 is the restricted model, and Model 2 is the unrestricted one, and the unrestricted model has more parameters than Model 1, which is also called the naive model. The *F* statistic is calculated as shown in Eq. (4):

$$F = \frac{\left(\dfrac{RSS_1 - RSS_2}{p_2 - p_1}\right)}{\left(\dfrac{RSS_2}{n - p_2}\right)} \tag{4}$$

where *RSSi* is the residual sum of squares of model *i*. The null hypothesis is that Model 2 does not provide a significantly better fit than model 1. In that case *F* will have an *F* distribution, with $(p_2 - p_1, n - p_2)$ degrees of freedom. The null hypothesis is rejected if the *F* calculated from the data is greater than the critical value of the *F*-distribution for the level of significance we choose.

The essence models in the ARDL bounds test framework are the following unrestricted error correction models in Eqs. (5), (6):

$$\Delta LY_t = a_0 + a_1 t + \sum_{i=1}^{m} \alpha_{2i} \Delta LY_{t-i} + \sum_{i=0}^{n} a_{3i} \Delta LX_{t-i} + a_4 LY_{t-1} + a_5 LX_{t-1} + \mu_{1t} \tag{5}$$

$$\Delta LX_t = \beta_0 + \beta_1 t + \sum_{i=1}^{m} \beta_{2i} \Delta LX_{t-i} + \sum_{i=0}^{n} \beta_{3i} \Delta LY_{t-i} + \beta_4 LX_{t-1} + \beta_5 LY_{t-1} + \mu_{2t} \tag{6}$$

Δ is the first difference operator and μ is the error term that must be a white noise, or put in other words, it represents the residual term that is supposed to be well behaved (serially independent, homoskedastic and normally distributed). All α and β coefficients are nonzero with a_4 and β_4 also being negative (this represents the speed of adjustment). The parameters α_{2i} and a_{3i} represent the short-run dynamic coefficients, while a_4 and a_5 are long-run coefficients in the energy-growth nexus relationship. α_0 and β_0 are drift components, μ_{1t} and μ_{2t} are white noise. Overall, we observe in Eqs. (5), (6) that each variable is represented as dependent on the past values of itself, the past values of the other variable(s), and the past values of differenced values of itself and the past values of differenced values of the other variable(s). Models 5 and 6 can be formulated either as intercept or trend ARDL models or both. Eqs. (5), (6) contain both. Halicioglou (Halicioglu, 2007) writes that it is possible to end up with two models, one with trend and one with not a trend. There is a method described in Bahmani-Oskooee and Goswami (2003) according to which one ends up with a single long-run relationship through consecutive eliminations of the rest of the relationships.

So at the end of this research stage, the researcher should produce one's results in a table whose exemplar model is presented in Table 1.

Table 1 Exemplar presentation of ARDL estimates (first stage).

Constant	ΔY		ΔX	
	Coefficient	t-Statistic (or P-value)	Coefficient	t-Statistic (or P-value)
Trend				
$\Delta(Y_{-1})$...				
$\Delta(Y_{-n})$				
$\Delta(X_{-1})$...				
$\Delta(X_{-n})$				
Y_{-1}				
X_{-1}				
R^2				
$\bar{R}^2$				
AIC				
SIC				
DW				
F-statistic				

Notes: It is typical to assign (*), (**), and (***) to significant coefficients for level 10%, 5%, and 1% of significance, respectively.

Flashback 4: What does a well-behaved residual term mean?

Residuals from a regression (or the error term) are created when the model does not fully represent the actual relationship between the independent variables and the dependent variables. It is almost impossible for the model ever to fully represent the actual underlying relationship. Thus there is always a residual. For the residuals, we make the following assumptions: their error variance V-$(u_i) = \sigma^2$ for all I and the error terms are serially independent. The regression relationship is linear (Maddala and Lahiri, 2009).

The first stage of the ARDL estimation produces a $(p+1)^k$ number of regressions so that the optimal lag length for each variable is obtained, with p being the maximum number of lags and k is the number of variables in the equation. In our simplistic example, there is only one X_t variable.

In the framework described in Eqs. (5), (6), we carry out the ARDL bounds cointegration test. These equations are estimated with ordinary least squares (OLS).

Flashback 5: Cointegration in simple words

When we don't have stationary time series, the regression between the variables X and Y is spurious. However, in spite of the fact that the two variables may not be stationary by themselves, their linear combination can be a stationary variable. There is also the case where one variable can be stationary, and the other is not, but again, their linear combination turns out to be a linear combination.

The economic importance of cointegration lies in the fact that the variables have a long-run economic relationship between them, if they are found to be cointegrated. The cointegration relationship does not generate directly information on the short-run equilibrium of the variables, but it

Continued

can contribute to the configuration of the information in the short run. This occurs through the error correction model paradigm.

Let two variables x_t and y_t, which are $I(d)$, namely, they are integrated of degree d; this means there is a number β so that $y_t - \beta x_t = u_t$; and the u_t has an integration order lower than d, then x_t and y_t are cointegrated with a cointegration order lower than d. Thus, when the variables x_t and y_t are integrated of order 1 and cointegrated, we don't have to transform the level values in differences, and we can directly apply the least square method and estimate the relationship $y_t = \alpha + \beta x_t + u_t$.

If we take differences of a variable, which is I(1), we are foregoing long-run information, so it is meaningful to study the variables only in the short run. An alternative method that contains information about the short-run and the long-run information (when the variables are cointegrated) is the error correction model. This is the quintessence of the Granger theorem. The error correction model can be written as follows in Eqs. (7), (8):

$$\Delta lny_t = a_1 + \sum_{i=1}^{l} a_{11}\Delta Ly_{t-i} + \sum_{j=0}^{m} a_{22}\Delta x_{t-j} + n_1 ECT_{t-1} + \mu_{1i} \tag{7}$$

$$\Delta lnx_t = a_1 + \sum_{i=1}^{l} a_{21}\Delta Lx_{t-i} + \sum_{j=0}^{m} a_{22}\Delta y_{t-j} + n_2 ECT_{t-1} + \mu_{2i} \tag{8}$$

The differences of x and y are functions if their lagged values, n_1 and n_2 are never zero (they should be lower than zero for convergence to exist in the long run), and the size of n describes the convergence speed, while the μ_s represent the errors which are white noise.

2.1.2 The second step in the ARDL analysis

The second step is as follows: If the existence of cointegration is confirmed in Eqs. (5), (6), then we estimate the long-run and the short-run models and derive both long- and short-run elasticities, namely, the ARDL equivalent of the UECM (unrestricted error correction model).

Cointegration, in the ARDL bounds test approach, is examined under the following hypothesis set up as shown in Eqs. (9), (10):

$$H_0 : a_1 = a_2 = a_n = 0 \tag{9}$$

$$H_1 : a_1 \neq a_2 \neq a_n \neq 0 \tag{10}$$

The hypotheses set up are read as follows: there is cointegration if the null hypothesis is rejected. The F-statistics for testing are compared with the critical values developed by Pesaran et al. (2001). Narayan critical values are more appropriate for small samples.

Pesaran et al. (2001) provide a table enumerated as CI and entitled: "Asymptotic critical value bounds for the F-statistic. Testing for the existence of a levels relationship" in five versions. These are (i) no intercept and no trend, (ii) restricted intercept and no trend, (iii) unrestricted intercept and no trend, (iv) unrestricted intercept and restricted trend, and (v) unrestricted intercept and unrestricted trend. They also provide a table CII entitled "Asymptotic critical value bounds for the t-statistic. Testing for the existence of a levels relationship" in three versions: (i) no intercept and no trend, (ii) unrestricted intercept and no trend, and (iii) unrestricted intercept and unrestricted trend. Next, we reproduce a part of these tables (CIiii and CIv) to explain how the decision for cointegration was made in Bölük and Mert (2015) based on Pesaran tables. Note that Pesaran tables are not valid for I(2) variables (Ali et al., 2016).

Case study 1. Nepal, R., Indra al Irsyad, M., Nepal, S.K., 2019. Tourist arrivals, energy consumption, and pollutant emissions in a developing economy implications for sustainable tourism. Tourism Manag. 72, 145–154

It is very insightful to present the ARDL model results in a comprehensive and concise way such as in the following table (Table 2) compiled by Nepal et al. (2019) who study the tourism-growth nexus in Nepal. Tourism demand is depicted through tourist arrivals, and economic growth is represented with per capita output. As covariates are employed the energy consumption, emissions and capital formation. They employ time series data with a 40 year span from 1975 to 2014 from Nepal Statistics Service and the World Development Indicators.

The configuration presented in the first column of Table 2 is very convenient. It reveals in a comprehensive way which variable is assumed as dependent and which variables are assumed as independent. Also the inclusion of lag numbers in a parenthesized form, beside the initials of the ARDL method, is also very informative. The presentation of critical values throws light to the cognitive action behind the significance of ARDL and allows reviewers and readers higher transparency in a manuscript.

Although the purpose of the presentation of case study 1 is to show that the method is employed in other areas beside the close energy-growth nexus, the most important reason for demonstrating it here is for its layout. However, it is worthwhile reporting the gist of the results in this paper: the results from Nepal et al. (2019) provide strong evidence of "an economy-driven tourism sector where expansion in economic output leads to expansion in tourist arrivals. More tourist arrivals, in turn, generate positive impacts on gross capital formation. Energy consumption negatively affects tourist arrivals, calling for increased attention toward improving energy efficiency and energy diversity."

Table 2 An ARDL model results indicative format presentation.

	Critical value bounds		
ARDL models	**1%**	**5%**	**10%**
FE (E|G, CO_2, K, T)=3.63***, ARDL (3,1,0,4,4)	3.74–5.06	2.86–4.01	2.45–3.52
FG (G|E, CO_2, K, T)=5.25*, ARDL (3,0,0,1,0)	3.81–4.92	3.05–3.97	2.68–3.53
FCO_2 (CO_2|E, G, K, T)=4.25**, ARDL (1,0,0,0,1)	3.29–4.37	2.56–3.49	2.20–3.09
FK (K|E, G, CO_2, T)=2.44, ARDL (2,0,2,0,0)	3.29–4.37	2.56–3.49	2.20–3.09
FT (E|G, CO_2, K)=5.03*, ARDL (1,1,0,0,0)	3.29–4.37	2.56–3.49	2.20–3.09

As aforementioned, we present next extracts of Pesaran tables, for the interested reader. These are Tables 3 and 4.

Table 3 Snapshot of Pesaran et al. (2001) Case CI (iii) entitled as unrestricted intercept and no trend.

k	0.100		0.050		0.025		0.010		Mean		Variance	
	I(0)	I(1)	I(0)	I(1)	I(0)	I(1)	I(0)	I(1)	I(0)	I(1)	I(0)	I(1)
0	−2.57	−2.57	−2.86	−2.86	−3.13	−3.13	−3.43	−3.43	−1.53	−1.53	0.72	0.71
1	−2.57	−2.91	−2.86	−3.22	−3.13	−3.50	−3.43	−3.82	−1.53	−1.80	0.72	0.81
2	−2.57	−3.21	−2.86	−3.53	−3.13	−3.80	−3.43	−4.10	−1.53	−2.04	0.72	0.86
3	−2.57	−3.46	−2.86	−3.78	−3.13	−4.05	−3.43	−4.37	−1.53	−2.26	0.72	0.89
4	−2.57	−3.66	−2.86	−3.99	−3.13	−4.26	−3.43	−4.60	−1.53	−2.47	0.72	0.91
5	−2.57	−3.58	−2.86	−4.19	−3.13	−4.46	−3.43	−4.79	−1.53	−2.65	0.72	0.92

Modified from Pesaran, M.H., Shin, Y., Smith, R.J., 2001. Bounds testing approaches to the analysis of level relationships. J. Appl. Economet. 16, 289–326.

Table 4 Snapshot of Pesaran et al. (2001) case CI (iii) entitled as unrestricted intercept and unrestricted trend.

k	0.100		0.050		0.025		0.010		Mean		Variance	
	I(0)	I(1)	I(0)	I(1)	I(0)	I(1)	I(0)	I(1)	I(0)	I(1)	I(0)	I(1)
0	-3.13	-3.13	-3.41	-3.41	-3.65	-3.66	-3.96	-3.97	-2.18	-2.18	0.57	0.57
1	-3.13	-3.40	-3.41	-3.69	-3.65	-3.96	-3.96	-4.26	-2.18	-2.37	0.57	0.67
2	-3.13	-3.63	-3.41	-3.95	-3.65	-4.20	-3.96	-4.53	-2.18	-2.55	0.57	0.74
3	-3.13	-3.84	-3.41	-4.16	-3.65	-4.42	-3.96	-4.73	-2.18	-2.72	0.57	0.79
4	-3.13	-4.04	-3.41	-4.36	-3.65	-4.62	-3.96	-4.96	-2.18	-2.89	0.57	0.82
5	-3.13	-4.21	-3.41	-4.52	-3.65	-4.79	-3.96	-5.13	-2.18	-3.04	0.57	0.85

Modified from Pesaran, M.H., Shin, Y., Smith, R.J., 2001. Bounds testing approaches to the analysis oflevel relationships. J. Appl. Economet. 16, 289–326.

Narayan and Smyth (2005) on the other hand has estimated critical values for the bounds test for four cases at three significance levels and up to seven independent variables up to 80 observations. The critical values of the four cases are entitled as (i) Case II, restricted intercept and no trend; (ii) Case III, unrestricted intercept and no trend; (iii) Case IV, unrestricted intercept and restricted trend; and (iv) Case V, unrestricted intercept and unrestricted trend. Bölük and Mert (2015) use Cases III and V. In Narayan tables, k stands for the number of regressors, and n is the sample size—I(0), stationary at levels, and I(1), stationary at first differences. These are shown in Tables 5 and 6 in an extract form. The full tables can be found in their respective sources.

Case study 2. Bölük, G., Mert, M., 2015. The renewable energy, growth, and environmental Kuznets curve in Turkey: An ARDL approach. Renew. Sustain. Energy Rev. 52, 587–595

Bölük and Mert (2015) use a Kuznets curve hypothesis framework to study the effect of renewable energies in reducing the impact of greenhouse gas emissions in Turkey. Thus they employ a model that contains greenhouse gas emissions as a dependent variable and income and renewable energies as independent variables. They apply the bounds test for seven lags, both in the intercept and the "intercept and trend" model. The decision on which model and lag configuration to select is based on AIC and SIC criteria and the F-statistic for the bounds test. Minimum AIC and SIC are accomplished in the sixth lag. The F statistic for this model is higher than the upper critical values of Pesaran and Narayan. In particular, $F = 5.656 > 4.35$ and $5.656 > 4.70$, which are the critical values in Pesaran and Narayan tables accordingly. Also, $F = 5.69 > 5.07$ and $5.6 > 55.545$ that are the critical values in Pesaran and Narayan tables accordingly (Table 7).

If the calculated F-statistic exceeds the upper bound of the critical values, the null hypothesis is rejected. Conversely, if it is lower than the lower bounds value, then the null hypothesis cannot be rejected. If the F value lies between the two bounds, the "verdict" about cointegration is inconclusive. In such a case the decision about cointegration will be based on the error correction term (Kremers et al., 1992; Banerjee et al., 1998) and whether it fulfills certain criteria, for example, the negative value.

When no cointegration is confirmed, we can proceed with simple Granger causality (unrestricted VAR). The VAR equation should be specified on stationary data. There are various reasons why cointegration is not confirmed. This may be due to the fact that there is no relationship between the examined variables or there might be omitted variables. The Toda Yamamoto test is a solution for Granger causality testing in this case. We discuss this option in a separate chapter. After all, even when a long-run relationship does not exist in the data, this does not mean

Table 5 Critical values for the bounds test by Narayan and Smyth (2005); Case III, unrestricted intercept and no trend, significance level 5%.

n	k = 0		k = 1		k = 2		k = 3		k = 4		k = 5		k = 6		k = 7	
	I(0)	I(1)	I(0)	I(1)	I(0)	I(1)	I(0)	I(1)	I(0)	I(1)	I(0)	I(1)	I(0)	I(1)	I(0)	I(1)
30	8.770	8770	8395	6350	4267	5473	3710	5018	3354	4774	3125	4608	2970	4499	2875	4445
35	8.640	8640	5290	6175	4183	5333	3615	4913	3276	4630	3037	4443	2864	4324	2753	4209
40	8570	8570	5260	6160	4133	5260	3548	4803	3202	4544	2962	4338	2797	4211	2676	4130
45	8590	8590	5235	6135	4083	5207	3535	4733	3178	4450	2922	4268	2764	4123	2643	4004
50	8510	8510	5220	6070	4070	5190	3500	4700	3136	4416	2900	4218	2726	4057	2593	3941
55	8390	8390	5125	6045	3987	5090	3408	1623	3068	4334	2848	4160	2676	3999	2556	3904
60	8460	8460	5125	6000	4000	5057	3415	4615	3062	4314	2817	4097	2643	3939	2513	3823
65	8490	8490	5130	5980	4010	5080	3435	4583	3068	4274	2835	4090	2647	3921	2525	3808
70	8370	8370	5055	5915	3947	5020	3370	4545	3022	4256	2788	4073	2629	3906	2494	3786
75	8420	8420	5140	5920	3983	5060	3408	4550	3042	4244	2802	4065	2637	3900	2503	3768
80	8400	8400	5060	5930	3940	5043	3363	4515	3010	4216	2787	4015	2627	3864	2476	3746

Source: Narayan, P. K., Smyth, R., 2005. Electricity consumption, employment and real income in Australia evidence from multivariate granger causality tests, Energy Policy 33, 1109–1116.

Table 6 Critical values for the bounds test by Narayan and Smyth (2005); Case V, unrestricted intercept and unrestricted trend, significance level 5%.

n	k = 0		k = 1		k = 2		k = 3		k = 4		k = 5		k = 6		k = 7	
	I(0)	I(1)	I(0)	I(1)	I(0)	I(1)	I(0)	I(1)	I(0)	I(1)	I(0)	I(1)	I(0)	I(1)	I(0)	I(1)
30	12.740	12.740	7.360	8.265	5.550	6.747	4.683	5.980	4154	5540	3818	5253	3576	5065	3394	4939
35	12.580	12.580	7.210	8.055	5.475	6.570	4.568	5795	4036	5304	3673	5002	3426	4790	3251	4640
40	12.510	12.510	7.135	7.980	5.387	6.437	4.510	5643	3958	5226	3577	4923	3327	4700	3121	4564
45	12.400	12.400	7.080	7.910	5.360	6.373	4.450	5560	3890	5104	3532	4800	3267	4584	3091	4413
50	12.170	12.170	6.985	7.860	5.247	6.303	4.368	5545	3834	5064	3480	4782	3229	4536	3039	4339
55	12.170	12.170	6.930	7.785	5.190	6.223	4.313	5425	3794	4986	3442	4690	3197	4460	2989	4271
60	12.200	12.200	6.905	7.735	5.190	6.200	4.298	5445	3772	4956	3407	4632	3137	4393	2956	4230
65	11.960	11.960	6.890	7.660	5.137	6.173	4.268	5415	3732	4920	3372	4613	3137	4363	2924	4206
70	12.000	12.000	6.860	7.645	5.110	6.190	4.235	5363	3720	4904	3368	4590	3107	4343	2913	4168
75	12.080	12.080	6.880	7.675	5.140	6.153	4.253	5333	3724	4880	3382	4567	3111	4310	2915	4143
80	12.060	12.060	6.820	7.670	5.067	6.103	4.203	5320	3678	4840	3335	4535	3077	4284	2885	4111

From Narayan, P. K., Smyth, R., 2005. Electricity consumption, employment and real income in Australia evidence from multivariate granger causality tests, Energy Policy 33, 1109–1116.

Table 7 Lag selection based on the AIC and SIC tests and the F bounds test.

Lag	Intercept model			Intercept and trend model		
	AIC	SIC	F bounds test	AIC	SIC	F bounds test
1	−2.1529	−1.6851	4.943	- 2.1125	−1.6057	4.623
2	−2.0201	−1.3908	3.376	−1.9926	−1.3234	2.871
3	−2.1055	−1.3104	4.059	−2.0621	−1.2272	2.866
4	−2.0928	−1.1293	2.656	−2.0602	−1.0565	2.108
5	−2.1984	−1.0630	3.525	−2.1693	−0.9934	3.363
6	−3.0263	−1.7157	5.656	−3.0670	−1.7183	5.692
7	−2.9813	−1.4919	0.897	−2.9475	−0.4167	0.761

Note: In the source, this is numbered as Table 5 in page 592.
From Bölük, G., Mert, M., 2015. The renewable energy, growth and environmental kuznets curve in Turkey: an ARDL approach, Renew. Sust. Energ. Rev. 52, 587–595.

that no short-run relationship exists either. For an illustrative analysis of these steps, please consult Case study 3. Also, it needs to be remembered that the cointegration equation provides the long-run elasticities. Short-run elasticities are presented by the coefficients of the first differenced variables. In cases where more than one coefficient for a particular variable has been estimated for the short-run case, these are added, and their joint significance is tested with a Wald test (Fuinhas and Marques, 2012).

Case study 3. Tiwari, A., 2011. Primary energy consumption, CO_2 emissions and economic growth: Evidence from India. South East Eur. J. Econ. Bus. 6, 99–117

Tiwari (2011) investigated the relationship between primary energy consumption, gross domestic product, and CO_2 emissions in India. The data span is from 1970 to 2007. He finds cointegration among the variables in the presence of endogenously determined structural breaks. Thus he employs a VAR causality framework with Toda and Yamamoto and Dolado and Lütkepohl test approaches.

Based on results from Table 8, we observe that emissions cause income growth, while emissions and energy jointly cause income growth. Also, income growth causes energy consumption.

Continued

Table 8 VAR Engle-Granger causality analysis.

Independent variables	VEC Granger causality short run/block exogeneity (Wald test/χ^2)		
	Dependent variables		
	Ln (GDPPC)	Ln (PECPC)	Ln (CO$_2$PC)
Ln (GDPPC)	–	10.379**	5.673
Ln(PECPC)	2.013	–	2.789
Ln(CO$_2$PC)	10.056**	4.666	–
Joint hypothesis	15.359**	11.005	11.824

Notes: Ln (GDPPC) stands for the gross domestic product per capita, Ln (PECPC) stands for primary energy consumption per capita, and Ln (CO$_2$PC) stands for the CO$_2$ emissions per capita. All of these variables are expressed in logs. One asterisk denotes significance at 1% level, while two asterisks denote significance at 5% level.
Adapted from Tiwari, A., 2011. Primary energy consumption, CO$_2$ emissions and economic growth: evidence from India, South East Eur. J. Econ. Bus. 6, 99–117, p. 107.

However, if cointegration is the case (which occurs very commonly, when there is a known and established theoretical connection between some variables), then we can proceed with the establishment of the error correction mechanism (ECM). Evidence of cointegration implies that there is a long-run relationship between the variables and their connection is not a short-lived situation, but a more permanent one, which can be recovered every time there is a disturbance.

Alternatively to the aforementioned F-test, a Wald test can be applied, which is used to test the null hypothesis of no cointegration when there is more than one short-run coefficient of the same variable (Tursoy and Faisal, 2018).

2.1.3 Diagnostic tests after cointegration

Typical diagnostic χ^2 tests follow to investigate the goodness of fit, stability, parsimoniality, functional form, and a well-behaved model in general. Note the Breusch-Godfrey serial correlation LM test, the Breusch-Pagan-Godfrey Heteroskedasticity test or the White test, and the Jarque-Bera test are some of the tests encountered in these applications. Also the Ramsey reset test is used for the functional form. Also the variance inflation factor (VIF) for multicollinearity might be useful in cases where there is suspicion of multicollinearity.

Flashback 6: Remember the ARCH, CUSUM, and CUSUMSQ tests?

The autoregressive conditional heteroskedasticity (ARCH): The test for an ARCH effect was devised originally by Engle, (1982) and is similar to the Lagrange multiplier (LM) test for autocorrelation. The ARCH effect is modeled by $\sigma_t^2 = \alpha_0 + \alpha_1 u_{t-1}^2$ with σ^2 being the conditional variance and u is the error term. This is termed as ARCH(1) because it contains one lagged value of the error term. To estimate the earlier relationship, first we estimate $y_t = \lambda y_{t-1} + \beta x_t + \varepsilon_t, \varepsilon_t \sim IN(0, \sigma_t^2)$ by OLS. The significance of the DW test does not necessarily imply serial autocorrelation, but it could also die to the ARCH effect. For disentangling this effect the interested reader is advised to read Maddala (1992), p. 264.

The CUSUM and CUSUMSQ tests: They examine the stability of the estimated models. They consist in displaying the cumulative sum of recursive residuals and the cumulative sum of squares of recursive residuals. This method recursively calculates the regression coefficients and residuals at particular thresholds (break points of the model). If the plots lie within the 5% critical values, then there is model stability. Also, if the plot deviates a bit from the critical values bands but in a transitory way, namely, it returns within the aforementioned bands, again we consider this to be a stable model. This is an important step followed in ARDL analysis because it is also used for prediction of the presence of a stable long-run relationship. CUSUM tests are based on Brown et al., (1975) because Chow stability requires a priori knowledge of structural breaks.

2.1.4 The impulse response function

The impulse response function shows what happens when the model is transferred to the one side of the dummy variable. For example, if 1 represents war time and 0 represents peace time, then if we take the ones or zeros only and separately, we have an impulse response function, one for war time and one for peace time. Thus they are also a useful tool to test the stability of a model across structural breaks.

Case study 4. Rauf, A., Zhang, J., Li, J., Amin, W., 2018. Structural changes, energy consumption, and carbon emissions in China: Empirical evidence from ARDL bound testing model. Struct. Change Econ. Dyn. 47, 194–206

This study investigates the energy-growth nexus with additional covariates being the agriculture value added, the industrial values added, the service value added, trade openness, financial development, urbanization, and environmental degradation in China, for the years from 1968 to 2016. The study employs the ADRD method, and they have tabulated the model diagnostic tests in Table 9. It is advisable to present the diagnostic test results in this way.

Continued

Table 9 Typical model diagnostic test results.

Tests	χ^2	Probability
Breusch-Godfrey serial Correlation LM test	1.499	0.473
Breusch-Pagan-Godfrey Heteroskedasticity test	17.852	0.214
ARCH test	0.195	0.907
Ramsey RESET	0.0004	0.985
Jarque-Bera test	1.073	0.584

Adapted from Rauf, A., Zhang, J., Li, J., Amin, W., 2018. Structural changes, energy consumption and carbon emissions in China: empirical evidence from ardl bound testing model, Struct. Chang. Econ. Dyn. 47, 194–206, p. 202.

Although the reason we refer to this study is Table 9, it is worthwhile reporting the main results of this study for the interested reader. Industry, agriculture, services, energy consumption, and trade openness have a positive and significant impact on carbon emissions. The economic growth and urbanization negatively affect the environment. Financial development has not been significant in any of the long-run or short-run horizons.

There are various hypotheses that underlie the models after cointegration is confirmed. After the identification of the long-run relationship in Eqs. (5), (6), we can continue with the examination of the short-run and the long-run Granger causality. The Granger causality refers to a situation where the past can be used to predict the future. Thus, if past values of X_t significantly contribute to forecasting future values of Y_t, the X_t is said to Granger cause the Y_t. However, evidence of correlation is not necessarily evidence for causality.

2.1.5 Combined cointegration methods for the robustness of the ARDL model

In the particular case of a unique order of integration, Bayer and Hanck (2013) have developed a test that borrows elements from a variety of previously developed cointegration tests. The combined test borrows elements from Engle and Granger (1987), Johansen, (1988), Boswijk, (1994), and Banerjee et al. (1998). The combined cointegration test uses Fisher's formulae and the P-values of the aforementioned individual tests in Eqs. (11), (12).

$$Engle\&Granger - Johansen = -2\left[\ln\left(P_{Engle\ \&\ Granger}\right) + \ln\left(P_{Johansen}\right)\right] \quad (11)$$

$$\begin{aligned} Engle\ \&\ Granger - Johansen - Boswijk - Banerjee\,et\,al. \\ = -2\left[ln\left(P_{Engle\ \&\ Granger}\right) + ln(P_{Johansen}) + ln\left(P_{Boswijk}\right) + ln\left(P_{Banerjee}\right)\right] \end{aligned} \quad (12)$$

The null hypothesis of no cointegration is rejected if the aforementioned Fisher statistic exceeds the critical value as produced by Bayer and Hanck (2013).

The aforementioned test balances the decisions produced by the independent tests, which suffer from particular drawbacks, each one of them. Tursoy and Faisal (2018) employ this test, and we present its application in Case study 5.

Case study 5. Tursoy, T., Faisal, F., 2018. The impact of gold and crude oil prices on stock market in Turkey: Empirical evidences from ARDL bounds test and combined cointegration. Resour. Policy 55, 49–54

This study investigates the relationship between stock prices, gold prices, and crude oil prices in Turkey. They apply monthly data from January 1986 to November 2016. Table 10 presents the results from a combined cointegration method by Bayer and Hanck (2013).

Results from Table 10 state that the three statistics are greater than both critical values. This entails that the hypothesis of no cointegration is rejected. In this case study the findings from Table 10 show that the Bayer-Hanck cointegration test coincides with the results from the ARDL bounds test.

Overall the results of this study show that both the short-run and the long-run results confirm the negative relationship between the gold price and stock prices and a positive relationship between crude oil.

Table 10 Bayer-Hanck cointegration test result.

Model specification	Fisher statistics ENG & GRA	ENG and GRA-JOHAN-BOS-BDM	Cointegration decision
$F_{LEQ} = f(LEQ/LCB,LG)$	10.3758*	22.8797**	Cointegration exists
Significance level	Critical values		
At 1%		16.651	31.793
At 5%		10.838	20.776
At 10%		8.457	16.171

Notes: One asterisk and two asterisks denote significance at 10% and 5% level, respectively. From Tursoy, T., Faisal, F., 2018. The impact of gold and crude oil prices on stock market in Turkey: empirical evidences from ardl bounds test and combined cointegration, Resour. Policy 55, 49–54, p. 52.

2.2 Causality after the ARDL bounds test

2.2.1 The importance of the error correction term (ECT)

The lagged error correction term is derived from the cointegration equation. Thus the long-run information, which is missed through the differencing of the variables for stationarity purposes, is reintroduced in the system of causality equations. This is a necessary step when variables are cointegrated. Cointegration implies that there must be causality of some direction; however, it does not reveal to which direction that causality goes, and thus additional causality analysis is required. Thus, before going to the estimation of Eqs. (3), (4) in the succeeding text, one needs to run another set of regressions in to get the residuals that will be inserted to Eqs. (3), (4) as the ECT term.

There are many strategies to follow in the examination and direction of causality. One such strategy is the VECM approach (vector error correction model), which is a restricted form of unrestricted VAR and is suitable once the variables are integrated at I (1). According to this model setup, the dependent variable is dependent on its own lagged values, as well as the lagged values of the independent variables, the error correction term, and the residual term. This is shown in the following set of Eqs. (13), (14).

$$\Delta lnY_t = a_1 + \sum_{i=1}^{l} a_{11}\,\Delta LY_{t-i} + \sum_{j=0}^{m} a_{22}\Delta X_{t-j} + n_1 ECT_{t-1} + \mu_{1i} \tag{13}$$

$$\Delta lnX_t = a_1 + \sum_{i=1}^{l} a_{21}\,\Delta LX_{t-i} + \sum_{j=0}^{m} a_{22}\Delta Y_{t-j} + n_2 ECT_{t-1} + \mu_{2i} \tag{14}$$

Residual terms are assumed to distribute normally. The coefficient of the ECT must be negative to assure system convergence from the short run toward the long run. An ECT equal to $x\%$ is interpreted as such that $x\%$ of economic growth is corrected by deviations in the short run that lead eventually to the long-run equilibrium path. The significant variables on the right hand side of each equation show short-run causality for the dependent variable.

Case study 5. Marques, A.C., Fuinhas, J.A., Menegaki, A.N., 2014. Interactions between electricity generation sources and economic activity in Greece: A VECM approach. Appl. Energy 132, 34–46

This study deals with the investigation of the relationship between electricity generation sources and the industrial production in Greece. The study employs monthly data from August 2004 to October 2013. The interaction of the variables and their endogeneity has been investigated with a VEC model (Table 11).

Table 11 The estimated VEC model.

	DLORP	DLRES	DLHYDRO	DLIPI	DLRXM
DLORP	0.341	0.083	0.988	−0.114	−0.411
	(3.494)	(0.279)	(2.696)	(−2.060)	(−2.999)
DLORP	0.428	0.175	−0.094	0.057	−0.081
	(4.339)	(0.581)	(−0.254)	(1.023)	(−0.588)
DLRES	0.090	−0.227	0.174	0.002	0.050
	(3.382)	(−2.786)	(1.735)	(0.126)	(1.333)
DLRES	0.032	−0.145	−0.088	−0.001	0.014
	(1.323)	(−1.978)	(−0.971)	(−0.042)	(0.403)

Table 11 The estimated VEC model—cont'd

	DLORP	DLRES	DLHYDRO	DLIPI	DLRXM
DLHYDRO	0.131 (4.497)	0.256 (2.886)	0.051 (0.463)	0.008 (0.497)	−0.106 (−2594)
DLHYDRO	0.070 (2.191)	0.188 (1.920)	−0.106 (−0.885)	0.014 (0.782)	−0.05 (−1.270)
DLIPI	0.033 (0.158)	1.797 (2.856)	−1.655 (−2.139)	−0.390 (−3.329)	0.120 (0.415)
DLIPI	−0.045 (−0.241)	0.872 (1.442)	−0.781 (−1.049)	−0.071 (−0.633)	0.065 (0.234)
DLRXM	−0.121 (−1.723)	0.140 (0.656)	−0.285 (−1.085)	0.062 (1.546)	−0.278 (−2.832)
DLRXM	−0.135 (−1.958)	0.478 (2.261)	0.491 (1.888)	−0.105 (−2.670)	−0.095 (−0.974)
DLPUMP	0.027 (2.513)	−0.023 (−0.692)	−0.129 (−3.139)	0.004 (0.588)	−0.013 (−0.819)
DLPUMP	0.001 (0.128)	0.062 (1.842)	−0.037 (−0.887)	−0.008 (−1.240)	−0.011 (−0.707)
ID0705	−0.080 (−0.956)	−2.579 (−10.191)	0.297 (0.954)	−0.023 (−0.492)	0.072 (0.617)
SD0904	0.018 (1.379)	0.126 (3.164)	0.030 (0.610)	0.001 (0.066)	0.023 (1.249)
ID1201	0.055 (0.682)	−0.063 (−0.258)	−0.060 (−0.200)	−0.121 (−2.658)	−0.425 (−3.776)
ECT1	−1.014 (−8.386)	0.160 (0.433)	−0.835 (−1.837)	−0.099 (−1.436)	0.532 (3.135)
ECT2	−0.102 (−3.894)	−0.437 (−5.484)	−0.207 (−2.110)	−0.099 (−1.436)	−0.050 (−1.366)
R-squared	0.598	0.745	0.386	0.383	0.401
Adj R-squared	0.520	0.696	0.268	0.265	0.286
F-statistic	7.701	15.141	3.264	3.225	3.476

Notes: t-statistics are in parenthesis. LORP, electricity generated from lignite, oila and gas (MWh); LRES, electricity generated from renewable energy sources (without hydropower, MWh); HYDRO, electricity generated from hydropower (MWh); LIPI, seasonally adjusted industrial production index (manufacturing); LRXM, rate of coverage of imports by exports; LPUMP, electricity consumption in water pumping systems (MWh); all variables are expressed in natural logarithms.
Adapted from Marques, A. C., Fuinhas, J.A., Menegaki, A.N., 2014. Interactions between electricity generation sources and economic activity in Greece: a vecm approach, Appl. Energy 132, 34–46., in p. 40.

Based on the results in this study, in the short run, economic growth is caused by conventional fossil sources. Also economic growth causes renewable energy both in the long run and the short run. Renewable energy does not cause economic growth.

2.2.2 FMOLS and DOLS estimators for robustness

The FMOLS (fully modified OLS) and the DOLS (dynamic OLS) were developed by Phillips and Hansen (1990) and Stock and Watson (1993). They lead to the generation of asymptotically efficient coefficients because they take into account the serial autocorrelation and endogeneity. They are applied only in the I(1) case for all variables. The latter makes them less flexible and attractive methods. OLS is biased when variables are cointegrated but nonstationary, while FMOLS is not. DOLS performs better than the FMOLS approach (Kao and Chiang, 2000) for several reasons: DOLS is computationally simpler, and it reduces bias better than FMOLS. The t-statistic produced from DOLS approximates the standard normal density better than the statistic generated from the OLS or the FMOLS. DOLS estimators are fully parametric and do not require preestimation and nonparametric correction. Ali et al., 2017a, 2017b reports that the most significant benefit of DOLS is that the test considers the mixed order of integration of variables in the cointegration framework.

2.2.3 Additional ways to study causality

Literature reports additional types of causality: (a) the weak causality/short-run causality, (b) the long-run causality, (c) the strong causality (joint causality), and (d) the pairwise causality. Each one serves a particular purpose.

(a) Weak causality/short-run causality

Each variable is caused by its own past only.

(b) Long-run causality

The error correction term is zero. This is a vector autoregression (VAR) causality leading to Toda-Yamamoto method.

Granger causality can be checked for existence through a VAR model (note that data are not in differences, namely, they are in level form) in Eqs. (15)–(18):

$$Y_t = g_0 + \alpha_1 Y_{t-1} + \ldots + \alpha_p Y_{t-p} + b_1 X_{t-1} + \ldots + b_p X_{t-p} + u_t \tag{15}$$

$$X_t = h_0 + c_1 Y_{t-1} + \ldots + c_p Y_{t-p} + d_1 X_{t-1} + \ldots + d_p X_{t-p} + v_t \tag{16}$$

$$H_0 : b_1 = b_2 = \ldots = b_p = 0 \tag{17}$$

$$H_1 : X\,Granger\,causes\,Y \tag{18}$$

A similar hypothesis set up can be constructed for the second equation, but this will not be done here for space considerations. Please note the following rationale:

If $b_i \neq 0$ and $d_i = 0$, then X_t will lead Y_t in the long run.
If $b_i = 0$ and $d_i \neq 0$, then Y_t will lead X_t in the long run.
If $b_i \neq 0$ and $d_i \neq 0$, then the feedback relationship is present.
If $b_i = 0$ and $d_i = 0$, then no cointegration exists.

After we have calculated the diagnostics of the model and we have verified that the model is well behaved, then the next step is the bounds test. The existence of a long-run relationship can be further corroborated with the investigation of significance of the individual terms.

(c)   Strong causality: The joint causality investigation process

This is the case (a) and (b) together. The joint causality test also known as strong causality test (Lee and Chang, 2008) identifies two sources of causation, one the short run and the other the long run to which the variables readjust after a short-run perturbation. This is tested with the short-run coefficients of the lagged variables and the significance of the lagged error correction term. Granger causality can be investigated in two other know ways: it can be investigated with the F-test to decide about the significance of first difference stationary variables (Asafu-Adjaye, 2000; Masih and Masih, 1996) or by including the ECT as a source of variation. This is most commonly checked with a *t*-test.

(d)   Pairwise Granger causality test

This is another solution toward the investigation of causality when cointegration is not confirmed. It can also be used for corroboration of VECM results. Menegaki and Tugcu (2016) have employed this method for the investigation of the energy-sustainable growth nexus in sub-Saharan African countries for the years 1985–2013. In addition to that, Menegaki and Tugcu (2018) have employed the same method for the investigation of the energy-sustainable growth nexus in Asian countries (Menegaki and Tugcu, 2018).

2.2.4 The asymmetric nonlinear ARDL approach: the NARDL approach
This version of ARDL was introduced by Shin et al., (2011) and is an extension of the method introduced by Pesaran et al. (2001). The nonlinear ARDL is used for testing whether the positive shocks of the independent variables have the same effect as their negative shocks on the dependent variables. Thus the ARDL relationship is formulated as follows in Eq. (19):

$$y_t = a^+ x_t^+ + a^- x_t^- + \varepsilon_t \tag{19}$$

The alphas are the long-run parameters, while x_t is the following vector regressor in Eq. (20):

$$x_t = x_0 + x_t^+ + x_t^- \tag{20}$$

With x_t^+ being the positive partial sum and x_t^- being the negative partial sum as follows in Eqs. (21), (22):

$$x_t^+ = \sum_{i=1}^{t} \Delta x_i^+ = \sum_{i=1}^{t} \max(\Delta x_i, 0) \tag{21}$$

$$x_t^- = \sum_{i=1}^{t} \Delta x_i^- = \sum_{i=1}^{t} \max(\Delta x_i, 0) \tag{22}$$

This means that the corresponding error correction model can be written as in Eqs. (23)–(24):

$$\Delta y_t = \rho y_{t-1} + \theta^+ x_{t-1}^+ + \theta^- x_{t-1}^- + \sum_{i=1}^{j-1} \varphi_i \Delta y_{t-i} + \sum_{i=0}^{p} \left(\pi_i^+ \Delta x_{t-i}^+ + \pi_i^- \Delta x_{t-i}^- \right) + \varepsilon_t \qquad (23)$$

$$\text{where } \theta^+ = \frac{\alpha^+}{\rho y_{t-1}} \text{ and } \theta^- = \frac{\alpha^-}{\rho y_{t-1}} \qquad (24)$$

The procedure steps are exactly as the conventional ARDL approach that has been already presented in this chapter. In addition to that, the method provides the cumulative dynamic multiplier effects of x^+ and x^- on y_t as follows in Eq. (25):

$$m_k^+ = \sum_{i=0}^{k} \frac{\partial y_{t+i}}{\partial x_t^+} \text{ and } m_k^- = \sum_{i=0}^{k} \frac{\partial y_{t+i}}{\partial x_t^-} \qquad (25)$$

When k increases to infinity, the multipliers converge to the alphas. This method has not been applied by Shahbaz (2018) in a case study for the energy-growth nexus in Pakistan and Al-hajj et al. (2018) for the investigation of the oil price and stock returns nexus in Malaysia. The NARDL method is applicable if all variables are integrated at I(1) or they have a flexible order of integration. The approach also solves multicollinearity through the choice of the appropriate lag length of variables. A complete account of asymmetric causality is presented in Apergis (2018) who provides a detailed account also on linear versus the nonlinear causality.

2.2.5 The pool mean group (PMG) estimator for panel data

The pool mean group allows for heterogeneity only in the short-run compared with the mean group that allows for heterogeneity both in the short and the long run. The pool mean group estimates are superior to the fixed effects estimates because they are robust to endogeneity and to the presence of unit roots. Overall the PMG is an estimator that allows pooling and averaging.

3 Indicative literature review of the last decade ARDL studies in the broad energy-growth nexus: A snapshot

This section contains a review of 35 studies in the energy-growth nexus that have employed the ARDL cointegration method. Publication dates range from 2004 to 2018. The percentages of the studies belonging to each year in the current sample of studies are as follows: 2004 (2.86%), 2007 (2.86%), 2008 (2.86%), 2009 (8.57%), 2010 (5.71%), 2011 (2.86%), 2012 (8.57%), 2013 (11.43%), 2014 (11.43%), 2015 (14.29%), 2016 (8.57%), 2017 (14.29%), and 2018 (5.71%). There is a clear upward trend in the latest years. With respect to their separation in single and multiple country studies, 71% of them are single country ones. This means that researchers are mostly interested in answering individual country questions rather than contributing to the formation of global relationships. Only a small percentage of the studies (11%) employ monthly data, while the rest employ yearly data. This of course depends on the nature of the investigated problem. Besides aggregate energy consumption and real GDP growth that stands for income, there is a variety of covariates employed in the energy-growth model equation. These are the separation between renewable and nonrenewable energy consumption, labor, capital, electricity consumption, carbon dioxide emissions, oil energy consumption, domestic credit, exports of goods and services, financial development, foreign direct investment, globalization, oil prices, the interest rate and the exchange rates, natural gas consumption, nuclear energy consumption, consumer prices, capital stock, agriculture sector growth, and modern sector growth. From the studies in the 35 paper sample, all use the real GDP per capita as an independent variable with some exceptions: 8.6% use the industrial production, 2% use the sustainable income growth, 2% are in essence energy demand functions that employ the energy demand as a dependent variable, and 17% employ the carbon emissions, namely, they are studies that deal with the investigation of the environmental Kuznets curve. As far as the four hypotheses findings, 40% find evidence for the feedback hypothesis, 22% find evidence for the growth hypothesis, 5% find evidence for the conservation hypothesis, and 11% find evidence for the neutrality hypothesis while the rest have mixed findings (Table 12).

4 What are the ARDL implementation strategies to follow in my energy-growth nexus paper?

This chapter deals with the general outline of the research in the ARDL analysis and not the specific direction that various studies may end up with due to specific handlings dictated by data, theory, and research demands. For example, Liu et al. (Liu, 2009) end their ARDL analysis with a factor decomposition model (FDM) analysis that shows the yearly causal contribution of each variable onto the dependent variable. This is not how most ARDL energy-growth nexus studies end with. The outline of most of these studies is an investigation of the integrational properties of the variables, followed by an ARDL cointegration analysis and ends with a causality analysis. In the following two tables (Tables 13 and 14), ARDL implementation strategies are provided with guidelines for every step and variant. Table 13 contains guidelines for the time series data, while Table 14 contains guidelines for the panel data version of ARDL implementation. More detailed discussions on time series and panel data causality tests are dependent on cointegration and integration results; the reader is advised to also consult the studies by Tugcu, 2018 and Apergis, 2018 in the Book by Menegaki (2018) entitled as "The Economics and the Econometrics of the Energy-Growth Nexus."

    Readers with some experience will have so far realized that the panel data are many shorter time-series data, pooled together. The data generation process may be or may not be the same across panels (subgroups of data). Thus many time-series tests and procedures have been adapted from time series into panel data through a kind of averaging across panels (groups of data). Panel data are a convenient way in energy economics to overcome problems such as collinearity. Also, they provide

Table 12 Literature review of the ARDL studies in the broad energy-growth nexus.

S. No.	Study	Data span	Cointegration econometric method	Dependent variable	Covariates	Single country	Multiple countries	Result
1	Fuinhas and Marques (2012)	1965–2009	ARDL bounds test approach	GDP per capita	E		PIGST: Portugal, Italy, Greece, Spain, and Turkey	Feedback hypothesis
2	Ibrahiem (2015)	1980–2011	ARDL bounds test approach	GDP per capita (at constant 2005 US$)	RES	Egypt	–	Feedback hypothesis
3	Shahbaz et al. (2012)	1972–2011	ARDL bounds test approach Gregory and Hansen (1990) structural break cointegration approach Clemente-Montanes-Reyes (1998) structural break unit root test for the robustness of the ARDL results	Domestic output in real terms-real GDP per capita	RES, non-RES, L, K (the population variable is used to transform the data as to per capita)	Pakistan	–	Feedback hypothesis
4	Odhiambo (2009)	1971–2006	VECM approach ARDL bounds test approach	Real GDP per capita	Energy consumption per capita, electricity consumption per capita	Tanzania	–	Growth Hypothesis

#	Author	Period	Method					Result
5.	Rahman and Kashem (2017)	1972–2011	ARDL bounds test approach	CO_2 growth	Energy consumption per capita, industrial production per capital	Bangladesh	–	Neutrality hypothesis
6	Ozturk and Acaravci (2011)	1971–2006	ARDL bounds test approach / ADF-WS for unit roots	Real GDP	Electricity consumption	–	11 MENA countries	Neutrality hypothesis
7	Cherni and Essaber Jouini (2017)	1990–2015	ARDL bounds test approach	CO_2 emissions	RES, economic growth	Tunisia	–	Bidirectional between RES and GDP, GDP, and CO_2
8	Bildirici and Kayikçi (2013)	1993–2010	ARDL bounds test approach	GDP per capita (real)	Oil production	–	Oil exporting Eurasian countries: Azerbaijan, Kazakhstan, Russian Federation, Turkmenistan	Neutrality hypothesis
9	Menegaki et al. (2017)	2000–12	ARDL bounds test approach / Dynamic Driscoll-Kraay estimator	GDP per capita and ISEW per capita	Road energy consumption, domestic credit, CO_2 emissions, labor, exports of goods and services, capital	–	Europe (26 countries)	Feedback hypothesis
10	Marques et al. (2016)	Aug 08–2014 02	ARDL bounds test approach	Industrial production	RES, non-RES	Greece	–	Feedback hypothesis

Continued

Table 12 Literature review of the ARDL studies in the broad energy-growth nexus—cont'd

S. No.	Study	Data span	Cointegration econometric method	Dependent variable	Covariates	Single country	Multiple countries	Result
11	Bölük and Mert (2015)	1961–2010	ARDL Bounds test approach	GHG emissions	RES electricity,	Turkey	–	The existence of a U shaped relationship between greenhouse gas emissions and income.
12	Ali et al., 2017a, 2017b	1971–2012	ARDL bounds test approach & DOLS (Dynamic ordinary least squares)	CO_2 emissions	GDP per capita, financial development, trade openness, foreign direct investment, energy consumption	Malaysia	–	The existence of the EKC is confirmed Energy consumption and CO_2 have a bidirectional relationship Unidirectional causality from trade openness and FDI to economic growth
13	Marques et al. (2017a,b)	1971–2013	ARDL bounds test approach	Gross domestic product per capita	Economic, political, and social globalization, primary energy consumption	–	43 countries	Feedback hypothesis
14	Shahbaz (2018)	$1985Q_I$–$2016Q_{IV}$	Nonlinear asymmetric ARDL	GDP per capita	Energy consumption, oil prices, capital, labor	Pakistan	–	

#	Author (year)	Period	Method	Dependent variable	Independent variables	Country	Countries	Findings
15	Al-hajj et al. (2018)	January 1990–November 2016 and May 2000 to November 2016	Nonlinear asymmetric ARDL	Oil price	Interest rate, exchange rate, industrial production, inflation	Malaysia (9 sectors and aggregate)	–	There is a long-run asymmetric link between oil price shocks, and all the included variables
16	Furuoka (2016)	1980–2012	ARDL	Economic growth	Natural gas consumption, domestic credit to private sector over GDP	–	China and Japan	China: growth hypothesis Japan: feedback hypothesis
17	Chandran et al. (2010)	1971–2003	ARDL	Real gross domestic product	Electricity consumption	Malaysia	–	Growth hypothesis
18	Wolde-Rufael (2010)	1969–2006	ARDL, Toda, and Yamamoto causality	Real GDP per capita	Nuclear energy consumption, labor, capital	India	–	Growth hypothesis
19	Ghosh (2009)	1970–2006	ARDL, Toda, and Yamamoto causality	Real GDP per capita	Electricity	India	–	Growth hypothesis
20	Squalli (2007)	1980–2003	ARDL, Toda, and Yamamoto causality	Real GDP per capita	Electricity, population	Indonesia	–	Growth hypothesis
21	Bildirici and Bakirtas (2014)	1980–2011	ARDL	Real GDP per capita	Oil, natural gas, and coal energy consumption	–	BRICTS: India, China, Russia, Brazil, Turkey, South Africa	Feedback
22	Nasreen and Anwar (2014)	1980–2012	ARDL	CO_2	GDP, energy consumption, F, population	–	Asian countries	EKC(yes)

Continued

Table 12 Literature review of the ARDL studies in the broad energy-growth nexus—cont'd

S. No.	Study	Data span	Cointegration econometric method	Dependent variable	Covariates	Single country	Multiple countries	Result
23	Saboori and Sulaiman (2013)	1971–2009	ARDL	CO_2	GDP, energy consumption		ASEAN counties: Indonesia, Malaysia, Philippines, Singapore, Thailand	EKC(yes), feedback between energy consumption and CO_2 emissions
24	Islam et al. (2013)	1971–2009	ARDL, VECM	Energy consumption	GDP, population, financial development	Malaysia	–	Feedback
25	Fatai et al. (2004)	1960–1999	ARDL	Real GDP per capita	Coal consumption, consumer prices		Australia, New Zealand	Conservation, neutrality
26	Sari et al. (2008)	2001:1–2005:6M	ARDL	Industrial production	Fossil fuel consumption, renewable energy consumption, labor	USA	–	Growth
27	Ziramba (2009)	1980–2005	ARDL	Industrial production	Coal consumption, industrial production, labor	South Africa	–	Neutrality, conservation
28	Kumar and Shahbaz (2012)	1971–2009	ARDL	Real GDP per capita	Real capital stock, coal consumption	Pakistan	–	Feedback
29	Heidari et al. (2013)	1972–2007	ARDL	Real GDP per capita	Real gross capital formation, labor, natural gas consumption	Iran	–	Feedback

	Study	Period	Method	Dependent variable	Independent variables	Country		Conclusion
30	Farhani et al. (2014)	1980–2010	ARDL	Real GDP per capita	Real gross capital formation, real trade, Natural gas consumption	Malaysia	–	Growth
31	Lean and Smyth (2014)	1980–2011	ARDL	Real GDP per capita	Gross capital formation, natural gas consumption	Malaysia	–	Growth
32	Rafindadi and Ozturk (2015)	1971–2012	ARDL	Real GDP per capita	Real gross capital formation, Labor, Real exports, Natural gas consumption	Malaysia	–	Neutrality
33	Solarin and Shahbaz (2015)	1971–2012	ARDL	Real GDP per capita	Real gross capital formation, real foreign direct investment	Malaysia	–	Feedback
34	Dogan (2015)	1995–2012	ARDL	Real GDP per capita	Trade openness, natural gas consumption, real gross capital formation, labor	Turkey	–	Feedback between income and gas
35	Shahbaz et al. (2016)	1972–2011		Economic growth	Financial development, energy consumption, agriculture, and modern sectors	Pakistan	–	Conservation
36	Halicioglu (2007)	1968–2005	ARDL	(Residential) Energy demand	Income, price, urbanization	Turkey	–	Only long-run causality from income, price, and urbanization to energy demand

Source: Author's compilation.

Table 13 ARDL implementation for time series data in the energy-growth nexus.

	Stages in time-series ARDL implementation	
	First: Stationarity and order of integration	
	ADF: augmented Dickey-Fuller, PP: Philips-Perron (Have low power properties; but since literature is still using them, it is good to use them as reference)	
	KPSS: Kwiatowksi-Phillips-Schmidt-Shin	
	ADF-WS: augmented Dickey-Fuller-Weighted symmetric (Good size and power properties)	
	LS: Lee and Strazicish for breaks	
	When contradictory results are reached, observing the correlogram is a good idea	
	Are the series $I(0)$ or $I(1)$? If yes, proceed with ARDL cointegration	
Yes: Stationarity		No: Stationarity
	Second stage: Cointegration	
	Maximum lag value is decided on AIC and BIC basis and HQC. The F value for the cointegration test should be applied for all criteria (BIC, AIC, and HQC)	
Yes: Cointegration	If cointegration evidence is inconclusive, then the decision about the long-run relationship is based on the ECT	No: Cointegration
	Are long-run coefficients significant? Do they have the correct sign?	
We need to augment the Granger-type causality test model with one period lagged ECT		If we find no evidence of cointegration, then the specification will be a vector autoregression

Table 13 ARDL implementation for time series data in the energy-growth nexus—cont'd

	Stages in time-series ARDL implementation	
		(VAR) in first difference form (Liu et al.)
		Even if the ECT is incorporated in all equations of the Granger causality model, only in the equations where the null hypothesis of no cointegration is rejected will be estimated with an ECT (Narayan and Smyth, 2006)
	Is the cointegration equation robust? Answer: Use the FMOLS, DOLS to check	
	Third stage: Causality	
	Granger causality is ideal both for small and large samples (Geweke et al., 1983)	
	The ECT model allows the inclusion of the lagged ECT derived from the cointegration equation. Thus the long-run information lost through differencing is reintroduced	
	Does the ECM have a negative sign?	
	Are the estimated coefficients stable?	
	Work with diagnostics to prove robustness of your model	

Source: Author's compilation. Note: BIC, Bayesian (Schwarz) information criterion; AIC, Akaike informationcriterion; HQC, Hannan–Quinn criterion; ECT, error correction model; FMOLS, fully modified OLS; DOLS, dynamic OLS.

Table 14 ARDL implementation for panel data in the energy-growth nexus.

	Stages in panel data ARDL Implementation	
	First: cross-sectional dependence This is examined with various tests: Breusch-Pagan LM test (Breusch and Pagan, 1980) Pesaran-scaled LM test (Pesaran, 2004) Pesaran CD test (Pesaran, 2004) Baltagi et al. bias corrected scaled LM test (Baltagi et al., 2012)	
No: cross-sectional dependence		Yes: cross-sectional dependence
	Second: Stationarity and order of integration	
Apply tests assuming cross-sectional independence (first generation) *Examples*: Im et al. (2003) Levin et al. (Levin et al., 2002) Choi (Choi, 2001) Breitung (Breitung, 2000) Maddala et al. (Maddala et al., 1999) Hadri (Hadri, 2000)	LS for two structural breaks and large size of data	Apply tests assuming cross sectional dependence (second generation) *Examples*: Pesaran (Pesaran, 2007) Moon and Perron (Moon and Perron, 2004) Bai and Ng (Bai and Ng, 2004) Chang (Chang, 2002) Harris and Sollis (2003) CIPS
Yes: Stationarity		No: Stationarity
	Third stage: Panel cointegration There are residual based tests, likelihood based tests and error correction based tests	
No: Cross-sectional dependence *Examples of tests*: Gutierrez (Gutierrez, 2003) Larsson et al. (2001) Pedroni (higher explanatory power- mostly preferred with seven		Yes: Cross-sectional dependence *Examples of tests*: Groen and Kleibergen (Groen and Kleibergen, 2003). It allows for multiple cointegration equations

Table 14 ARDL implementation for panel data in the energy-growth nexus—cont'd

	Stages in panel data ARDL Implementation	
statistics) (Pedroni, 2001, 2004) McCoskey and Kao (McCoskey and Kao, 1998) (ideal for small samples) Kao (ideal for small samples) (Kao, 1999)		Westerlund (Westerlund, 2007) four statistics (good for structural breaks)
	Use a resilient estimator such as Driscoll and Kraay (1998) Is cointegration confirmed?	
Yes: Cointegration FMOLS DOLS MG PMG (does not consider cross-sectional dependence; constrains long-run coefficients be the same across units) CCEP (allows cross-sectional dependence, endogeneity, serial correlation) CCEMG (as above but better for small cross sections)		No: Cointegration Pooling is a good idea: Opt between random effects models or fixed effects models depending on Hausman test
	Fourth stage: Panel causality	
	Granger causality: It is a traditional method that assumes panels are homogeneous with no interconnections among cross-section units	Hurlin and Dumitrescu, (2012): good sample properties and cross-sectional dependence resilient. Able to report individual specific causal linkages Bai & Kao CUP-FM

Source: Author's compilation. Note: FMOLS, fully modified OLS; DOLS, dynamic OLS; MG, mean group (estimator); PMG, panel mean group (estimator); CIPS, Cross sectionally augmented Im Pesaran and Shin; CCEP, common correlated effects pooled (estimator); CCEMG, common correlated effects mean group (estimator); CUP-FM, continuously updated fully modified (estimator).

more degrees of freedom, they provide a more informed speed of adjustment, and one can control for heterogeneity and efficiency in the identification and measurement of economic issues (Tugcu, 2018). Of course panel data suffer from limitations such as the cross-sectional dependence phenomenon, which is attributed to globalization and unification of policies across panel units (e.g., countries). The other limitation comes from the fact that panel data are in essence two entry level data and thus the error term in modeling contains both unit (e.g., country)-specific information and time-specific information. This may contribute to the endogeneity problem if the aforementioned error components are correlated to explanatory variables. However, these drawbacks do not discourage researchers from using panel data, which are the main type of data to expect in the energy-growth nexus research field.

5 Conclusion

The energy-growth nexus economics is a field that attracts major research attention for the reasons I have explained in Chapter 1 of this book and in Chapter 16. The ARDL method has been mostly favored and used in the past decade due to its merits (flexibility, interpretability, eloquence, and statistical properties that are explained in the introduction of this chapter. The chapter is structured in a way that it will meet the needs of two groups of researchers:

(i) The new researchers who have recently started using the ARDL method and some points of its implementation have not been fully clarified to them yet, because they are fragmented in various research papers and lecture notes in the Internet. This causes delays in research and paper writing and always leaves room for journal reviewers to reject a paper or advise major reviews.

(ii) The more experienced researchers who have used the method a lot of times but there is always an aspect in the method that would be benefited from throwing additional light to it. Besides the method is continuously enriched it its applied dimension and reading this chapter by experienced researchers will grant them the opportunity to stay up-to-date.

The chapter is seething with applied work and knowledge through the case studies and the flashbacks it makes throughout its length. Sometimes, it happens that even experienced researchers are using a test of a statistical concept, whose exact meaning needs brushing up since the days they learned that during their undergraduate years at university.

Furthermore the chapter guides the ARDL energy-growth researcher about the steps that need to be taken and the exact way that results should be presented and written in a paper to create the readers a feeling of transparency when they read a research paper. Also, this point will offer comparability among papers and will facilitate meta-analysis that is so valuable for the progress of science and the evolution of society.

The chapter can also serve as a textbook chapter for postgraduate students who write their MA/MSc (not lest PhD) dissertation and need to employ this method. The quintessence of the chapter lies in the last two tables in Section 4, which separate the

ARDL steps between the time-series and panel-data frameworks. Integration, cointegration, and causality steps are explained and presented in a vertebrate and well-tied nature and relieves students from the stress of selecting the correct test in every step of the implementation.

Last but not least the content of this chapter is useful not only for the researchers of the energy-growth nexus but also for the researchers of other fields such as the tourism-growth nexus or the broader environment-growth nexus and the Kuznets curve studies.

References

Al-hajj, E., Al-Mulali, U., Solarin, S.A., 2018. Oil price shocks and stock returns nexus for Malaysia: fresh evidence from nonlinear ardl test. Energy Rep. 4, 624–637.

Ali, W., Abdullah, A., Azam, M., 2017a. The dynamic relationship between structural change and CO2 emissions in Malaysia: a cointegrating approach. Environ. Sci. Pollut. Res. 24, 12723–12739.

Ali, W., Abdullah, A., Azam, M., 2017b. Re-visiting the environmental Kuznets curve hypothesis for Malaysia: fresh evidence from ARDL bounds testing approach. Renew. Sust. Energ. Rev. 77, 990–1000.

Apergis, N., 2018. Testing for causality: a survey of the current literature. In: The Economics and Econometrics of the Energy-Growth Nexus.

Asafu-Adjaye, J., 2000. The relationship between energy consumption, energy prices and economic growth: time series evidence from asian developing countries. Energy Econ. 22, 615–625.

Bahmani-Oskooee, M.M., Goswami, G.G., 2003. A disaggregated approach to test the j-curve phenomenon: Japan versus her major trading partners. J. Econ. Financ. 27, 102–113.

Bai, J., Ng, S., 2004. A panic attack on unit roots and cointegration. Econometrica 72, 1127–1177.

Baltagi, B.H., Feng, Q., Kao, C., 2012. A Lagrange multiplier test for cross-sectional dependence in a fixed effects panel data model. J. Econ. 170, 164–177.

Banerjee, A., Dolado, J.J., Mestre, R., 1998. Error-correction mechanism tests for cointegration in a single-equation framework. J. Time Ser. Anal. 19, 267–283.

Bayer, C., Hanck, C., 2013. Combining non-cointegration tests. J. Time Ser. Anal. 34, 83–95.

Bildirici, M.E., Bakirtas, T., 2014. The relationship among oil, natural gas and coal consumption and economic growth in brics (Brazil, Russian, India, China, Turkey and South Africa) countries. Energy 65, 134–144.

Bildirici, M.E., Kayikçi, F., 2013. Effects of oil production on economic growth in eurasian countries: panel ardl approach. Energy 49, 156–161.

Bölük, G., Mert, M., 2015. The renewable energy, growth and environmental kuznets curve in Turkey: an ARDL approach. Renew. Sust. Energ. Rev. 52, 587–595.

Boswijk, H.P., 1994. Testing for an unstable root in conditional and structural error correction models. J. Economet. 63, 37–60.

Breitung, J., 2000. The local power of some unit root tests for panel data. In: Baltagi, B. (Ed.), Nonstationary Panels, Panel Cointegration and Dynamic Panels, Advances in Econometrics. vol. 15. JAI, Amsterdam, pp. 161–178.

Breusch, T.S., Pagan, A.R., 1980. The Lagrange multiplier test and its applications to model specification in econometrics. Rev. Econ. Stud. 47, 239–253.

Brown, R.L., Durbin, J., Evans, J.M., 1975. Techniques for testing the constancy of regression relationshipsover time. J. Roy. Statist. Soc. B 37, 149–163.

Chandran, V.G.R., Sharma, S., Madhavan, K., 2010. Electricity consumption-growth nexus: the case of Malaysia. Energy Policy 38, 606–612.

Chang, Y., 2002. Nonlinear iv unit root tests in panels with cross-sectional dependency. J. Econ. 110, 261–292.

Cherni, A., Essaber Jouini, S., 2017. An ardl approach to the co2 emissions, renewable energy and economic growth nexus: Tunisian evidence. Int. J. Hydrog. Energy 42, 29056–29066.

Choi, I., 2001. Unit root tests for panel data. J. Int. Money Financ. 20, 249–272.

De Vita, G., Endresen, K., Hunt, L.C., 2006. An empirical analysis of energy demand in Namibia. Energy Policy 34, 3447–3463.

Dogan, E., 2015. Revisiting the relationship between natural gas consumption and economic growth in Turkey. Energy Sources Part B 10, 361–370.

Driscoll, J.C., Kraay, A.C., 1998. Consistent covariance matrix estimation with spatially dependent panel data. Rev. Econ. Stat. 80, 549–559.

Engle, R.F., 1982. Autoregressive conditional heteroskedasticity with estimates of the variance of United Kingdom inflation. Econometrica 50 (4), 987–1008.

Engle, R.F., Granger, C.W.J., 1987. Cointegration and error correction representation: estimation and testing. Econometrica 55, 251–276.

Farhani, S., Shahbaz, M., Arouri, M., Teulon, F., 2014. The role of natural gas consumption and trade in tunisia's output. Energy Policy 66, 677–684.

Fatai, K., Oxley, L., Scrimgeour, F.G., 2004. Modelling the causal relationship between energy consumption and gdp in New Zealand, Australia, India, Indonesia, the Philippines and Thailand. Math. Comput. Simul. 64, 431–445.

Fuinhas, J.A., Marques, A.C., 2012. Energy consumption and economic growth nexus in Portugal, Italy, Greece, Spain and Turkey: an ARDL bounds test approach (1965–2009). Energy Econ. 34, 511–517.

Furuoka, F., 2016. Natural gas consumption and economic development in China and Japan: an empirical examination of the asian context. Renew. Sust. Energ. Rev. 56, 100–115.

Geweke, J., Meese, R., Dent, W., 1983. Comparing alternative tests of causality in temporal systems. Analytic results and experimental evidence. J. Econ. 21, 161–194.

Ghosh, S., 2009. Electricity supply, employment and real gdp in India: evidence from cointegration and granger-causality tests. Energy Policy 37, 2926–2929.

Groen, J.J.J., Kleibergen, F., 2003. Likelihood-based cointegration analysis in panels of vector error-correction models. J. Bus. Econ. Stat. 21, 295–318.

Gutierrez, L., 2003. On the power of panel cointegration tests: a Monte Carlo comparison. Econ. Lett. 80, 105–111.

Hadri, K., 2000. Testing for stationarity in heterogeneous panel data. Econ. J. 3, 148–161.

Halicioglu, F., 2007. Residential electricity demand dynamics in Turkey. Energy Econ. 29, 199–210.

Harris, R., Sollis, R., 2003. Applied Time Series Modelling and Forecasting. Wiley, West Sussex.

Haug, A.A., 2002. Temporal aggregation and the power of cointegration tests: a monte carlo study. Oxf. Bull. Econ. Stat. 64, 399–412. +312-313.

Heidari, H., Katircioglu, S.T., Saeidpour, L., 2013. Natural gas consumption and economic growth: are we ready to natural gas price liberalization in Iran? Energy Policy 63, 638–645.

Hurlin, C., Dumitrescu, E., 2012. Testing for granger non-causality in heterogeneous panels. Working Papers halshs-00224434, HAL.

Ibrahiem, D.M., 2015. Renewable electricity consumption, foreign direct investment and economic growth in Egypt: an ARDL approach. Proc. Econ. Financ. 30, 313–323.

Im, K.S., Pesaran, M.H., Shin, Y., 2003. Testing for unit roots in heterogeneous panels. J. Econ. 115, 53–74.

Islam, F., Shahbaz, M., Ahmed, A.U., Alam, M.M., 2013. Financial development and energy consumption nexus in Malaysia: a multivariate time series analysis. Econ. Model. 30, 435–441.

Jalil, A., Ma, Y., 2008. Financial development and economic growth: time series evidence from Pakistan and China. J. Econ. Cooperat. Islam. Countries 29, 29–68.

Johansen, S., 1988. Statistical analysis of cointegration vectors. J. Econ. Dyn. Control. 12, 231–254.

Johansen, S., Juselius, K., 1990. Maximum likelihood estimation and inference on cointegration—with applications to the demand for money. Oxf. Bull. Econ. Stat. 52, 169–210.

Kao, C., 1999. Spurious regression and residual-based tests for cointegration in panel data. J. Econ. 90, 1–44.

Kao, C., Chiang, M.H., 2000. On the estimation and inference of cointegrated regression in panel data. In: Baltagi, B.H. (Ed.), Nonstationary Panels, Panel Cointegration, and Dynamic Panels, Advances in Econometrics. vol. 15, pp. 179–222.

Kremers, J.J.M., Ericsson, N.R., Dolado, J.J., 1992. The power of cointegration tests. Oxf. Bull. Econ. Stat. 54, 325–348.

Kumar, S., Shahbaz, M., 2012. Coal consumption and economic growth revisited: structural breaks, cointegration and causality tests for Pakistan. Energy Explor. Exploit. 30, 499–521.

Larsson, R., Lyhagen, J., Lothgren, M., 2001. Likelihood-based cointegration tests in heterogeneous panels. Econ. J. 108, 1–24.

Lean, H.H., Smyth, R., 2014. Disaggregated energy demand by fuel type and economic growth in Malaysia. Appl. Energy 132, 168–177.

Lee, C.C., Chang, C.P., 2008. Energy consumption and economic growth in asian economies: a more comprehensive analysis using panel data. Resour. Energy Econ. 30, 50–65.

Lee, J., Strazicich, M.C., 2003. Minimum lagrange multiplier unit root test with two structural breaks. Rev. Econ. Stat. 85, 1082–1089.

Levin, A., Lin, C.F., Chu, C.S.J., 2002. Unit root tests in panel data: asymptotic and finite-sample properties. J. Econ. 108, 1–24.

Liu, Y., 2009. Exploring the relationship between urbanization and energy consumption in China using ARDL (autoregressive distributed lag) and FDM (factor decomposition model). Energy 34, 1846–1854.

Maddala, G.S., Lahiri, K., 2009. Introduction to Econometrics, fourth edn. Wiley Publications.

Maddala, G.S., Wu, S., Liu, P., 1999. Do panel data rescue purchasing power parity (ppp) theory? In: Krishnakkumar, J., Ronchetti, E. (Eds.), Panel Data Econometrics: Future Directions. Elsevier.

Marques, A.C., Fuinhas, J.A., Menegaki, A.N., 2016. Renewable vs non-renewable electricity and the industrial production nexus: evidence from an ARDL bounds test approach for Greece. Renew. Energy 96, 645–655.

Marques, L.M., Fuinhas, J.A., Marques, A.C., 2017a. Augmented energy-growth nexus: economic, political and social globalization impacts. Energy Procedia 136, 97–101.

Marques, L.M., Fuinhas, J.A., Marques, A.C., 2017b. On the dynamics of energy-growth nexus: evidence from a world divided into four regions. Int. J. Energy Econ. Policy 7, 208–215.

Masih, A.M.M., Masih, R., 1996. Energy consumption, real income and temporal causality: results from a multi-country study based on cointegration and error-correction modelling techniques. Energy Econ. 18, 165–183.

McCoskey, S., Kao, C., 1998. A residual-based test of the null of cointegration in panel data. Econ. Rev. 17, 57–84.

Menegaki, A.N., 2018. The Economics and Econometrics of the Energy-Growth Nexus. Academic Publishing, Elsevier.

Menegaki, A.N., Tugcu, C.T., 2016. Rethinking the energy-growth nexus: proposing an index of sustainable economic welfare for Sub-Saharan Africa. Energy Res. Soc. Sci. 17, 147–159.

Menegaki, A.N., Tugcu, C.T., 2018. Two versions of the index of sustainable economic welfare (ISEW) in the energy-growth nexus for selected asian countries. Sustain. Prod. Consum. 14, 21–35.

Menegaki, A.N., Marques, A.C., Fuinhas, J.A., 2017. Redefining the energy-growth nexus with an index for sustainable economic welfare in Europe. Energy 141, 1254–1268.

Moon, H.R., Perron, B., 2004. Testing for a unit root in panels with dynamic factors. J. Econ. 122, 81–126.

Narayan, P.K., Smyth, R., 2005. Electricity consumption, employment and real income in Australia evidence from multivariate granger causality tests. Energy Policy 33, 1109–1116.

Narayan, P.K., Smyth, R., 2006. Higher education, real income and real investment in China: evidence from granger causality tests. Educ. Econ. 14, 107–125.

Nasreen, S., Anwar, S., 2014. Causal relationship between trade openness, economic growth and energy consumption: a panel data analysis of Asian countries. Energy Policy 69, 82–91.

Nepal, R., Al Irsyad, M.I., Nepal, S.K., 2019. Tourist arrivals, energy consumption and pollutant emissions in a developing economy–implications for sustainable tourism. Tour. Manag. 72, 145–154.

Odhiambo, N.M., 2009. Energy consumption and economic growth nexus in Tanzania: an ARDL bounds testing approach. Energy Policy 37, 617–622.

Ozturk, I., Acaravci, A., 2011. Electricity consumption and real GDP causality nexus: evidence from ardl bounds testing approach for 11 mena countries. Appl. Energy 88, 2885–2892.

Pedroni, P., 2001. Critical values for cointegration tests in heterogeneous panels with multiple regressors. Oxf. Bull. Econ. Stat. 61, 653–670.

Pedroni, P., 2004. Panel cointegration: asymptotic and finite sample properties of pooled time series tests with an application to the PPP hypothesis. Economet. Theor. 20, 597–625.

Pesaran, M.H., 2004. General Diagnostic Tests for Cross Sectional Dependence in Panels, Cambridge Working Papers in Econometrics, No:0435. Faculty of Economics, University of Cambridge.

Pesaran, M.H., 2007. A simple panel unit root test in the presence of cross-section dependence. J. Appl. Econ. 22, 265–312.

Pesaran, M.H., Shin, Y., 1999. An autoregressive distributed lag modelling approach to cointegration Aaalysis. In: Strøm, S. (Ed.), Econometrics and Economic Theory in the 20th Century: The Ragnar Frisch Centennial Symposium. Cambridge University Press, Cambridge.

Pesaran, M.H., Shin, Y., Smith, R.J., 2001. Bounds testing approaches to the analysis of level relationships. J. Appl. Economet. 16, 289–326.

Phillips, P.C.B., Hansen, B.E., 1990. Statistical inference in instrumental variables regression with i(1) processes. Rev. Econ. Stud. 57, 99–125.

Rafindadi, A.A., Ozturk, I., 2015. Natural gas consumption and economic growth nexus: is the 10th malaysian plan attainable within the limits of its resource? Renew. Sust. Energ. Rev. 49, 1221–1232.

Rahman, M.M., Kashem, M.A., 2017. Carbon emissions, energy consumption and industrial growth in Bangladesh: empirical evidence from ardl cointegration and granger causality analysis. Energy Policy 110, 600–608.

Saboori, B., Sulaiman, J., 2013. CO2 emissions, energy consumption and economic growth in association of Southeast Asian nations (Asean) countries: acointegration approach. Energy 55, 813–822.

Sari, R., Ewing, B.T., Soytas, U., 2008. The relationship between disaggregate energy consumption and industrial production in the United States: an ARDL approach. Energy Econ. 30, 2302–2313.

Shahbaz, M., 2018. Current issues in time-series analysis for the energy-growth nexus (egn); asymmetries and nonlinearities case study: Pakistan. In: The Economics and Econometrics of the Energy-Growth Nexus.

Shahbaz, M., Zeshan, M., Afza, T., 2012. Is energy consumption effective to spur economic growth in Pakistan? New evidence from bounds test to level relationships and granger causality tests. Econ. Model. 29, 2310–2319.

Shahbaz, M., Islam, F., Butt, M.S., 2016. Finance–growth–energy nexus and the role of agriculture and modern sectors: evidence from ardl bounds test approach to cointegration in Pakistan. Glob. Bus. Rev. 17, 1037–1059.

Shin, Y., Yu, B., Greenwood-Nimmo, M., 2011. Modelling asymmetric cointegrationand dynamic multiplier in a nonlinear ARDL framework. In: Festschrift in Honor of Peter Schmidt. SSRN, Rochester.

Solarin, S.A., Shahbaz, M., 2015. Natural gas consumption and economic growth: the role of foreign direct investment, capital formation and trade openness in Malaysia. Renew. Sust. Energ. Rev. 42, 835–845.

Squalli, J., 2007. Electricity consumption and economic growth: bounds and causality analyses of opec members. Energy Econ. 29, 1192–1205.

Stock, J.H., Watson, M.W., 1993. A simple estimator of cointegrating vectors in higher order integrated systems. Econometrica 61 (4), 783–820.

Tiwari, A., 2011. Primary energy consumption, CO2 emissions and economic growth: evidence from India. South East Eur. J. Econ. Bus. 6, 99–117.

Tugcu, C.T., 2018. Panel data analysis in the energy-growth nexus (egn). In: The Economics and Econometrics of the Energy-Growth Nexus.

Tursoy, T., Faisal, F., 2018. The impact of gold and crude oil prices on stock market in Turkey: empirical evidences from ardl bounds test and combined cointegration. Resour. Policy 55, 49–54.

Westerlund, J., 2007. Testing for error correction in panel data. Oxf. Bull. Econ. Stat. 69, 709–748.

Wolde-Rufael, Y., 2010. Bounds test approach to cointegration and causality between nuclear energy consumption and economic growth in India. Energy Policy 38, 52–58.

Ziramba, E., 2009. Disaggregate energy consumption and industrial production in South Africa. Energy Policy 37, 2214–2220.

A note on the VECM approach in applications of the energy-growth nexus

1 Introduction

Throughout the construction and compilation of this book, I have stressed the importance of compiling a reference book that should be found at the work station of every new energy-growth researcher. New entrants in the field find themselves overwhelmed with a bulk of knowledge, methods, and results, and they must be able to read efficiently enough up to a degree that will equip them with the knowledge and tools necessary to write their own papers. New energy-growth researchers who are at the last year of their undergraduate studies or their master degrees or new PhD students do not have knowledge of all the methods, and sometimes this defect deprives them of the opportunity of reading and understanding other literature. Although students and practitioners may be focusing on specific methodologies, they need to have at least a working knowledge of all methodologies appearing in the energy-growth nexus, because they must be in the position of understanding at least the basic stuff and be able to compare the studies among them. A literature review requires a comparison to be made among causality directions and elasticity magnitudes, so it is vital to be able to derive these fundamental results from an energy-growth nexus paper and not be hindered by deficiencies in reading and comparing across different approaches. The same applies for reviews asked from various journals publishing energy-growth nexus material. In cases it has been quite some time that a researcher has used a certain methodology, one needs some quick brush up to make sure that one has been reminded of the basic information that can be derived from a methodology.

Under this framework, this short chapter serves the purpose of becoming a quick reminder on the implementation of the VECM approach and uses examples from three case studies, which have followed slightly different estimation and methodological routes, but they all end up using the VECM approach. This is one of the shortest chapters of the book because some of the points covered here have already been covered in other chapters, and we only provide a quick hint here. The reason I thought it is important to include such a chapter, albeit a short one, is that the title "A VECM Approach" is accompanying many papers in the field, and I guess some students will find it confusing and may deem it as a completely different approach.

After this brief introduction that motivates the chapter and justifies its size, I provide a Section 2 with the basic implementation route followed in papers

A Guide to Econometric Methods for the Energy-Growth Nexus. https://doi.org/10.1016/B978-0-12-819039-5.00006-9

claiming to be using the VECM approach; Section 3 contains three case studies, and Section 4 offers some concluding remarks.

2 The basics of the VECM approach in the energy-growth nexus

Studies that employ the VECM approach usually follow some stylized steps: After the investigation of unit roots, they build a VAR model based on Granger (1988) that is recommended (if variables are stationary) or a VECM (if variables are not stationary) with cointegration investigation. According to Engle and Wranger (1987), if variables are each integrated of order 1 and cointegrated, then there is a causal relationship between them, at least at one direction. When cointegration is not confirmed, then we cannot speak of a long-run relationship between the variables. One way to investigate cointegration is through the Johansen maximum likelihood ratio test (Johansen, 1988; Johansen and Juselius, 1990), another with the ARDL method or others. These types of cointegration tests are examined in other chapters of this book, and hence, I will not devote more space explaining them again now at this point. The VAR and VECM setups will have equal number of simultaneous equations, but the VECM approach uses differenced variables and one additional variable in the right hand side equations, which is the error correction term, the residual from the cointegration regression. In the VECM approach the short-run dynamics are captured by the coefficients of the differenced variables. The specification of the VAR model may have some difficulties, but these can be solved through the Akaike Information Criterion (Akaike, 1974) and the Schwarz Bayesian Criterion (Schwartz, 1978).

The VAR (p) process can take the following simple example form shown in Eq. (1):

$$\begin{matrix} y_{1,t} \\ y_{2,t} = \\ y_{3,t} \end{matrix} \begin{matrix} c_1 \\ c_2 + \\ c_3 \end{matrix} \begin{bmatrix} a_{1,1} & a_{1,2} \\ a_{2,1} & a_{2,2} \\ a_{3,1} & a_{3,2} \end{bmatrix} \begin{bmatrix} y_{1,t-1} \\ y_{2,t-1} \\ y_{3,t-1} \end{bmatrix} + \begin{bmatrix} a_{1,2} & a_{2,2} \\ a_{2,2} & a_{3,2} \\ a_{3,2} & a_{4,2} \end{bmatrix} \begin{bmatrix} y_{1,t-1} \\ y_{2,t-1} \\ y_{3,t-1} \end{bmatrix} + \cdots \begin{matrix} e_{1,t} \\ e_{2,t} \\ e_{3,t} \end{matrix} \tag{1}$$

3 An indicative selection of case studies bearing the title of "A VECM approach" in the energy-growth nexus

This part contains three case studies from three papers in the energy-growth nexus that contain the phrase "A VECM Approach" in their titles. I provide summaries and quick references to the implementation of the VECM equations and tables with useful reminders to their result commentaries. Case study 1 is based on Mahadevan and Asafu-Adjaye (2007), Case study 2 is based on Mandal and Madheswaren (2010), and Case study 3 is built by Marques et al. (2014).

Case study 1: Energy, economy, and prices

Country/countries: 20 countries. Net energy exporters' group contains three developed countries (Australia, Norway, and the United Kingdom) and eight developing countries (Argentina, Indonesia, Kuwait, Malaysia, Nigeria, Saudi Arabia, and Venezuela). Net energy importers group contains three developed countries (Japan, Sweden, and the United States) and seven developing countries (Ghana, India, Senegal, South Africa, South Korea, Singapore, and Thailand).

Data span: 1971–2002 (WDI).

Covariates: Real GDP per capita (constant 2000 US$), energy consumption (energy use in kilogram of oil equivalent per capita), and the consumer price index with base year 2000 (as proxy of energy prices).

Methodology: Pedroni's panel cointegration and the panel-based VECM. The study uses 10 net energy importing countries and 10 energy exporting countries. Each category comprises seven developing countries and three developed countries. Thus, this is a qualitatively balanced sample. The main novelty of the study is in that it compares the panel causality results (short and long run) with a separate estimation of the VECM for each country. The study starts with an IPS panel unit root test with the conclusion that the series is nonstationary and integrated of order one. They continue with the implementation of a Pedroni's heterogeneous panel test and a Johansen test that rejects the null hypothesis of no cointegration at 5% level of significance for 15/20 of the countries (Fig. 1) (Table 1).

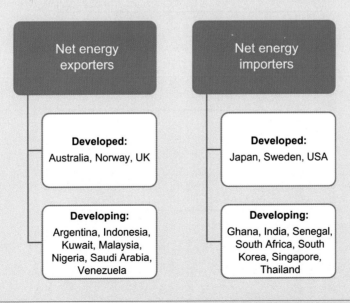

FIG. 1

The four groups of countries in the study by Mahadevan and Asafu-Adjaye (2007).

Continued

Table 1 Results from panel VECM estimation.

Null hypothesis	Full sample		Developed countries		Developing countries	
	Short-run causality test	Strong exogeneity test	Short-run causality test	Strong exogeneity test	Short-run causality test	Strong exogeneity test
Net energy exporters						
$\Delta en \rightarrow \Delta gdp$	8.34*	3.56	4.68*	4.23*	5.91*	3.24
$\Delta gdp \rightarrow \Delta en$	5.28*	4.56*	12.11*	8.08*	18.40*	16.81*
$\Delta p \rightarrow \Delta en$	0.30	0.72	1.98	1.46	2.19	2.67
$\Delta en \rightarrow \Delta p$	0.27	1.78	1.35	2.85	2.17	2.26
Net energy exporters						
$\Delta en \rightarrow \Delta gdp$	17.15*	11.78*	25.47*	17.72*	17.34*	11.56*
$\Delta gdp \rightarrow \Delta en$	7.67*	2.11	6.62*	2.17	1.38	1.11*
$\Delta p \rightarrow \Delta en$	0.79	6.50*	1.63	10.95*	2.29	5.42*
$\Delta en \rightarrow \Delta p$	1.49	1.34	2.27	1.15	2.47	2.37

Notes: One asterisk denotes significance at 1% level. According to the authors of the study, the relationship between prices and GDP has been reported because it does not add to the discussion.

Main results are as follows:

- From the energy exporting countries, two of them, namely, Nigeria and Venezuela, do not confirm the long-run relationship between the crucial magnitudes.
- From the energy importing countries, South Korea, Senegal, and Thailand do not confirm the long-run relationship between the crucial magnitudes.
- However, a more detailed presentation of results is shown in Table 2.

Table 2 provides a comparison of the results from panel data and individual countries results. Although differences are not striking, it is evident that results are not identical either, and thus when we come to individual countries, panel data results may be misleading. As far as energy exporter countries are concerned, there are not any differences across individual developed countries and panel data countries, either in the short run or the long run.

Table 2 Comparison of hypotheses results between panel data and individual countries.

Panel data		Individual countries	
Net energy exporters		Short run	Long run
Developed countries	Feedback	Australia, feedback	Australia, feedback
		Norway, feedback	Norway, feedback
		UK, feedback	UK, feedback
Developing countries	Feedback	Argentina, feedback	Argentina, feedback
		Indonesia, feedback	Indonesia, conservation
		Kuwait, feedback	Kuwait, coservation
		Malaysia, feedback	Malaysia, feedback
		Nigeria, feedback	NA
		Saudi Arabia, feedback	Saudi Arabia, feedback
		Venezuela, feedback	NA
Net energy importers			
Developed countries	Feedback	Japan, feedback	Japan, growth
		Sweden, feedback	Sweden, growth
		USA, feedback	USA, feedback

Continued

Table 2 Comparison of hypotheses results between panel data and individual countries—cont'd

Panel data		Individual countries	
Developing countries	Growth	Ghana, growth	Ghana, feedback
		India, growth	India, growth
		Senegal, growth	Senegal, NA
		South Africa, growth	South Africa, feedback
		South Korea, growth	South Korea, NA
		Singapore, NA	Singapore, feedback
		Thailand, growth	Thailand, NA

Adapted from Mahadevan, R., Asafu-Adjaye, J., 2007. Energy consumption, economic growth and prices: a reassessment using panel VECM for developed and developing countries. Energy Policy 35, 2481–2490.

Regarding the net energy importer countries, there are no differences in the short run. However, there are differences in the long run. Only for the United States and India do results remain the same, namely, the provide support for the feedback and the growth hypotheses, respectively. Albeit small the difference when looking at the global picture, these differences in the hypotheses outcomes will be of utmost importance when one is interested in individual country policy making.

Energy policy making can be a challenging task with a variety of complications and must take into account the balance of payments, the security of supply, the healthy finances of national fuels industries, and many others. The authors of the study report two cases for consideration, one for energy importing countries and one for energy exporting countries. They state that, for the former, energy consumption contributes to economic growth, but again, it is not certain that energy conservation will impede economic growth, because many other parameters count for this result and should be considered. On the other hand, in energy exporting developing economies, energy conservation may retard economic growth, but other measures can be used to reduce excessive energy demand, and this will not retard growth in the long run.

Modified from Mahadevan, R., Asafu-Adjaye, J., 2007. Energy consumption, economic growth and prices: a reassessment using panel VECM for developed and developing countries. Energy Policy 35, 2481–2490.

Case study 2: Energy consumption and output in the Indian cement sector

Country/countries: India (cement industry).

Data span: 1979–2005 with 18 major cement-producing states.

Covariates: energy consumption, output growth.

Methodology: Pedroni's cointegration approach, panel VECM.

This is one of the few sectoral studies present in the energy-growth nexus field. As will be seen next, a major finding of the study is that energy conservation can be implemented in this industry. The industry has a lot of potential for improvement in its energy efficiency by lowering the clinker-cement ratio. Panel data were preferred due to the short span of time series data. The authors of the study employ solely the Breitung (2000) panel unit root test because it has the highest power and the smallest size distortions among all panel unit root tests (Hlouskova and Wagner, 2006). The variables were turned into first differences to become stationary at 1% level of significance. Afterwards the Pedroni panel cointegration tests were performed, which proved the existence of the long-run relationship.

Based on results from Table 3, there is both short-run and long-run causality between energy consumption and output growth in the cement industry of India, in both equation formation setups. The coefficients of energy consumption and ECT were significant at 1% level. Also the coefficients of income and ECT were also significant at 1% level. The ECT combined with the joint tests of energy consumption, capital, labor, and imports were significant at 1%. On the other hand, in the energy equation, the joint tests of ECT with other variables were significant except for labor. This entails that only capital and material are significant and thus affect energy demand, either in the short or the long run.

Table 3 Panel causality test results.

Dependent variable	Sources of causation					
	Short run ΔY	ΔE	ΔK	ΔL	ΔM	
ΔY	–	23.59*	37.28*	11.84*	31.25*	
ΔE	57.49*	–	43.36*	6.17	26.37*	
	Long run ECT	(ECT,Y)	(ECT,E)	(ECT,K)	(ECT,L)	(ECT,M)
ΔY	6.59*	–	24.04*	38.24*	11.95**	31.43*
ΔE	6.70*	58.37*	–	44.85*	7.15	28.38*

One asterisk denotes 1% level. Two asterisks denote 5% level.
From Mandal, S.K., Madheswaren, S., 2010. Causality between energy consumption and output growth in the Indian cement industry: an application of the panel vector error correction model (VECM), Energy Policy 38, 6560–6565.

Continued

Table 4 Fully modified OLS estimates.

Dependent variables	Independent variables				
	Y	E	K	L	M
Y	–	0.34 (23.74)*	0.15 (6.03)*	0.05 (6.48)*	0.58 (37.64)*
E	0.62 (24.39)*	–	−0.13 (5.68)*	0.11 (1.09)	0.77 (13.97)*

One asterisk denotes 1% level.
From Mandal, S.K., Madheswaren, S., 2010. Causality between energy consumption and output growth in the Indian cement industry: an application of the panel vector error correction model (VECM), Energy Policy 38, 6560–6565.

Table 4 describes the long-run elasticities. The fully modified OLS estimates were used because this approach takes into account of the endogeneity and provides unbiased estimates of the long-run elasticities. In the output equation the elasticity of output with respect to energy consumption has been estimated to be 0.34, which means that 1% increase in energy consumption increases output by 0.34%. The elasticity of energy consumption with respect to output is 0.62, which means that 1% increase in output causes an increase in energy consumption by 0.62%. The negative sign in the capital coefficient implies that the employment of more capital corresponds to the consumption of less energy, and this may constitute an indication that energy saving is a capital-intensive process (Mandal and Madheswaren, 2010).

Modified from Mandal, S.K., Madheswaren, S., 2010. Causality between energy consumption and output growth in the Indian cement industry: an application of the panel vector error correction model (VECM), Energy Policy 38, 6560–6565.

Case study 3: Interactions between electricity generation and economic activity

Country/countries: Greece.
 Data span: August 2004–October 2013.
 Covariates: LORP, electricity from lignite, oil, and gas (MWh); LRES, electricity from renewable energy (MWh); HYDRO, electricity from hydropower (MWh); LIPI, seasonality adjusted industrial production index; LRXM, the rate of coverage of imports by exports; LRUMP, electricity consumption in water pumping systems (MWh).

Methodology: Johansen cointegration, VECM, VAR block exogeneity, variance decomposition.

The study aims to inform energy policy makers in the incorporation of national technology into the development of renewables and on whether electricity consumption can be implemented without reducing economic activity growth. As the study finds, economic growth is caused by conventional fossil sources in the short run. Also, there is a causal effect from economic growth onto renewable energy in the short run. The authors warn that this finding (without a reverse causal effect) might indicate that some of the resources freed up in the economy are allocated for the deployment of renewable, but these funds do not stimulate economic growth itself.

The study starts with the investigation of unit roots. It employs an augmented Dickey-Fuller (ADF), a Phillips-Perron (PP), and a Kwiatkowski-Phillips-Schmidt-Shin (KPSS) tests. Detailed results are not presented here due to space considerations. The interested reader should refer directly to the relevant article (Marques et al., 2014, Table 2, p. 39). Based on those results, all variables contain a unit root. Thus, given the nonstationarity of the data, the cointegration analysis must take place within a certain framework. The VAR Johansen's cointegration test reveals the existence of two cointegrating vector among the variables, which generate important long-run elasticities. Again, because the focus of this case study is to comment on the VECM approach, we skip the presentation of these equations, and we move on directly to the VECM results (the short-run results).

The most important findings from Table 5 are as follows:

- The high values of the ECT indicate quick (within 1 month) adjustment of a disequilibrium.
- The negative sign of the ECT means stability and equilibrium convergence.
- Residuals were searched and used to look for outliers, which were corrected with dummies. These were May 2007, January 2012, and April 2009. Dummies were found to associate with policy issuances and their starting dates.
- Furthermore the structures of causal relationships among the variables have been analyzed with Granger causality results and block exogeneity tests.
- The results from block exogeneity tests have confirmed the existence of endogeneity and the appropriateness of VEC modeling.
- The variance decomposition analysis (in the original paper) further strengthened the causality results showing the dynamics of adjustment after a shock and of endogeneity.

Modified from Marques, A.C., Fuinhas, J.A., Menegaki, A.N., 2014. Interactions between electricity generation sources and economic activity in Greece: a VECM approach, Appl. Energy 132, 34–36.

Table 5 The estimated VECM (VEC model).

	DLORP	DLRES	DLHYDRO	DLIPI	DLRXM
DLORP (−1)	0.3409 (3.4942)	0.081 (0.2788)	0.9881 (2.6956)	−0.1144 (−2.0601)	−0.4109 (−2.9989)
DLORP (−2)	0.4278 (4.3392)	0.1750 (0.5814)	−0.0940 (−0.2538)	0.0574 (1.0225)	−0.0814 (−0.5882)
DLRES (−1)	0.0904 (3.3816)	−0.2274 (−2.7864)	0.1742 (1.7351)	0.0019 (0.1263)	0.0500 (1.3329)
DLRES (−2)	0.0318 (1.3228)	−0.1453 (−1.9775)	−0.0878 (−0.9711)	−0.0006 (−0.0423)	0.0136 (0.4026)
DLHYDRO (−1)	0.1306 (4.4969)	0.2559 (2.8859)	0.0505 (0.4633)	0.0082 (0.4965)	−0.1058 (−2.5942)
DLHYDRO (−2)	0.0701 (2.1914)	0.1876 (1.9198)	−0.1064 (−0.8851)	0.0142 (0.7822)	−0.0571 (−1.2701)
DLIPI (1)	0.0326 (0.1584)	1.7971 (2.8578)	−1.6548 (−2.1389)	−0.3902 (−3.3287)	0.1201 (0.4153)
DLIPI (−2)	−0.0478 (−0.2411)	0.8724 (1.4421)	−0.7810 (−1.0494)	−0.0714 (−0.6329)	0.0650 (0.2335)
DLRXM (−1)	−0.1205 (−1.7226)	0.1401 (0.6558)	−0.2852 (−1.0850)	0.0616 (4.5460)	−0.2782 (−2.8315)
DLRXM (−2)	−0.1354 (−1.9575)	0.4778 (2.2614)	0.4908 (1.8879)	−0.1052 (−2.6702)	−0.0946 (−0.9739)
DLPUMP (−1)	0.0274 (2.5130)	−0.0231 (−0.6924)	−0.1288 (−3.1389)	0.0037 (0.5884)	−0.0126 (−0.8189)
DLPUMP (−2)	0.0014 (0.1276)	0.0621 (1.8416)	−0.0368 (−0.8868)	−0.0078 (−1.2399)	−0.0110 (−0.7069)
ID0705	−0.0795 (−0.9560)	−2.5786 (−10.1909)	0.2970 (0.9539)	−0.0232 (−0.4924)	0.0718 (0.6168)
SD0904	0.0180 (1.3788)	0.1258 (3.1641)	0.0299 (0.6104)	0.0005 (0.0659)	0.0228 (1.2494)
ID1201	0.0546 (0.6817)	−0.0631 (−0.2580)	−0.0600 (−0.1995)	−0.1212 (−2.6583)	−0.4246 (−3.7762)
ECT1	−1.0141 (−8.3856)	0.1600 (0.4333)	−0.8346 (−1.8368)	−0.0989 (−1.4361)	0.5324 (3.1349)
ECT2	−0.1015 (−3.8935)	−0.4366 (−5.4840)	−0.2067 (−2.1104)	−0.0989 (−1.4361)	−0.0500 (−1.3656)
R-squared	0.5975	0.7448	0.3862	0.3834	0.4012
Adj R-squared	0.5199	0.6956	0.2679	0.2645	0.2858
F-statistic	7.7007	15.1408	3.2639	3.225	3.4756

Note: t-statistics are in parentheses.
From Marques, A.C., Fuinhas, J.A., Menegaki, A.N., 2014. Interactions between electricity generation sources and economic activity in Greece: a VECM approach, Appl. Energy 132, 34–36.

4 Concluding remarks

This short chapter offers a quick reference and reminder of the setup of "A VECM Approach" entitled paper in the energy-growth nexus field. The rationale of the VECM approach is provided in an eloquent down-to-earth explanation, and various case studies are provided. Overall, this chapter serves the general overarching aim of the book that is to remind junior energy-growth researchers of the basics of the VECM approach and enables a sufficient reading and comparison of an energy-growth nexus paper that employs this methodology and provides a quick reminder for somebody reviewing a paper using this method.

References

Akaike, H., 1974. A new look at the statistical model identification. IEEE Trans. Autom. Control 19, 716–723.

Breitung, J., 2000. The local power of some unit root test for panel data. Adv. Econ. 15, 161–167.

Engle, R.F., Wranger, C.W.J., 1987. Co-integration and error correction: representation, estimation and testing. Econometrica 55 (2), 251–276.

Granger, C.W.J., 1988. Some recent developmentsin a concept of causality. J. Econ. 39 (1–2), 199–211.

Hlouskova, J., Wagner, M., 2006. The performance of panel unit root and stationarity tests: results from a large scale simulation study. Econom. Rev. 25, 85–116.

Johansen, S., 1988. Statistical analysis for cointegration vectors. J. Econ. Dyn. Control. 12, 231–254.

Johansen, S., Juselius, K., 1990. Maximum likelihood estimation and inference on cointegration with application to the demand formoney. Oxf. Bull. Econ. Stat. 52, 169–210.

Mahadevan, R., Asafu-Adjaye, J., 2007. Energy consumption, economic growth and prices: a reassessment using panel VECM for developed and developing countries. Energy Policy 35, 2481–2490.

Mandal, S.K., Madheswaren, S., 2010. Causality between energy consumption and output growth in the Indian cement industry: an application of the panel vector error correction model (VECM). Energy Policy 38, 6560–6565.

Marques, A.C., Fuinhas, J.A., Menegaki, A.N., 2014. Interactions between electricity generation sources and economic activity in Greece: a VECM approach. Appl. Energy 132, 34–36.

Schwartz, R., 1978. Estimating the dimension of a model. Ann. Stat. 6, 461–464.

Further reading

Hatanaka, M., 1996. Time Series Based Econometrics: Unit Roots and Cointegration. Oxford University Press, Oxford.

Adjustment speeds, elasticities, and semielasticities: Their importance in the energy-growth nexus

5

1 Introduction

The estimation of the elasticity of energy consumption to GDP belongs to the core of the energy-growth nexus research. Together with this elasticity, we also estimate a variety of elasticities of the rest of the parameters in the production function or the demand function, but most importantly, we are interested in the relationship between energy consumption and economic growth, since one of the sustainability goals pertinent in all economies and societies nowadays is the reduction of energy consumption and together with that, the reduction of greenhouse gas emissions.

Irrespective of whether you are new entrant researchers in the energy-growth nexus research field, or recurring reviewers in relevant journals, you will have realized that in almost all research papers, the magnitudes are transformed in natural logarithms so that they can directly be used for elasticity calculations. Since the purpose of this whole book is to summarize all the fundamental information required in the energy-growth nexus analysis for the new researchers so that they can write their papers effectively, and a in short time, I regard as important to host the elasticity, semielasticity, and the error correction mechanism or speed of adjustment into the pages of this chapter. In case new researchers need some refreshing of their knowledge on this specific matter, this chapter, together with the whole book, will be at your disposition as a first aid reference.

The rest of this chapter is structured as follows: After this very brief introduction (Section 1), I continue with Section 2, which accommodates all the required technical information and definitions about elasticities, semielasticities, and the speed of adjustment. Section 3 is an indicative selection of four case studies with modified extracts from relevant papers and can show or remind new researchers how to format their results and how to make their result statements on this matter. Last, Section 4 offers some concluding remarks for the chapter.

A Guide to Econometric Methods for the Energy-Growth Nexus. https://doi.org/10.1016/B978-0-12-819039-5.00009-4

2 Background material

Before going to the main part of this short chapter, which would give examples of papers for the interpretation of elasticities, semielasticities, and the speed of adjustment, it is useful to recall some technical knowledge about these concepts. Thus this part is divided into two subsections. Section 2.1 deals with the elasticities and semielasticities, while Section 2.2 deals with the technical knowledge about the error correction mechanism.

2.1 Elasticities and semielasticities

The definition of elasticity is simple and common knowledge. But let me repeat that at this point, in case some of the students using this manual need a reminder; the elasticity is the percentage change of one economic variable with respect to a change in another, or even better, in response to a change in the other. Therefore, when we speak of an elastic variable, we refer to a variable that responds proportionally and even more than that to a change in the other variable. Conversely, with the term inelastic variable, we refer to a variable that changes less than proportionally in response to changes in the other. When we use the elasticities, we need absolute magnitudes. The sign only refers to whether we have an increase or decrease.

In the energy-growth nexus research field, we use the concept of elasticity to calculate how much will be the effect of a change in energy consumption to economic growth. It is a very popular tool and lies in the heart of the energy-growth nexus research. This is shown in Eq. (1):

$$E_{E.EG} = \frac{\partial(\text{economic growth})}{\partial(\text{energy consumption})} \tag{1}$$

If the earlier variables were discrete, which is not the case, but it could be for specific covariates, then the formula would change into Eq. (2):

$$E_{E.EG} = \frac{\%\text{change in Economic quantity}}{\%\text{change in Energy consumption}} \tag{2}$$

Also, it is good to remember that the following cases may be applicable for the relationship:

- $E_{E.EG} > 1$, elastic with Economic Growth changing more than Energy Concumption
- $E_{E.EG} < 1$, elastic with Economic Growth changing less than Energy Concumption
- $E_{E.EG} = 1$, elastic with Economic Growth changing as much as Energy Concumption

where E stands for elasticity, E as subscript stands for economic growth, and EG stands for energy consumption. In economics, there are also two cases that, based on my up-to-date experience, I have not come across yet. This is the perfectly elastic response in which $E_{E.\ EG} \to \infty$ and that would mean that economic growth would have an infinite response to whatever the change in energy consumption. In my understanding, this situation would only be approaching a situation of an economy at the first stage of electrification. Imagine, for example, a village in an underdeveloped country where no electricity is available and suddenly after the intervention of provision of structural financial aid from a national organization, electrification becomes available. But again, this situation of perpetual increase of economic growth would not be realistic, since it could last for only a time snapshot. So, I cannot think of any other situation that the perfectly elastic response of $E_{E.\ EG}$ would be suitable.

On the other hand, there is another extreme case of a perfect inelastic variable in which $E_{E.\ EG} = 0$. This entails that economic growth does not respond to any change in energy consumption. As in the other extreme case, I would suggest that this situation would apply to a highly developed economy with a lot of progress in energy efficiency with a low and slow economic growth as happens in most highly developed economies. But again, I have not come across any such case, and I cannot say anything more unless I have a realistic context. Both these extreme cases are explained in imaginary situations and have not been validated empirically (to the best of my knowledge).

The transformation with logarithms not only is directly convenient for the calculation of the so-longed for elasticities but also is useful for smoothing nonlinear relationships between energy consumption and economic growth. On top of that, this handling enables a transformation of highly skewed variables into ones that approach more the normal distribution (Benoit, 2011). Also, it is an easy remedy for solving heteroskedasticity. So there are more than one advantages in using the logarithms. The only hindrance in using logarithms is that the involved variable should not be negative. In situation such as these, negative variables must be dropped, and the zeros might need to be transformed into very tiny figures, maybe equal to 0.00001 just to avoid dropping these variables altogether and thus avoid to further reducing the sample. However, these are very rare cases, but it is nevertheless good to have some knowledge of how to confront them when they appear.

Various forms of logarithm transformation that can be encountered in empirical literature (though not necessarily in the energy-growth nexus) are the following, after we assume that the linear model is, for example,

$$Y_i = a + \beta X_i + \varepsilon_i \tag{3}$$

$$Y_i = a + \beta \log X_i + \varepsilon_i \text{ known as the linear} - \log \text{ transformation} \tag{4}$$

$$\log Y_i = a + \beta X_i + \varepsilon_i \text{ known as the log} - \text{linear transformation} \tag{5}$$

$$\log Y_i = a + \beta \log X_i + \varepsilon_i \text{ known as the log} - \log \text{ transformation} \tag{6}$$

The interpretation in Eq. (4) is as follows:

"A one unit increase in $\log X_i$ will cause an increase in Y_i in (the estimated) β units." The expected change in Y caused by a change in X can be calculated as follows: $\hat{\beta} \times \log\left(\frac{100+p}{100}\right)$ whereby p refers to the increase in X.

The interpretation in Eq. (5) is as follows:

"A one unit increase in X will cause a change in Y by $ep\hat{\beta}$ units". As above p refers to the % change in X. This case is more straightforward.

The interpretation in Eq. (6) is as follows:

"A % increase in X, will cause another percentage increase in Y." This is the type we commonly use in the energy-growth nexus empirical research field to receive the elasticities. However, it is good to have some working knowledge of the interpretation of the other transformations as well, because we may be confronted with some models sometimes. The semielasticity is calculated as the percentage change in a function, say economic growth with respect to an absolute change in another variable and say energy consumption. The semielasticity is defined algebraically as $\frac{f'(x)}{f(x)}$ for a function at point x (Wooldridge 2009). Next, we move on to Section 2.2 with relevant information on the speed of adjustment or the error correction mechanism (ECM).

2.2 The speed of adjustment

The adjustment speed is provided by the error correction mechanism (ECM). This relates the error, namely, the deviation from the long-run equilibrium to the short-run dynamics. Therefore the ECM produces the speed with which a dependent variable returns to equilibrium after a change in other variables.

One way to make variables Y_t and X_t stationary is to take first differences of the variables and regress each on the other one. This produces the short-run relationship between the variables as follows in Eq. (7):

$$\Delta y_t = \delta_0 + \delta_1 \Delta X_t + u_t \tag{7}$$

The long-run relationship is given by Eq. (8):

$$Y_t = c + \delta_1 X_t + \delta_2 X_{t-1} + \mu Y_{\tau-1} + u_t \tag{8}$$

However, the long-run relationship does not have an economic meaning and may also be a spurious regression, unless the Y_t and X_t are nonstationary.

If the two variables are cointegrated, then there is a long-run equilibrium relationship, which could be generally written as in Eq. (9):

$$Y^E = a + \beta X^E \tag{9}$$

However, if the Y_t is different from the equilibrium, then the long-run relationship is defined as in Eq. (10):

$$Y_t = c + \delta_1 X_t + \delta_2 X_{t-1} + \mu Y_{\tau-1} + u_t \tag{10}$$

Thus to make this relationship reliable and stable, we take first differences of Y_t (the left-hand side is written as $Y_t - Y_{t-1}$), and we rewrite the term $\mu Y_{\tau-1}$ as $-(1-\mu)Y_{t-1}$.

This can be further written as in Eq. (11)

$$\Delta y_t = c + \delta_1 \Delta X_\tau - \lambda(y_{t-1} - a - \beta X_{t-1}) + u_t \qquad (11)$$

whereby $\lambda = 1 - \mu$ and $\beta = \frac{\delta_1 + \delta_2}{1-\mu}$

If the long-run relationship exists, then the parenthesized term $y_{t-1} - a - \beta X_{t-1}$ in the previous relationship will be cointegtated and integrated of order 1.

The economic intuition behind the estimation of these models is that if $Y_{t-1} > a + \beta X_{t-1}$, then it will be above equilibrium, and then we take off some of the Y to correct for this disequilibrium as of Eq. (12):

$$\underset{Part\,1\,\rightarrow\,SR}{\Delta y_t = c + \delta_1 \Delta X_\tau} - \underset{Part\,2\,\rightarrow\,LR}{\lambda(y_{t-1} - a - \beta X_{t-1})} + u_t \qquad (12)$$

3 An indicative selection of energy-growth nexus case studies

This subsection briefly presents four case studies through which a junior energy-growth nexus researcher can recollect how the elasticities and the speed of adjustment are interpreted in the energy-growth nexus research field. This indicative collection contains (i) the renewable energy-growth nexus in a global relationship, (ii) the energy-growth nexus in South Africa, (iii) the electricity-growth nexus in Greece, and (iv) the energy and sustainable economic growth in G7 countries. This selection has been extracted and modified based on the original papers by Apergis and Payne (2012), Molele and Ncanywa (2018), Polemis and Dagoumas (2013), and Menegaki and Tugcu (2017), respectively.

Case study 1: The renewable energy-growth nexus in a global relationship

Country/countries: 80 countries

Data span: 1990–2007

Variables: Real GDP in billions of constant 2000 US dollars, total renewable energy consumption in million kilowatt hours, gross-fixed capital formation in billions of constant 2000 US dollars, and total labor force in millions. The variables have been transformed into natural logarithms.

Methodology: Pedroni (1999, 2004) panel cointegration tests and a panel vector error correction model with Engle and Granger (1987) two-step procedure.

The long-run renewable energy-growth relationship

The study by Apergis and Payne (2012) has produced the following relationship (Eq. 13):

Continued

$$Y = \frac{0.139}{(5.19)} + \frac{0.371}{(9.72)} \text{Renewable Energy} + \frac{0.384}{(22.3)} \text{Non renewable Energy}$$

$$+ \frac{0.388}{(41.5)} \text{Capital} + \frac{0.493}{(52.5)} \text{Labor} \qquad (13)$$

Note: The estimated regression is accompanied by information about various tests: $\text{Adj.}R^2 = 0.74$, $LM = 0.53$ (this is the Lagrange multiplier), $HE = 1.66$ (this is White's heteroskedasticity test), and $RESET = 0.8$ (this is Ramsey's test for the regression equation specification error test). The probability values for the LM, HE, and $RESET$ are $(0.62, 0.29, 0.40)$. The numbers in parentheses below the estimated parameters are t-values. As a rule of thumb, we take t values larger than two to indicate significance.

With respect to elasticity interpretation from the estimated equation (7), we have quoted the following statements from the paper by Apergis and Payne (2012):

- "A 1% increase in renewable energy consumption increases real GDP by 0.371%."
- "A 1% increase in nonrenewable energy consumption increases real GDP by 0.384%."
- "A 1% increase in capital increases real GDP by 0.388%."
- "A 1% increase in labor increases real GDP by 0.493%."

For the complete paper the interested readers are advised to refer directly to the paper by Apergis and Payne (2012).

Modified from Apergis, N., Payne, J.E., 2012. Renewable and non-renewable energy consumption-growth nexus: evidence from a panel error correction model. Energy Econ. 34, 733–738.

Case study 2: The energy-growth nexus in South Africa

Country/countries: South Africa

Data span: 1980–2012

Variables: EC, electricity consumption (in TWH); OILC, oil consumption (net oil imports in millions of metric tons); GDP (constant price 2010, in millions); NGE, net gold exports (in millions); SPI, subsidies on production in all industries (in million); IGS, South African Reserve Bank Assets (investment in government stock).

Methodology: Johansen cointegration method, VECM.

Based on Table 1 the speed of adjustment is 4.4% and 9.4% for the electricity and oil consumption models, respectively. Based on policy recommendations from the authors of the paper, South Africa should keep a high level of oil reserves for security reasons. Another one of their recommendations is electricity rationing, namely, a controlled distribution of electricity. Last the authors recommend electricity price increases to discourage wastage.

Table 1 Summary of VECM results, 1982–2012.

Variable	Coefficient
Cointegration (total model)	−0.003374 (−0.08294)
Constant	0.0116451 (2.70588)
Cointegration (electric consumption model)	−0.044148 (−1.34327)
Cointegration (oil consumption model)	−0.093655 (−1.12922)

Notes: t stats are in parentheses.
From Molele, S.B., Ncanywa, T., 2018. Resolving the energy-growth nexus in South Africa, J. Econ. Financ. Sci. 11(1), a162, Available from: https://jefjournal.org.za/index.php/jef/article/view/162/171, Accessed 03/06/2020.

Modified from Molele, S.B., Ncanywa, T., 2018. Resolving the energy-growth nexus in South Africa, J. Econ. Financ. Sci. 11(1), a162, Available from: https://jefjournal.org.za/index.php/jef/article/view/162/171, Accessed 03/06/2020.

Case study 3: The electricity-growth nexus in Greece

Country/countries: Greece

Data span: 1970–2011

Variables: Residential energy consumption (kWh), GDP (constant 2005 prices in euro), employment, low-voltage residential electricity price (Euros/MWh). Data have been extracted from the Public Power Corporation, The WorldBank Consumer Database and Eurostat.

Methodology: Johansen's cointegration, VECM approach, impulse response function (IRF), variance decomposition approach.

Greece is a country that depends on energy for its growth, while at the same time, carefully designed energy conservation policies can increase economic growth. The current study by Polemis and Dagoumas (2013) has identified a bidirectional relationship between electricity consumption and economic growth.

Based on the causality results based on Table 2, the following statements can be made about the electricity-growth nexus in Greece (Polemis and Dagoumas 2013):

– Electricity consumption is elastic to changes in real income and employment.
– Electricity consumption is inelastic to changes in electricity prices.
– Real income elasticities range from 4.13 to 4.45.
– Real employment elasticities range from 1.16 to 1.88.
– A 1% increase in the level of economic growth will increase the consumption of electricity by an average 1.6%.
– An increase in real electricity price leads to a decrease in electricity consumption from −0.17 to −0.29.
– A 1% increase in the energy price will decrease electricity consumption by 0.2% on average.

Continued

Table 2 Long-run and short-run elasticities for the electricity-growth nexus in Greece.

Long-run elasticities	GDP	Employment	Price (low-voltage residential electricity)	LFOIL (price of light fuel)	Cooling degree days	Heating degree days	
Ordinary least squares (OLS)	4.20* (6.68)	1.65* (6.30)	−0.22*** (−1.74)	−0.18* (−2.61)	−0.13 (−1.29)	0.33*** (1.73)	
Dynamic OLS	4.45*** (1.68)	1.16** (2.04)	−0.29 (−0.63)	−0.35* (−4.07)	−0.65** (−2.39)	−0.57 (−1.13)	
Fully modified OLS	4.13* (4.22)	1.88* (4.60)	−0.17*** (−1.83)	−0.20* (−3.10)	−0.16 (−1.01)	0.35*** (4.52)	
Canonical cointegrating regression	4.14* (3.02)	1.83* (3.61)	−0.19** (−1.98)	−0.21* (−2.40)	−0.21 (−0.87)	0.28 (0.97)	
Short-run elasticities	Δ(GDP)	Δ(Employment)	Δ(Price, low-voltage residential electricity)	Δ(Price of light fuel)	Δ(Cooling degree days)	Δ(Heating degree days)	ECT
Dependent variable ΔCONEL	0.19*** (1.89)	0.61** (2.45)	−0.08** (−1.95)	−0.04 (−0.82)	−0.15* (−3.70)	0.13*** (1.71)	−0.32* (−4.66)

Notes: One, two, and three asterisks denote significance at 1%, 5%, and 10% level, respectively.
From Polemis, M.L., Dagoumas, A.S., 2013. The electricity consumption and economic growth nexus: evidence from Greece, Energy Policy 62, 798–808.

– The short-run real income elasticity of electricity consumption is estimated at 0.19, while the elasticity with respect to electricity price is 0.08.
– In the short run the use of residential electricity is for heating purposes, because the coefficient of the heating degree days is 0.13.
– About the ECT: It is −0.13. Due to short-run deviations, electricity consumption adjusts to the long-run equilibrium, with 32% of the adjustment occurring in the first year.

Modified from Polemis, M.L., Dagoumas, A.S., 2013. The electricity consumption and economic growth nexus: evidence from Greece, Energy Policy 62, 798–808.

Case study 4: Energy and sustainable economic growth in G7 countries

Country/countries: G7 countries (Canada, France, Germany, Italy, Japan, the United Kingdom, and the United States)
   Data span: 1995–2013
   Variables: GDP per capita in US$ 2013, ISEW per capita in US$ 2013, gross-fixed capital formation in US$ 2013, total labor force, research and development expenditure per capita in US$ 2013, and energy consumption per capita (kg of oil equivalent). The RD is used as a proxy for education. All variables are expressed in natural logarithms.
   Methodology: ARDL, Dumitrescu-Hurlin-Granger causality
   This paper has been motivated by a whole branch of new research work that has compared the findings from the conventional energy-growth nexus to the energy-sustainable growth nexus. The ISEW has been constructed for the sampled countries by the authors, based upon data availability. Since the required data for the construction of the ISEW are not fully available for all countries and there are still theoretical issues about their measurement, the authors have estimated two versions of the ISEW, namely, the basic ISEW that contains economic variables only—these are more or less available for most countries— and the full or solid ISEW that contains as many as possible from the environmental parameters that typically constitute the ISEW.

• Based on the findings from Table 3, the joint Hausman test proves that the null hypothesis of the long-run homogeneity is accepted. The PMG estimator is consistent and efficient under the long-run homogeneity assumption for each model.
• The null hypothesis of no cross-sectional dependence is accepted for Models 2 and 3 but not for Model 1.
• All variables contribute to economic growth positively in all models, except for Model 2 in which only labor contributes in a negative way and in Model 3 in which energy contributes again in a negative way.
• Energy is significant at 10% in Models 1 and 2 at 10% level of significance and in Model 3 at 1% level.

Continued

Table 3 Results from Panel ARDL estimation for elasticities and semielasticities.

Dependent variables	GDP per capita (Model 1)	Full or solid ISEW per capita (Model 2)	Basic ISEW per capita (Model 3)
Long-run coefficients			
Capital	0.252 (5.438)	0.652 (24.850)	0.834 (39.089)
Labor	0.363 (0.899)	−1.256 (−8.363)	0.208 (0.747)
R&D	0.813 (14.559)	0.342 (17.331)	0.142 (6.151)
Energy	0.136 (1.552)	0.123 (1.801)	−0.267 (−4.532)
Joint Hausman test	2.51 [0.64]	3.50 [0.48]	6.75 [0.15]
CD test	2.888 [0.00]	1.243 [0.21]	0.691 [0.48]
Error correction parameter	−0.447 (−3.351)	−0.650 (−3.994)	−0.868 (−6.550)
Short-run coefficients			
Capital	0.113 (3.394)	0.424 (3.999)	0.723 (6.572)
Labor	0.162 (3.440)	−0.817 (−4.004)	0.180 (6.666)
R&D	0.363 (3.423)	0.223 (3.982)	0.123 (6.473)
Energy	0.061 (3.300)	0.080 (4.000)	−0.231 (−6.600)
dCapital	0.305 (3.142)	0.363 (2.861)	0.171 (1.631)
dLabor	−0.231 (−0.694)	−0.555 (−0.961)	−0.068 (−1.000)
dR&D	−0.040 (−0.921)	−0.108 (−2.245)	−0.013 (−0.431)
dEnergy	0.281 (1.259)	0.050 (0.540)	0.268 (3.204)
Constant	−3.958 (−3.228)	6.0.993 (4.075)	−12.905 (−6.509)

Notes: Numbers in parentheses are t-statistics, while numbers in brackets are p-values. The lag order for the first model is 1,1,0,0,0 the second model is 0,1,0,0,0 and the third model is 0,0,1,0,1. One, two, and three asterisks indicate significance at 1%, 10%, and 5%, respectively.
From Menegaki, A.N., Tugcu, C.T., 2017. Energy consumption and sustainable economic welfare in G7 countries; A comparison and the conventional nexus; Renew. Sust. Energ. Rev. 69, 892–901, p. 897.

- In the long run, energy contributes in a negative way to sustainable economic growth.
- Capital is significant at 1% level in all models with an ascending size from Models 1–3, while the R&D size has a descending size.
- Each of the estimated models has a stable equilibrium, proved by the negative and statistically significant error correction coefficients.
- The short-run causalities are few.

For more information about the causality results and details about the ISEW set-up the interested reader should refer directly to the original paper.

Modified from Menegaki, A.N., Tugcu, C.T., 2017. Energy consumption and sustainable economic welfare in G7 countries; A comparison and the conventional nexus; Renew. Sust. Energ. Rev. 69, 892–901.

4 Concluding remarks

The long past of the energy-growth nexus field and the controversial results it has received so far, guarantee that this energy economics field will have a long future and a wide scope of application and experimentation. This entails that more researchers will be involved herein, and these people need to be quickly equipped, reminded, and updated with the essentials of the methodology, because this is the only way they can use their research time to move the field forward. This short chapter in particular and the whole book in general aim to put the new researcher of the energy-growth nexus field quickly up to date and facilitate one's route to the construction of new horizons. Thus the chapter serves the purpose of a quick reminder of certain concepts, which happen to be the very essence of the research papers in this field; namely the elasticities of the variables with respect to economic growth and most importantly the elasticity of the variable representing energy consumption with respect to economic growth. Together with the elasticities and semielasticities, the chapter also deals with a brief presentation of the theoretic background of the speed of adjustment through the error correction mechanism, which is also accompanied by an indicative set of case studies. The chapter is also useful to journal paper reviewers who need to be reminded some tools as quickly as possible and speed up their review process.

References

Benoit, K., 2011. Linear Regression Models With Logarithmic Transformations. Methodology Institute, London School of Economics. Available from: https://kenbenoit.net/assets/courses/ME104/logmodels2.pdf. (Accessed 3 June 2020).

Engle, R.F., Granger, C.W.J., 1987. Cointegration and error correction: representation, estimation, and testing. Econometrica 55, 251–276.

Menegaki, A.N., Tugcu, C.T., 2017. Energy consumption and sustainable economic welfare in G7 countries; A comparison and the conventional nexus. Renew. Sust. Energ. Rev. 69, 892–901.

Pedroni, P., 1999. Critical values for cointegration tests in heterogeneous panels with multiple regressors. Oxford Bull. Econ. Stat. 61, 653–670.

Pedroni, P., 2004. Panel cointegration: asymptotic and finite sample properties of pooled time series tests with an application to the PPP hypothesis: new results. Economet. Theor. 20, 597–627.

Polemis, M.L., Dagoumas, A.S., 2013. The electricity consumption and economic growth nexus: evidence from Greece. Energy Policy 62, 798–808.

Wooldridge, J.M., 2009. Introductory Econometrics, A Modern Approach, fourth ed. Southwestern.

Quantile regression approach: A new approach in the energy-growth Nexus with substantial benefits in asymmetry accounting

6

1 Introduction

The quantile regression has started relatively recently being applied in the energy-growth nexus literature. In the past, it has been used extensively in pediatric medicine (offering an optimistic perspective for precision medicine), survival and duration time studies (Huang et al., 2017), the determination of wages, discrimination effects, and income inequality. Also, it has been used in the finance literature in studies that dealt with bank failure and the time occurrence of this failure (Schaeck, 2008). Regarding the more recent application in the energy-growth nexus field, it is not well documented in the relevant studies why asymmetries would be present in the way income and wealth is generated in different countries given the consumption of energy in those countries and other stylized parameters. One reason, quite understandable, why to use this method, is for testing whether poorer countries will be affected the same way by energy conservation measures as the rich ones. Another reason as stated by Troster et al. (2018) in their study on renewable energy, oil prices, and economic growth for the United States is that their study would allow them to determine whether extremely low or high changes in energy consumption prices would lead economic growth. Therefore we can have very specific and accurate answers to what will happen if there is 1% energy reduction in poor countries. This information would otherwise have to be included in dummy variables and other forms of robust estimation that assign less weight to observations that are characterized as outliers. Among the various other statistical twists offered by the method, the quantile regression may be favored because it does not assume a parametric distribution and it estimates the entire conditional distribution of the independent variable. Generally, this method is regarded as more versatile and informative (Rodriguez and Yonggang, 2017). The rest of this chapter is organized as follows—After the brief introduction that motivates the chapter in brief, the rest of the chapter is structured as follows: Section 2 provides support of the reasons and the forms of the asymmetries in the energy-growth nexus, Section 3 offers a thorough presentation of the essentials for the usage of the quantile regression, Section 4 offers selected case studies that have applied the method, and Section 5 concludes the chapter and challenges further research.

A Guide to Econometric Methods for the Energy-Growth Nexus. https://doi.org/10.1016/B978-0-12-819039-5.00005-7

2 Reasons and forms for asymmetries in the energy-growth nexus

As economic development proceeds and grows, the same does the middle-class population in emerging economies. This entails that continually more people around the world aim and will continue aiming at living a life with all the comforts and facilities that are available due to energy use in the modern world. The easy solution in the needed energy production is fossil fuel energy, but since this is becoming scarce and polluting, new solutions need to be arrived at to get reach of affordable and clean energy sources. Giving emphasis to the new infrastructure and the building of smart grids will reconcile demand and supply in better and more efficient terms, will prevent energy access inequality, and will safeguard energy security for all nations and parts of world population.

Since 2000 the United States and the EU have terminated the operation of many coal plants to stabilize or reduce the CO_2 emissions and the climate change situation from aggravation (Morris, 2015). More specifically, about 80% of new energy investments have taken place for green energy, while only 19% have taken place for fossil fuel plants between 2000 and 2013.

By 2030 investment in renewable energy sources will have outpaced fossil fuel generation by 60% (Schneider Electric, 2020). This, combined with the falling costs of renewables, promises already a larger expansion of renewables in the future. The future is also envisaged with a large number of distributed generators contrary to a small number of central distributors. This may contribute to asymmetries, unless it is established correctly from the beginning. Moreover, 70% of new capacity additions will have been implemented as renewable by 2040 (Schneider Electric, 2020). Digitalization of the energy systems and the establishment of new storage technologies will contribute to balancing energy and demand, so this will contribute to the reduction of asymmetries, but this positive outcome will take some time to fully materialize in the future. Of course in many countries and parts of the world that have fallen behind with the development of technologies and the Internet of Things (IoT), digitalization is not expected to reduce asymmetries soon.

According to BP energy scenarios (BP, 2019), a situation will apply that the following characteristics will be present:

– World GDP will more than double in 2040.
– Energy demand will be mainly driven by India, China, and other Asian countries, which will constitute more than 65% of the total global increase.
– Three quarters of the energy increase will be absorbed in primary energy sector destined for the power sector.
– By 2040 renewable energies will have become the main and largest source of power. However, their penetration depends on technical progress and the retirement rate of fossil-fueled plants.
– Three quarters of the world population in 2040 still live in countries with a very low energy consumption per capita (less than 100GJ per capita).

- Energy for industry and households will count for three quarters of energy consumption. Thus they are important actors for the energy transition.
- The share of passenger vehicle kilometers powered by electricity increases to 25% by 2040.
- Liquefied natural gas (LNG) is continuously expanding.
- Carbon emissions will continue to rise (will be about 7% by 2040), which requires a comprehensive energy policy to be addressed.
- The tightening in the regulation of plastic reduction and ban will also contribute to the reduction in oil demand.

Albeit the increasing production of renewable energies and the increasing income, there are still a considerable number of energy-impoverished people. According to the Council of the Europe Development Bank (2019), 30 million Europeans live in energy poverty, while 18 countries are positioned at the bottom 20% of income scale. Income grows more slowly than the energy price levels. High-income countries consume more than 4000 kWh per capita per year, while this amount for Ghana is only 350 kWh and a meager 150 kWh in Nigeria. Therefore this situation describes the one factor forming different elasticities for citizens across countries and within countries. Furthermore, different policies applicable in the different countries worldwide contribute to asymmetries too. Just, as an example, in Europe there are 451 active energy efficiency policies. Of course they are in line with basic directives, but they are nevertheless different from each other.

Overall, asymmetries in energy consumption arise due to the different starting point of development each country is at. There may appear different circumstances such as geographical, climatological, and weather conditions that will determine a different energy behavior of citizens in different countries. Foremost, each country follows a different energy transition path from fossil energy toward renewable energy depending on the aims and objectives it sets, the international environmental agreements each country has cosigned, the environmental problems each country is facing due to greenhouse gas emissions, its energy security needs, and goals together with the energy poverty its citizens are confronted with. All these factors reflect differently on the mode of reaction of countries in front of energy conservation measures. This difference or the so-called asymmetry can generate completely different results in the energy-growth nexus relationship we are studying across the distribution of energy consumption and economic growth.

2.1 Are there extreme events in energy consumption?

After the lengthy discussions on energy conservation, it is understandable that different countries, groups of countries, industries, and specific sectors in an economy may react differently to these reductions, either conservation measures take the form of energy efficiency or replacement of conventional fuels with renewable energy sources. Consequently, energy conservation policies may have heterogeneous implications. They may constitute a push factor for advanced economies, but they may also constitute a pull factor for poor and underdeveloped economies. Namely, imposing the reduction on energy consumption may induce the weaker economies to additional weakness and deeper poverty. While researchers in the energy-growth nexus studies always find a common point of reference for the countries they include in their panels, these countries can never be absolutely the same. Moreover, some studies do not pay much attention to the similarities of the economic structure and the level of economic development as well as geographic and climatic details of the involved countries, but they only care about data availability and are driven by it in the inclusion of countries in their studied samples. The quantile regression method can help toward the generation of country-specific results. Therefore the quantile regression perspective can localize even the studies of global relationships in the energy-growth nexus, which are highly probable in containing tail behaviors. Extreme values in energy consumption or production may occur due to climate change and extreme weather conditions. Irrespective of whether fossil energy consumption itself causes and contributes to climate change, it may also contribute to the occurrence of aberrant behaviors in energy consumption due to extreme events such as droughts, floods, and other natural catastrophes. According to Contreras-Lisperguer and de Cuba (2008), climate change can have several impacts to the energy systems: increases or decreases in temperature can lead to blackouts due to a burden in electricity demand and the peaks that are formulated because of changes in precipitation and temperature patterns. Droughts can have repercussions on hydropower generation or the buried infrastructure of power plants through ground shifting, while extreme events such as wildfires, tornados, and hurricanes can damage energy infrastructures (power stations, transmission lines, oil refineries, oil and gas platforms, and pipelines) and capital investment, which again may generate outliers in an energy-growth data set. The aforementioned phenomena besides affecting energy consumption patterns also affect the income patterns. For more information on the effects of extreme events in communities and properties, the interested reader could refer to Huang and Nguyen (2017).

3 Presentation of the quantile regression

The conditional quantile regression contributes at modeling the conditional distribution of a dependent variable as a function of the independent variables. In a similar fashion the least squares estimation is based on mean models, and the quantile regression estimation is based on conditional quantile functions. Generally, median regression methods (the most common form of quantile regression) are based on minimizing sums of absolute residuals and can be formulated as linear programming problems, solved with simplex algorithm (Koenker and Hallock, 2001). According to Huang et al. (2017), the quantile regression is attractive for being able to give information about the possibly heterogeneous effects of the independent variables at the different quantiles of the dependent variable, and this advantage applies for all types of data. The same authors also claim that although mean regression-based modeling

Table 1 Statistical methods and rule of thumb for the existence of outliers.

Statistical methods	Formula	Rule of thumb
Leverage statistics	$b_t = \frac{1}{T} + (x_t - \bar{x})/[(T-1)s_x^2]$	$>2/\text{sqrt}(T)$
Influence statistics	$Dif\ beta_{j(-i)} = [b_j - b_j(-i)/SE_{b_j}]$	$>(2K+2)/T$
Cook's D	$D_j = \sum_j \left[\hat{y}_j - \frac{\hat{y}_j(-i)}{K} K\ MSE \right]$	$>4/T$

Notes: T is the number of independent variables, and MSE is the mean square error of the regression model. bj (−i) is the recalculation of beta after removing the outlier i.
Adapted from www.bauer.uh.edu

will dominate the statistical modeling in the end, it is this alternative method of quantile regression that should be viewed as a critical extension and complement when asymmetries and outliers are implied, which certainly violate the typical linear regression parametric assumptions. *In the case of normally distributed data, roughly 1 in 370 data points will deviate from the mean by 3xSD (standard deviations). Suppose T = 1000. Then, 9 data points deviating from the mean by more than 3xSD indicates outliers* (Source: www.bauer.uh.edu). There are various ways to identify outliers. Some of them are through the standardized residuals, leverage statistics, influence statistics, Cook's D statistic, and of course the eyeball method, which can be tedious and not quite accurate. For this reason, Table 1 provides a useful reminder for the statistical methods used to identify outliers and their decision rules formulated as rule of thumb.

It is worthwhile to continue the presentation of the quantile regression with a reminder on what happens in the linear regression framework. This is essential because it puts the reader gradually to the conception and the setup framework of the quantile regression. Therefore the traditional linear regression model assumes a form of the following type (Eq. 1):

$$\mu_{yx} = E(y \mid x_1, x_2, ..., x_k) = x^T \beta = \beta_0 + \beta_1 x_1 + \beta_2 x_2 + ... + \beta_k x_k \tag{1}$$

The estimator $\hat{\beta}_{LS}$ is a solution to the equation that follows in Eq. (2):

$$\hat{\beta}_{LS} = arg \min_{\beta \in R^p} \sum_{i=1}^{n} (y_i - x_i^T \beta)^2 \tag{2}$$

Eq. (2) provides information about the mean relationship between a dependent and one or more independent variables. Given that the aforementioned conditional mean model can provide spurious results when extreme values and outliers are present, the solution of the quantile regression is suggested.

3.1 What is a quantile? Some primer material

This brief subsection continues with equipping the reader with background material and definitions, necessary for the understanding of the quantile regression. So, let's visit first the concept of the quantile in simple statistics.

If the cumulative distribution function of a real valued random variable Y is provided by Eq. (3):

$$F_Y(y) = P(Y \leq y) \tag{3}$$

Also, you may recall that that the cumulative distribution function of a parameter $x(\gamma, \sigma)$ is defined by the Eq. (4):

$$F(x) = 1 - \left(1 + \gamma \frac{x}{\sigma}\right)^{\frac{1}{\gamma}}, \gamma, \sigma > 0, x > 0 \tag{4}$$

While the corresponding probability density function is defined by Eq. (5):

$$f(x) = \sigma^{-1}\left(1 + \gamma \frac{x}{\sigma}\right)^{\frac{1}{\gamma} - 1}, \gamma, \sigma > 0, x > 0 \tag{5}$$

whereby gamma is a shape parameter and sigma is a scale parameter.

Then, connecting back to Eq. (3), the τth quantile of Y is provided as.

$$Q_Y(\tau) = F_Y^{-1}(\tau) = \inf\{y : F_Y(y) \geq \tau\} \text{ with } \tau \in (0, 1) \tag{6}$$

Also the τth conditional linear quantile regression of y for x representing a set of independent variables as shown in Eq. (7):

$$Q_y(\tau \mid x) = Q_\tau(y \mid x_1, x_2, ..., x_k) = F^-(\tau \mid x) = x^T \beta(\tau), \text{given that } x = (1, x_1, x_2, ...x_k)^T \tag{7}$$

and $0 < \tau < 1$.

Define the loss function as $\rho_\tau(y) = y(\tau - \|_{(y<0)})$, with the symbol letter $\|$ defined as an indicator function. The loss function equals to $y(\tau - 1)$, when $y < 0$ and equals to $y\tau$ when $y > 0$ or $= 0$.

The solution to the quantile can be found by minimizing the loss function of $Y - u$ with respect to u, namely, perform the following calculation in Eq. (8):

$$\underset{u}{min} \, E(\rho_\tau(Y - u)) = \underset{u}{min} \left\{ (\tau - 1) \int_{-\infty}^{u} (y - u) dF_y(y) + \tau \int_{u}^{\infty} (y - u) dF_Y(y) \right\} \tag{8}$$

This translates into solving the function to 0 and with respect to q_τ in Eq. (9):

$$0 = (1 - \tau) \int_{-\infty}^{q_\tau} dF_Y(y) - \tau \int_{q_\tau}^{\infty} dF_Y(y) \tag{9}$$

This in turn entails that $F_Y(q_\tau) = \tau$. This means that q_τ is the τth quantile of the Y.

3.2 The quantile regression

Quantile regression is an extension of the ordinary least squares (OLS) linear regression but remains a semiparametric method, because it avoids the parametric distribution of the error process as we will see in the succeeding text. Foremost the standard linear regression focuses on the average relationship between a set of regressors and the dependent variable y, based on the conditional mean function, $E(y/x)$ as aforementioned. This means that the conditional mean regression analysis focuses on a single part of the conditional distribution and does not provide information for the entire conditional distribution. This information gap is covered by the quantile approach through a continuum of quantile functions (Troster et al., 2018), which can describe the relationship at different points in the conditional distribution of y. In addition to this, tail causality may be different from mean causality, and this requires the exploration of the whole range of quantiles. The quantile framework provides the information on whether extreme values affect the dependent variable. So this method provides more robust results when outliers are present. This variable is economic growth in the energy-growth nexus and may be affected asymmetrically from the independent variables, the most important of which is energy consumption connected with other covariates such as labor and capital, most importantly.

The method is useful because it offers the opportunity to examine together the unequal variation of one variable for different ranges of another variable. Although it is basically a conditional median regression instead of a mean conditional regression, it can host other measures of central tendency too. The most known conditional median function refers to the median measure that corresponds to the 50th percentile of the empirical distribution. In this sense the quantile q is defined from y splitting the data into q below y and $1-q$ above that. This entails that Eq. (10) applies:

$$F(y_q) = q \text{ and } y_q = F^{-1}(q) : \text{for the median, } q = 0.5 \qquad (10)$$

The quantile regression may also be known as the least-absolute deviations (LAD) regression, which minimizes the sum of the prediction errors, $\sum i |e_i|$. Quantile regression minimizes this sum of errors and assigns different penalties for overprediction and underprediction as of $(1-q)|e_i|$ and $q|e_i|$ accordingly (Baum, 2013).

The quantile regression estimator minimizes the following objective function in Eq. (11):

$$Q(\beta_q) = \sum_{i:y_i \geq x_i'\beta}^{N} q|y_i - x_i'\beta_q| + \sum_{i:y_i < x_i'\beta}^{N} (1-q)|y_i - x_i'\beta_q| \qquad (11)$$

Given the aforementioned, in essence, the quantile regression has minimized a weighted sum of the positive and negative error terms. According to APTECH (2019) the method can be used to study the distributional relationship of variables; it can detect heteroskedasticity; it can deal with censored variables and is more robust to outliers. The interpretation of the estimated model is the same as the linear regression model, only with the special caveat that we get regression coefficients that estimate the independent variables' effect on a specified quantile of the dependent variable. The latter is economic growth in the energy-growth nexus, if there is a production function specification in the model or energy demand if the model is specified as a demand function.

Huang et al. (2017) reported another approach in the quantile regression framework. Besides the minimization of weighted absolute deviations, they refer to the maximization of a Laplace likelihood. Thus a dependent variable Y follows the asymmetric Laplace distribution (ALD), if its probability density function with parameters μ, σ, and τ is given by Eq. (12):

$$f(y|\mu, \sigma, \tau) = \frac{\tau(1-\tau)}{\sigma} \exp\left\{-\rho_t\left(\frac{y-\mu}{\sigma}\right)\right\} \tag{12}$$

The following notation applies in Eq. (12):

(i) $\rho_\tau(u) = u(\tau - I(u < 0))$ is the so-called check or loss function, playing the role of q in the previously shown minimization problem (Eq. 11) and which formulates the quantile regression as solutions to a linear programming model.

(ii) $I(\bullet)$ is the indicator function.

(iii) $0 < \tau < 1$ is the skewness parameter.

(iv) $\sigma > 0$ is the scale parameter.

(v) $-\infty < \mu < \infty$ is the location parameter denoting the τth quantile, because $P_t(y \leq \mu)$ and $P_t(y > \mu) = 1 - \tau$.

Various estimators have been proposed for the nonlinear quantile regression (Powell, 1986 Manski, 1975; Machado and Mata, 2000), which generally follow the manner in Eq. (13):

$$\hat{\theta}(\tau) = argmin_\theta \sum_{i=1}^{n} \rho_\tau(y_i - g(x_i, \theta)) \tag{13}$$

The following table recapitulates the main differences between the quantile regression and the linear regression. To recapitulate, Table 2 sums up and compares the characteristics of the quantile regression and the linear regression.

3.3 The quantile autoregressive distributed lag framework

This book has devoted a whole chapter in the ARDL approach (Chapter 3), and the reader is advised to have read this before going into this subsection. The quantile autoregressive distributed lag (QARDL) approach was developed quite recently by Cho et al. (2015).

Table 2 Comparison of the quantile regression vis-à-vis the linear regression.

The quantile regression	The linear regression
Deals with the prediction of conditional quantiles Q. Y jX/	It is concerned with the prediction of conditional mean E.Y jX/
Requires a large data set	It can work even with a small data set
It does not assume normality	It assumes normality
Robust to outliers	Sensitive to outliers
Computationally intensive	Computationally less intensive
Keeps $Q_\tau = (Y|X)$/under transformation	Does not keep $E(Y|X)$ under transformation

Modified from Rodriguez, R.N., Yonggang, Y., 2017. Five Things You Should Know About Quantile Regression, Paper SAS525-2017, SAS Institute Inc, Available from: https://support.sas.com/resources/papers/proceedings17/SAS0525-2017.pdf, Accessed 20/01/2020.

Shahbaz et al. (2018a,b) identify the reasons why QARDL model is superior to its linear counterpart. They identify at least four reasons, and these are as follows:

(1) This version of model takes into account locational asymmetry.
(2) The model simultaneously considers the long-term and the short-term dynamics across quantiles of the conditional distribution of the relevant variables.
(3) This model allows the cointegration coefficient to vary over the innovation quantile as caused by shocks.
(4) This model is superior even to the nonlinear autoregressive distributed lag (NARDL) model in which nonlinearity is exogenously defined, because the threshold is set to zero instead of being data driven.

This chapter will not devote more space describing the model, since there is a whole chapter in this book about the ARDL method. However, only the basic model setup for reference reasons will be provided in Eq. (14):

$$Q_{Y_t} = a(\tau) + \sum_{i=1}^{p} \varphi_i(\tau) Y_{t-i} + \sum_{i=0}^{q_1} \omega_i(\tau) X_{1t-i} + \sum_{i=0}^{q_2} \lambda_i(\tau) X_{2t-i} + \sum_{i=0}^{q_3} \theta_i(\tau) X_{3t-1} + \varepsilon_t(\tau) \quad (14)$$

with $\varepsilon_t(\tau) = Y_t - Q_{Y_t}(\tau/F_{t-1})$ and $Q_{Y_t}(\tau/F_{t-1})$ being the τth quantile of the Yth, conditional on the information set F_{t-1} and $X_1..._n$ being the independent variables and Y the dependent variable in the energy-growth nexus.

3.4 The quantile-on-quantile (QQ) approach

This subsection will briefly provide the quantile-on-quantile (QQ) approach of Sim and Zhou (2015). This is a generalization of the quantile regression method, which combines the conventional regression method with nonparametric estimations (Shahbaz et al., 2018b). Nonparametric methods help avoid the problems of dimensionality. Thus the methodology starts with a nonparametric energy-growth framework as in Eq. (15):

$$Y_t = \beta^\theta X_t + u_t^\theta \quad (15)$$

The following notation applies for Eq. (15):

(i) Y_t is typically the income variable at period t in the energy-growth nexus models or the energy consumption variable in demand-related energy-growth models.
(ii) X_t is the energy consumption variable at period t in the energy-growth nexus models or the income variable in demand related energy-growth models.
(iii) θ is the θth quantile of the conditional distribution of the independent variable
(iv) u_t^θ is the quantile residual term whose conditional θth quantile is assumed be zero.
(v) $\beta^\theta(\bullet)$ is an unknown function, and hence, it can be shown as a first-order Taylor expansion around a quantile of the independent variable as follows in Eq. (16):

$$\beta^\theta(X_t) \approx \beta^\theta(X^\tau) + \beta^{\theta'}(X^\tau)(X_t - X^\tau) \quad (16)$$

(vi) The slope coefficient $\beta^{\theta'}$ is the partial derivative of $\beta^{\theta}(X_t)$ and shows the marginal effect of this variable. Noteworthy is the dual indexation in $\beta^{\theta}(X^{\tau})$ and $\beta^{\theta'}(X^{\tau})$, which gives the right to write the aforementioned equation (Eq. 15) as of Eq. (17):

$$\beta^{\theta}(X_t) \approx \beta_0(\theta, \tau) + \beta_1(\theta, \tau)(X_t - X^{\tau}) \tag{17}$$

For more details on this version of the quantile regression model, the interested reader should either refer to Sim and Zhou (2015) or read Case study 3 on this chapter.

3.5 Selecting the appropriate weight for the nonparametric quantile function

The idea behind the nonparametric attribute of the quantile regression is to approximate results locally with a series of quantile regressions based on a subset of the observations, which are close to the independent values with more weight placed on observations close to these values. Larger distances imply that the weights decline and approach zero. Common kernel functions appropriate for weighting are shown in the Table 3.

3.6 Adapting to heteroskedasticity with the conformalized quantile regression

The approach of conformalized quantile regression combines the advantages of the quantile regression with conformal prediction. This method enables quantifying the certainty of the estimated intervals with a high probability. Conformal prediction has the virtue of providing a nonasymptotic, distribution-free coverage guarantee. Now we can try describing the idea behind this method using a hypothetical example from the energy-growth nexus field. Suppose we have n training samples for the dependent variable, Y being the income, and the independent variable X being energy consumption. We represent all variables with $\{(X_i, Y_i)\}_{i=1}^{n+1}$, which are drawn i.i.d. from a joint distribution of X and Y from a rational set. Given a miscoverage rate a *(alpha)* that we intend to tolerate, we would like that $P\{Y_{n+1} \in C(X_{n+1})\} \geq 1 - a$ for any joint

Table 3 Common kernel functions appropriate for weighting in the quantile regression.

Kernel	Kernel function $K(z)$
Rectangular	$\frac{1}{2}I(|Z| < 1)$
Triangular	$(1 - |Z|)I(|Z| < 1)$
Epanechnikov	$\frac{3}{4}(1 - Z^2)I(|Z| < 1)$
Bisquare	$\frac{15}{16}(1 - Z^2)^2 I(|Z| < 1)$
Gaussian	$2\pi^{-0.5}e^{-z^2/2}$

Modified from McMillen, D.P., 2013. Quantile Regression for Spatial Data, Springer, p. 69, open book.

distribution P_{XY} and any sample size n. For this level of alpha, a quantile of the empirical distribution of the absolute residuals is computed as in Eq. (18):

$$Q_{1-a}(R, I_2) = (1-a)(1+1/|I_2|) - \text{the empirical quantile of } \{R_i : i \epsilon I_2\} \qquad (18)$$

The data set is divided into two disjoint subsets: the training set $\{(X_i, Y_i) : i \in I_1\}$ and calibration set $\{(X_i, Y_i) : i \in I_2\}$. For more details on the implementation of the method, the interested reader should refer to Romano et al. (2019). To the best of my knowledge, no studies have been performed in the energy-growth nexus up to date that have employed this method.

4 The employment of the quantile approach in indicative energy-growth nexus case studies

This section provides authors with simplified case studies in the employment of the quantile approach in selected energy-growth studies. Noteworthy is that very few studies have employed the method and hence it is a method of ample scope when researchers find good reason in using it.

Case study 1: A renewable energy-growth nexus with oil prices

Country: The United States.

    Data span: July 1989–July 2016, 331 monthly observations.

    Variables: Oil prices (OP), US industrial production index (IPI) as a measure of economic activity, renewable energy consumption (R). All variables have been sourced from Datastream.

    This study investigates the relationship between renewable energy, energy prices, and economic growth in the United States, with the aim to find out whether extremely low or extremely high changes in energy consumption or prices lead economic growth in the United States for the period between July 1989 and July 2016. Results from this study find that negative shocks in oil prices affect the consumption of renewable energy sources. However, no evidence is present for high oil prices to be affecting renewable energy consumption. The authors also found evidence of lower tail causality from large decreases in economic activity to changes in renewable energy consumption. This entails that the economic growth in the United States provides asymmetric incentives to develop renewable energy consumption. This also suggests that renewable energy consumption in the United States is favored in periods of economic recession, while the economy would need that to happen in periods of economic expansion. The finding renders the energy policies not necessary in the periods of recession, but only in the period of expansion. With the information the study receives from the tails' causality, it is understandable that large decreases in renewable energy consumption will reduce economic growth and large increases in renewable energy production contribute to

Continued

economic growth. Large decreases and increases of renewable energy production are denoted by the lowest and highest quantiles of the distribution.

The importance of the quantile framework can be stressed by the fact that there appeared to be no Granger causality between variations in renewable energy, economic activity, and energy prices, when all quantiles had been taken together as a single distribution. Evidence of bidirectional causality between renewable energy and economic growth at the lowest quantiles of the distribution and unidirectional causality from renewable energy to economic growth at the highest tail of the distribution were produced as causality results under the quantile framework. Causality results also found support for unidirectional causality from energy prices to economic growth at the extreme quantiles of the distribution. Last but not least, causality was found from energy prices to renewable energy in the lower tail of the distribution.

Past studies with the United States in the renewable energy-growth nexus

According to the literature review section of this study, the relationship of renewable energy growth nexus in the United States has been studied in at least 14 past studies within a panel of other countries and in at least 20 single country studies, while the oil prices and economic growth nexus have been studied in at least 49 studies in the past, either single country or panel data studies.

Methodological hints

The authors investigate unit root processes separately in the whole time series and in each quantile separately (as of Koenker and Xiao, 2004) and Galvao (2009). Then they employ the Johansen cointegration test (Johansen, 1991, 1995) and a quantile cointegration test (Xiao, 2009).

The applicability of the quantile approach is proved through the Jarque-Bera normality test (Jarque and Bera, 1980), which rejects the null hypothesis for normality at 1% level of significance, for all the employed series. This is an indispensable tool in quantile regression studies that supports the necessity of using the method.

Unit root testing

Results from unit root testing show that in the conventional framework that treats each series as a whole, none of the series is stationary. Not much differently, results under the quantile framework show that oil prices and economic activity are nonstationary at 5% level of significance for all quantiles, while the same procedure for renewable energy consumption reveals a somewhat different result. This variable is nonstationary at the lowest quantiles of the distribution, but the situation is reversed from the medium to higher quantiles.

Cointegration

The linear cointegration test of Johansen (1991, 1995) does not support cointegration in the variables. The authors include two lags and two leads of $(\Delta Z_t, \Delta Z_t^2)$ in the following quantile cointegrating model in Eq. (19):

$$Q_\tau^Y\left(Y_t \mid I_t^Y, I_t^Z\right) = a(\tau) + \beta(\tau)'Z_t + \gamma(\tau)'Z_t^2 + \sum_{l=-K}^{K} \Delta Z_{t-j}' \Pi_j + \sum_{j=-K}^{K} \Delta Z_{t-j}^{2l} \Gamma_j F_u^{-1}(\tau)$$

$$(19)$$

The following notation applies for Eq. (18):

(i) $\beta(\tau)$ is a vector of constants.
(ii) $I_t^Y = (Y_{t-1}, \ldots, Y_{t-s}) \in R^s$ is the past information of Y_t.
(iii) $\alpha(\tau)$ is a persistence parameter.

F_u^{-1} is the inverse conditional distribution of the errors for each quantile $\tau \in T[0,1]$. The quantile cointegration results are shown in Table 4.

The variables in Table 4 are in logarithms. The test deals with the stability of the coefficients beta (β) and gamma (γ) in the quantile cointegration model. CV1–3 refer to critical values. Results of the sup test in Column 3 show that the null hypothesis is rejected at all times. Xiao (2009) has proposed a supremum form of the absolute value of the difference $\hat{V}_n(\tau) = (\hat{\beta}(\tau) - \hat{\beta})$ as a test statistic within the framework of the null hypothesis that $H_0: \beta(\tau) = \beta$. For more details the interested reader should refer to this specific study itself.

Table 4 The Xiao (2009) quantile cointegration test.

Model (column 1)	Coefficient (column 2)	$\sup_T \lvert \hat{V}n(\tau) \rvert$ (column 3)	CV1 = 1% (column 4)	CV5 = 5% (column 50	CV10 = 10% (column 6)
Opt vs IPlt	β	32,630.50	10,286.49	8361.47	7094.76
	γ	3685.03	1041.44	685.60	516.65
Opt vs Rt	β	17,653.73	2104.60	1368.62	1075.01
	γ	1367.67	159.27	91.10	66.97
IPlt vs Rt	β	4500.36	4500.36	317.36	6.08
	γ	338.10	37.67	23.09	17.09

From Troster, V., Shahbaz, M., Salah Uddin, G., 2018. Renewable energy, oil prices, and economic activity: a granger-causality in quantiles analysis, Energy Econ. 70, 440–452.

Modified from Troster, V., Shahbaz, M., Salah Uddin, G., 2018. Renewable energy, oil prices, and economic activity: A Granger-causality in quantiles analysis, Energy Economics 70, 440–452.

Case study 2: The environment-/energy-growth nexus

Country: 30 countries worldwide: Europe and Central Asia (13), South Asia (2), North America (2), Latin America and Caribbean (3), East Asia and Pacific (6), Middle East and North Africa (3), and sub-Saharan Africa (1).
Data span: 1980–2014.

Continued

Variables: CO_2 emissions from energy (thousand tons), total primary energy consumption (tons of oil equivalent), renewable energy consumption (tons of oil equivalent), technological innovation through the proxy of total patent applications, real GDP per capita (in constant 2010 US$), financial development through the proxy of domestic credit to private sector as percent of GDP, trade as percent of GDP, and foreign direct investment as percent of net inflows to GDP and population size. Variables have been sourced from World Bank, EIA, and the BP statistical review.

By 2030 carbon emissions will have increased by a gloomy range between 40% and 110% (Intergovernmental Panel on Climate Change IPCC, 2007). Admittedly the energy sector is the largest producer of these emissions, but research that focuses only on the relationship among energy, economic growth, and emissions is not quite transparent on the exact mechanism that can work toward the mitigation of emissions without hindering economic growth. Therefore the nexus must be enriched with additional explaining variables and covariates that can correct statistically for the missing variables bias. The study uses renewable energy, since its utilization can contribute to sustainable development and it uses technological innovation, because this is regarded as a prerequisite for the improvement of energy efficiency, which will in turn lead economies to using less energy and achieving more growth simultaneously. This is a novel approach because the majority of these studies focus on the investigation of the validity of the environmental Kuznets curve (EKC), while other environment-/energy-growth nexus studies are still inconclusive on the drivers that affect and are affected by carbon emissions. Thus this controversy justifies carrying out new research with new variables and covariates that hopefully will throw light to the studied phenomenon from a different angle and eventually will lead to the formation of a widely agreed global relationship.

Unit root testing

The study has used the Levin-Lin-Chu (LLC) test, the Breitung test, the Im-Pesaran-Skin (IPS) test, Fisher-ADF test, and the Fisher-PP test. The estimated results show that variables are nonstationary, and thus they become first differenced to solve the problem.

Reasons for using the quantile regression

The authors of the study base their decision to use the quantile regressions on four elements of statistical evidence:

(i) For data normality the skewness should equal to zero. However, their estimated coefficient of skewness reveals that the variables are skewed with thicker concentration than the normal distribution.
(ii) For data normality, kurtosis should be 3. However, the data reveal the existence of longer tails.
(iii) The Bera-Jarque result also reveals nonnormality.
(iv) The visual observation of the scatter plot reveals the existence of nonlinearity. For all the aforementioned four reasons, the authors of the study felt their decision to use the quantile regression method was a reasonably justified one.

Before applying the quantile regression, the study uses the Johansen Fisher panel cointegration test and finds at least two cointegration relationships between carbon emissions and all the independent variables.

The model

The conditional quantile of y_i has been set up as the following fixed effects model in Eq. (20):

$$Q_{y_{it}}(\tau \mid \alpha_i, \xi_t, x_{it}) = a_i + \xi_t + \beta_{1\tau}(\text{Primary energy consumption})$$
$$+ \beta_{2\tau}(\text{renewable energy consumption})$$
$$+ \beta_{3\tau}(\text{technological innovation}) + \beta_{4\tau}(\text{real GDP})$$
$$+ \beta_{5\tau}(\text{financial development}) + \beta_{6\tau}(\text{trade})$$
$$+ \beta_{7\tau}(\text{foreign direct investment}) + \beta_{8\tau}(\text{population}) \quad (20)$$

The study employs equally weighted quantiles with $w_k = \frac{1}{K}$ and $\lambda = 1$. The last four variables in the aforementioned equation (Eq. 19) have been used as control variables to avoid any omitted variable bias. The results reported in Table 5 justify completely the usage of the quantile regression. Briefly, this case study highlights the most important findings.

Carbon emissions: Apparently the OLS results under- or overestimate the effects of all independent variables on the dependent variable, being the emissions.

→ **Policy recommendation**: Reduction policies should be aimed in different patterns and quantities for different countries. Global decisions made at international level for binding deadlines must be more flexible and tailored made for different countries.

Nonrenewable energy: It has the greatest effect across all quantiles.

→ **Conclusion and policy recommendation:** Although renewable energy has increased in usage in many countries that are characterized by high emissions, the proportion of renewable energy in the total energy mix of these countries is still small, and therefore their mitigating effect is not that obvious.

Renewable energy: For countries that produce high carbon emissions, there is a stronger effect on emissions compared with countries that produce low carbon emissions.

→ **Conclusion and policy recommendation:** As aforementioned.

Economic growth: Its impact on carbon emissions is positive. This effect decreases from countries with low emissions to countries with high emissions.

→ **Conclusion and policy recommendation:** Government regulations should be reformed for countries that are still high carbon emitters irrespective of their high stage of development. These countries have the economic strength to invest in mitigation technologies and the replacement of conventional fossil

Continued

Table 5 Results from the fixed effects panel quantile regression.

						Quantile regression				
	OLS regression	Tau = 0.1 (10th)	Tau = 0.2 (20th)	Tau = 0.3 (30th)	Tau = 0.4 (40th)	Tau = 0.5 (50th)	Tau = 0.6 (60th)	Tau = 0.7 (70th)	Tau = 0.8 (80th)	Tau = 0.9 (90th)
Primary energy consumption	1.02639*	0.96930*	1.03544*	0.98822*	0.95406*	0.95882*	0.94865*	1.04490*	1.11623*	1.12541*
Renewable energy consumption	−0.03425*	−0.06910*	−0.05123*	−0.04355*	−0.03177*	−0.0322*	−0.02112*	0.02279*	−0.01138*	−0.01622*
Technological innovation	−0.00158	0.00436	0.00386	−0.00803*	−0.0080*	−0.01225*	−0.02240*	−0.03750*	−0.04836*	−0.04732*
Real GDP	0.13875*	0.22627*	0.15909*	0.12646*	0.11678*	0.09731*	0.09376*	0.02926*	0.01709*	0.00390*
Financial development	−0.00038	−0.00683*	0.00112*	0.00168*	−0.0005*	0.00063*	0.00016	0.00163	0.00324*	−0.00187*
Trade	0.00043	0.00205*	0.00138*	0.00079*	0.00077*	0.00078*	0.00106*	0.00043*	−0.00051*	−0.00064*
Foreign direct investment	−0.00024*	0.00029*	0.00072*	0.00048*	0.00044*	−0.0006*	−0.00027*	−0.00039*	−0.00025*	−0.00006*
Population	0.12175*	0.04671*	0.03363*	0.10208*	0.13124*	0.12977*	0.15366*	0.09468*	0.13427	0.15321*

Note: The asterisk denotes significance at 5%.

Adapted from Chen, W., Lei, Y., 2018. The impacts of renewable energy and technological innovation on environment-energy-growth nexus: new evidence from a panel quantile regression, Renew. Energy 123: 1–14.

fuels with renewable energies. High economic growth countries, which are also high carbon emitters, have easy and cheap access to technological innovation.

Technological innovation: It bears a larger negative effect on countries with higher carbon emissions compared with the countries with low emissions.

→ **Conclusion and policy recommendation:** Technology progress contributes in a fundamental way toward the reduction of carbon emissions. High emitting rich countries can make the difference toward the reduction of carbon emissions through their accumulated knowledge, which drives energy efficiency and the building of renewable energy infrastructure.

Trade and foreign direct investment: They have a larger reducing impact for countries that are high carbon emitters.

→ **Conclusion and policy recommendation:** Trade and foreign direct investment contribute to significant technology spillover and thus make the transition to renewable energies and energy efficiency a quicker and easier process.

Modified from Chen, W., Lei, Y., 2018. The impacts of renewable energy and technological innovation on environment-energy-growth nexus: New evidence from a panel quantile regression, Renew. Energy 123, 1–14.

Case study 3: Variations in the energy-growth relationship among the top 10 energy-consuming countries

Countries: Brazil, Canada, China, France, Germany, India, Japan, Korea, Russia, and the United States.

Data span: 1960q1–2015q4 (Note that they have been converted from annual observations into quarterly ones with a quadratic match-sum method.)

Variables: Energy consumption (kilogram of oil equivalent) per capita, real gross domestic product (in constant 2010 US$) per capita.

This study employs the quantile-on-quantile approach (QQ) by Sim and Zhou (2015) as described shortly in a previous subsection of this chapter. The study does not devote much detail in explaining the necessity of using the method in advance, but the results seem to justify it. The authors explain that the QQ approach is a combination of the quantile regression with nonparametric estimations, and they wish to impose a linear regression locally around the neighborhood of each data point in their sample and provide higher weights to each point's immediate neighbor. The local linear regression is estimated by the minimization of the following problem in Eq. (21):

$$min_{b_0,b_1} \sum_{i-1}^{n} \rho_\theta \left[EC_t - b_0 - b_1 \left(G\hat{D}P_t - G\hat{D}P^\tau \right) \right] K \left(\frac{F_n \left(G\hat{D}P_t - \tau \right)}{h} \right) \quad (21)$$

Continued

The following notation applies for the aforementioned equation (Eq. 21):

(i) $\rho_\theta(u)$ is the quantile loss function depicted as $\rho_\theta(u) = u(\theta - I(u < 0))$.
(ii) I is the indicator function.
(iii) $K(\bullet)$ is the kernel function.
(iv) h is the bandwidth parameter of the kernel function.

For more details on the setup of this function (Eq. 20) and all the previous steps, the interested reader is advised to refer directly to the original paper by Shahbaz et al. (2018a,b).

The paper does not provide the estimated results in a table form, but it provides an eloquent graph of the results from which an extract has been conceded for educative purposes to the current chapter. The extract shows the results for the United States and Russia. The rest of the countries are not shown in Fig. 1, but their main results are presented as follows: Note that when one is reporting the quantile location of one magnitude, one must complement it with the location of the quantile for the other magnitude. In this case study, when this is not reported, this means that we are referring to the same quantile location for both magnitudes.

China: Energy consumption leads economic growth.

The United States: Economic growth affects energy consumption, and this is shown in all quantiles. The positive effect is stronger at low quantiles and a bit moderate in higher quantiles. The results of this country can be directly observed in Fig. 1. High economic growth in the United States may signify that either technology has led to fuel efficiency or that the good production has moved from energy intensive sectors to less energy-intensive sectors.

Russia: This is the second country depicted in Fig. 1. According to results from it, the feedback hypothesis applies for this country only in high quantiles of both magnitudes. Consequently, in these quantiles, energy conservation will slow down economic growth. As far as the findings from the middle quantiles of economic growth are concerned, there is a strong effect of the conservation hypothesis (with the higher quantiles of energy consumption), namely, economic growth affecting positively energy consumption. The lower quantiles of economic growth reveal only a weak relationship between energy and growth. As aforementioned, due to space considerations, the rest of the country graphs are not shown here and can be found in the source paper.

India: Evidence of the feedback and neutrality hypothesis. At low quantiles of economic growth, there is a quite meager relationship between the two magnitudes. At high quantiles of economic growth, there is a significant effect of economic growth on energy consumption.

Japan: Energy consumption and economic growth have a strong positive effect on each other at their upper quantiles.

Canada: Generally the feedback effect becomes supported in the middle quantiles of both magnitudes.

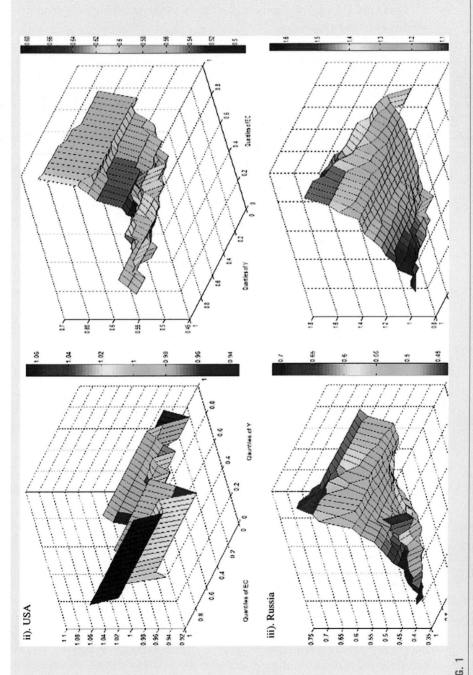

ii). USA

iii). Russia

FIG. 1

Extract from Fig. 4 in Shahbaz et al. (2018a,b): impact of economic growth on the energy consumption of the investigated countries—here it is about only the United States and Russia.

Germany: Generally the growth effect becomes supported in the upper quantiles of both magnitudes.

Brazil: Generally the growth effect becomes supported in the upper quantiles of both magnitudes.

France: Similar findings with Germany.

Korea (South): Energy appears as nonimportant for the economic development in South Korea. The results maybe tend toward the support of the neutrality hypothesis.

Overall, this study attributes the huge variation of the energy-growth relationship across the quintiles of the two variables, to the differences in the relative importance of energy in the various countries, the energy efficiency levels each a country has reached, the production capacity constraints of each one and the negative externalities of the energy consumption. Once again, this quantile regression method offers opportunities for tailored-made energy conservation policies, depending on the economic phase each economy is found at.

Modified from Shahbaz, M., Zakaria, M., Shahzad, S.H.S., Mahalik, M.K., 2018. The energy consumption and economic growth nexus in top ten energy-consuming countries: Fresh evidence from using the quantile-on-quantile approach, Energy Econ. 71, 282–301.

5 Conclusion and new challenges

The energy-growth nexus literature has been blamed for lack of precision and controversial results. Major meta-analysis in the field has not managed to systemize the gained knowledge so far, due to this chaotic difference across studies of the same object (country or group of countries). Since this is the case, researchers still experiment on the methods that could drive unification and eventually consensus.

The quantile regression offers hope for new order and precision in the field and tailored-made recommendations for countries and other entities. Through the revolution of the big data era, the richness and availability of energy-growth data is bound to increase.

The quantile method has not been used extensively in the energy-growth nexus in the way other econometric methods have. So, there is ample new scope for usage, experimentation, and comparison. However, given the small number of studies at hand and the even smaller number of case studies in this chapter, I have the feeling that the energy-growth nexus studies do not justify fully their usage of the quantile regression. The method should not be used just for the sake of it, but mostly after justification of the inappropriateness of the linear regression model. Foremost a scatterplot may offer tangible evidence for the existence of outliers and extreme values. Naturally the table of descriptive statistics is effective enough in proving that, but unless there is a serious distorting effect from the values of certain variables, even the quintile method will not perform miracles. On top of that the current studies are not very convincing that they are using the method because of outliers. Results from new studies should be presented and tested with and without outliers to decide whether the problem is solved in a better way by simply dropping the outlier value or by taking the pains in incorporating it in the model with a quantile regression.

Actually and most importantly the merit of the quantile regression approach will be realized only if the estimates of this approach are presented in result tables alongside linear regression results. This will enable a comparison of coefficient and their standard errors, and we will be able to gradually build our knowledge of the contribution of this method to macroeconomic data, which are much different from human behavior data or medical data where the quantile method has already flourished.

References

APTECH, 2019. The Basics of Quantile Regression. Available from: www.aptech.com. (Accessed 8 January 2020).

Baum, C.F., 2013. Quantile regression, Lecture notes, EC 823: Applied Econometrics. Available from: www.bc.edu/EC-C/S2013/823/EC823.S2013.nn04.slides.pdf.

BP, 2019. BP Energy Outlook, 2019 ed. Available from: https://www.bp.com/content/dam/bp/business-sites/en/global/corporate/pdfs/energy-economics/energy-outlook/bp-energy-outlook-2019.pdf. Available from: 27/01/2020.

Cho, J.S., Kim, T.-H., Shin, Y., 2015. Quantile cointegration in the autoregressive distributed-lag modeling framework. J. Econ. 188, 281–300.

Contreras-Lisperguer, R., de Cuba, K., 2008. The Potential Impact of Climate Change on the Energy Sector in the Caribbean Region. Available from: https://www.oas.org/dsd/Documents/Effects_of_Climate_on_Energy_DSD_Energy_Division.pdf. (Accessed 20 January 2020).

Council of the Europe Development Bank, 2019. Energy Poverty in Europe, How Efficiency and Renewable Can Help. Available from: https://coebank.org/media/documents/CEB_Study_Energy_Poverty_in_Europe.pdf. (Accessed 28 January 2020).

Galvao, A.F., 2009. Unit root quantile autoregression testing using covariates. J. Econ. 152, 165–178.

Huang, M.L., Nguyen, C., 2017. High quantile regression for extreme events. J. Stat. Distribut. Appl. 4, 4. https://doi.org/10.1186/s40488-017-0058-3.

Huang, Q., Zhang, H., Chen, J., He, M., 2017. Quantile regression models and their applications: a review. J. Biomet. Biostat. 8, 3. https://doi.org/10.4172/2155-6180.1000354.

Intergovernmental Panel on Climate Change (IPCC), 2007. Climate change 2007, impacts, adaptation and vulnerability. Available from: https://www.ipcc.ch/site/assets/uploads/2018/03/ar4_wg2_full_report.pdf], accessed on 29/08/2020.

Jarque, C.M., Bera, A.K., 1980. Efficient tests for normality, homoscedasticity and serial in dependence of regression residuals. Econ. Lett. 6, 255–259.

Johansen, S., 1991. Estimation and hypothesis testing of cointegration vectors in Gaussian vector autoregressive models. Econometrica 59, 1551–1580.

Johansen, S., 1995. Likelihood-Based Inference in Cointegrated Vector Autoregressive Models. Oxford University Press.

Koenker, R., Hallock, K.F., 2001. Quantile regression. J. Econ. Perspect. 15 (4), 143–156.

Koenker, R., Xiao, Z., 2004. Unit root quantile autoregression inference. J. Am. Stat. Assoc. 99, 775–787.

Machado, J., Mata, J., 2000. Box-Cox quantile regression and the distribution of firm sizes. J. Appl. Econ. 15, 253–274.

Manski, C., 1975. Maximum score estimation of the stochastic utility model of choice. J. Econ. 3, 205–228.

Morris, C., 2015. Five megatrends for a global energy transition. In: Energy Transition. The Global Energiewende. available from: https://energytransition.org/2015/07/5-megatrends-for-a-global-energy-transition. (Accessed 27 January 2020).

Powell, J.L., 1986. Censored regression quantiles. J. Econ. 32, 143–155.

Rodriguez, R.N., Yonggang, Y., 2017. Five Things You Should Know About Quantile Regression, Paper SAS525-2017. SAS Institute Inc. Available from: https://support.sas.com/resources/papers/proceedings17/SAS0525-2017.pdf. (Accessed 20 January 2020).

Romano, Y., Patterson, E., Candes, E.J., 2019. The conformalized quantile regression. In: 33rd Conference on Neural Information Processing Systems (NeurIPS 2019), Vancouver, Canada.

Schaeck, K., 2008. Bank liability structure flick loss and time to failure. A quantile regression approach. J. Financ. Serv. Res. 33, 163–179.

Schneider Electric, 2020. 3 Megatrends Shaping the New World of Energy. Available from: https://perspectives.se.com/aem/3-megatrends-shaping-the-new-world-of-energy. (Accessed 27 January 2020).

Shahbaz, M., Lahiani, A., Salah Abosedra, S., Hammoudeh, S., 2018a. The role of globalization in energy consumption: a quantile cointegrating regression approach. Energy Econ. 71, 161–170.

Shahbaz, M., Zakaria, M., Shahzad, S.H.S., Mahalik, M.K., 2018b. The energy consumption and economic growth nexus in top ten energy-consuming countries: fresh evidence from using the quantile-on-quantile approach. Energy Econ. 71, 282–301.

Sim, N., Zhou, H., 2015. Oil prices, US stock return, and the dependence between their quantiles. J. Bank. Financ. 55, 1–8.

Troster, V., Shahbaz, M., Salah Uddin, G., 2018. Renewable energy, oil prices, and economic activity: a granger-causality in quantiles analysis. Energy Econ. 70, 440–452.

Xiao, Z., 2009. Quantile cointegrating regression. J. Econ. 150, 248–260.

Further reading

Bauer.uh.edu, 2020. Lecture 10, Robust and Quantile Regression. Available from: https://www.bauer.uh.edu/rsusmel/phd/ec1-25.pdf. (Accessed 20 January 2020).

Chen, W., Lei, Y., 2018. The impacts of renewable energy and technological innovation on environment-energy-growth nexus: new evidence from a panel quantile regression. Renew. Energy 123, 1–14.

Koenker, R., 2000. Quantile Regression. Available from: http://www.econ.uiuc.edu/~roger/research/rq/rq.pdf. (Accessed 8 January 2020).

Koenker, R., 2017. Quantile regression: 40 years on. Annu. Rev. Econ. 9, 155–176.

McMillen, D.P., 2013. Quantile Regression for Spatial Data. Springer, p. 69.

Moss, T., 2019. Ending Global Energy Poverty—How Can We Do Better? World Economic Forum. Available from: https://www.weforum.org/agenda/2019/11/energy-poverty-africa-sdg7. (Accessed 28 January 2020).

Troster, V., 2016. Testing for granger-causality in quantiles. Econ. Rev. 37, 1–17.

Time-varying Fourier analysis in the energy-growth nexus or the X-variable-growth nexus

1 Introduction

As the years pass in the evolution of the investigation of the relationship of the energy-growth nexus or the X-variable-growth nexus, researchers keep using more sophisticated methods and concepts from mathematics and physics to describe the energy-growth relationship in a deeper way and reach consensus across the different methodologies. The involvement of structural breaks and data interdependencies are of common incidence in the energy-growth field. For example, history has revealed many time periods that oil prices have changed due to geopolitics or supply outages that have been transmitted into the energy consumption and the energy-growth relationship. Furthermore, nowadays, most countries have become environmental conscious, and their energy consumption is dictated by decarbonization goals and objectives that signify the generation of a new pattern in the energy-growth nexus. The same applies with technological innovation that contributes to energy efficiency, which is also a requirement and objective for many countries or economic sectors. Therefore the issuance of various directives or the signature of international agreements with binding deadlines for the aforementioned may signify oscillations for the energy-growth relationship or the "X-variable"-growth relationship, which is worth observing within the Fourier framework that assumes these oscillations resemble the smooth sine and cosine function oscillations.

The framework has not been applied in many energy-growth applications so far, so we cannot generalize and make reliable literature statements as to whether the method is superior to others. However, the framework can be poured to many cointegration and causality methodologies to experiment on whether breaks are ideally hosted in the energy-growth relationship. It is certainly worth trying it when there is grounded belief that the relationship is characterized by breaks. And as it has been mentioned earlier, this relationship, particularly when data spans are long, is permeated by structural changes, more than anything else.

As the purpose of this book dictates, it is appropriate to write a short chapter on the Fourier approximation. Although the detailed econometrics are well described in purely mathematics of physics textbooks, it is convenient to have the basic knowledge and paraphernalia available in brief at first need. Sometimes, irrespective of whether we primarily and genuinely use the Fourier method in our research or we

149

A Guide to Econometric Methods for the Energy-Growth Nexus. https://doi.org/10.1016/B978-0-12-819039-5.00015-X

are simply reading the up-to-date energy-growth literature in an attempt to write a literature review or compare our results with the ones in literature, we need to have the Fourier basics collected somewhere and easily available and comprehensible. The same applies when we are required to act as paper or chapter reviewers in Fourier approximated energy-growth nexus studies. This chapter enables a quick reminder and help for students, researchers, and practitioners.

The rest of this short paper consists of three additional parts besides the introduction (Section 1). The second part provides the basic notions and concepts in Fourier analysis, which can put the new energy-growth researcher into context quickly. The third part encompasses two case studies with the gist from their using the Fourier approximation. Last the fourth part offers some concluding remarks.

2 A simple definition of Fourier analysis

To start with a bit of history, Fourier analysis investigates the way general functions can be represented by sums of trigonometric functions. This type of analysis was named after Joseph Fourier who first showed that this approximation made simpler the study of heat transfer. Thus, in essence, Fourier analysis can decompose a function into oscillary components (Fourier analysis), while forming the function back together from these components is called Fourier synthesis. In the relevant bibliography the decomposition is called Fourier transformation. Among its many applications in positive sciences (mainly physics and mathematics), Fourier analysis has found fertile ground recently in the energy-growth nexus in energy economics. Gradually, it is adopted in other branches such as the tourism-growth nexus or the environment-growth nexus or the general field of studies I call with one word as the X-variable-growth nexus.

It would be useful to provide some definitions at the beginning to make reading more comfortable for all levels of readership. Thus we need first to define the terms Fourier series and Fourier transform. As far as the first term is concerned, the Fourier series is a discrete sum of trigonometric or exponential functions with specific frequencies that is derived from a general well-behaved function that is periodic. As far as the second term is concerned, a Fourier transform is a continuous integral or trigonometric or exponential function with a continuum of possible frequencies that is derived from a general, well-behaved function that is not necessarily periodic (Morin, 2009). To make the aforementioned more tangible for somebody to understand, suppose we have a function $f(x)$ that is periodic in the interval $0 \leq x \leq L$, then Fourier's theorem entails that the $f(x)$ can be written in a trigonometric series as follows in Eq. (1):

$$f(x) = a_0 + \sum_{n=1}^{\infty} \left[a_0 \cos\left(\frac{2\pi n x}{L}\right) + b_n \sin\left(\frac{2\pi n x}{L}\right) \right] \tag{1}$$

To start from a simpler basis, let's have a look at the following figure (Fig. 1). It depicts a periodic function that evolves in cycles in every pi interval of time or more

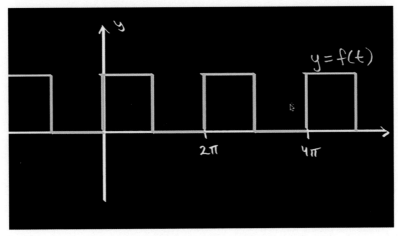

FIG. 1

An example of a periodic function that evolves in cycles in every pi interval of time.

specifically *sec*onds of time. It is easy to observe the periodicity of the function and the similarity of periodicity with the sine and cosine functions in Figs. 2 and 3.

Thus, returning to Fig. 1, the period of this function is $T = 2\pi$ sec/cycle, and its frequency is Freq $= 1/2\pi^*$ cycles/s. This function can be represented as an infinite sum of sines and cosines of different periods and frequencies. Thus a function of f(x) could be written as follows:

$$f(t) = a_0 + a_1 \cos(t) + a_2 \cos(2t) + a_3 \cos(3t) + \cdots + b_1 \sin(t) + b_2 \sin(2t)$$
$$+ b_3 \sin(3t) + \cdots \tag{2}$$

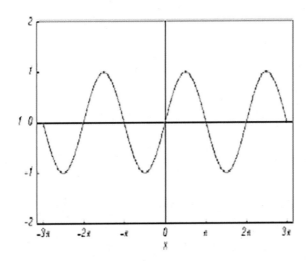

FIG. 2

An example of a sin function.

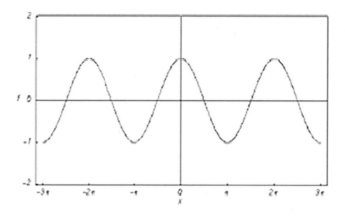

FIG. 3

An example of a cosine function.

With visual observation only, it becomes clear that the function in Fig. 1 can be better approximated by the sin function in Fig. 2, because the period matches better. The cosine function (Fig. 3) in this case appears to be out of phase with the function depicted in Fig. 1.

The following rules apply:

$$a_0 = \frac{1}{2\pi} \int_{-\pi}^{\pi} f(x) dx \tag{3}$$

$$a_n = \frac{1}{\pi} \int_{-\pi}^{\pi} f(x) \cos\left(\frac{n\pi}{\pi} x\right) dx \tag{4}$$

$$b_n = \frac{1}{\pi} \int_{-\pi}^{\pi} f(x) \sin\left(\frac{n\pi}{\pi} x\right) dx \tag{5}$$

With $n = 1, 2\ldots$

Eqs. (3)–(5) are justified because to integrate a step function such as the $f(x)$ we see in Fig. 1, we have to break it into pieces. If $f(-x) = -f(x)$, we have an odd function, and we model with sine terms. If $f(-x) = f(x)$, we have an even function, and we model with cosine terms (Hernandez, 2020).

3 Examples with case studies from the energy-growth nexus

This section encompasses summarized and modified extracts from two energy-growth studies. Their most important elements are presented in a compact form for quick reference.

Case study 1: Asymmetries in the convergence of carbon dioxide emissions

Countries: 21 OECD countries (Austria, Australia, Belgium, Canada, Finland, France, Greece, Hungary, Italy, Japan, Korea, the Netherlands, New Zealand, Norway, Poland, Portugal, Spain, Sweden, Switzerland, the United Kingdom, and the United States).

Data span: 1950–2014.

Variables: CO_2 emissions (sourced from the Carbon dioxide information analysis center (http:/cdiac.ornl.gov).

Methodology: Quantile unit root analysis with Fourier function.

This study employs the methodology suggested by Enders and Lee (2012), and Bahmani-Oskooee et al. (2017) recommend the usage of Fourier approximation to capture the time-varying smooth process of a variable. The terms $a_k \sin\left(\frac{2\pi kt}{T}\right)$ and $\beta_k \cos\left(\frac{2\pi kt}{T}\right)$ can be used for the approximation of the breaks. The parameters a_k and β_k refer to the amplitude and displacement of the frequency component. Thus the term d(t) can be written as follows:

$$d(t) = c + at + a_k \sin\left(\frac{2\pi kt}{T}\right) + \beta_k \cos\left(\frac{2\pi kt}{T}\right) \tag{6}$$

The following notation applies in Eq. (6):

c is the constant.
k is the frequency of the Fourier function.
t is the time trend.
T is the sample size by sequence.
$\pi = 3.1416$.

With that in mind, a model that could be written as $y_t = d(t) + \varepsilon_t$, namely, a deterministic trend, a stationary error term, and zero mean, are now formulated as follows:

$$y_t = c + at + a_k \sin\left(\frac{2\pi kt}{T}\right) + \beta_k \cos\left(\frac{2\pi kt}{T}\right) + \varepsilon_t \tag{7}$$

In continuation to this step, Bahmani-Oskooee et al. (2017) produce an adjusted series y_t^{ad} that excludes the deterministic trend. The adjusted series is poured into the ADF regression model, which is rewritten in its quantile counterpart as follows in Eq. 8:

$$Q_{y_t}^{ad}\left(\tau \mid y_{t-1}^{ad}, \cdots, y_{t-p}^{ad}\right) = Q_e(\tau) + \theta(\tau)y_{t-1}^{ad} + \sum_{i=1}^{p} \varphi_i \Delta y_{t-i}^{ad} \tag{8}$$

After the approximation of smooth breaks with a Fourier function, they find that $\theta(\tau)$ has an increasing trend in Austria, Belgium, Finland, France, Italy, and Norway without rebounds. Thus results provide more neat information with Fourier analysis because only 6 out of the 21 countries show explosive

Continued

performance compared with the results of 16 out of 21 that was supported without the Fourier approximation.

Regarding the second panel of Table 1, the statistic $t_n(\tau_i)$ reveals that stationarity is supported for more countries in lower quantiles.

For more information and details on the implementation of the Fourier approximation in this framework, the interested reader is advised to refer directly to the original study (Cai et al., 2018).

Table 1 Results for Fourier approximated quantile unit roots in Cai et al., (2018).

Quantiles	0.1	0.25	0.5	0.75	0.9
Panel A. Results for persistence					
Australia	0.918*	0.934*	0.961	0.948	0.971
Austria	0.835*	0.924	0.940	0.986	1.043
Belgium	0.665**	0.822*	0.939	0.970	0.937
Canada	0.914*	0.895**	0.838***	0.859**	0.936
Finland	0.845**	0.902**	0.930	1.036	1.083
France	0.905	0.864**	0.943	1.028	1.079
Greece	0.935**	0.963	0.998	1.005	0.989
Hungary	0.900*	0.911*	0.945	0.992	0.998
Italy	0.987	0.959	0.960	0.956	0.972
Japan	0.938	0.955	0.971	0.989	1.050
Korea	0.949	1.000	1.023	1.049	1.090
Netherlands	0.903**	0.903***	0.941*	1.000	1.069
New Zealand	0.974	0.958	0.982	1.007	1.021
Norway	0.693	0.934	0.992	1.060	1.168
Poland	0.770***	0.900***	0.991	0.993	1.012
Portugal	0.946	0.949	0.983	1.021	1.042
Spain	0.905**	0.965	0.982	1.008	0.989
Sweden	0.884	0.841*	0.927	1.014	1.013
Switzerland	0.813**	0.818**	0.778***	0.828**	0.831*
UK	0.936	1.035	0.986	1.056	1.096
USA	0.807***	0.844**	0.879**	0.891**	1.028
Panel B. Results for unit roots					
Australia	−3.223	−1.804	−1.140	−1.682	−1.674
Austria	−2.806	−1.487	−1.309	−0.301	1.056
Belgium	−3.464	−1.401	−0.672	−0.318	−0.983
Canada	−5.718*	−2.459*	−2.916**	−2.531*	−2.808
Finland	−2.549**	−2.061*	−1.648	0.656	1.522

Table 1 Results for Fourier approximated quantile unit roots in Cai et al., (2018)—cont'd

Quantiles	0.1	0.25	0.5	0.75	0.9
France	−1.467	−1.806	−1.051	0.550	4.306
Greece	−4.951**	−2.086	−0.122	0.313	−1.506
Hungary	−2.691	−2.268	−1.458	−0.198	−0.135
Italy	−0.599	−1.786	−1.898	−1.618	−0.236
Japan	−2.856	−1.874	−1.124	−0.340	1.391
Korea	−1.223*	0.000	2.207	3.102	7.497
Netherlands	−0.768	−3.559***	−1.824	0.000	0.524
New Zealand	−0.421	−0.694	−0.427	0.125	0.182
Norway	−2.549**	−0.606	−0.229	1.046	0.848
Poland	−1.232	−1.499	−0.303	−0.323	0.417
Portugal	−4.393*	−2.783**	−0.894	0.804	2.471
Spain	−3.304**	−1.207	−0.710	0.434	−0.326
Sweden	−3.528	−2.528*	−1.139	0.251	0.334
Switzerland	−10.312**	−2.445*	−3.317***	−1.878	−1.178
UK	−0.546	0.417	−0.234	0.592	0.150
USA	−7.969**	−2.351	−1.975	−2.333	0.654

Notes: Three, two, and one asterisks stand for significance at 1%, 5%, and 10% accordingly. Modified from Adapted from Cai, Y., Chang, T., Inglesi-Lotz, R., 2018. Asymmetric persistence in convergence for carbon dioxide emissions based on quantile unit root test with Fourier function. Energy 161, 470–481.

Case study 2: A modern application financial development and energy consumption with Fourier Toda-Yamamoto estimation

Countries: 21 emerging countries (Brazil, Chile, China, Colombia, Egypt, Greece, India, Indonesia, South Korea, Malaysia, Mexico, Pakistan, Peru, Philippines, South Africa, Thailand, Turkey, United Arab Emirates, Czech Republic, Hungary, and Poland) as classified by Morgan Stanley Capital International (MSCI).

Data span: 1971–2014.

Variables: Financial development, energy consumption, and economic growth.

Methodology: Fourier-Toda-Yamamoto approximation.

The investigation of the relationship between financial development and economic growth started relatively early after the first world war with works of Shumpeter (1932), Goldsmith (1969), McKinnon (1973), and Shaw (1973). They have supported in their work the fundamental role played by banks in encouraging innovation and the funding of productive projects. Financial markets reduce risk because they contribute to portfolio diversification

Continued

(Levine, 1991), they improve financial intermediation, and they provide incentives for corporate control (Rousseau and Wachtel, 2000; Demirguc-Kunt and Levine, 1996).

Financial development refers to the size of capital flows in financial institutions, capital markets, and foreign direct investment (FDI). Financial development also influences environmental quality through the aforementioned mechanisms, but we should not forget that environmental quality also affects tourism and is affected by tourism. When financial intermediation is efficient, not only tourism businesses can borrow at cheaper rates, but also consumers can borrow to finance some of their costly consumption items such as holiday packages. It has been stated in Levine (2002) that banks play their role in improving economic growth at initial levels of economic development and particularly under weak institutional environments on the condition that this does not lead to domestic capital leakages and the subsequent fragilities (Ahmed, 2013) that the weak institutional environment can lend to the system. The latter occurs because banks offer services such as project evaluation, savings mobilization through various schemes of terms and interest rates, risk diversification and sharing, and transaction intermediation. These services help create the environment of safety necessary for technological progress and economic development to flourish. Financial development promotes economic growth, that is, capital accumulation and total factor productivity (TFP). Financial liberalization results in the improvement of the monetary transmission mechanism, and this encourages savings and investment and then increases economic growth (Beakert et al., 2005).

Let y_t being the energy consumption, x_t the financial development, and z_t the economic growth. However, when structural breaks are not accounted for, inferences may be misleading. Breaks may exist both in y_s and x_s, or they may impact on each other at various lags. Thus, to overcome the limitations inherent under the VAR framework (Enders and Jones, 2016), we employ the new strategy suggested in Durusu-Ciftci et al., (2020) who also extend the standard Granger causality model with a Fourier approximation. The Toda-Yamamoto procedure suggested therein estimates a VAR $(p + d)$ model with level data and d being the maximum integration order of variables. More specifically, under this framework, the assumption that the intercept term is constant is relaxed and the VAR $(p + d)$ model is defined in Eq. (9):

$$y_t = a(t) + \beta_1 y_{t-1} + \cdots + \beta_{p+d} y_{t-(p+d)} + \varepsilon_t \tag{9}$$

Apparently the intercept is time variant and signifies the structural shifts in y_t. The gradual shifts that are not known to us in none of their identification characteristics (number, date, and form) are captured now through the Fourier approximation in Eq. (10):

$$a(t) \equiv a_0 + \sum_{k=1}^{n} a_{1k} \sin\left(\frac{2\pi kt}{T}\right) + \sum_{k=1}^{n} a_{2k} \cos\left(\frac{2\pi kt}{T}\right) \tag{10}$$

n denotes the number of frequencies, and α_{1k} and α_{2k} represent the amplitude and displacement of the frequency. After substitution of (10) into (9), we get the following relationship as of Eq. (11):

$$y_t = a_0 + \sum_{k=1}^{n} a_{1k} \sin\left(\frac{2\pi kt}{T}\right) + \sum_{k=1}^{n} a_{2k} \cos\left(\frac{2\pi kt}{T}\right) + \beta_1 y_{t-1} + \cdots$$
$$+ \beta_{p+d} y_{t-(p+d)} + \varepsilon_t \tag{11}$$

Overall, given the three variables employed in our study, $y=$GDPC, $x=$Tourism Development Index, $z=$Financial Development Index, we can rewrite relationship (11) in its constituent parts in Eqs. (12)–(14):

$$y_t = \alpha_{1,0} + \sum_{k-1}^{n} \alpha_{1,1k} \sin\left(\frac{2\pi kt}{T}\right) + \sum_{k-1}^{n} \alpha_{1,2k} \cos\left(\frac{2\pi kt}{T}\right)$$
$$+ \sum_{j=1}^{p+d} \beta_{1,1j} y_{t-j} + \sum_{j=1}^{p+d} \beta_{1,2j} x_{t-j} + \sum_{j=1}^{p+d} \beta_{1,3j} z_{t-j} + \varepsilon_{1,t} \tag{12}$$

$$x_t = \alpha_{2,0} + \sum_{k-1}^{n} \alpha_{2,1k} \sin\left(\frac{2\pi kt}{T}\right) + \sum_{k-1}^{n} \alpha_{2,2k} \cos\left(\frac{2\pi kt}{T}\right)$$
$$+ \sum_{j=1}^{p+d} \beta_{2,1j} x_{t-j} + \sum_{j=1}^{p+d} \beta_{2,2j} y_{t-j} + \sum_{j=1}^{p+d} \beta_{2,3j} z_{t-j} + \varepsilon_{2,t} \tag{13}$$

$$z_t = \alpha_{3,0} + \sum_{k-1}^{n} \alpha_{3,1k} \sin\left(\frac{2\pi kt}{T}\right) + \sum_{k-1}^{n} \alpha_{3,2k} \cos\left(\frac{2\pi kt}{T}\right)$$
$$+ \sum_{j=1}^{p+d} \beta_{3,1j} z_{t-j} + \sum_{j=1}^{p+d} \beta_{3,2j} y_{t-j} + \sum_{j=1}^{p+d} \beta_{3,3j} x_{t-j} + \varepsilon_{3,t} \tag{14}$$

Under the Toda-Yamamoto specification, the null hypothesis of Granger noncausality is based on zero restrictions on the first p parameters, and respective Wald statistic has an asymptotic $\chi 2$ distribution with p degrees of freedom. If the Wald statistic depends on k frequency, the solution is suggested in Becker et al., (2004) with the corresponding bootstrap distribution of Wald statistic (Hatemi-J, 2002; Balcilar et al., 2010). We set the number of Fourier frequency to n^{max} and the number of lags to p^{max} and select the optimal of n and p that yields the smallest information criterion value (Akaike or Schawarz). Moreover, to test whether the trigonometric terms are significant, we carry out the F-test for the restriction $a_{1k}=a_{2k}=0$ $(k=1,...n)$ with the alternative hypothesis of nonlinear terms with a given frequency. If the null hypothesis cannot be rejected, then the model in Eq. (11) reduces to the VAR model in the Toda-Yamamoto framework.

Table 2 is only an extract of the results. The table consists of two more panels (Panel B and C that are not reported here for space considerations). Panel B presents causality results between financial development and economic growth, and Panel C presents causality results between economic growth and energy consumption. The equation system has been estimated using one to four lags with a choice among them based on the minimization

Continued

Table 2 Extract from original Fourier-Toda-Yamamoto result table in Durusu-Ciftci et al., (2020).

	H0: Financial development does not cause energy consumption				H0: Energy consumption does not cause financial development			
		Bootstrap critical values				Bootstrap critical values		
	Wald	10%	5%	1%	Wald	10%	5%	1%
Brazil	0.749	9.214	13.506	24.927	0.350	5.790	8.452	15.320
Chile	6.530	5.591	8.059	15.046	0.208	5.775	8.373	14.149
China	2.035	5.876	8.230	15.030	0.835	4.623	6.680	12.834
Colombia	1.718	11.018	16.023	35.522	0.016	11.233	15.804	27.852
Egypt	6.216	8.999	13.079	22.864	0.946	4.637	6.638	11.955
Greece	4.279	5.209	7.511	13.445	1.963	4.982	7.257	13.060
India	15.757	7.629	10.679	18.688	5.066	6.706	9.581	17.070
Indonesia	2.132	7.239	10.373	19.643	0.245	4.846	6.803	12.156
South Korea	2.106	4.747	6.907	12.609	8.732	4.481	6.384	11.246
Malaysia	0.460	9.341	13.459	22.857	0.004	8.277	11.980	21.238
Mexico	1.822	8.715	12.187	20.717	0.086	5.772	8.408	16.045
Pakistan	12.253	9.553	13.718	24.673	1.966	4.502	6.393	11.134
Peru	4.010	11.067	15.139	26.548	0.239	10.707	14.899	25.432
Philippines	6.608	8.706	12.281	22.289	0.097	9.007	13.021	23.014
South Africa	0.066	5.355	7.692	13.685	10.424	7.847	11.041	19.399
Thailand	0.573	6.577	9.486	17.924	0.285	7.469	10.931	19.636
Turkey	0.346	6.503	9.459	17.357	0.876	17.310	22.651	36.328
United Arab Emirates	0.644	5.400	7.778	13.578	0.159	6.767	9.821	17.666

Modified from: Durusu-Ciftci, D., Soytas, U., Nazlioglu, S., 2020. Financial development and energy consumption in emerging markets: smooth structural shifts and causal linkages. Energy Econ. 87, 104729.Modified from: Durusu-Ciftci, D., Soytas, U., Nazlioglu, S., 2020. Financial development and energy consumption in emerging markets: smooth structural shifts and causal linkages. Energy Econ. 87, 104729.

of the Schwarz-Bayesian Criterion. For additional details of the estimation strategies in this paper, the interested reader is advised to refer to Durusu-Ciftci et al. (2020)

The empirical findings of this study have shown that it is important taking into account structural shifts for the causal linkages between financial development and energy consumption. The causality analysis without structural breaks supported causality between financial development and energy consumption only in 4 out of 21 countries, the analysis with breaks confirmed that in half cases. We provide an extract from the published result table, only to enable a visual representation of result setup.

4 Conclusion

The Fourier analysis has been introduced recently in the energy-growth nexus field, because the field is seeking ways to understand the long-run and short-run relationships in a more thorough way, particularly when structural breaks are present. The Fourier analysis, although fruitful in signal processing, is regarding the relationship between the energy-growth series and their covariates as a bunch of sine and cosine waves with various frequencies and phases. Therefore Fourier analysis allows researchers identify the frequencies of the relationship together with their magnitude and phase. Due to their smooth functions, these approximations are ideal in cases of structural changes. This short chapter is a convenient summary that serves as a first aid tool to the new energy-growth researchers who may become overwhelmed by the multitude of approaches and manipulations present to depict the fundamental energy-growth relationship. Particularly, the student or new researcher studies the existent literature to make comparisons. Most of the times, researchers are experts in certain methodologies and are not aware of all of them. Thus, this chapter will be quite beneficial for somebody who needs to get a quick grasp of the method and facilitate his own study.

References

Ahmed, A.D., 2013. Effects of financial liberalization on financial market development and economic performance of the SSA region: an empirical assessment. Econ. Model. 30, 261–273.

Bahmani-Oskooee, M., Chang, T., Elmi, Z., Ranjbar, O., 2017. Re-testing Prebischesinger hypothesis: new evidence using Fourier quantile unit root test. Appl. Econ. 50 (4), 1–14.

Balcilar, M., Ozdemir, Z.A., Arslanturk, Y., 2010. Economic growth and energy consumption causal nexus viewed through a bootstrap rolling window. Energy Econ. 32, 1398–1410.

Beakert, G., Harvey, C.R., Lundblad, C., 2005. Does financial liberalization spur growth? J. Financ. Econ. 77, 3–55.

Becker, R., Enders, W., Hurn, S., 2004. A general test for time dependence in parameters. J. Appl. Econ. 19, 899–906.

Cai, Y., Chang, T., Inglesi-Lotz, R., 2018. Asymmetric persistence in convergence for carbon dioxide emissions based on quantile unit root test with Fourier function. Energy 161, 470–481.

Demirguc-Kunt, A., Levine, R., 1996. Stock markets, corporate finance and economic growth: an overview. World Bank Econ. Rev. 10, 223–239.

Durusu-Ciftci, D., Soytas, U., Nazlioglu, S., 2020. Financial development and energy consumption in emerging markets: smooth structural shifts and causal linkages. Energy Econ 87, 104729.

Enders, W., Jones, P., 2016. Grain prices, oil prices, and multiple smooth breaks in a VAR. Stud. Nonlinear Dyn. Econ. 20, 399–419.

Enders, W., Lee, J., 2012. A unit root test using a Fourier series to approximate smooth breaks. Oxf. Bull. Econ. Stat. 74 (4), 574–599.

Goldsmith, R., 1969. Financial Structure and Development. Yale University Press, New York.

Hatemi-J, A., 2002. Export performance and economic growth nexus in Japan: a bootstrap approach. Jpn. World Econ. 14, 25–33.

Hernandez, S.R., 2020. Fourier Series of Videos. Available from: https://www.youtube.com/channel/UCHsrpPzUxC2vqVQgCTx40rw. (Accessed 10 May 2020).

Levine, R., 1991. Stock markets, growth, and the tax policy. J. Financ. 46, 1445–1465.

Levine, R., 2002. Bank-based or market-based financial systems: which is better? In: Working paper #9138. 1050 Massachusetts Avenue, Cambridge, MA 02138, USA. National Bureau of Economic Research.

McKinnon, R., 1973. Money and Capital in Economic Development. Brookings Institution, Washington, DC.

Morin, D., 2009. Chapter 2: Fourier Analysis. Available from: https://scholar.harvard.edu/files/david-morin/files/waves_fourier.pdf. (Accessed 10 May 2020).

Rousseau, P.L., Wachtel, P., 2000. Equity market and growth: cross-country evidence on timing and outcomes 1980–1995. J. Bank. Financ. 24, 1933–1957.

Shaw, E., 1973. Financial Deepening in Economic Development. Oxford University Press, New York.

Shumpeter, J., 1932. The Theory of Economic Development. Harvard University Press, Cambridge, MA, US.

Further reading

Sachs, J., Warner, A., 1995. Economic reform and the process of global economic integration. Brook. Pap. Econ. Act. 26 (25th Anniversary Issue), 1–118.

Ways of treatment of cross-sectional dependence in the energy-growth nexus and the X-variable growth nexus

1 Introduction

The notion of cross-sectional dependence was founded initially as a spatial approach concept with a distance metric, which was later replaced with economic distance in applications of regional economics (Sarafidis and Wansbeek, 2010) or policy distance (Conley and Topa, 2002). As panel data empirical applications increased, the error cross-sectional dependence became the new panel data worry. This approach relies on the error term containing a total of unobserved factors that influence each country, economic sector, or other object of analysis, separately. If a model is correctly specified with a correctly specified cross-sectional dependence across countries, the error is idiosyncratic and uncorrelated across countries. Estimating an energy-growth nexus model without taking into account the cross sectional dependence would entail that the produced estimators are inconsistent, inefficient, and biased. Philips and Sul (2003) describe the most striking effect of cross-sectional dependence in that the pooled ordinary least squares (OLS) approach is of little gain in precision terms compared with the single equation approach with crossed-sectional dependence existent but ignored.

1.1 The spatial approach

In the spatial approach, specific moving average, autoregression, and error components' processes have been set up and adapted for their spatial nature, but we are not presenting them at this point, due to space considerations. The interested reader should refer directly to Sarafidis and Wansbeek (2010).

1.2 The factor structure approach

The factor structure approach relies on the presence of an unobserved common error component, which is a liner combination of other parameters. This is written as follows in Eq. (1):

$$v_{it} = \lambda_i' \varphi_t + \varepsilon_{it} \tag{1}$$

161

A Guide to Econometric Methods for the Energy-Growth Nexus. https://doi.org/10.1016/B978-0-12-819039-5.00008-2

The following notation applies in the previous equation:

φ_t is a vector of unobserved factors.
λ_i is a vector of factor loadings.
ε_{it} is idiosyncratic with $E(\varepsilon_{it})=0$ and $E(\varepsilon_{it}\varepsilon_{js})=\sigma_e^2$ for $t=s$ and $i=j$ and $E(\varepsilon_{it}\varepsilon_{js})=0$ if otherwise.

Depending on the size of the panel and the time structure, namely, the number of countries sampled in the energy-growth (or X-variable-growth nexus) relationship each time, and the dataspan, which happens to be short in these models, typically 10–15 years, different model specifications arise. Therefore, conversely to time series, the asymptotic statistical theory for panel data initially had been derived for fixed T and N going to infinity (Smith and Fuertes, 2016).

Particularly, when new and more sophisticated variables are needed to be included in the energy-growth relationship, such as financial or institutional, these magnitudes provide values only for very short data spans, since statistical agencies have started relatively recently the collection and upkeep of those data. Notwithstanding the panel and time structure, model setup will foremost depend on the type and strength of correlation between the lambda and phi with x. The energy-growth nexus studies do not present or discuss this background information, and the cross-sectional dependence works as a black box. Statistical tests confirm or do not confirm the existence of it. Then, appropriate adaptations are made in empirical modeling, as well as vague conjectures about the practical origin of the phenomenon, which consumes itself in attributing the dependence to convenience suggestions, which are not corroborated though. Various tests support the cross-sectional dependence and that becomes the reason for using special unit root tests and special cointegration or causality tests that can prevent spurious regressions from occurring, but the researcher does not spend any effort discovering or showing the exact type of cross-sectional dependence, which would be interesting to know from a policy making perspective, because it gives an idea of spillover for many variables of interest. Noteworthy is that the seemingly unrelated regression (SUR) by Zellner is a good example of error cross-sectional dependence, where there is no need to impose a factor structure in the error term, because regressors are assumed as exogenous in the case of a misspecified model and N and T are infinite. This chapter will not expand on SUR structures, because there is a separate chapter in this book that does.

The rest of this chapter is structured as follows: After this brief introduction, Section 2 follows, which discusses the definition of the cross-sectional dependence and the occurrence of the cross-sectional dependence phenomenon. Section 3 discussed the ways through which we can identify the problem through the employment of various tests; Section 3 presents four empirical case studies, which have dealt with the detection of the problem and the ways it has been confronted with unit root test, cointegration, and causality procedures that were resilient to the problem of cross-sectional dependence, because they have been designed to cope with it. Last, Section 5 is a conclusion.

2 The cross sectional dependence: Definition, occurrence, and reason

Why should appear cross-sectional dependence in energy consumption in EU, G7, or other various geographic or political and institutional entities that are examined together? The answer lies in the globalization era that characterizes the world today both in economic and social aspects, and the environmental ones. There are groups of economies that form coalitions such as the European countries that have chosen to participate to the European Economic Union (EU). This coalition is mainly an economic one, but gradually has become social and political. Other countries belong to other unions or organizations partly because they have stipulated to certain conditions and promised to comply with rules and behaviors. These behaviors are either the reasons they qualified for participation or they have promised to develop them with certain deadlines. The endorsement of international environmental agreements also drives to unanimous behavior and attitudes toward the reduction of pollution, the increase of energy efficiency, and the replacement of conventional fossil energy sources with renewable energy sources. Of course, each economy structure is different; the level of its development is also different and thus can fulfill these goals with a different rhythm and speed or with different means. So the similarities and homogeneity across the countries that are sampled in the energy-growth nexus should neither be neglected nor taken for granted. Most of the times, as we will observe in Section 4, cross-sectional dependence is present. Therefore the measures and remedies suggested in Sections 3 and 4 should be employed by energy-growth nexus researchers and practitioners to gain robust results.

Basak and Das (2018) differentiate between strong (common factor), semistrong, and weak cross-sectional dependence (idiosyncratic). According to Sarafidis and Wansbeek (2010), however, there is no unique definition about the strength of the cross-sectional dependence, and this is also reflected in the succeeding text. Let us see in the succeeding text exactly what holds.

Suppose y_{it} is the dependent variable in the energy-growth nexus, which most of the times, it happens to be an income-related variable. As i defines the countries with $i = 1,2, \dots N$, because most of the times, the studies in the energy-growth nexus use groups of countries in their samples, either due to lack of data and lack of long time series that would enable the study of a relationship only for a single country, or due to the interest and wish to study global relationships that contribute to the formation of the relevant theory. As always, t represents time with $t = 1,2, \dots T$. Then, if we assume a model of the type shown in Eq. (2),

$$y_{it} = f(x_{i,t}, \theta) + \varepsilon_{it} \tag{2}$$

The error term is independently and normally distributed with $E(\varepsilon_t) = 0$ and $E(e_t \acute{e}_t) = \Omega$. Denoting as λ_i the eigenvalues of the omega matrix, then the aforementioned cases of strong, semistrong, and weal cross-sectional dependence are defined as follows:

Strong cross-sectional dependence: when $\lambda_N = O(N)$ or when either of the following conditions applies as in Eqs. (3), (4), and (5):

$$\max\left(\sum_{j=1}^{N}|\omega_{ij}|_i = O(N)\right) \tag{3}$$

$$\sqrt{\frac{1}{N}\sum\sum\omega_{ij}^2} = O(N) \tag{4}$$

$$\frac{1}{N}\sum\sum|\omega_{ij}| = O(N) \tag{5}$$

Note: lowercase omegas are elements of the maximum eigenvalue Ω.

Semistrong cross-sectional dependence: when $\lambda_N = O(h_N)$ with $\frac{h_N}{N} \to 0$ as $N \to \infty$ or when either of the following conditions applies as per Eqs. (6), (7), and (8):

$$\max\left(\sum_{j=1}^{N}|\omega_{ij}|_i = O(h_N)\right) \tag{6}$$

$$\sqrt{\frac{1}{N}\sum\sum\omega_{ij}^2} = O(h_N) \tag{7}$$

$$\frac{1}{N}\sum\sum|\omega_{ij}| = O(h_N) \tag{8}$$

Weak cross-sectional dependence: when $\lambda_N = O_\rho(1)$. Therefore this type of cross-sectional dependence could be identified as independence. Weak cross-sectional dependence is the case when either of the following conditions applies as per Eqs. (9), (10), and (11):

$$\limsup_{N}\ \max_{i}\left(\sum_{j=1}^{N}|\omega_{ij}| < \infty\right) \tag{9}$$

$$\limsup_{N}\sqrt{\frac{1}{N}\sum\sum\omega_{ij}^2} < \infty \tag{10}$$

$$\limsup_{N}\frac{1}{N}\sum\sum|\omega_{ij}| < \infty \tag{11}$$

Furthermore, as we will see in the following section, the separation of pure cross-sectional dependence from the case of both cross-sectional dependence and time dependence is possible and advisable to deal with the problem more effectively. Next, we will also provide in sufficient detail, the various tests for the diagnosis of the problem in its various forms and origins.

3 The cross-sectional dependence: The diagnosis

This part presents and briefly discusses seven tests and strategies used for the identification of cross-sectional dependence in energy-growth and tourism-growth case studies. More or less, there are standard steps followed in this process, but the cases provide useful insights and guidance to anybody writing a paper in this field currently. The tests and strategies analyzed here are the following: Friedman's test (Section 3.1), Pesaran CD test (Section 3.2), Frees' test (Section 3.3), Driscoll and Kraay (Section 3.4), Philips and Sul (Section 3.5), The Feasible Generalized Least Squares (Section 3.6), and the panel-corrected standard error (Section 3.7).

3.1 Friedman's (FR) test statistic (Friedman, 1937)

This test is based on Spearman's rank correlation coefficient. The average rank of $\{u_{i,1}, \ldots u_{i,T}\}$ is equal to $(T+1)/2$. The FR test is defined as per Eq. (12):

$$FR = \frac{2}{N(N-1)} \sum_{i=1}^{N-1} \sum_{j=i+1}^{N} \hat{r}_{ij} \tag{12}$$

The $\hat{r}_{ij}$ is the sample estimate of the rank correlation coefficient of the residuals.

Warning: There is high probability that this test misses occasions with cross-sectional dependence, because correlations of different sign cancel out each other.

3.2 Pesaran CD test (Pesaran, 2004, 2006)

This is an *LM* statistic defined as $LM = T \sum_{i=1}^{N-1} \sum_{j=i+1}^{N} \hat{p}_{ij}^2$ with $\hat{p}_{ij}$ being the pairwise correlation of the residuals and is shown as per Eq. (13):

$$\hat{p}_{ij} = \hat{p}_{ji} = \frac{\sum_{t=1}^{T} \hat{u}_{it} \hat{u}_{jt}}{\left(\sum_{t=1}^{T} \hat{u}_{it}^2\right)^{\frac{1}{2}} \left(\sum_{t=1}^{T} \hat{u}_{jt}^2\right)^{\frac{1}{2}}} \tag{13}$$

Variables under hats are estimates of the initial variables they represent. *LM* follows a χ^2 distribution with $N(N-1)/2$ degrees of freedom. This test is valid for a fixed N and T going to infinity. An alternative test with N being infinitely large and T sufficiently large was provided by Pesaran in 2004 (Pesaran, 2004) in Eq. (14):

$$CD = \sqrt{\frac{2T}{N(N-1)}} \left(\sum_{i=1}^{N-1} \sum_{j=i+1}^{N} \hat{p}_{ij}\right) \tag{14}$$

This test has a mean equal to zero and can be adapted to accommodate unbalanced panels too.

Warning: There is high probability that this test misses occasions with cross-sectional dependence, because correlations of different sign cancel out each other.

3.3 Frees' test (Frees, 1995, 2004)

This test is based on the sum of the squared rank correlation coefficients and is provided by the following formula in Eq. (15):

$$FRE = \frac{2}{N(N-1)} \sum_{i=1}^{N-1} \sum_{j=i+1}^{N} \hat{r}_{ij}^2 \tag{15}$$

This follows a joint distribution of two independent χ^2 variables with $T-1$ and $T(T-3)/2$ degrees of freedom, respectively. The H_0 is rejected if $FRE > (T-1)^{-1} + Q_q/N$.

3.4 Driscoll and Kraay (1998)

Standard errors from Driscoll and Kraay (1998) are better calibrated in the presence of cross-sectional dependence. Particularly, they have invented a covariance matrix estimator, which not only generated heteroskedasticity robust standard errors, but also is more; this robustness applies to spatial and temporal dependence. Basically, this is a nonparametric statistic. This test has been adapted for unbalanced panel data sets by Hoechle (2007). Driscoll and Kraay (1998) suggest *a Newey-West type correction to the sequence of cross-sectional averages of the moment conditions.* In essence the square roots of the diagonal elements of the robust covariance matrix are shown in the following Eq. (16):

$$V(\hat{\theta}) = (\acute{X}X)^{-1} \hat{S}_T (\acute{X}X)^{-1} \tag{16}$$

where the $\hat{S}_T$ is the aforementioned Newey and West (1987) correction, which can be written as per Eq. (17):

$$\hat{S}_T = \hat{\Omega}_0 + \sum_{j=1}^{m(T)} w(j,m) \left[\hat{\Omega}_j + \hat{\Omega}_j' \right] \tag{17}$$

The following notation applies for Eq. (17):

$m(T)$: is the lag length through which the residuals can be autocorrelated.
w: stands for Bartlett weights.
$\hat{\Omega}_j$: is a $(K+1) \times (K+1)$ matrix, which is defined in Eq. (18):

$$\Omega_j = \sum_{t=j+1}^{T} h_t(\hat{\theta}) h_{t-j}(\hat{\theta})' \text{ with } h_t(\hat{\theta}) = \sum_{i=1}^{N(t)} h_{it}(\hat{\theta}) \tag{18}$$

For additional material on the construction of this test, the interested reader might find useful to refer to Hoechle (2007).

3.5 Philips and Sul (2003)

This is a panel unit root test that is based on a notion of median unbiased estimation (Andrews, 2003) that uses the invariance property and the median function of panel pooled OLS estimator, which is written as $m(p) = m_{T,N}(p)$. The panel median estimator can be written as per Eq. (19):

$$\hat{p}_{med} = \begin{cases} 1 \ if & \hat{p}_{OLS} > m(1) \\ m^{-1}(\hat{p}_{OLS}) & m(-1) < \hat{p}_{OLS} \le m(1) \\ -1 & \hat{p}_{OLS} \le m(-1) \end{cases} \tag{19}$$

Instrumental variable approaches: Find instruments correlated with the regressor, but uncorrelated with the unobserved factors.

3.6 The feasible generalized least squares (FGLS) if $T > N$

When other bias and cross-sectional dependence coexist, one obtains the $\hat{p}_{med}$ and the error variance estimate $\hat{V}_{med}$ and then applies the panel GLS as per Eq. (20):

$$p_{pfGLS} = \frac{\sum_{t=1}^{T} \hat{y}_{t-1} \hat{V}_{med}^{-1} \hat{y}_t}{\sum_{t=1}^{T} \hat{y}_{t-1} \hat{V}_{med}^{-1} \hat{y}_{t-1}} \tag{20}$$

3.7 The panel corrected standard error (PCSE) if $N > T$

This is proposed by (Beck and Katz, 1995) as a sandwich type panel data estimator of the covariance matrix of the estimated parameters being robust to the so-called spherical errors. The spherical error assumption is defined as $\Omega = \sigma^2 I$, with I being the identity matrix. PCSEs are calculated with the square root of the diagonal elements of Eq. (21)

$$PCSE = (X^T X)^{-1} X^T \hat{\Omega} X (X^T X)^{-1} \tag{21}$$

With Ω being estimated as per $\hat{\Omega} = \hat{\Sigma} \times I_T$, the sign of multiplication represents the Kroenecker product (Bailey and Katz, 2020). This estimator reminds of the heteroskedasticity consistent estimator.

Having briefly considered basic diagnostics and strategies to identify and adapt to cross-sectional dependence, we will proceed now with a selection of indicative case studies from the energy-growth nexus and the tourism-growth nexus since we generally show interest for studies in the broader X-variable-growth nexus.

4 Energy-growth and X-variable-growth nexus case studies facing cross-sectional dependence

This part contains three case studies from the energy-growth nexus field and one from the tourism-growth nexus field. They are summarized and analyzed in their basic steps facing cross-sectional dependence. Also, they are accompanied by other basic information that make the studies serve as useful guidance and reference tools when one is writing his own paper.

Case study 1: The energy-growth nexus in energy importing and exporting countries

Country/ies: 29 net energy importers and 19 net energy exporter countries. The latter are Albania, Algeria, Australia, Bolivia, Canada, Colombia, Ecuador, Egypt, Gabon, Indonesia, Iran, Nigeria, Norway, Syria, Trinidad, the United Arab Emirates (UAE), Venezuela, Sudan, and South Africa. The former are Austria, Belgium, Bangladesh, Brazil, Chile, China, Czech Republic, Germany, Denmark, Spain, Finland, France, the United Kingdom, Hungary, India, Italy, Japan, Korea, Sri-Lanka, the Netherlands, New Zealand, Pakistan, the Philippines, Portugal, Sweden, Thailand, Turkey, the United States (US), and Vietnam.

Data span: 1970–2012.

Variables: Real GDP per capita, real energy consumption, trade openness (total value of imports and exports as percentage of GDP), gross fixed capital formation and/or net capital stock (with the perpetual inventory method), and real investment to GDP ratio, depending on the results the latter three generate, while aiming at robustness.

Unit root testing

(Maddala and Wu, 1999), (Breusch and Pagan, 1980), Lagrange multiplier (LM), Pesaran (2004) cross-sectional dependence test, and (Bai and Carrion-i-Silvestre, 2009) for both cross-sectional dependence and shocks.

Homogeneity versus heterogeneity

The study applies the Swamy statistic and the adjusted Swamy statistic to decide about heterogeneity. The test result supports homogeneity at 1% level of significance.

Cointegration

The study employs the Westerlund (2007) panel cointegration test (Table 1), which is applicable in the presence of cross-sectional dependence and heterogeneous data. The only disadvantage of this test is that it cannot host structural breaks. To confront that too, the study employs the Westerlund and Edgerton (2008) test (Table 2). Also the study employs Mean Group (MG), Pooled Mean Group (PMG), and Common Correlated Effects Mean Group (CCEMG) for the calculation of long-run elasticities but concludes that the results of PMG are the best to follow for policy making.

Causality:

The study employs a Pooled Mean Group (PMG) estimator with the following results:

(i) Energy importing countries: Growth hypothesis.
(ii) Energy exporting countries: Feedback hypothesis.

The speed of adjustment varies from 0.02 for Albania to 0.6 for New Zealand, which has the following explanation: For Albania, 2% of the

Table 1 Westerlund panel cointegration test.

	H_0: No cointegration				H_0: No cointegration		
	Energy net exporter				Energy net importer		
Statistic	Value	P-Value	Robust	Value	P-Value	Robust
Gt	−3.9829	0.0437	0.0002	−3.5993	0.0628	0.0001
Ga	−5.3751	0.1486	0.0007	−4.7701	0.0085	0.0000
Pt	−8.8647	0.0081	0.0015	−7.2994	0.0005	0.0001
Pa	−11.3036	0.0019	0.0001	−12.2150	0.0061	0.0000

From Jalil, A., 2014. Energy-growth conundrum in energy exporting countries: Evidence from heterogeneous panel methods robust to cross-sectional dependence, Energy Econ. 44, 314–324.

Table 2 Panel cointegration test (Westerlund and Edgerton, 2008) results with structural breaks and cross-sectional dependence.

Model	$Z_\varphi(N)$	P-Value	$Z_\tau(N)$	P-Value
No break	6.6951	0.007035	2.4248	0.0142
Mean shift	2.7804	0.002619	1.7850	0.0281
Regime shift	3.0880	0.001321	1.8417	0.0920

Note: The test follows Campbell and Perron (1991) for lag length selection.
From Jalil, A., 2014. Energy-growth conundrum in energy exporting countries: Evidence from heterogeneous panel methods robust to cross-sectional dependence, Energy Econ. 44, 314–324.

disequilibrium of the previous year shock is adjusted back to the long run equilibrium in the current year. This adjustment is 60% for New Zealand. However, another interpretation reveals that Albania is more sensitive to a depletion of its energy reservoirs or the sudden stop of energy import.

Modified from Jalil, A., 2014. Energy-growth conundrum in energy exporting countries: Evidence from heterogeneous panel methods robust to cross-sectional dependence, Energy Econ. 44, 314–324.

Case study 2: The clean energy-growth nexus in sub-Saharan African countries
Country/ies: 11 sub-Saharan African countries (Cameroon, Congo [RDC], Côte d'Ivoire, Ghana, Kenya, Nigeria, South Africa, Sudan, Togo, and Zambia).

Continued

Table 3 Pesaran CD results for the clean energy-growth nexus in sub-Saharan countries.

Specification	Real GDP		Clean energy consumption	
	Statistic result	*P*-Value	Statistic result	*P*-Value
AR(1)	4.501***	0.000	1.727*	0.084
AR(2)	2.929***	0.003	1.627	0.104
AR(3)	2.897***	0.004	1.652*	0.098

Notes: One asterisk represents significance at 10%, while three asterisks denote significance at 1%. Adapted from Hamit-Haggar, M., 2016. Clean energy-growth nexus in sub-Saharan Africa: Evidence from cross-sectionally dependent heterogeneous panel with structural breaks, Renew. Sustain. Energy Rev. 57, 1237–1244.

Data span: 1971–2007.

Variables: Clean energy consumption per capita (aggregate consumption of hydropower and nuclear, geothermal, wind and solar consumption, among others, in kilogram of oil equivalent, divided by the number of population). Real GDP per capita series is expressed in constant 2000 US dollars. The study employs the Pesaran CD test, whose results are shown in Table 3.

The null hypothesis is posed as of no cross-sectional dependence and is rejected at 1% and 10% for real GDP and clean energy, respectively. Since the cross-sectional dependence is confirmed, the study proceeds with unit root testing and cointegration procedures that show resilience in cross-sectional dependence.

Unit root modeling

The study employs the Carrion-i-Silvestre et al. test, which can accommodate both cross-sectional dependence and breaks. This test statistic is constructed by averaging the Kwiatkowski et al. test and is defined by the following formula in Eq. (22):

$$LM(\lambda) = N^{-1} \sum_{t=1}^{N} \hat{\omega}_i^{-2} T^{-2} \sum_{i=1}^{N} \hat{S}_{it}^2 \qquad (22)$$

with $\hat{S}_{it} = \sum_{j=1}^{t} \hat{\varepsilon}_{ij}$ being the partial sum process from OLS residuals. $\hat{\omega}_i^2$ is a consistent estimate of the long-run variance of the residuals.

Cointegration

The investigation of cointegration with cross-sectional dependence has been examined with Westerlund and Edgerton cointegration tests. The results are shown in Table 4.

Table 4 Westerlund and Edgerton cointegration tests.

| Specification | LMτ | | LMφ | |
	Test result	P-Value	Test result	P-Value
No break	−0.087	0.465	−1.039	0.149
Level break	−1.627*	0.052	−4.376***	0.000
Regime shift	0.157	0.574	−4.606***	0.000

Notes: One asterisk represents significance at 10%, while three asterisks denote significance at 1%. Adapted from Hamit-Haggar, M., 2016. Clean energy-growth nexus in sub-Saharan Africa: Evidence from cross-sectionally dependent heterogeneous panel with structural breaks, Renew. Sustain. Energy Rev. 57, 1237–1244.

Putting aside the situation with no breaks, which does not support cointegration, the other two cases with level breaks and regime shift are affirmative in their support about cointegration. Afterward, four methods have been employed for the estimation of the long-run estimates: (i) the ordinary least squares (OLS), (ii) the dynamic ordinary least squares (DOLS), (iii) the fully modified OLS (FMOLS), and (iv) the dynamic seemingly unrelated regression (DSUR). All of them were significant, while the largest coefficient was produced with the OLS.

Causality

The bootstrap corrected Engle and Granger causality test was used to find short-run and long-run causalities. These are as follows:

Long-run: growth hypothesis (clean energy drives economic growth).
Short-run growth hypothesis (clean energy also drives economic growth).

The potential of clean energy types in their contribution to economic growth becomes clear in this study. As a result, policy makers responsible for energy sub-Saharan Africa should take that into consideration for favoring and promoting clean energies.

Modified from Hamit-Haggar, M., 2016. Clean energy-growth nexus in sub-Saharan Africa: Evidence from cross-sectionally dependent heterogeneous panel with structural breaks, Renew. Sustain. Energy Rev. 57, 1237–1244.

Case study 3: Carbon emissions, income, energy and tourism in EU countries

Country/ies: 25 EU countries and candidate ones (Austria, Belgium, Bulgaria, Cyprus, Germany, Denmark, Spain, Estonia, France, Greece, Croatia, Ireland, Italy, Lithuania, Luxemburg, Latvia, Malta, the Netherlands, Poland, Portugal, Romania, Slovenia, Turkey, and the United Kingdom).

Continued

Data span: 1995–2011.

Variables: CO_2 emissions (metric tons), gross domestic product (in constant 2005 US$), energy consumption (kilogram of oil equivalent), and tourism (international tourist arrivals). All data have been sourced from World Development Indicators. All data have been transformed in natural logarithms.

This case study is motivated by the fact that tourism contributes to energy consumption and pollution in various direct and indirect ways. According to the World Tourism Organization (UNWTO), tourism is responsible for 4.6% of global warming and 5% of the produced emissions. The authors of the study selected Europe as the object of their study, because this continent attracts half of the world's international tourists.

Homogeneity vs heterogeneity

The authors employ the homogeneity test by Pesaran and Yamagata and the CD test of Pesaran. Afterward, they employ the Covariance Augmented Dickey Fuller (CADF) and the Cross-sectionally augmented IPS (CIPS) unit root tests, the LM bootstrap cointegration test, and the Emirmahmutoglu-Kose Granger causality test. Furthermore, for robustness, they employ multiple estimators such as the group-mean DOLS, the group-mean FMOLS, and the mean-group estimator. The homogeneity and cross-sectional dependence results are shown in Table 5, which has been adapted from Dogan and Aslan (2017).

The homogeneity test is based on Swamy approach, which estimates the delta and adjusted delta and tests the null hypothesis, which supports slope homogeneity ($H_0 : \beta_t = \beta$ against an alternative, which supports the slope heterogeneity ($H_1 : \beta_i \neq \beta_j$) for a nonzero fraction of pair-wise slopes with $i \neq j$. Thus, based on Table 5, the hypothesis of homogeneity cannot be supported. Also the data are characterized by cross-sectional dependence.

Table 5 Homogeneity test and cross-sectional dependence test results.

	Carbon emissions	Income	Energy consumption	Tourism
$\tilde{\Delta}$		16.34*	11.32*	12.45*
$\tilde{\Delta}_{adj}$		17.90*	12.40*	13.65*
CD dependence test	8.84* (0.00)	67.78* (0.00)	16.44* (0.000)	46.31* (0.00)

Notes: Numbers in parentheses in the CD dependence test are P-values. The asterisks denote significance at 1%.

Causality

Based on the causality results from Table 6, there is one-way causality from growth to tourism, from tourism to emissions, and from economic growth to energy consumption. Moreover, there is bidirectional causality between emissions and energy consumption and between real income and carbon emissions.

Information for policy making

Energy policies should be directed to energy efficiency and the increase of the share of renewables in the energy mix. The authors advise the direction of research and development for energy efficiency technologies and the propagation of sustainable tourism.

Table 6 Causality results based on Emirmahmutoglu-Kose test.

Hypothesis	Fisher-statistic	Conclusion
Income → carbon emissions	77.46 (0.00)	Two-way causality
Carbon emissions → income	149.79 (0.00)	
Energy → emissions	93.38 (0.00)	Two-way causality
Emissions → energy	81.47 (0.00)	
Tourism → emissions	64.51 (0.08)	One-way causality from tourism to emissions
Emissions → tourism	50.52 (0.45)	
Energy → income	55.33 (0.28)	One-way causality from income to energy
Income → energy	67.81 (0.04)	
Tourism → income	56.86 (0.23)	One-way causality from income to tourism
Income → tourism	108.31 (0.00)	
Tourism → energy	54.26 (0.31)	No causality between tourism and energy
Energy → tourism	50.92 (0.43)	

Note: One, two, and three asterisks represent significance at 10%, 5%, and 1% level of significance. From Dogan, E., Aslan, A., 2017. Exploring the relationship among CO2 emissions, real GDP, energy consumption and tourism in the EU and candidate countries: Evidence from panel models robust to heterogeneity and cross-sectional dependence, Renew. Sustain. Energy Rev. 77, 239–245.

Case study 4: The tourism-growth nexus in the countries around the Mediterranean Sea (one X-variable-growth nexus)

Country: European, Asian, and African Mediterranean countries (the European countries are Albania, Bosnia and Herzegovina, Croatia, France, Greece, Italy, Malta, Monaco, Montenegro, Slovenia, Spain, and Turkey. The Asian countries are Cyprus, Israel, Lebanon, and Syria. The African countries are Algeria, Egypt, Libya, Morocco and Tunisia).

   Data span: 1998–2011.

   Variables: Annual real GDP per capita growth, international tourism receipts in current US$, and international tourism expenditure in current US$. The data have been exported from the World Bank Development Indicators.

Unit root testing

The author has used the Levine, Lin, and Chu (LLC) and the Im, Pesaran, and Shin (IPS) tests. He has found first difference stationarity.

Cross sectional dependence

As a next step the author has used the Pesaran CD test for checking cross-sectional dependence. He has found strong cross sectional dependence, since the null hypothesis of nondependence was rejected at 1% level of significance.

Causality

The study employed the Dumitrescu and Hurlin (2012) test, which is resilient to both cross-sectional dependence and heterogeneity. This test is based on the individual Wald statistic of Granger noncausality averaged across the countries. The model setup is shown below in the Eq. (23):

$$y_{i,t} = a_i + \sum_{j=1}^{J} \lambda_i^j y_{i,t-j} + \sum_{j=1}^{J} \beta_i^j x_{i,t-j} + \varepsilon_{i,t} \tag{23}$$

The following notation applies for Eq. (23):

Y is the income variable.
X stands for tourism vector (receipts and expenditures).
ε is the disturbance term.

   Detailed causality results can be found in Table 7. Evidence of the feedback hypothesis has been generated between income and carbon emissions as well as emissions and energy consumption. In addition to these findings, there is one-way causality running from tourism to carbon emissions, from income to energy consumption, and from income to tourism. No evidence is there for a causal relationship between tourism and energy consumption.

Modified from Dogan, E., Aslan, A., 2017. Exploring the relationship among CO2 emissions, real GDP, energy consumption and tourism in the EU and candidate countries: Evidence from panel models robust to heterogeneity and cross-sectional dependence, Renew. Sustain. Energy Rev. 77, 239–245.

Table 7 Causality results for the tourism-growth nexus in the Mediterranean region.

Countries	H0: Tourism receipts do not cause growth		H0: Growth does not cause tourism receipts		H0: Tourism expenditure does not cause growth		H0: Growth does not cause tourism expenditure	
	Wald test	Decision	Wald test	Decision	Wald test	Decision	Wald test	Decision
Europe	13.843*	Reject	6.585*	Reject	13.640*	Reject	5.016*	Reject
Albania	16.489*	Reject	7.376**	Reject	1.880	Accept	2.554	Accept
Bosnia & Herzegovina	2.431	Accept	3.223	Accept	2.937	Accept	3.281	Accept
Croatia	7.667**	Reject	6.080**	Reject	20.408*	Reject	6.455**	Reject
France	6.094**	Reject	2.824	Accept	5.250***	Reject	5.020***	Reject
Greece	4.803***	Reject	11.213*	Reject	0.393	Accept	0.522	Accept
Italy	6.558**	Reject	0.662	Accept	4.931***	Reject	0.921	Accept
Malta	0.652	Accept	0.722	Accept	1.395	Accept	7.436**	Reject
Monaco	12.872*	Reject	1.471	Accept	2.214	Accept	4.958***	Reject
Montenegro	1.762	Accept	0.218	Accept	1.701	Accept	6.531**	Reject
Slovenia	1.455	Accept	5.533***	Reject	2.004	Accept	2.814	Accept
Spain	14.965*	Reject	2.867	Accept	16.479*	Reject	3.944	Accept
Turkey	2.659	Accept	0.323	Accept	7.454**	Reject	2.913	Accept
Asia	1.885***	Reject	−0.529	Accept	1.647***	Reject	2.443**	Reject
Cyprus	2.181	Accept	0.615	Accept	2.441	Accept	1.870	Accept
Israel	0.075	Accept	0.091	Accept	1.159	Accept	8.689*	Reject
Lebanon	1.399	Accept	0.295	Accept	4.272**	Reject	0.165	Accept
Syria	5.677**	Reject	1.498	Accept	0.785	Accept	0.185	Accept
Africa	−0.066	Accept	−0.226	Accept	0.443	Accept	−1.195	Accept
Algeria	1.332	Accept	1.939	Accept	2.195	Accept	0.081	Accept
Egypt	0.028	Accept	0.090	Accept	0.426	Accept	0.080	Accept
Libya	1.924	Accept	0.726	Accept	0.319	Accept	0.107	Accept
Morocco	2.284	Accept	0.093	Accept	1.331	Accept	0.427	Accept
Tunisia	0.168	Accept	1.237	Accept	0.021	Accept	0.029	Accept

Notes: One, two and three asterisks indicate significance at 1%, 5%, and 10% respectively.
From Tugcu, C.T., 2014. Tourism and economic growth nexus revisited: a panel causality analysis for the case of the Mediterranean region, Tour. Manag. 42, 207–212.

5 Conclusion

In the last decades the world has experienced an increasing economic, financial, social, and cultural integration due to globalization. This implies the existence of strong interdependence and interlinkages across countries, sectors, and economic entities, and this reflects on their statistical data. This can have various explanations, but less research has taken place on this aspect, compared with the microeconomic applications, where the object of study is the individual, whose behavior can be explained with various psychology and sociology theories, such as imitation, herd behavior, and neighborhood effects. Of course the unobservable common factors that typically enter the energy-growth nexus panel data are easier to discover compared with human behavior and social norms.

At the opposite end of cross-sectional dependence is the heterogeneity concern. Inasmuch as the cross-sectional dependence may be a problem in energy-growth nexus modeling so will be the heterogeneity across the sampled countries. Heterogeneous countries in their energy consumption or heterogeneous economic sector or other entities cannot be sampled together to build one and single model for informing policy making. This heterogeneity must be taken into account too, either by making allowance for it through special econometric structures or by separating countries based on their degree of homogeneity, which can lead to economic and energy policies that are designed based on groups characteristics, which are common across the group. This promises more effectiveness of the policies.

This chapter has provided a brief explanation of the concept of cross-sectional dependence, together with diagnostics and solutions with handlings shown in four difference case studies, three energy-growth nexus ones, and one on the tourism-growth nexus, simply to show the wide spectrum of applications that can be informed from the older energy-growth nexus.

This chapter can serve as a quick reference for students and junior researchers who need a handy and quick look up on concepts and methods regarding cross-sectional dependence.

References

Andrews, D.W.K., 2003. Tests for parameter instability and structural change with unknown change point: a corrigendum. Econometrica 71, 395–397.

Bai, J., Carrion-i-Silvestre, J.L., 2009. Structural changes, common stochastic trends, and unit roots in panel data. Rev. Econ. Stud. 76 (2), 471–501.

Bailey, D., Katz, J.N., 2020. Implementing Panel-Corrected Standard Errors in R: The pcse Package. Available from: https://cran.r-project.org/web/packages/pcse/vignettes/pcse.pdf. (Accessed 3 February 2020).

Basak, G.K., Das, S., 2018. Understanding Cross-Sectional Dependence in Panel Data. Cornell University. Available from: https://arxiv.org/pdf/1804.08326.pdf. (Accessed 2 February 2020).

Beck, N., Katz, J.N., 1995. What to do (and not to do) with times-series-cross-section data in comparative politics. Am. Polit. Sci. Rev. 89 (3), 634–647.

Breusch, T.S., Pagan, A.R., 1980. The lagrange multiplier test and its applications to model specification in econometrics. Rev. Econ. Stud. 47 (1), 239–253.

Campbell, J., Perron, P., 1991. Pitfalls and opportunities: what macroeconomists should know about unit roots. In: Blanchard, O.J., Fischer, S. (Eds.), NBER Macroeconomic Annual. MIT Press, Cambridge, MA, pp. 141–201.

Conley, T.G., Topa, G., 2002. Socio-economic distance and spatial patterns in unemployment. J. Appl. Econ. 17 (4), 303–327.

Driscoll, J.C., Kraay, A.C., 1998. Consistent covariance matrix estimation with spatially dependent panel data. Rev. Econ. Stat. 80, 549–560.

Dumitrescu, E.I., Hurlin, C., 2012. Testing for granger non-causality inheterogeneous panels. Econ. Model. 29 (4), 1450–1460.

Frees, E.W., 1995. Assessing cross-sectional correlation in panel data. J. Econ. 69, 393–414.

Frees, E.W., 2004. Longitudinal and Panel Data: Analysis and Applications in the Social Sciences. Cambridge University Press, Cambridge.

Friedman, M., 1937. The use of ranks to avoid the assumption of normality implicit in the analysis of variance. J. Am. Stat. Assoc. 32, 675–701.

Hoechle, D., 2007. Robust standard errors for panel regressions with cross-sectional dependence. Stata J., 1–31. Available from: http://fmwww.bc.edu/repec/bocode/x/xtscc_paper. (Accessed 3 February 2020).

Maddala, G.S., Wu, S., 1999. A comparative study of unit root tests with panel data and a new simple test. Oxford Bull. Econ. Stat. 61, 631–652.

Newey, W.K., West, K.D., 1987. A simple, positive semi-definite, heteroskedasticity and autocorrelation consistent covariance matrix. Econometrica 55, 703–708.

Pesaran, M.H., 2004. General diagnostic tests for cross section dependence in panels. In: University of Cambridge, Faculty of Economics, Cambridge Working Papers in Economics no.0435.

Pesaran, M.H., 2006. Estimation and inference in large heterogeneous panels with a multifactor error structure. Econometrics 74, 967–1012.

Philips, P.C.B., Sul, D., 2003. Dynamic panel estimation and homogeneity testing under cross section dependence. Econ. J. 6, 217–259.

Sarafidis, V., Wansbeek, T., 2010. Cross-Sectional Dependence in Panel Data Analysis. The University of Sydney. Available from: https://mpra.ub.uni-muenchen.de/20815/1/Cross_Sectional_Dependence_in_Panel_Data_Analysis.pdf. (Accessed 2 February 2020).

Smith, R.P., Fuertes, A.M., 2016. Panel time series. Working Paper. Birkbeck University of London. Available from http://www.bbk.ac.uk/ems/faculty/smith/ron-smith-downloads/RSpanel.pdf.

Westerlund, J., 2007. Testing for error correction in panel data. Oxf. Bull. Econ. Stat. 69, 709–748.

Westerlund, J., Edgerton, D.L., 2008. A simple test for cointegration in dependent panels with structural breaks. Oxf. Bull. Econ. Stat. 70, 665–704.

Further reading

Baltagi, B.H., Pesaran, M.H., 2007. Heterogeneity and cross section dependence in panel data models: theory and applications. J. Appl. Econ. 22, 229–232.

Conley, T.G., 1999. GMM estimation with cross sectional dependence. J. Econ. 92, 1–45.

Emirmahmutoglu, F., Kose, N., 2011. Testing for granger causality in heterogeneous mixed panels. Econ. Model. 28 (3), 870–876.

Parks, R., 1967. Efficient estimation of a system of regression equations when disturbances are both serially and contemporaneously correlated. J. Am. Stat. Assoc. 62 (318), 500–509.

Pesaran, M.H., Yamagata, T., 2008. Testing slope gomogeneity in large panels. J. Econ. 42 (1), 50–93.

Zellner, A., 1962. An efficient method of estimating seemingly unrelated regressions and tests for aggregation bias. J. Am. Stat. Assoc. 57, 348–368.

The low profile of simultaneous equation modeling in the energy-growth nexus

1 Introduction

One of the major problems in the energy-growth nexus field is that there is no mature and roundly tested theory underpinning it. This means that researchers, up to a large degree, behave through a trial and error process when it comes to the selection of variables, econometric methods, and functional forms. This has led to the generation of a vast empirical output of research, which despite its size and continuity since the very first paper in 1950s, has not managed to reach consensus.

There are two major approaches in the energy-growth model setup: One is the production function approach, and the other is the demand function approach. Also another literature branch is the environmental Kuznets curve approach. In the first an income-related variable (mostly GDP) is the dependent variable with various other variables being the independent variables. These are typical factors of production such as labor, capital, and the centerpiece energy, followed by many covariates, which vary from study to study. In the second, namely, the demand type model, brings forth energy consumption as a dependent variable, while the independent variables are GDP and energy prices and the variety of the rest of the variables is endless. Analogously, in the third, namely in a carbon emissions Kuznets curve type model, the emissions are placed as a dependent variable, while the independent ones are income, energy, and many other, still not finalized in nature and type.

Needless to say that the variables that should be enclosed in the energy-growth modeling are still at an experimental level with some, of course, well established such as labor, capital, and energy in the case of a production function approach or income and energy prices in the energy demand type model. However, researchers always try new variables based on the availability and the characteristics of the economy they are studying, in an attempt to better depict the relationship of interest.

Therefore, when researchers construct their energy-growth models, sometimes it happens that the so-called independent variables are not completely independent of the error term, because the independent variables themselves may be affected by other magnitudes. This entails that the ordinary least squares (OLS) estimation is not reliable to use, because it will lead to the generation of inconsistent estimates. Foremost, we cannot study in isolation a variable that is affected or affects a

179

A Guide to Econometric Methods for the Energy-Growth Nexus. https://doi.org/10.1016/B978-0-12-819039-5.00017-3

magnitude in more than one ways and through more than one model setups. In such circumstances the solution of the SEM approach is advisable.

This brings into the current discussion the situations of endogeneity and exogeneity in the variables for the energy-growth nexus. It is common knowledge that endogeneity is a situation that the variables are determined by the energy-growth nexus model itself, while the exogeneity situation means that the variables are affected from the outer world and factors outside the energy-growth nexus model. Exogeneity guarantees in variables that they are independent of the error term. To avoid the computational burden and the nonlinear solutions generated by methods used for the estimation of systems, such as the maximum likelihood estimation (MLE) method or the full information maximum likelihood (FIML) method, there is a preference for using single equation estimation methods such as the ordinary least squares method (OLS), the indirect method of least squares (ILS), and the two-stage least squares method (2SLS) or the three-stage least squares method (3SLS). The ILS and the 2SLS are briefly discussed here. The rest of the methods are not very often used, and they can be found in more advanced econometric textbooks by the interested reader.

Up to date the energy-growth nexus has very few studies to show in the SEM framework despite the reasonable ground it offers. The reasons for this deficit are not quite clear nor have been commented by energy-growth theorists or applied researchers.

The rest of this chapter is organized as follows: After this brief introduction that motivates the chapter, Section 2 proceeds with a short, reference-type description of the aforementioned single-type equation methods and simultaneously provides insights for the application of this method in the energy-growth and the X-variable growth nexus field. Section 3 provides a selection of simplified case studies in the energy-growth nexus, which have used the SEM framework. This chapter is thus structured so as to provide quick reference to researchers who need a first aid type reminder of the method or a first aid acquaintance with the method before going into further details. Section 4 offers the conclusion.

2 The brief econometrics of the simultaneous equations method

The energy-growth nexus field offers a justified ground for the usage of the SEM, because there is a simultaneous equation nature in the fundamental production function type and the energy demand function setups. Nevertheless, the framework remains at large in the shadow, and only few energy-growth researchers have applied it. In this section, I provide summaries of the single equation estimations, which have been used in energy-growth nexus literature so far, omitting the system estimations, which are cumbersome in estimation and interpretation. Thus this subsection contains summary reference for the indirect least squares (ILS), the instrumented equations, and the two stage least squares method. The reader needs to know that this section is brief, it is used as a reminder of how the method works, but the detail is saved for purely econometrics textbooks whereto the reader should refer to when one needs a "from scratch" learning tool.

2.1 The indirect least squares method

This method relies in the calculation of the reduced-form equations to be led to consistent estimation through the structural equations. The reduced forms do not necessarily make sense in economic theory terms, because they are a rearrangement of the initial structural equations, so that the independent variables appear as exogenous and allow the researcher to apply the OLS, which in this case, will generate unbiased and consistent estimates. Of course, when we employ estimations with reduced form equations, what we end up estimating may not be the variable we were interested in originally.

Example: Let $y = a_0 + a_1 x_1 + a_2 x_2 + u_1$ be an energy-growth nexus relationship through a production function approach. Also, suppose $y = b_0 + b_1 x_1 + b_2 x_3 + u_2$ is an energy-growth nexus relationship through a demand function approach, with y being an income variable (e.g., GDP) and x_1 the energy consumption variable. The rest of the magnitudes are other variables typically entering the energy-growth nexus relationship, either in its production function form or the demand function form and which are exogenous. If we solve the previous equations for y and x_1 (endogenous variables) with respect to x_2 and x_3 (the exogenous variables), the reduced form equations are shown in Eqs. (1), (2):

$$y = \frac{a_0 b_1 - b_0 a_1}{b_1 - a_1} + \frac{a_2 b_1}{b_1 - a_1} x_2 - \frac{b_2 a_1}{b_1 - a_1} x_3 + u_1 \tag{1}$$

$$x_1 = \frac{a_0 - b_0}{b_1 - a_1} + \frac{a_2}{b_1 - a_1} x_2 - \frac{b_2}{b_1 - a_1} x_3 + u_2 \tag{2}$$

These equations can now be solved with OLS, and this will give us consistent estimates. But Maddala (2008) warns that it may not always be possible to get solutions or we may get multiple solutions and researchers have to choose among those solutions with carefully balanced criteria.

So, one could summarize the ILS steps as follows: (i) first, one assumes the reduced form equations, which originate from the structural ones, so that the dependent variable in each of the equations is the only endogenous variable and depends on a series of exogenous or lagged endogenous variables, and (ii) the second step involves the usage of OLS estimation in each of the reduced form equations. This is a legitimate statistical procedure, because the independent variables are taken to be uncorrelated with the disturbance. The estimators in the ILS may be biased, but the biasedness decreases as the sample increases (Gujarati and Porter, 2009).

2.2 Single-equation methods or limited information methods

Conversely to full information methods that use information on the restrictions of all equations composing a system of them, the limited information method does not take into account the variables missing from other equations. Hence the term "limited" juxtaposed to the "full information" that will not be presented in this chapter due to its cumbersome calculations. Thus this subsection will only deal with instrument variable models and the two-stage least squares method.

2.2.1 Instrumentation

One broadly used single equation method for parameter estimation in a system of simultaneous equations is the instrumental variable method, which is about a variable that is correlated with the error term, but uncorrelated with the explanatory variable. Suppose we have the following energy-growth nexus simultaneous equation system in Eqs. (3), (4):

$$y_1 = a_1 y_2 + c_1 x_1 + c_2 x_2 + u_1 \tag{3}$$

$$y_2 = a_2 y_1 + c_3 x_3 + u_2 \tag{4}$$

ys are endogenous, and xs are exogenous in Eq. (3), which we take it to be a production function type energy-growth nexus model, and in Eq. (4), which we take it to be an energy demand type function model. It also applies that $cov(x_1, u_1) = 0$ and $(x_2, u_1) = 0$, but for y and u, it applies that $cov(y_2, u_1) \neq 0$. In this case, we use x_3 as instrumental variable of y_2, because $cov(x_3, u_1) = 0$. Thus we receive the following three normal equations (Eqs. 5–7), the first two being the same as in the ordinary least squares method; while with the addition of the third equation, we build the instrumental variable model in Eqs. (5)–(7).

$$\frac{1}{n} \sum x_1 (y_1 - a_1 y_2 - c_1 x_1 - c_2 x_2) = 0 \tag{5}$$

$$\frac{1}{n} \sum x_2 (y_1 - a_1 y_2 - c_1 x_1 - c_2 x_2) = 0 \tag{6}$$

$$\frac{1}{n} \sum x_3 (y_1 - a_1 y_2 - c_1 x_1 - c_2 x_2) = 0 \tag{7}$$

Since this is a guide and reference book, we will not expand further, because this material can be found in sufficient detail in standard econometrics textbooks, while the purpose of the current book is to serve as a first aid resource to brushing up necessary knowledge for the understanding of case studies and for the building of one's own new energy-growth models.

2.2.2 The two stage least squares method

This method gives the same results as the method of instrumentation. However, the variables that are used as instruments, in this case of 2SLS, are used as regressors. There are two stages in this process because of the following: first we estimate the reduced form equations by OLS and receive the predicted y_s, namely, the $\hat{y}_s$. Second, we replace the right hand side endogenous variables by the predicted y_s and estimate the equation by OLS again. Now, let us move to a much simpler energy-growth model (Eq. 8) in which the difference between the instrument variable model and the 2SLS model will be much more straightforward to show in Eq. (8):

$$y_1 = \beta y_2 + u_1 \tag{8}$$

With y_1, y_2 being endogenous variables, the reduced form equation for y_2 can be written as $y_2 = \hat{y}_2 + v_2$. The instrumental variable estimator for β is provided from the following Eq. (9):

$$\sum \hat{y}_2 (y_1 - \beta y_2) = 0 \tag{9}$$

The 2SLS estimator for β is provided from the following equation (Eq. 10):

$$\sum \hat{y}_2 (y_1 - \beta \hat{y}_2) = 0 \tag{10}$$

2.2.3 System methods or full information methods

While in the OLS approach, we aim at getting parameter estimators that minimize the sum of the squared error, in the Full Information maximum likelihood method (FIML), we aim at parameters that maximize the likelihood function for a case i, as shown in Eq. (11):

$$\log L_i = K_i - \frac{1}{2} \log \left| \sum i \right| - \frac{1}{2} (x_i - \mu_i)' \sum_i^{-1} (x_i - \mu_i) \tag{11}$$

The following notation applies for the previous equation:

x_i: is the raw data vector for case i.
μ_i: parameter mean vector.
Σ_i: parameter covariance matrix.

3 Case studies of energy-growth nexus studies that use the SEM framework

This section presents three case studies in the energy-growth nexus that have employed the SEM framework. They have been summarized in their basic foundations and results. It should be noted that since the theoretical underpinnings of the energy-growth nexus are not quite solid, the justification for using the SEM is neither clear nor insufficient. When the theory is still trying to find its foundations, econometric experimentation is more than welcome. Thus we cannot ignore the alleged interlinkages in the energy-growth nexus (production function orientation and energy demand function orientation), but we cannot fervently support them either. The same attitude is held in the three case studies too that follow next.

Case study 1: Environmental quality, energy, and growth in MENA countries

Country/ies: Fourteen MENA countries: Algeria, Bahrain, Egypt, Iran, Jordan, Kuwait, Lebanon, Morocco, Oman, Qatar, Saudi Arabia, Syria, Tunisia, and United Arab Emirates (UAE).

Data span: 1990–2011

Variables: CO_2 emissions (metric tons per capita), energy consumption (kg of oil equivalent per capita), economic growth (constant 2000 USD), trade openness (imports and exports as % of GDP) labor (% of the total population), capital (constant 2000 USD), financial development (total credit to private sector as a ratio of GDP), and urbanization (as % of urban population of the total population and population. The data have been sourced from the World Development Indicators of World Bank.

The author recognizes the endogeneity of the three key variables and recommends setting up a three-way interconnection among the variables of GDP, energy consumption, and environmental degradation. Energy has a direct contribution to the formation of a country's income. This contribution occurs through the constituents of income and aggregate demand such as consumption, investment, and net imports. Carbon emissions also contribute (positively and negatively) to the formation of national income. Last, capital and income are determinants of economic growth. Also the study reports various supporting literature about the endogeneity of the variables involved in these three models. This interconnection is widely understood in the energy-growth nexus, since it can take these configurations. More specifically, he has estimated the following set of three simultaneous equations (Eqs. 12–14):

$$
\begin{aligned}
\ln(\text{GDP})_{it} = {} & \beta_0 + \beta_{1i} \ln(\text{Energy consumption})_{it} \\
& + \beta_{2i} \ln(\text{Carbon emissions})_{it} + \beta_{3i} \ln(\text{Capital})_{it} \\
& + \beta_{4i} \ln(\text{Labor})_{it} + u_{it}
\end{aligned}
\tag{12}
$$

$$
\begin{aligned}
\ln(\text{Energy concumption})_{it} = {} & \gamma_0 + \gamma_{1i} \ln(\text{GDP})_{it} \\
& + \gamma_{2i} \ln(\text{Carbon emissions})_{it} \\
& + \gamma_{3i} \ln(\text{Capital})_{it} + \gamma_{4i} \ln(\text{Labor})_{it} \\
& + \gamma_{5i} \ln(\text{Foreign direct investment})_{it} \\
& + \gamma_{5i} \ln(\text{Population})_{it} + \varepsilon_{it}
\end{aligned}
\tag{13}
$$

$$
\begin{aligned}
\ln(\text{Carbon emissions})_{it} = {} & \delta_0 + \delta_{1i} \ln(\text{GDP})_{it} \\
& + \delta_{2i} \ln(\text{Energy consumption})_{it} \\
& + \delta_{3i} \ln(\text{Urbanization})_{it} \\
& + \delta_{4i} \ln(\text{Trade openness})_{it} + \theta_{it}
\end{aligned}
\tag{14}
$$

The coefficients of the equations reveal the returns to scale through the elasticities. The study employs the Generalized Method of Moments (GMM) with instruments to address endogeneity.

Table 1 Results with GDP as dependent variable.

	Intercept	Energy consumption	Carbon emissions	Capital	Labor
Algeria	−0.515***	0.412*	−0.036	1.135*	−0.067
Bahrain	−3.565*	0.831*	−0.078***	0.371*	−0.466*
Egypt	5.177*	−0.179***	−0.541*	0.092	0.117
Iran	−11.201*	0.441*	−0.199***	0.561*	−0.201***
Jordan	−4.697*	0.211	−0.356	0.357***	−0.257**
Kuwait	13.055*	0.305**	−0.780*	0.059	−0.119
Lebanon	5.383*	−0.414*	−0.288**	0.142	0.331*
Morocco	5.998*	0.167	−0.089	0.291**	0.513***
Oman	7.667	0.380*	−0.279*	0.289***	−0.629*
Qatar	−3.811*	0.554*	−0.265*	0.411*	−0.348*
Saudi Arabia	7.761*	0.341*	−0.220**	0.177	−0.102
Syria	2.633**	0.101	−0.245	−0.188***	−0.148
Tunisia	2.497*	0.199***	−0.188**	0.064	0.402*
United Arab Emirates	3.381*	0.724*	−222**	−0.063	−0.306*
Panel	4.217*	0.321*	−0.304**	0.269***	−0.410*
Hansen test[a]	0.19	0.321*	−0.304**	0.269	−0.410*
Durbin-Wu-Hausman test[b]	0.04				
Pagan-Hall test	0.01				

[a]*Hansen test deals with testing the validity of instruments. The null hypothesis assumes overidentification of restrictions (Result: The null of overidentification cannot be rejected. Also this entails that the null hypothesis about the appropriateness of instruments cannot be rejected).*
[b]*The Durbin-Wu-Hausman test deals with the endogeneity issue. The Pagn-Hall test was used for the investigation of heteroskedasticity.*
Notes: One, two, and three asterisks denote significance at 1%, 5%, and 10%, respectively.
Modified from Omri, A., 2013. CO_2 emissions, energy consumption and economic growth nexus in MENA countries: evidence from simultaneous equations models. Energy Econ. 40, 657–664.

Based on Table 1 the following holds for the GDP model (with GDP as dependent variable): Energy consumption has a positive (significant) effect only for the following countries: Algeria, Bahrain, Iran, Kuwait, Oman, Qatar, Saudi Arabia, Tunisia, and the United Arab Emirates. Surprisingly, this effect is negative for Egypt and Lebanon. The significant coefficients, depending on their sign, they reveal by how much the income increases or decreases, by 1% of

Continued

energy consumption. Policy result: since the growth hypothesis applies for most of the MENA countries, policy makers cannot recommend reduction of energy consumption unless energy efficiency is in place. With respect to carbon emissions, they have a negative contribution for the GDP of the following countries: All except for Algeria, Jordan, Morocco, and Syria. The coefficient of capital is significant only in seven countries. Last labor contributes negatively to GDP in most MENA countries, which may be a result of the low quality of labor force that has remained in those countries, where from the best work force immigrate in pursuit of a better future.

The study offers detailed results in separate tables for each of the equations. For reasons of space the rest of the two tables is not provided in this excite, but the interested reader is advised to refer directly to the original source. However, the results of the other two models are briefly reported in the succeeding text: GDP affects positively energy consumption for nine countries and negatively for two countries. Carbon emissions have a positive contribution to energy consumption almost in all countries except for two of them. Capital has a positive impact on energy consumption for five countries. Labor has a significant impact only in two countries. Financial development has a positive impact on the energy consumption of all countries. Population also has a positive impact for most of the countries.

Results for the Energy consumption equation show that GDP affects positively carbon emissions for 10 countries. Energy consumption has a positive impact on carbon emissions for all countries. The urbanization also positively affects carbon emissions in four countries. Trade openness has a positive impact only in the emissions of one country, Iran.

The same author has also applied the same method in another study that investigates the relationship among nuclear energy, renewable energy, and economic growth in 17 developed and developing countries (Omri et al., 2015). This study is not provided as a separate case study here because it follows almost the same steps as in Omri (2013).

Modified from Omri, A., 2013. CO_2 emissions, energy consumption and economic growth nexus in MENA countries: evidence from simultaneous equations models, Energy Econ. 40, 657–664.

Case study 2: Biomass energy consumption, economic growth, and carbon emissions in West Africa

Country/ies: Eleven West African countries, namely, Benin, Burkina Faso, Cote d'Ivoire, Gambia, Ghana, Mali, Niger, Nigeria, Senegal, Sierra Leone, and Togo. Note: The analysis is conducted both at single country level and at geographical making sense panels such as West Africa, North Africa, East Africa, South Africa, and Central Africa.

Data span: 1980–2010

Variables: GDP per capita (constant 2005 US$), biomass consumption per capita (in kilogram), carbon emissions per capita (in kilograms), capital as gross fixed capital formation as % of GDP, human capital development (primary school enrolment as % of gross enrolment), financial development (domestic credit to private sector as % of GDP), trade openness (export of goods and services plus import of goods and services as % of GDP), and urbanization (urban population as % of total population). All data have been sourced from World Development Indicators and Global material flow database.

With the usage of a three-stage least square (3SLS) and a system generalized method of moments (sys-GMM), which gave the same results as the former, the study estimates the following three simultaneous Eqs. (15)–(17):

$$
\begin{aligned}
\ln(\text{GDP per capita})_{it} = \beta_0 \\
+ \beta_{1i} \ln(\text{Bioemass energy consumption per capita})_{it} \\
+ \beta_{2i} \ln(\text{Carbon emissions per capita})_{it} \\
+ \beta_{3i} \ln(\text{Capital per capita})_{it} \\
+ \beta_{4i} \ln(\text{Human capital development})_{it} + u_{it}
\end{aligned}
$$

(15)

$$
\begin{aligned}
\ln \text{Biomass energy consumption (per capita)} \\
= \gamma_0 + \gamma_{1i} \ln(\text{GDP per capita})_{it} \\
+ \gamma_{2i} \ln(\text{Carbon emissions per capita})_{it} \\
+ \gamma_{3i} \ln(\text{Capital per capita})_{it} \\
+ \gamma_{4i} \ln(\text{Human capital development})_{it} \\
+ \gamma_{5i} \ln(\text{Financial development})_{it} \\
+ \gamma_{6i} \ln(\text{Urbanization rate})_{it} + e_{it}
\end{aligned}
$$

(16)

$$
\begin{aligned}
\ln(\text{Carbon emissions per capita})_{it} \\
= \delta_0 + \delta_{1i} \ln(\text{GDP per capita})_{it} \\
+ \delta_{2i} \ln(\text{Biomass energy consumption per capita})_{it} \\
+ \delta_{3i} \ln(\text{Urbanization rate})_{it} \\
+ \delta_{4i} \ln(\text{Trade openness})_{it} + \varepsilon_{it}
\end{aligned}
$$

(17)

Main results of Eq. (4)

The biomass energy consumption positively affects GDP per capita in 7 out of 11 countries (in the single country version of the model) and in seven West African countries (in the panel version). Also, there is a positive impact of

Continued

carbon emissions on GDP in seven countries. Capital was not significant, while human development was significant with a positive sign only in one country.

For the panel estimation version of the model, biomass consumption and carbon emissions were a significant impact on GDP. Capital was not significant, but human capital (through the proxy of human development index) was positively significant.

Main results of Eq. (5)

GDP was positively significant in its impact on biomass energy consumption. Emissions had a diverse effect on the biomass energy consumption. Capital and financial development had negligible effects on biomass consumption. Human capital had diverse effect only on two countries and urbanization an effect on one country.

For the panel estimation version of the model, GDP and emissions have a positive effect on biomass consumption. None of the rest of the variables had a significant impact.

Main results of Eq. (6)

GDP significantly affected carbon emissions in all countries except for two. Biomass energy consumption had a positive effect on carbon emissions in four countries and a negative in seven of the countries. Trade openness was significant only in one country. The same applies for urbanization. So these two variables do very little in explaining the carbon emissions relationship with GDP. These results are also corroborated in the panel version of the model for West Africa. For space considerations and to avoid reproducing the exact result tables here, I will generate a result synopsis for the previous three Models (Eqs. 15–17) (Table 2).

Policy recommendations

The authors separate the following categories of countries: in West Africa, there is strong association between economic growth and biomass energy consumption with the corresponding high carbon emissions. Emphasis must be laid on energy efficiency and clean energies that will further reduce carbon emissions from biomass.

In countries with evidence of the growth hypothesis, namely, that biomass energy consumption contributes to economic growth without generating high emissions, energy conservation measures can be applied without hindering economic growth.

Last in counties wherein biomass consumption and emissions cause an economic growth reduction impact, they should employ energy conservation measures.

Modified from Adewyyi, A.O., Awodumi, U.B., 2017. Biomass energy consumption, economic growth and carbon emissions: fresh evidence from West Africa using a simultaneous equation model. Energy 119, 453–471.

Table 2 Synopsis of results from the simultaneous Eqs. (15)–(17).

	Number of countries
Biomass energy consumption ↔ GDP	Eight countries: Gambia, Ghana, Nigeria, Senegal, Benin, Burkina Faso, Mali, Togo and Panel version
Biomass energy consumption → GDP	None
GDP → biomass energy consumption	Two countries: Cote d'Ivoire, Sierra Leone
Carbon emissions ↔ biomass energy consumption	Six countries: Gambia, Mali, Nigeria, Senegal, Burkina Faso, Togo and Panel version
Carbon emissions → biomass energy consumption	Three countries: Cote d'Ivoire, Benin, Sierra Leone
Biomass energy consumption → carbon emissions	One country: Niger
Carbon emissions ↔ GDP	Seven countries: Gambia, Nigeria, Cote d'Ivoire, Benin, Burkina Faso, Mali, Niger, Togo and Panel version
Carbon emissions → GDP	One country: Sierra Leone
GDP → carbon emissions	Two countries: Senegal, Niger

Modified from Adewyyi, A.O., Awodumi, U.B., 2017. Biomass energy consumption, economic growth and carbon emissions: fresh evidence from West Africa using a simultaneous equation model. Energy 119, 453–471.

Case study 3: Income, energy, and trade in middle- and high-income countries

Country/ies: Twenty-four middle- and high-income countries (12 high incomes: Australia, Canada, France, Germany, Italy, Japan, the Netherlands, Portugal, Spain, Sweden, Switzerland, the United Kingdom, and the United States. Twelve low income: Algeria, Argentina, Brazil, Bulgaria, Chile, China, Colombia, Malaysia, Mexico, Thailand, Turkey, and Venezuela.

Data: 1990–2011

Variables: Real GDP per capita (constant 2005 US$), energy consumption per capita (kg of oil equivalent per capita), capital (gross capital formation as percentage of GDP), trade openness (sum of imports and exports as percentage of GDP), financial development (domestic credit to private sector as share of GDP), urbanization (urban population as percentage of total population), and FDI (net inflows as share of GDP). Data were sourced from World

Continued

Development Indicator database and have been expressed in logarithms for the known reasons.

The authors use the GMM estimation for the following three Eqs. (18)–(20):

$$\ln(\text{GDP})_{it} = \beta_0 + \beta_{1i} \ln(\text{Energy consumption})_{it} + \beta_{2i} \ln(\text{Trade})_{it} + \beta_{3i} \ln(\text{Capital})_{it} + u_{it} \tag{18}$$

$$\ln(\text{Energy concumption})_{it} = \gamma_0 + \gamma_{1i} \ln(\text{GDP})_{it} + \gamma_{2i} \ln(\text{Trade})_{it} + \gamma_{3i} \ln(\text{Financial development})_{it} + \gamma_{4i} \ln(\text{Population})_{it} + \varepsilon_{it} \tag{19}$$

$$\ln(\text{Trade})_{it} = \delta_0 + \delta_{1i} \ln(\text{GDP})_{it} + \delta_{2i} \ln(\text{Energy consumption})_{it} + \delta_{3i} \ln(\text{Foreign direct invetsment})_{it} + e_{it} \tag{20}$$

To save space the results of the three equations (Eqs. 7–9) are summarized in Table 3. The symbol (+) signifies a positive relationship, while the symbol (−) signifies a negative relationship. Apparently, in Eq. (7), energy positively affects GDP in two countries and negatively in five countries. Thus, in two countries, there is support for the growth hypothesis, while in five of them, there is evidence for the conservation hypothesis. In Portugal, there is mutual positive relationship between energy and GDP, and this gives rise to the feedback hypothesis. While trade was significant in Eq. (7) for most of the countries, this is significant in only few countries in Eq. (8). For some countries, such as the United States and the panel version of the model, most variables appear significant. Moreover, at panel scale, there is support for the feedback hypothesis between energy and income and trade and income.

Policy recommendations based on results from the simultaneous Eqs. (7)–(9)

The sampled countries should work toward diversifying their economic production so that they avoid the risk of depletion of their natural resources and protect themselves against the volatility of oil and natural gas resources. The gain of technology transfer through trade can help middle-income countries to build relevant technologies. Energy conservation policies will reduce energy consumption and imports and exports. These countries must balance their cheap energy supplies with low carbon emissions.

Table 3 Detailed results of the simultaneous Eqs. (18)–(20).

Country	Eq. (18)				Eq. (19)			Eq. (20)		
	Energy consumption	Trade	Capital	GDP	Trade	Financial development	Population	GDP	Energy consumption	Foreign direct investment
Australia	+	+ (**)	+ (*)	+	+	+	− (*)	+ (**)	−	+
Canada	− (***)	+ (*)	+ (*)	+	+ (*)	+	− (**)	−	+ (*)	+ (**)
France	−	+ (*)	−	−	+	−	+	+ (*)	+	+
Germany	−	+	+	+	+	+	+	+	+	−
Japan	+ (**)	+ (*)	− (**)	+	+	+	−	+ (*)	− (*)	+ (*)
Netherlands	+	+ (*)	+	−			+	+ (**)		−
Portugal	+ (*)	+ (*)	−	+ (*)	− (**)	−	−	+ (*)		+
Spain	−	+ (*)	+	+ (*)	−	− (*)	−	+	+	+ (*)
Sweden	− (**)	+ (*)	+	− (***)			−	+ (**)	+	−
Switzerland	− (**)	+ (*)	+ (*)	−	+	+	− (**)	+ (*)	+ (**)	+
United Kingdom	− (***)	+ (*)	+ (*)	+ (*)	+	− (***)	− (*)	−	− (**)	+ (**)
United States	− (***)	+	+	+ (*)	+	− (***)	−	+ (*)	− (*)	+ (*)
Panel	+ (*)	+ (**)	+ (***)	+ (**)	+	−	+ (*)	+ (*)	− (*)	+ (*)
Hansen test (p-value)	2.939 (.1745)				2.125 (.1265)			9.767 (.1163)		
Durbin-Wu-Hausman (DWH) (p-value)	16.790 (.0002)				11.532 (.0031)			34.930 (.0000)		

Notes: The constant estimates are not reported due to space considerations. One, two, and three asterisks in parentheses denote significance at 1%, 5%, and 10%, respectively. As aforementioned the Hansen test refers to the overidentification for the restrictions in GMM estimation. The DWH tests the endogeneity of variables. The null of the DWH test indicates that the endogenous regressors' effects on the estimates are significant, and this requires the usage of instruments. Also according to the Hansen test the null hypothesis of over identifying the restrictions cannot be rejected.
Modified from Tiba, S., Frikha, M., 2018. Income, trade openness and energy interactions: evidence from simultaneous equation modeling. Energy 147, 799–811.

4 Conclusion

This chapter has dealt with the presentation of the SEM framework in the energy-growth nexus. Inherently the dual nature of the energy-growth nexus (in a production function and a demand function approach) and maybe a triple nature through the environmental Kuznets curve, justifies the employment of the SEM approach in this field. However, it should also be borne in mind that the theoretical underpinnings of this field are not strong enough. This means that we cannot decide with certainty, which variables are endogenous and which of them are exogenous. Nevertheless, the contradiction and controversy characterizing the field more that welcomes this approach, because there is still much road to be covered until a global theory can be formulated. SEM has been applied only in few cases in the energy-growth nexus, and this explains the dearth in studies so far.

The chapter will allow newcomers to the field to realize the potential in this approach and use more of it in the future, so that there is a balance in the approaches used in the field. Only through a balanced usage of the different econometric methods we can get sufficient information about the possible effect of the econometric method on the diversity of the energy-growth nexus results.

Last the chapter serves as a quick reference guide for whoever needs to brush up the various concepts in the approach through a quick revision of the essentials of the methodology and at the same time through the simplified case studies. Thus the chapter is useful both to paper authors and paper reviewers.

References

Gujarati, D.N., Porter, D.C., 2009. Basic Econometrics, fifth ed. McGraw Hill Inc., New York.
Maddala, G.S., 2008. Introduction to Econometrics, third ed. Wiley Publications.
Omri, A., 2013. CO_2 emissions, energy consumption and economic growth nexus in MENA countries: evidence from simultaneous equations models. Energy Econ. 40, 657–664.
Omri, A., Mabroul, N.B., Sassi-Tmar, A., 2015. Modeling the causal linkages between nuclear energy, renewable energy and economic growth in developed and developing countries. Renew. Sust. Energ. Rev. 42, 1012–1022.

Further reading

Jian Li, M.A., 2010. Effects of Full Information Maximum Likelihood, Expectation Maximization, Multiple Imputation and Similar Response Pattern Imputation on Structural Equation Modeling With Incomplete and Multivariate Nonnormal Data (Ph.D. dissertation). The Ohio State University. Available from: https:/etd.ohiolink.edu/!etd.send_file?accession=osu1281387395&disposition=inline. (Accessed 23 February 2020).

The Johansen cointegration method and several others during the evolution of the energy-growth nexus and the broader "X-variable"-growth nexus

1 Introduction

Junior researchers, when reading literature on the energy-growth nexus or the broader "X-variable"-growth nexus, encounter numerous published papers that have employed various cointegration methods. While new researchers may be specializing to a particular cointegration method for the implementation of their dissertation or thesis, other methods exist before and after the method they are using, for which they must have adequate knowledge to go by. To be able to make sound comparisons of their results with results from other studies, one must be aware of what each method does, why it does it, and how it does it. Therefore it is necessary, irrespective of the method eventually employed by the researcher, to have a knowledge and understanding of the alternatives. Without this knowledge the researcher cannot answer why one has used one method instead of the other. Sometimes, researchers receive this as a question posed by peer reviewers when a paper returns from review. Notwithstanding the necessities of having at least some working knowledge of all the methods employed in a research field, it is realized that this cannot be achieved without hard pains. Therefore the purpose of this chapter is to introduce the researcher smoothly all through Johansen method steps and the rest of the cointegration methods to enable a quick and thorough understanding in one shot, through applications and explanations of all the tricky spots. The rest of the chapter is organized as follows: After the introduction (Section 1), Section 2 deals with the VAR models in general and the Johansen cointegration approach, Section 3 deals with the rest of the most important cointegration methods, and Section 4 is the conclusion.

193

A Guide to Econometric Methods for the Energy-Growth Nexus. https://doi.org/10.1016/B978-0-12-819039-5.00004-5

2 The Johansen cointegration approach

2.1 A head start with VAR models

A vector autoregressive (VAR) model is a generalization of univariate AR models for multiple time series. Within a VAR framework, all variables are represented by an equation that explains its evolution based on its own lags and the lags of the other variables in the multivariate framework. The number of variables k is measured over a period of time t as a linear evolution of their past values.

Thus, for an example, with two variables, Y_{1t} and y_{2t}, a reduced p order VAR(1) can be written as shown in Eq. (1):

$$\begin{bmatrix} y_{1t} \\ y_{2t} \end{bmatrix} = \begin{bmatrix} c_1 \\ c_2 \end{bmatrix} + \begin{bmatrix} A_{11} & A_{12} \\ A_{21} & A_{22} \end{bmatrix} \begin{bmatrix} y_{1,t-1} \\ y_{2,t-1} \end{bmatrix} + \begin{bmatrix} \varepsilon_{1t} \\ \varepsilon_{2t} \end{bmatrix} \tag{1}$$

This setup generates one equation for each of the two variables. A VAR (ρ) shows the depth of lags goes back to $t - \rho$.

When variables are cointegrated, the error correction term is included in the VAR, and the model becomes a restricted VAR in the form of an error correction model (VECM). On the other hand, if variables are not cointegrated, first differences are taken. The variables are cointegrated when a linear combination of variables is stationary when two or more series are separately nonstationary.

Due to their linearity and the sharing of the same lag order assumptions, VAR models can be analyzed and written as single equations. However, depending on the number of variables (m) and their lags (p), the models may end up with many regressors, which may also be collinear. This causes the interpretation of the coefficients to be hard and unreliable. Thus impulse response functions (IRF) may be of use because they reveal the effect of a standard deviation shock on the dependent variable. IRF are formed through the moving average (MA) of the VAR equation. The original Eagle-Granger cointegration procedure consists of three steps: (i) the identification of the integration order of each variable, (ii) the OLS estimation of the cointegration relationship, and (iii) test the residuals from this regression for stationarity.

2.2 The Johansen cointegration framework and implementation

Cointegration has been extensively studied through the methods of Eagle and Granger and Johansen and Juselius for bivariate and multivariate relationships. The Johansen-Juselius method can be regarded as a multivariate generalization of the Eagle and Granger method. If there are n variables with unit roots, there are at most $n-1$ cointegrating vectors according to this framework. Zolna et al. (2016) describe the Johansen-Juselius method as a sequential procedure based on maximum likelihood techniques, which is a combination of cointegration and error correction models in a vector error correction model (VECM).

The Johansen (1988) and Johansen-Juselius (J-J) method (1990) from this point and after, we will call both as J-J method for brevity—is a full information maximum likelihood-based approach, appropriate for large samples. It requires that all regressors be stationary with an equal order of integration. Otherwise the validity of the method is at stake. Particularly, its limitation is better perceived when the data generating process (DGP) may be affected by major economic events. Namely, in the presence of structural breaks, results about cointegration may be distorted, and the hypothesis of cointegration is rejected (Esso, 2010).

To understand better the J-J method, it is useful to compare it with the Engle and Granger method (1987). This is also a two-step approach that suffers from the same disadvantages as J-J, but it has one more drawback: it can be applied only if there is one cointegration relationship. The method relies on the likelihood ratio (LR) test statistic for cointegration, whose asymptotic distribution depends on the assumptions made with respect to the deterministic trends and a detailed assumption about the cointegration equations. The unit root analysis will reveal whether the series have a common deterministic trend. Then the optimal lag length for the cointegration equation is decided through the AIC[a] statistic.

2.2.1 A detailed representation of cointegration in the variables

Suppose that C_t is a vector containing (let's assume four) integrated series (at the same integration level) namely, $C_t = (X_t, Y_t, Z_t, \Lambda_t)$. Understandably, we need to test the long-run relationship of the variables contained in this vector. The vector can be formulated as of Eqs. (2), (3):

$$C_t = A_0 + \sum_{i=1}^{m} A_i C_{t-i} + u_t \tag{2}$$

$$\Delta C_t = A_0 + \Pi C_{t-1} + \sum_{i=1}^{m} \Gamma_i \Delta C_{t-i} + u_t \tag{3}$$

which constitutes a VAR (m), namely, a vector autoregressive process of order m. Long-run relationships are depicted in a (4×4) matrix Π, shown in Eq. (3). The long-run relationship among the four variables is examined through the existence of $r \leq 3$ cointegration relationships. Alternatively, this is examined through the testing of the hypothesis that the rank of matrix Π in Eq. (3) is at most r. Γ_i stands for (4×4) matrices that reveal the short-run dynamics of the model.

Eq. (3) can be also written as of Eq. (4):

$$\Delta C_t = A_0 + a\beta' C_{t-1} + \sum_{i=1}^{m} \Gamma_i \Delta C_{t-i} + u_t \tag{4}$$

with a being a matrix $(4 \times r)$ reflecting the speed of adjustment and β being a matrix $(4 \times r)$ representing the cointegrating vectors.

---

[a]This has been explained in detail in Chapter 3 on the ARDL approach.

Naser (2015) follows the parsimonious vector equilibrium correction model (PVECM), and he eliminates nonsignificant cointegrating vectors in his identified matrix. After dropping those vectors, he reestimates the following equation as of Eq. (5):

$$\Delta C_t = \hat{A}_0 + \hat{a}\left(\sum_{i=1}^{r}\hat{\beta}_i'C_{t-1}\right) + \sum_{i=1}^{m}\hat{\Gamma}_i\Delta C_{t-i} + u_t \tag{5}$$

2.2.2 The investigation of Johansen's cointegration with two tests

The investigation of Johansen's cointegration can take place through (i) the maximum eigenvalue test and (ii) the trace test. Both tests involve two statistics: r_0 is the number of cointegrating vectors, and $\lambda_{\max}$ is the maximum eigenvalue

(i) The maximum eigenvalue test

This is based on the following LR statistic, which is called the maximum eigenvalue statistic and is represented by Eq. (6):

$$\lambda_{\text{eigen}}(r, r+1) = -T\log(1 - \lambda_{r+1}) \tag{6}$$

The following notation applies for Eq. (6):

$T =$ the number of observations, $\lambda_i =$ the largest eigen value, and $r =$ the number of cointegrations.

The null hypothesis is that there are r cointegrating vectors. The alternative is that there are $k > r$ cointegrating vectors, and this is the same hypothesis for both tests.

Thus the maximum eigenvalue is calculated under the null hypothesis:

$H_0 : r_0 = r$ no cointegration

$H_1 : r_0 > r$ cointegration

In essence, this test conducts tests on each eigenvalue separately. The second test through which the investigation of Johansen's cointegration is performed is the trace test and is explained next.

(ii) The trace test

The name originates from the test statistics involved, which is the trace (the sum of the diagonal elements) of a diagonal matrix of generalized eigenvalues. The statistic of the test is provided by Eq. (7):

$$\lambda_{\text{trace}}(r) = -T\sum_{i=r+1}^{n}\log(1 - \lambda_i) \tag{7}$$

Also the trace test is calculated under the null hypothesis:

$H_0 : r_0 \leq r$ no cointegration

$H_1 : r_0 > r$ cointegration

The null hypothesis is that there are at most r cointegration vectors. The alternative is that there are $k > r$ cointegrating vectors, and this is the same hypothesis for both Johansen tests.

If the maximum eigenvalue statistic is above the 5% critical value, we reject the null hypothesis of no cointegration. The trace determines the number of cointegrating vectors among variables. There should be at least one cointegrating vector for a possible cointegration. Usually, we start by testing the existence of $r \leq m - 1$ cointegration relationships among the m variables in a model. According to Cheung and Lai (1993), the trace test is more robust than the maximum eigenvalue test.

Flashback 1: What is an eigenvalue?

Eigenvalues are a special set of scalars associated with a linear system of equations that are sometimes also known as characteristic roots, characteristic values. Each eigenvalue is paired with a corresponding so-called eigenvector (or a corresponding into a right eigenvector and a corresponding left eigenvector; there is no analogous distinction between left and right for eigenvalues).

The decomposition of a square matrix A into eigenvalues and eigenvectors is known in this work as eigen decomposition, and the fact that this decomposition is always possible as long as the matrix consisting of the eigenvectors of A is square is known as the eigen decomposition theorem.

Flashback 2: What is a trace?

The trace of a square matrix A is the sum of elements on the main diagonal (the diagonal from the upper left to the lower right) of A.

Case study 1: Cointegration and causality between energy and GDP in Tunisia

Belloumi (2009) employs Johansen's cointegration method to study the long-run relationship between energy consumption per capita (in kilogram of oil equivalent) and gross domestic product (in constant 2000 US$) in Tunisia for the period 1971–2004 and then continues with a vector error correction model (VECM) approach for the investigation of causality. The correlation between the two series is equal to 0.97. The study also employed the augmented Dickey-Fuller (ADF) test (1979) and the Phillips-Perron test (PP) test (1988) to investigate the existence of unit roots. The variables are nonstationary at levels, but they become stationary after they become first differenced, namely, they are $I(1)$. Through a variables' graph observation and the results of unit root tests, it has been assumed that the level data have no deterministic trends and the cointegration equations have intercepts. Two lag intervals have been used in first differences. Table 1 provides the results of the Johansen maximum likelihood cointegration tests.

Based on the results that are shown in Table 1, the maximum eigenvalue statistic is $21.669 > 15.892$, which is the critical value of 5%. Thus the null

Continued

Table 1 Johansen cointegration estimation results between energy consumption per capita and gross domestic product in Tunisia.

Number of cointegration	Eigenvalue	Trace statistic	5% critical value
Test 1: rank test (trace)			
None	0.502	28.076	20.261
At most 1	0.186	6.406	9.164
Test 2: rank test (maximum eigenvalue)			
Number of cointegration	Eigenvalue	Trace statistic	5% critical value
None	0.502	21.669	15.892
At most 1	0.186	6.406	9.164

From Belloumi, M., 2009, Energy consumption and GDP in Tunisia: cointegration and causality analysis. Energy Policy 37, 2745–2753.

hypothesis of no cointegration is rejected at 5%. The same result is produced through the trace test. Also, under $H_0: \leq 1$, the trace and maximum values are equal to $6.406 < 9.164$, which is the 5% critical value. Thus the null hypothesis that supports cointegration is accepted at 5% level of significance. According to these results the two variables, namely, the energy consumption and the gross domestic product, have one cointegrating equation. After cointegration is confirmed, the author also proceeds with a VECM causality testing. The interested reader is referred to the source of this study.

Modified from Belloumi, M., 2009. Energy consumption and GDP in Tunisia: cointegration and causality analysis. Energy Policy 37, 2745–2753.

Case study 2: The tourism-led growth hypothesis for Turkey

As it has been mentioned at the introduction of this book and this chapter, the energy-growth nexus has inspired other fields too. This is why one can broadly refer to these studies as the "X-variable"-growth nexus studies. One such strand of studies is the tourism-growth nexus, which investigates the tourism-led growth hypothesis. The current study (Case study 2) investigates the tourism-led growth hypothesis in Turkey for the years 1960–2006. It uses real gross domestic product (Y), total number of tourist inflows (T) to Turkey, and the real exchange rate (RER). It uses two cointegration methods, namely, both the Pesaran's bounds test and Johansen method, to corroborate results.

Katircioglou (2009) prefers to run the Johansen cointegration tests for a few different lags to find out whether the results are sensitive to the lag structure. Namely, he does not blindly consult the Akaike information criterion (AIC),

Bayes-Schwarz Information Criterion (BIC), or the Hannan-Quinn Information Criterion (HQIC) results (which in this case study advise in favor of lag $= 1$). He is based on a suggestion based on Pindyck and Rubinfeld (1991). Thus this is another approach that a researcher may follow and could also use, juxtaposed to the lags suggested by AIC, BIC, or HQIC results (Table 2).

The study does not conclude the existence of any long-run relationship between income and tourist flows in Turkey. Therefore no reason was documented for Turkish policy makers at the time of the study, to take measures for the promotion of tourism for that to contribute to growth. This finding contradicts results from other researchers such as Gunduz and Hatemi-J (2005) and Ongan and Demiröz (2005) who had found evidence for the growth and feedback hypotheses, respectively, for the tourism in Turkey.

Table 2 Cointegration tests based on Johansen approach.

Variables	Trace statistic	5% critical value	1% critical value
VAR lag:1			
Y, T, and RER			
$H_0: r = 0$	19.08	29.68	35.65
$H_0: r \leq 1$	8.67	15.41	20.04
$H_0: r \leq 2$	3.04	3.76	6.65
VAR lag:2			
Y, T, and RER			
$H_0: r = 0$	21.16	29.68	35.65
$H_0: r \leq 1$	10.70	15.41	20.04
$H_0: r \leq 2$	3.13	3.76	6.65
VAR lag:3			
Y, T, and RER			
$H_0: r = 0$	14.89	29.68	35.65
$H_0: r \leq 1$	6.77	15.41	20.04
$H_0: r \leq 2$	2.31	3.76	6.65
VAR lag:4			
Y, T, and RER			
$H_0: r = 0$	18.87	29.68	35.65
$H_0: r \leq 1$	7.73	15.41	20.04
$H_0: r \leq 2$	3.29	3.76	6.65

From Katircioglu, S.T., 2009, Revisiting the tourism-led-growth hypothesis for Turkey using the bounds test and Johansen approach for cointegration. Tour. Manag. 30, 17–20.

Modified from Katircioglu, S.T., 2009. Revisiting the tourism-led-growth hypothesis for Turkey using the bounds test and Johansen approach for cointegration. Tour. Manag. 30, 17–20.

2.3 The modified Johansen approach for small samples

Reinsel and Ahn (1992) and Reimers (1992) apply a small sample modification for the Johansen approach to correct the bias injected in small samples with the conventional Johansen approach. These authors suggest multiplying of the Johansen statistics with the scale factor $(T-pk)/T$, with T being the number of observations in the sample, p is the number of variables, and k is the lag order of the VAR. The critical values in this case are taken from Mackinnon et al. (1999). One such modification takes place in Belke et al. (2011).

Case study 3: The energy-growth relationship for 25 OECD countries

Belke et al. (2011) investigate the cointegration between energy consumption (kilograms of oil equivalent), real GDP per capita (2000 constant US$), and purchasing power parities as proxy for economic growth, for 25 OECD countries with a data span from 1981 to 2007. To distinguish between national and international development elements, they also employ a principal components analysis. In addition to these variables, they also use energy prices in US dollars. Results from the Johansen's cointegration results can be found in Table 3. They sourced all their data from the International Energy Agency.

Table 3 Johansen's cointegration results from the two basic tests.

H_0	Trace statistic	Critical value	Maximum eigenvalue statistic	Critical value
None	45.78*	42.92	26.93*	25.82
At most 1	19.85	25.87	13.93	19.39
At most 2	5.93	12.52	5.93	12.52

Note: One asterisk indicates significance at 5%. Critical values are taken from Mackinnon et al. (1999).
From Belke, A., Dobnik, F., Dreger, C., 2011, Energy consumption and economic growth: new insights into the cointegration relationship. Energy Econ. 33, 782–789.

They use the dynamic ordinary least squares method (DOLS) as the most appropriate to tackle the problem of endogeneity and serial correlation, and they estimate the following model in Eqs. (8)–(10):

$$E_{i,t} = a_{1i} + \delta_{1i}t + \beta_{1i}Y_{i,t} + \gamma_{1i}P_{i,t} + u_{i,t} \tag{8}$$

$$Y_{i,t} = a_{2i} + \delta_{2i}t + \beta_{2i}E_{i,t} + \gamma_{2i}P_{i,t} + \varepsilon_{i,t} \tag{9}$$

$$P_{i,t} = a_{3i} + \delta_{3i}t + \beta_{3i}E_{i,t} + \gamma_{3i}Y_{i,t} + \eta_{i,t} \tag{10}$$

The following notation applies for Eqs. (8)–(10):

i denotes the country, t denotes time, a_i denotes country-specific fixed effects, and.

δ_i denotes time trends.

The estimated results for the long-run horizon are as shown in Table 4:

- The elasticity of energy consumption is about 0.60 across the study periods. This means that 1% increase in real GDP increases energy consumption by 0.6%.
- The price elasticity is about−0.13, which means that energy consumption is relatively price inelastic.
- No significant differences appear among the various breaks, so the estimates are robust.

Table 4 Results from the DOLS estimation.

	1981–90	1991–2007	1981–2000	2001–07
β_1	0.64* (0.46)	0.59* (0.23)	0.58* (0.21)	0.63* (0.55)
γ_1	−0.12* (0.47)	−0.14* (0.34)	−0.14*(0.17)	−0.12* (0.45)
β_2	0.57* (0.42)	0.62* (0.39)	0.61* (0.09)	0.54* (0.31)
γ_2	0.04 (0.45)	0.02 (0.52)	0.04 (0.31)	0.02 (0.53)

Notes: One asterisk indicates significance at 1%.
Reproduced from Belke, A., Dobnik, F., Dreger, C., 2011, Energy consumption and economic growth: new insights into the cointegration relationship. Energy Econ. 33, 782–789.

2.4 The Johansen-Fisher panel cointegration test

This is a nonparametric test that does not assume homogeneity across the units of the panel. In analogy with its time-series counterpart, the test includes the trace statistic and the eigenvalue statistic. These are written as shown in Eqs. (11), (12):

$$\lambda_{\text{trace}} - \text{panel} = -2 \sum_{i=1}^{N} Ln(\pi_{\text{trace},i}) \sim \chi^2_{2N} \qquad (11)$$

$$\lambda_{\max} - \text{panel} = -2 \sum_{i=1}^{N} Ln(\pi_{\text{trace},i}) \sim \chi^2_{2N} \qquad (12)$$

Critical values for these tests are provided in Mackinnon et al. (1999).

3 Other cointegration methods in the broader "X-variable"-growth nexus

3.1 Threshold cointegration

Threshold cointegration is implemented in two steps. The first step decides whether there is a structural break in the cointegrating relationship. For this purpose the method employs the three (Hansen, 1992) stability tests: SupF, MeanF, and Lc. The SupF test is permeated by the rationale of the Chow test about stability. The MeanF test investigates whether the model is a stable relationship. Last the Lc is applied when the likelihood of the parameter variation is stable in the whole sample. For more about these tests, the interested reader can consult page 1388 in Esso (2010).

The second step in the threshold cointegration method is the application of the cointegration test with a break as recommended in Gregory and Hansen (1996). Depending on the on the type of shift present in the cointegration equation, four different model equations may be broadly applicable:

(i) the level shift equation
(ii) the level shift with trend equation
(iii) the regime shift equation
(iv) the regime and trend shift equation

Let B be a break due to a structural change, a cointegration equation for two series, Y_t and X_t, can be written as in Eq. (13):

$$\ln(Y_t) = \mu_1 + \mu_2 B + \beta_1 t + \beta_2 tB + a_1 \ln(X_t) + a_2 \ln(X_t)B + \varepsilon_t \tag{13}$$

The following notation applies for Eq. (13):

μ_1 is the intercept before the shift.
μ_2 is the intercept at the time of the shift.
β_1 is the trend slope before the shift.
β_2 is the trend slope at the time of the shift.
a_1 is the cointegrating slope coefficient before the regime shift.
a_2 is the cointegrating slope coefficient at the time of the regime shift.

The earlier model is the general, all inclusive case reported in (iv). The model herein collapses to all the other cases, (i), (ii), and (iii). The break, B, is treated as unknown and is the minimum of the unit root test statistics calculated on the subsample where the break is examined. After cointegration is confirmed, causality analysis follows.

Case study 4: Threshold cointegration: An application on sub-Saharan countries

Esso (2010) employs threshold cointegration in a sample of seven sub-Saharan countries during the period 1970–2007. Results are provided in Table 5. The study employs Gregory and Hansen cointegration tests for an endogenous structural break in the cointegration equation.

Table 5 Threshold cointegration test results.

Countries	Dependent variable: real GDP			
	Model 1	Model 2	Model 3	Model 4
Cameroon	−3.663 (1) [1986]	−3.657 (1) [1986]	−3.684 (1) [1986]	−4.621 (0) [1988]
Congo	−4.181 (0) [1985]	−4.163 (0) [1985]	−4.694 (0) [1985]	−5.099 (3) [1989]
Cote d'Ivoire	−2.731 (0) [1984]	−4.332 (0) [1979]	−5.352 (3) [1983]	−5.629 (3) [1986]
Ghana	−3.284 (0) [1997]	−3.891 (0) [1997]	−3.531 (0) [1998]	−5.710 (1) [1982]
Kenya	−4.899 (5) [1990]	−4.764 (5) [1990]	−4.518 (1) [1976]	−5.058 (6) [1993]
Nigeria	−4.749 (3) [1995]	−4.753 (3) [1995]	−4.316 (3) [2001]	−4.919 (0) [1982]
South Africa	−2.681 (2) [1985]	−3.331 (1) [1988]	−3.022 (0) [1987]	−5.210 (1) [1995]
Countries	Dependent variable: energy			
	Model 1	Model 2	Model 3	Model 4
Cameroon	−4.673 (1) [1982]	−4.628 (1) [1984]	−4.499 (1) [1984]	−4.572 (3) [1982]
Congo	−7.373 (0) [1984]	−7.375 (0) [1984]	−7.385 (0) [1984]	−7.357 (0) [1984]
Cote d'Ivoire	−3.553 (0) [1976]	−5.752 (4) [1977]	−3.463 (2) [1981]	−6.069 (3) [1978]
Ghana	−5.417 (1) [1980]	−5.878 (1) [1987]	−5.731 (1) [1988]	−5.576 (1) [1994]
Kenya	−3.756 (1) [1988]	−5.223 (3) [1999]	−3.997 (3) [1988]	−5.178 (0) [1998]
Nigeria	−4.413 (0) [1980]	−4.637 (0) [1995]	−4.885 (3) [1981]	−5.896 (0) [1988]
South Africa	−3.507 (0) [2001]	−3.741 (0) [1978]	−5.113 (1) [1984]	−5.625 (1) [1988]

Notes: Only ADF* is presented as threshold cointegration test statistic. The asterisk denotes the null of no cointegration at 5%. Numbers in parentheses are lag orders to include in equations. Time breaks are in brackets. The 5% critical values for Model 1, level shift; Model 2, level shift with trend; Model 3, regime shift; and Model 4, regime and trend shift based on Gregory and Hansen (1996) are −4.61, −4.99, −4.95, and −5.50, respectively.
From Esso, L.J., 2010. Threshold cointegration and causality relationship between energy use and growth in seven African countries. Energy Econ. 32, 1383–1391.

Continued

According to the results from Table 5, there is rejection of the null of no cointegration in Cameroon, Cote d'Ivoire, Ghana, Nigeria, and South Africa when energy is treated as endogenous. On the other hand, when GDP is treated as endogenous, there is evidence of threshold cointegration in Cote d'Ivoire, Ghana, and Nigeria. Time breaks are found to have occurred between 1977 and 1994 and coincide with events in most of sub-Saharan countries during the 1980s and 1990s.

Modified from Esso, L.J., 2010. Threshold cointegration and causality relationship between energy use and growth in seven African countries. Energy Econ. 32, 1383–1391.

Hatemi-J (2008) introduces another structural break setup with two dummies in Eq. (14).

$$\ln(Y_t) = \mu_1 + \mu_2 B1 + \mu_3 B2 + \beta_1 t + \beta_2 tB1 + \beta_3 tB2 + a_1 \ln(X_t) + a_2 \ln(X_t)B1 + a_3 \ln(X_t)B2 + \varepsilon_t \tag{14}$$

The following notation applies for Eq. (14):

μ_1: It is the base dummy.

μ_2: coefficient estimate of intercept dummy that is different from the common dummy μ_1. It represents the change in intercept for the first endogenous structural break.

μ_3: It represents the change from the base dummy due to the second structural break.

$\beta_1, \beta_2, \beta_3$ are base slope coefficients of X_t.

a_1, a_2, a_3 are differential slope coefficients due to endogenous structural breaks.

$B1, B2$ are the break dummies which are formed endogenously at time $t = 1, 2, \dots$ n and they can be further written as $B1t$, $B2t$.

With respect of their time occurrence, the dummy breaks can be represented as follows:

$$B1t = 0 \quad \text{if } t \leq [n_{t1}]$$

$$B1t = 1 \quad \text{if } t > [n_{t1}]$$

$$B2t = 0 \quad \text{if } t \leq [n_{t2}]$$

$$B2t = 1 \quad \text{if } t > [n_{t2}]$$

With $t1$ and $t2$ being unknown parameters belonging to the set $(0, 1)$ and stand for the occurrence timing of the break.

The testing of the null hypothesis of no cointegration takes place through a residual based technique. For the two variables of the aforementioned paradigm, to be cointegrated, they must be integrated of order one, and their residual must be integrated of order zero, namely, stationary (Engle and Granger, 1987).

Case study 5: International crude oil prices and the stock prices of clean energy and technology companies

Bondia et al. (2016) use stock prices of alternative energy companies, the variable called NEX, (through the weekly WilderHill New Energy Global Innovation Index) and stock prices of technology companies, the variable called PSE, through the New York Stock Exchange Arca Tech 100 Index) as well as oil prices, the variable called AOP, interest rates (through a 10 year treasury constant maturity rates) for a data span ranging from January 3, 2003, to June 5, 2015, the variable called INT. The study period contains a recession in 2008 when there was a sudden drop in these variables.

The study employs two models of the type shown in Eqs. (8), (9), and they estimate the cointegration relationships with OLS. The residuals are examined with three tests, the ADF*, the Z_t^*, and the Z_a^*. The latter two have been proposed by Perron (1989). Understandably the aforementioned statistics are bias corrected modified to their original counterparts. They test the following cointegrating relationships of their underlying variables as shown in Eqs. (15)–(17):

$$\underset{(\tau)\in T}{ADF^*} = \inf ADF(\tau) \tag{15}$$

$$\underset{(\tau)\in T}{Z_t^*} = \inf Z_t(\tau) \tag{16}$$

$$\underset{(\tau)\in T}{Z_\alpha^*} = \inf Z_\alpha(\tau) \tag{17}$$

The aforementioned Eqs. (15)–(17) are used to test the residuals corresponding to the estimations for each structural break. They are the Phillips and Ouliaris tests (1990). The lowest value of the three is compared with the critical values for one break (Gregory and Hansen, 1996) and two breaks (Hatemi-J, 2008) as shown in the Table 6 with the critical values contained in Tables 7 and 8.

Table 6 Threshold cointegration results.

NEXt = f (PSEt, AOPt, INTt)	ADF*	Z_t^*	Z_a^*
Gregory and Hansen (GH) test	−6.15[a] (0.44)	−5.65 (0.44)	−62.07 (0.44)
Hatemi-J (HJ) test	−8.79[a] (0.26, 0.31)	−7.60[a] (0.26, 0.31)	−110.89[a] (0.26, 0.31)

Notes: Numbers in parentheses stand for the break points. Superscript "a" stands for 5% level of significance. The critical values for GH and HJ are available in Gregory and Hansen (1996, pp. 109), and Hatemi-J (2008, pp. 501).
From Bondia, R., Ghosh, S., Kanjilal, K., 2016. International crude oil prices and the stock prices of clean energy and technology companies: evidence from non-linear cointegration tests with unknown structural breaks. Energy 101, 558–565.

Continued

Table 7 Snapshot of approximate asymptotic critical values for tests of cointegration with two regime shifts.

Number of independent variables	Test statistic	1% critical value	5% critical value	10% critical value
$m = 1$	ADF*, Z_t^*	−6.503	−6.015	−5.653
	Z_a^*	−90.794	−76.003	−52.232
$m = 2$	ADF*, Z_t^*	−6.928	−6.458	−6.224
	Z_a^*	−99.458	−83.644	−76.806
$m = 3$	ADF*, Z_t^*	−7.833	−7.352	−7.118
	Z_a^*	−118.577	−104.860	−97.749

Modified from Hatemi-J, A., 2008, Tests for cointegration with two unknown regime shifts with an application to financial market integration. Empir. Econ. 35, 497–505.

Table 8 A snapshot of asymptotic critical values for cointegration tests with two regime shifts.

	Level	0.01	0.025	0.05	0.10	0.975
$m = 1$	**ADF*, Z_t^***					
	C	−5.13	−4.83	−4.61	−4.34	−2.25
	C/T	−5.45	−5.21	−4.99	−4.72	−2.72
	C/S	−5.47	−5.19	−4.95	−4.68	−2.55
	Z_a^*					
	C	−50.07	−45.01	−40.48	−36.19	−1.63
	C/T	−57.28	−52.09	−47.96	−43.22	−15.90
	C/S	−57.17	−51.32	−47.04	−41.85	−13.15
$m = 2$	**ADF*, Z_t^***					
	C	−5.44	−5.16	−4.92	−4.69	−2.61
	C/T	−5.88	−5.51	−5.29	−5.03	−3.01
	C/S	−5.97	−5.73	−5.50	−5.23	−3.12
	Z_a^*					
	C	−57.01	−51.41	−46.98	−42.49	−14.27
	C/T	−64.77	−58.57	−53.92	−48.94	−19.19
	C/S	−68.21	−63.28	−58.33	−52.85	−19.72

Table 8 A snapshot of asymptotic critical values for cointegration tests with two regime shifts—cont'd

	Level	0.01	0.025	0.05	0.10	0.975
$m = 3$	**ADF*, Z_t^***					
	C	−5.77	−5.50	−5.28	−5.02	−2.96
	C/T	−6.05	−5.79	−5.57	−5.33	−3.33
	C/S	−6.51	−6.23	−6.00	−5.75	−3.65
	Z_a^*					
	C	−63.64	−57.96	−53.58	−48.65	−18.20
	C/T	−70.27	−64.26	−59.76	−54.94	−22.72
	C/S	−80.15	−73.91	−68.94	−63.42	−26.64

Modified from Gregory, A.W., Hansen, B.E., 1996. Residual-based tests for cointegration in models with regime shifts. J. Econ. 70, 99–126.

According to Table 6 the null hypothesis of no cointegration is rejected at 5%, both for one and two breaks. Thus there is a long-run relationship among the studied variables with two breaks endogenously determined. Therefore the relationship is not the same throughout the investigated period, but it changes three times. Overall, this type of analysis is more robust. Tables 7 and 8 contain the asymptotic critical values for Hatemi-J and Gregory and Hansen tests.

Modified from Bondia, R., Ghosh, S., Kanjilal, K., 2016. International crude oil prices and the stock prices of clean energy and technology companies: evidence from nonlinear cointegration tests with unknown structural breaks. Energy 101, 558–565.

3.2 Panel cointegration tests

Johansen cointegration method is sometimes used with another cointegration method so that results are rendered robust. Four panel cointegration methods are often used:

(i) the Kao method (Kao, 1999)
(ii) the Pedroni method (Pedroni, 2001)
(iii) the Johansen-Fisher developed by Maddala and Wu (2001)
(iv) the Westerlund (2007) method

The first assumes homogeneity on cross-sectional units and is based on the Engle-Granger two-step procedure. Cointegration is tested with the ADF test. The second encompasses seven tests, which are residual based. These are as follows:

- the v-statistic,
- the p-statistic,
- the pp-statistic,
- the ADF statistic (the latter three are called within-dimension statistics),

- the group rho-statistic,
- the group pp-statistic and
- the group ADF statistic (the latter three are also called between dimension statistics).

The first four statistics are based on the within approach, and the last three are based on the between approach. Their null hypothesis is that of no cointegration. The tests reject the null hypothesis when they have large negative values. This does not apply for the panel-v test, which rejects the null when it has a large positive value (Quedraogo, 2013).

The statistics of the third test are provided in a paragraph earlier. The Westerlund statistic (Fourth statistic) provides four alternatives:

- Gt and Ga (for the existence of cointegration individual panels),
- Pt and Pa (the existence of cointegration in the whole panel).

Westerlund test results are not robust to the lag and lead lengths when the time dimension is short (Persyn and Westerlund, 2008). The DOLS method (Kao and Chiang, 2001) is a parametric approach appropriate for panel estimation. However, since it does not consider cross-sectional heterogeneity, FMOLS (Pedroni, 2000) which is a nonparametric approach, is the ideal estimation strategy, because this method acknowledges heterogeneity across units, serial correlation, and endogeneity issues. Given the facts that FMOLS cannot estimate short-run relationships, an alternative estimation strategy is the pooled mean group estimation (PMG), which can estimate both short-run and long-run relationships while also taking into account possible heterogeneity. Thus the panel cointegration approach is very convenient. Otherwise, we would have to run a heterogeneous regression for each individual to avoid the homogeneity of coefficients that would be assumed with a single regression (Zoundi, 2017).

Case study 6: CO_2 emissions, renewable energy, and the environmental Kuznets curve with panel data

Zoundi employs a panel cointegration analysis to investigate the impact of renewable energy (wind, solar, hydro, geothermal, and heat pumps) on carbon emissions (metric tons per inhabitant) in the framework of a Kuznets curve analysis for 25 African countries during the period 1980–2012. He employs a bulk of panel cointegration tests displayed in Table 9.

Based on the earlier results in Table 9, all tests reject the null hypothesis of no cointegration, except for rho (both panel and group) and Westerlund Ga statistics. The lag length has been determined with Schwarz Information Criterion (SIC) in the Pedroni and Kao tests, while in the Westerlund test, the lag has been set to one.

Furthermore the study employs DOLS and FMOLS estimation to estimate the long-run relationships between the associated variables. To further estimate the short-run relationships, the study employs a GMM approach together with a dynamic fixed effect (DFE), a mean group (MG), and a pooled mean group (PMG) estimation for reason of robustness proof. Based on the results

Table 9 Cointegration tests.

	Cointegration test	Statistics
Pedroni	Panel-v	1.39*
	Panel-rho	0.84
	Panel-PP	−8.87***
	Panel-ADF	−9.57***
	Group-rho	3.86
	Group-PP	−19.30***
	Group-ADF	−11.98***
Kao	t	−7.58***
Westerlund	Gt	−2.935***
	Ga	−6.672
	Pt	−13.138
	Pa	−11.207

Notes: *Pedroni and Kao have been generated in Eviews and Westerlund has been generated in Stata with a number of bootstrap replicates in the Westerlund test to be reduced from the maximum of 800–300. One, two, and three asterisks indicate significance at 10%, 5%, and 1% respectively.*
From Zoundi, Z., 2017. CO2 emissions, renewable energy and the environmental kuznets curve, a panel cointegration approach. Renew. Sustain. Energy Rev. 72, 1067–1075.

(which are not presented here for space considerations), 1% increase in renewable energy can reduce CO_2 emissions by 0.13%. Also, 1% increase in primary energy increases emissions by 0.85%. This has a consequence that the two types of energy consumption lead to air quality depletion by 0.72% (0.85–0.13). Last the EKC is not confirmed for all countries in the sample (Zoundi, 2017).

Modified from Zoundi, Z., 2017. CO$_2$ emissions, renewable energy and the Environmental Kuznets Curve, a panel cointegration approach. Renew. Sustain. Energy Rev. 72, 1067–1075.

3.3 The continuously updated fully modified (Cup-FM) estimation

Bai et al. (2009) have proposed the Cup-FM estimation to allow for cross-sectional dependence in the panel data. According to Bai and Kao (2006), the panel regression with cross-sectional dependence can be written as in Eq. (18):

$$y_{it} = a_i + \beta X_{it} + e_{it} \tag{18}$$

wherein

$$e_{it} = \lambda_i' F_t + u_{it}$$

The CUP-FM estimator is provided in Eq. (19):

$$\hat{\beta}_{Cup} = \left[\sum_{i=1}^{N} \left(\sum_{t=1}^{T} \hat{y}_{it}^{+} (\hat{\beta}_{Cup}) (X_{it} - \overline{X}_i)' - T \left(\lambda_i' (\hat{\beta}_{Cup}) \hat{\Delta}_{Fei}^{+} (\hat{\beta}_{Cup}) + \hat{\Delta}_{uei}^{+} (\hat{\beta}_{Cup}) \right) \right) \right]$$
$$\times \left[\sum_{i=1}^{N} \sum_{t=1}^{T} (X_{it} - \overline{X}_i)(X_{it} - \overline{X}_i)' \right]^{-1} \tag{19}$$

The following notation applies in Eq. (19):

$$\hat{y}_{it}^+ = y_{it} - \left(\hat{\lambda}_i' \hat{\Omega}_{Fei} + \hat{\Omega}_{uei}\right) \hat{\Omega}_{ei}^{-1} \Delta X_{it}$$

$\hat{\Omega}_{Fei}$ and $\hat{\Omega}_{uei}$ are the estimated long-run covariance matrices.

$\hat{\Delta}_{Fei}^+$ and $\hat{\Delta}_{uei}^+$ are the estimated one-sided long-run covariance.

The estimator is calculated by repeatedly estimating parameters, and the long-run covariance matrix and loading until convergence are reached (Fang and Chang, 2016).

Case study 7: Energy, human capital, and economic growth in Asian Pacific countries

The study investigates the cointegration relationship for 16 Asian Pacific countries over the period 1970–2011 using the augmented production function between energy consumption (million tons oil equivalent) and economic growth (constant 2005 GDP, national prices in millions), also using capital and human capital. The latter is measured as the number of workers and human capital index that is measured based on years of schooling.

The aforementioned study employs both the CUP-FM and the FMOLS to find out about the seriousness of the problem of cross-sectional dependence. The results in Table 10 show that capital is significant for growth and 1% increase in capital increases growth by 0.5%. The elasticity of output with energy consumption is 0.04, while the rest of the variables do not appear to be important for growth. The scale of economy is underestimated with FMOLS with the sum of input elasticities equal to 0.802, which is much smaller than 0.975 from the Cup-FM estimators.

Table 10 CUP-FM and FMOLS panel estimation results.

	CUP-FM		FMOLS	
	Coefficient	t-Statistics	Coefficient	t-Statistics
lnK (capital)	0.508***	16.511	0.495***	24.271
lnL (labor)	0.212	0.982	−0.099	0.252
lnH (human capital)	0.215	1.170	0.301	1.118
lnE (energy consumption)	0.040**	2.113	0.105***	4.765

***, Denote the significance level of 1% and **, denote the significance level of 5%.
From Fang, Z., Chang, Y., 2016. Energy, human capital and economic growth in asia pacific countries—evidence from a panel cointegration and causality analysis. Energy Econ. 56, 177–184.

Modified from Fang, Z., Chang, Y., 2016. Energy, human capital and economic growth in Asia Pacific countries—evidence from a panel cointegration and causality analysis. Energy Econ. 56, 177–184.

3.4 The threshold autoregressive and the momentum threshold autoregressive asymmetric cointegration models with breaks

If asymmetric cointegration between variables is present, then both cointegration and causality tests are misspecified. The asymmetric adjustment is a significant source of nonlinearity. Thus threshold autoregressive (TAR) and momentum threshold autoregressive (MTAR) models are used to test for asymmetric cointegration and then use asymmetric error correction terms to study the direction of causality (Enders and Siklos, 2001). Suppose we have two variables Y_t and X_t that are connected with the following linear equation relationship in Eqs. (20)–(22):

$$Y_t = a_0 + a_1 X_t + \varepsilon_t \tag{20}$$

$$\Delta \varepsilon_t = \rho \varepsilon_{t-1} + \sum_{i=1}^{k} \beta_i \Delta \varepsilon_{t-i} + v_t \tag{21}$$

If ε_t is stationary and $a_1 < 0$, this is evidence for cointegration. Eq. (16) is modified as follows to account for asymmetries as in Eq. (22):

The following notation applies for Eq. (22):

$$\Delta \varepsilon_t = \rho^+ M_t \varepsilon_{t-1} + \rho^- (1 - M_t) \varepsilon_{t-1} + \sum_{i=1}^{k} \beta_i \Delta \varepsilon_{t-i} + u_t \tag{22}$$

M_t is the heavyside indicator.

ρ^+, ρ^- are upward and downward adjustment of parameters.

ε_t is the residuals from the DOLS procedure.

Eqs. (8), (10) contain a specification of an error correction model that is termed as threshold autoregressive model (TAR). The MTAR is based on a different rule for the heavyside indicator. The rule for the TAR model is shown in Eq. (23), while the rule for the MTAR model is shown in Eq. (24).

$$M_t = \begin{cases} 1, & if \ \varepsilon_{t-1} \geq \tau \\ 0, & if \ \varepsilon_{t-1} < \tau \end{cases} \tag{23}$$

$$M_t = \begin{cases} 1, & if \ \Delta \varepsilon_{t-1} \geq \tau \\ 0, & if \ \Delta \varepsilon_{t-1} < \tau \end{cases} \tag{24}$$

Namely, the threshold in Eq. (24) (the MTAR version) depends on the previous period change on ε_{t-1}. Note that tau is the value of the threshold. Enders and Siklos (2001) perform a financial application (the term structure of interest rates in the United States) with two cases: one with $\tau = 0$ and the other with τ being unknown. Their results showed that the power of the MTAR test was superior and is showed that the federal funds rate and the 10-year yield on government bonds were cointegrated, something that was not confirmed with the TAR test approach.

Flashback: What's a heaviside indicator?

The Heaviside indicator function, usually denoted by H, is a discontinuous function, named after - Oliver Heaviside (1850–1925), whose value is zero for negative arguments and one for positive arguments. The function was first developed in operational calculus for the solution of differential equations, where it signaled a function switch on at a specified time that remained on indefinitely (Davies, 2002).

Case study 8: The value of the US dollar and its impact on oil prices

This study investigates the relationship between real oil price (WTI and Brent) and the US real effective exchange rate (REER). The employed method addresses asymmetric cointegration with structural breaks using a TAR and an MTAR model. Cointegration is evident with significant asymmetric error correction adjustments, and the REER appears to be slightly exogenous in this relationship (McLeod and Haughton, 2018). They use monthly data from January 1995 to June 2016 on consumer price index, the monthly World Texas Intermediate (WTI) crude oil spot price, and the monthly global Brent crude oil spot price. The selection of the two oil indexes was done due to robustness considerations.

Based on results from the earlier table (Table 11), cointegration is confirmed in both panels, namely, for both the WTI-REER and the Brent-REER relationships in both TAR and MTAR model configurations. In the first panel, cointegration in the TAR model is found through the rejection of the null hypothesis ($H_0: \rho^+ = \rho^- = 0$), which represents the no-cointegration hypothesis. This is shown by all significant statistics at 5% level of significance. The same applies for the MTAR configuration. However, we observe that the F test is not significant at 5%, which constitutes evidence for asymmetry (the hypothesis of symmetry is rejected). Almost similar results can be found for the Brent model in Panel B. In this case the asymmetry is evidenced at 10% level of significance. According to McLeod and Haughton (2018), as far as the estimated threshold values for both equations are concerned, these are reasonable estimates due to their proximity to zero.

Table 11 Asymmetric cointegration tests.

	τ	ρ^+	ρ^-	Φ_μ^*	t-max	F-equal
Panel A: WTI-USREER						
TAR (3)	−0.064	−0.145* (0.049)	−0.224* (0.052)	12.086*	−2.982*	1.414
MTAR (3)	−0.026	−0.100* (0.045)	−0.314* (0.057)	16.575*	−2.208*	9.642*

Table 11 Asymmetric cointegration tests—cont'd

	τ	ρ^+	ρ^-	Φ_μ^*	t-max	F-equal
Panel B: Brent-USREER						
TAR (3)	−0.032	−0.136 (0.044)	−0.200* (0.055)	10.452*	−3.101*	0.926
MTAR (7)	0.009	−0.018 (0.065)	−0.212* (0.046)	10.965*	−0.279	7.253**

Notes: ρ^+ and ρ^- are the asymmetric adjustment coefficients, τ is the optimum threshold, Φ_μ^* is the test statistic for the null hypothesis of no cointegration (H_0: $\rho^+=\rho^-=0$), and F-equal is the test statistic for the null hypothesis of symmetry (H_0: $\rho^+=\rho^-$). t-max is the secondary (less powerful) test of cointegration. Numbers in brackets are standard errors. Numbers in brackets in the first column represent the chosen lag lengths. One asterisk and two asterisks denote statistical significance at the 5% and 10% level, respectively, using Monte Carlo simulations with 10,000 repetitions.

Modified from McLeod, R.C.D., Haughton, A.Y., 2018. The value of the US dollar and its impact on oil prices: evidence from a non-linear asymmetric cointegration approach. Energy Econ. 70, 61–69.

3.5 Sparse cointegration

Sparse estimation means that some of the cointegrating vectors are estimated to be exactly zero. This method is applicable in high dimensional settings where the data span is short, but the number of the series is large (Wilms and Croux, 2016). These data sets are usually attractive, because they can be found for free in the Internet. Also, some other methods, such as the Johansen cointegration, cannot be applied in cases where the number of series exceeds their data span.

The method is relied on a penalized negative log-likelihood. Without the penalties the objective function is the one applicable in the Johansen cointegration. Thus the objective function in the penalized case can be written as in Eq. (25):

$$L(\Gamma, \Pi, \Omega) = \frac{1}{T} tr\left((\Delta Y - \Delta Y_L \Gamma - Y\Pi') \times \Omega (\Delta Y - \Delta Y_L \Gamma - Y\Pi')'\right) - \log|\Omega| + \lambda_1 P_1(\beta)$$
$$+ \lambda_2 P_2(\Gamma) + \lambda_3 P_3(\Omega)$$

$$(25)$$

The following notation applies for Eq. (25):

tr(.) is the trace

$$\Omega = \Sigma^{-1}$$

P_1, P_2, P_3 are three penalty functions

$$P_1(\beta) = \sum_{i=1}^{q} \sum_{j=1}^{r} |\beta_{ij}|$$

Γ stands for the short-run effects.

In the earlier objective function, the aim is to select Γ, Π, Ω so as to minimize Eq. (20) subject to the constraint $\Pi = \alpha\beta'$, with a and β are $q*r$ matrices of full column rank r. The normalization $a'\Omega a = Ir$ is imposed for identifiability purposes. The method may suffer from multicollinearity and interpretation issues, but in the simulation made by Wilms and Croux (2016), it has outperfomed the conventional Johansen cointegration method.

3.6 Another nonlinear cointegration application

While having seen much of that already, an interesting definition about nonlinear cointegration is the following: If two or more series are of extended memory (i.e., its information does not decay through time) but a nonlinear transformation of them is short memory, then the series are said to be nonlinearly cointegrated (Escanciano and Escribano, 2009). Or, in a more classical way, we can say that two series are nonlinearly cointegrated, if there is a nonlinear function of them that is stationary. Since nonlinearity is closely related to nonstationarity but there are difficulties in studying them together, the concepts of long memory and short memory have been inserted into the discussion. In this subsection the homoskedastic nonlinear cointegration is presented as a special case.

3.6.1 The homoskedastic nonlinear cointegration

Zolna et al. (2016) use an adapted Breusch-Pagan test to test the presence of heteroskedasticity in the cointegration residuals received from nonlinear cointegration in a case study of structural health monitoring. Thus, if there is a nonlinear cointegration relationship described as in Eq. (26):

$$z_t = f(x_t) - y_t \tag{26}$$

$x_t, y_t =$ the two series.

$z_t =$ residual becomes an approximate zero series, then z_t turns into the modified cointegration residual that is approximately zero mean and homoskedastic as shown in Eq. (27)

$$z_t^* = \frac{f(x_t) - y_t}{\sqrt{1 + [f'(x_t)]^2}} \tag{27}$$

The adapted Breush-Pagan test proposed by Zolna et al. (2016) entails an auxiliary regression as in Eq. (28):

$$[\varepsilon_t - E(\varepsilon_t)]^2 = \beta_0 + \beta_1 y_t + \text{error} \tag{28}$$

If the bracketed term on the left is independent of y on the right, residuals are homoskedastic with respect to y. For more on this implementation, the interested reader is referred to the quite interesting paper by Zolna et al. (2016).

3.7 The Bayer and Hanck's cointegration

It combines the tests of Engle and Granger and Johansen, the error correction f-test of (Boswijk (1994)) and the error correction t-test of (Banerjee et al. (1998)). It requires all the variables having the same order of integration equal to one. We will not expand further on the test, which is based on Fisher's equation, and it is presented with sufficient detail in Chapter 2.

---

4 Conclusion

Quite often, energy-growth nexus researchers are confronted with methods they are not familiar with. New doctoral offsprings are sometimes specialized in a limited number of methods while working and writing their doctoral thesis. Thus it is useful to have a quick reference guide, when encountering a new cointegration method for the first time. Most importantly, it is useful to have that in a brief, quick, and simple enough form for the novice to understand. This is the purpose not only of this book but also of this chapter too in respect to the topic its title declares to be handling: cointegration methods.

Overall, this chapter had dealt with a detailed presentation of Johansen cointegration with various applications. On the other side of this method is the ARDL method, and they are very often used together in research papers to corroborate study findings.

An interesting fact remains that while many new approaches have been in the meanwhile developed that claim to be addressing the handicaps of the Johansen method, the method is still among the most preferred one among researchers.

The rest of the cointegration methods that are briefly presented in this chapter are as follows:

- the Johansen Fisher panel cointegration,
- the modified Johansen cointegration for small samples,
- the Gregory-Hansen,
- the Hatemi-J
- the continuously updated fully modified estimation,
- the momentum threshold autoregressive with breaks method,
- the threshold autoregressive method,
- the threshold cointegration method,
- the sparse cointegration method,
- the homoskedatsic nonlinear cointegration method,
- the Bayer and Hanck cointegration method.

Most importantly the chapter hosts indicative case studies that besides these methods also employ various steps and twists that are rarely included in full and in sufficient detail, and thus they leave junior researchers puzzled with the series of steps that must be followed and the best-practice examples that need to be followed to receive the least possible number of negative comments by journal reviewers due to the obscure aspects they leave. This chapter also suggests the steps that need to be taken before the Johansen method takes place and the steps that should be taken afterward with respect to causality investigation and robust analysis. Foremost the paper explains why researchers could still use the Johansen method instead of the newer ARDL method, depending on the research context.

References

Bai, J., Kao, C., 2006. On the estimation and inference of a panel cointegration model with cross-sectional dependence. In: Baltagi, B.H. (Ed.), Panel Data Econometrics: Theoretical Contributions and Empirical Applications. Elsevier Science, Amsterdam, pp. 3–30.

Bai, J., Kao, C., Ng, S., 2009. Panel cointegration with global stochastic trends. J. Econ. 149, 82–99.

Banerjee, A., Dolado, J.J., Mestre, R., 1998. Error-correction mechanism tests for cointegration in a single-equation framework. J. Time Ser. Anal. 19, 267–283.

Belke, A., Dobnik, F., Dreger, C., 2011. Energy consumption and economic growth: new insights into the cointegration relationship. Energy Econ. 33, 782–789.

Belloumi, M., 2009. Energy consumption and GDP in Tunisia: cointegration and causality analysis. Energy Policy 37, 2745–2753.

Bondia, R., Ghosh, S., Kanjilal, K., 2016. International crude oil prices and the stock prices of clean energy and technology companies: evidence from non-linear cointegration tests with unknown structural breaks. Energy 101, 558–565.

Boswijk, H.P., 1994. Testing for an unstable root in conditional and structural error correction models. J. Econom. 63, 37–60.

Cheung, Y., Lai, K., 1993. Finite-sample sizes of Johansen's likelihood ratio tests for co-integration. Oxf. Bull. Econ. Stat. 55 (3), 313–328.

Davies, B., 2002. "Heaviside Step Function". Integral Transforms and their Applications, third ed. Springer, p. 369.

Dickey, D., Fuller, W., 1979. Distribution of the estimators for autoregressive time series with a unit-root. J. Am. Stat. Assoc. 74, 427–431.

Enders, W., Siklos, P., 2001. Cointegration and threshold adjustment. J. Bus. Econ. Stat. 19, 166–176.

Engle, R.F., Granger, C.W.J., 1987. Cointegration and error correction: representation, estimation and testing. Econometrica 55, 251–276.

Escanciano, J.C., Escribano, A., 2009. Econometrics: nonlinear cointegration. In: Encyclopedia of Complexity and Systems Science. Springer, Berlin, Germany, pp. 2757–2769.

Esso, L.J., 2010. Threshold cointegration and causality relationship between energy use and growth in seven african countries. Energy Econ. 32, 1383–1391.

Fang, Z., Chang, Y., 2016. Energy, human capital and economic growth in asia pacific countries—evidence from a panel cointegration and causality analysis. Energy Econ. 56, 177–184.

Gregory, A.W., Hansen, B.E., 1996. Residual-based tests for cointegration in models with regime shifts. J. Econ. 70, 99–126.

Gunduz, L., Hatemi-J, A., 2005. Is the tourism-led growth hypothesis valid for Turkey? Appl. Econ. Lett. 12, 499–504.

Hansen, B.E., 1992. Tests for parameter instability in regressions with I(1) processes. J. Bus. Econ. Stat. 10, 321–335.

Hatemi-J, A., 2008. Tests for cointegration with two unknown regime shifts with an application to financial market integration. Empir. Econ. 35, 497–505.

Johansen, S., 1988. Statistical analysis of cointegration vectors. J. Econ. Dyn. Control 12, 231–254.

Johansen, S., Juselius, K., 1990. Maximum likelihood estimation and inference on cointegration—with applications to the demand for money. Oxf. Bull. Econ. Stat. 52, 169–210.

Kao, C., 1999. Spurious regression and residual-based tests for cointegration in panel data. J. Econ. 90, 1–44.

Kao, C., Chiang, M.-H., 2001. On the estimation and inference of a cointegrated regression in panel data. In: Baltagi, B.H., Fomby, T.B., Carter Hill, R. (Eds.), Nonstationary Panels, Panel Cointegration, and Dynamic Panels (Advances in Econometrics). vol. 15. Emerald Group Publishing Limited, Bingley, pp. 179–222. https://doi.org/10.1016/S0731-9053 (00)15007-8.

Katircioglu, S.T., 2009. Revisiting the tourism-led-growth hypothesis for Turkey using the bounds test and johansen approach for cointegration. Tour. Manag. 30, 17–20.

Mackinnon, J.G., Haug, A.A., Michelis, L., 1999. Numerical distribution functions of likelihood ratio tests for cointegration. J. Appl. Economet. 14, 563–577.

Maddala, G.S., Wu, S., 2001. A comparative study of unit root tests with panel data and a new simple test. Oxf. Bull. Econ. Stat. 61, 631–652.

McLeod, R.C.D., Haughton, A.Y., 2018. The value of the us dollar and its impact on oil prices: evidence from a non-linear asymmetric cointegration approach. Energy Econ. 70, 61–69.

Naser, H., 2015. Analysing the long-run relationship among oil market, nuclear energy consumption, and economic growth: an evidence from emerging economies. Energy 89, 421–434.

Ongan, S., Demiröz, D.M., 2005. The contribution of tourism to the long-run turkish economic growth. Ekonomicky casopis 53, 880–894.

Pedroni, P., 2000. Fully modified OLS for heterogeneous cointegrated panels. Adv. Econom., 93–130.

Pedroni, P., 2001. Critical values for cointegration tests in heterogeneous panels with multiple regressors. Oxf. Bull. Econ. Stat. 61, 653–670.

Perron, P., 1989. The great crash, the oil price shock and the unit root hypothesis. Econometrica 57 (6), 1361–1401.

Persyn, D., Westerlund, J., 2008. Error-correction-based cointegration tests for panel data. Stata J. 8 (2), 232–241.

Phillips, P.C.B., Ouliaris, S., 1990. Asymptotic properties of residual based tests of cointegration. Econometrica 58, 165–193.

Phillips, P.C.B., Perron, P., 1988. Testing for a unit root in time series regression. Biometrika 75, 335–346.

Pindyck, R.S., Rubinfeld, D.L., 1991. Models and Economic Forecasts. Mcgraw-Hill Inc.

Quedraogo, N.S., 2013. Energy consumption and human development: evidence from a panel cointegration and error correction model. Energy 63, 28–41.

Reimers, H.E., 1992. Comparisons of tests for multivariate cointegration. Stat. Pap. 33, 335–359.

Reinsel, G.C., Ahn, S.K., 1992. Vector autoregressive models with unit roots and reduced rank structure: estimation. Likelihood ratio test, and forecasting. J. Time Ser. Anal. 13, 353–375.

Westerlund, J., 2007. Testing for error correction in panel data. Oxf. Bull. Econ. Stat. 69, 709–748.

Wilms, I., Croux, C., 2016. Forecasting using sparse cointegration. Int. J. Forecast. 32, 1256–1267.

Zolna, K., Dao, P.B., Staszewski, W.J., Barszcz, T., 2016. Towards homoscedastic nonlinear cointegration for structural health monitoring. Mech. Syst. Signal Process. 75, 94–108.

Zoundi, Z., 2017. CO_2 emissions, renewable energy and the environmental kuznets curve, a panel cointegration approach. Renew. Sustain. Energy Rev. 72, 1067–1075.

How does the wavelet approach satisfy the required deliverables in the energy-growth nexus studies?

11

1 Introduction

Quite often, readers of energy-growth papers encounter new methodologies to which they are not much acquainted, because they are not mainstreamed. Some of them are interdisciplinary, and they are borrowed from other sciences. In everyday research life, it happens than not all researchers master the same econometric methods. Of course, it is never too late to learn and even master a new method. But before mastering a method, it is useful that readers can read and understand these papers that also happen to be using strange nomenclature and terminologies. One such new method in the energy-growth nexus and the broader "X-growth" nexus is the wavelet approach. Irrespective of whether an energy-growth researcher plans to use the wavelet method itself, one must be able to read and understand their results and the messages they convey for policy making.

Trying to decipher unknown nomenclature can be very tedious when one has limited time. Usually, students and researchers read the literature to find out what novelties go on and how they could contribute something new themselves. Thus understanding the various new method papers appearing on databases is crucial, and when this understanding is prevented from happening because of a cumbersome nomenclature and terminology, this can be very frustrating. In those moments, researchers need somebody to put them quickly into the cadre. Explain them the story in a few, succinct words. This is the main and primary purpose of this chapter. The secondary purpose of the chapter is to pose new challenges to the already established researchers in the field and the wavelet method and give them a few hints on how this method looks like from the outside, what would the uninitiated reader need to know to read their wavelet method paper easily, and how should the wavelet method experienced author in the energy-growth nexus write, to make one's paper more readable. Making one's paper more readable, not only increases citations but also reduces the workload when the paper is under review in a journal or other publication outlet.

Therefore this chapter adopts an illustrative purpose and structure and starts with a down-to-earth explanation and presentation of the method, appropriate for social sciences and researchers with no strong mathematical background. Therefore it

219

A Guide to Econometric Methods for the Energy-Growth Nexus. https://doi.org/10.1016/B978-0-12-819039-5.00003-3

presents the gist of most nomenclature in the section that follows (Section 2) and then continues with indicative and diverse case studies (Section 3), discussion first of the way the method is applied and second the way it should be applied in the energy-growth nexus field (Section 4), and a conclusion (Section 5).

2 Basic methodology and nomenclature in the standard wavelet procedure: A survival map

This section deals with a brief but all inclusive presentation of the basic tools and methods in the wavelet approach. Researchers can use it as a first needed toolkit when they first encounter the method or as reference pages to refresh their existing knowledge.

The wavelet approach has strong roots and connections with physics and engineering.

The word "wavelet" refers to a wavelike oscillation (Picture 1). The oscillation begins from a zero position, increases, and then through backward movement returns to the initial zero position. If there is an unknown signal (from random perturbation), the wavelet will eventually correlate with the signal, if they happen to have the same frequency. This is the reason correlation finds itself at the heart of wavelet methodology. The Fourier transform can be seen as a special category of the continuous wavelet transform. If wavelets are compared with sine waves, we get Fourier transforms (MathWorks, 2019). However, the Fourier transform converts the time series into a frequency domain, but says nothing about location and time. As a result of that, the Fourier transform says which frequencies are present, but does not say when they occur (Tangborn, 2019).

The wavelet is a mathematical function which can divide a function (a signal) into different scale components. The best and more easily grasped definition I have

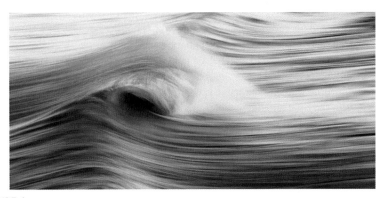

PICTURE 1

A wavelet is like a wavelike oscillation.

Courtesy: http:/Pixabay.com, code 1905610.

encountered is by Graps (1995): "Wavelets are mathematical functions that cut up data into different frequency components, and then study each component with a resolution matched to its scale."

Next, three figures by Tangborn represent schematically the differences among an original signal (data series) in Fig. 1, the Fourier Transform in Fig. 2, and the wavelet transform in Fig. 3. One can describe the original signal in Fig. 1 as different frequencies located across time in a static way (vertical lines go down the time axis). The Fourier transform is represented in Fig. 2 as horizontal distributions across time, and this reveals the dynamic nature of this representation. The wavelet transform in Fig. 3 has both vertical and horizontal lines with respect to the time axis, and the vertical lines define even smaller divisions and subdivisions as if one is trying to observe what is going on in them through a magnifying glass.

In essence the wavelet methodology deals with transforming a time series into a time-frequency space, whereby the researcher can observe the time series both in respect of time and frequency and this makes a very comprehensive visualization of the evolution of the time series. The evolution takes place in:

Low frequency bands → Long-term horizon
High frequency bands → Short-term horizon

The method performs well both with stationary and nonstationary time series, as well as when breaks are present. This is because the method allows for a decomposition of all the periodic characteristics of the time series to be a function of time (this element means that unit root analysis is not a prerequisite in these studies). Furthermore, the

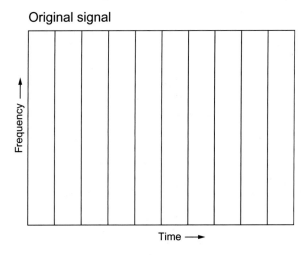

FIG. 1

Representation of an original signal.

Reproduced from Tangborn, A., 2019. Wavelet Transforms in Time Series Analysis, Global Modeling and Assimilation Office, Goddard Space Flight Center, Available from: https:/www.atmos.umd.edu/~ekalnay/syllabi/ AOSC630/Wavelets_2010.pdf. (Accessed 18 August 2019).

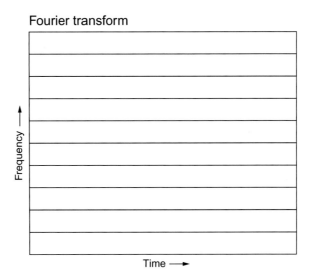

FIG. 2

Representation of the Fourier transform.

Reproduced from Tangborn, A., 2019. Wavelet Transforms in Time Series Analysis, Global Modeling and Assimilation Office, Goddard Space Flight Center, Available from: https:/www.atmos.umd.edu/~ekalnay/syllabi/ AOSC630/Wavelets_2010.pdf. (Accessed 18 August 2019).

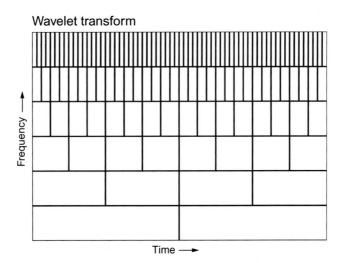

FIG. 3

Representation of the wavelet transform.

Reproduced from Tangborn, A., 2019. Wavelet Transforms in Time Series Analysis, Global Modeling and Assimilation Office, Goddard Space Flight Center, Available from: https:/www.atmos.umd.edu/~ekalnay/syllabi/ AOSC630/Wavelets_2010.pdf. (Accessed 18 August 2019).

method of wavelets consists in "dilation" and "translation" of a pair of "mother" and "father" wavelet functions, which are represented as Eqs. (1), (2), respectively:

$$\int \varphi(t)dt = 1 \text{ with } \varphi_{j,k}(t) = 2^{j/2} \varphi \left(2^j t - k\right) \tag{1}$$

$$\int \psi(t)dt = 0 \text{ with } \psi_{j,k}(t) = 2^{j/2} \psi \left(2^j t - k\right) \tag{2}$$

Wavelet "fathers" approximate the smooth components of a series, while wavelet "mothers" approximate the noise components. The main purpose of the mother wavelet is to provide a source function to generate the daughter wavelets (translated and scaled versions of the mother wavelet). The main purpose of the father wavelet is the scaling in the time domain. A father wavelet reconstructs the low-frequency component of the series and integrates to unity. The mother wavelet represents short-run variation from the trend and integrates to zero (Ha et al., 2018).

The following notation applies for the Eqs. (1), (2):

$j = 1, 2, \dots J$ stands for the scale.
$k = 1, \dots 2^j$ stands for the translation.

$f(t)$ is the signal (series), and this can be written as:

$$f(t) = \sum_k S_{j,k} \varphi_{j,k}(t) + \sum_k d_{j,k} \psi_{j,k}(t) + \sum_k d_{j-1,k} \psi_{j-1,k}(t) + \dots + \sum_k d_{1,k} \psi_{1,k}(t) \tag{3}$$

Additional notation for Eq. (3) is provided as follow:

$\varphi_{j, k}$ = the scaled version of φ
$\psi_{j, k}$ = the translated version of ψ
$S_{j, k}$ = the smooth coefficient
$d_{j, k}$ = the detailed coefficient

High dilation entails larger stretching of the wavelet, and this enables the visualization of lower frequencies (the long-run horizon).

2.1 The wavelet continuous transform

The wavelets can be divided into continuous and discrete versions. The former is in most frequent use than the latter. The continuous wavelets also divided into real values and complex valued ones. In few words the continuous wavelet function is a signal representation with the translation and scale parameters of the wavelet varying continuously. The continuous wavelet transform of a function $x(t)$, at scale a, with $a > 0$ and translation value b (a real number) is expressed with an integral of the following type (Eq. 4):

$$X_w(a, b) = \frac{1}{|a|^{1/2}} \int_{-\infty}^{+\infty} x(t) \overline{\psi} \left(\frac{t-b}{a}\right) dt \tag{4}$$

The following additional notation applies for the Eq. (4):

ψ = a continuous function and the mother wavelet.
x = the signal.
X = the processed signal.
α = the scale (equal to the size of the window).
b = the translation.

In the continuous wavelet transform, one can set the scale and translation in an arbitrary way (Ryan, 2019). To explain how translation works, we need to insert the term "window" into this presentation. A larger "window" refers to low frequency. A smaller "window" refers to high frequency. Next the "translation" refers to how far we open the window from its initial point. The window ranges over the length of the input signal. Overall, windowing refers to a type of weighting that gives less emphasis and weight to the interval's endpoints than in the middle. The effect of the "window" is to localize the signal in time (Graps 1995).

2.2 The cross-wavelet transform

The cross-wavelet transform is in fact a correlation formula that provides information about the association of two random variables at different time scales. This function captures the local covariance of two time series in each frequency. It is shown in Eq. (5) (Jammazi and Aloui, 2015):

$$D\left(\frac{\left|W_n^X(s)W_n^{Y*}(s)\right|}{\sigma_X \sigma_Y} < p\right) = \frac{Z_\nu(p)}{\nu}\sqrt{P_k^X P_k^Y} \tag{5}$$

The following additional notation applies for Eq. (5):

σ_X = standard deviation of x.
σ_Y = standard deviation of y.
$Z_\nu(p)$ = the confidence interval related to the probability p for a probability density function defined by the square root of the product of two χ^2 distributions.

2.3 Multiple and partial wavelet coherence ratio transforms

The multiple and partial wavelet coherence functions are more rarely used. Nevertheless, they are worthy of including them in the current guide pages. In this version, they have been sourced from Bilgili (2015) as Eqs. (6), (7).

$$R_{1(23...p)}^2 = 1 - \frac{\gamma^d}{S_{11}\gamma_{11}^d} \tag{6}$$

$$\sigma_{1j.qj} = -\frac{\gamma_{j1}^d}{\left(\gamma_{11}^d \gamma_{jj}^d\right)^{\frac{1}{2}}} \tag{7}$$

The following additional notation applies for Eqs. (6), (7):

$R^2_{1(23\ldots p)}$ = squared multiple wavelet coherence.
γ^d = determinant of γ.
$\sigma_{1j.\ qj}$ = complex partial wavelet function.

2.4 The wavelet power spectrum

The wavelet power spectrum measures the local variance of each variable. The distribution of a local power spectrum can be written as shown in Eq. (8):

$$D\left(\frac{\left|W^X_t(s)\right|^2}{\sigma^2_X} < p\right) \rightarrow \frac{1}{2}P_f \chi^2_v \tag{8}$$

The following additional notation applies for Eq. (8):

t = time
s = scale
P_f = the mean spectrum at the Fourier frequency f that corresponds to the wavelet scale s.
v assumes the value 1 or 2 for real or complex wavelets.
δ^2_χ = the variance of the corresponding variable.

2.5 The wavelet coherence ratio transform

The wavelet coherence ration transform is defined as the localized correlation coefficient between the series in a time-frequency space. This is computed as shown in Eq. (9):

$$R^2(u, s) = \frac{\left|S\left(s^{-1}W_{xy}(u, s)\right)\right|^2}{S\left(s^{-1}|W_x(u, s)|^2 S\left(s^{-1}|W_y(u, s)|^2\right)\right)} \tag{9}$$

The following additional notation applies for Eq. (9):
S = the smoothing parameter with $0 \le R^2(u,s) \le 1$. A value equal to 1 indicates perfect correlation, while a value equal to zero indicates no correlation.

2.6 The phase of the wavelet coherence

The phase of the wavelet allows examining the lead-lag relations between the variables at the different frequencies. The phase is defined as shown in Eq. (10) (Uddin et al., 2018):

$$\theta_{\varepsilon\tau}(o, u) = \tan^{-1}\left(\frac{Z\{Q(\varepsilon^{-1}W_{\varepsilon,\tau}(o, u))\}}{R\{Q((\varepsilon^{-1}W_{\varepsilon,\tau}(o, u)))\}}\right) \tag{10}$$

The following additional notation and conditions apply for Eq. (10):

Z = the imaginary parts of the wavelet coefficients.

R = the real parts of the wavelet coefficients.

When $\theta_{\varepsilon\tau}(o,u) = 0$, the series move together at time and frequency.

When $\theta_{\varepsilon\tau}(o,u) \in (0, \frac{\pi}{2})$, the series move in phase, but variable $o(t)$ leads $u(t)$.

When $\theta_{\varepsilon\tau}(o,u) \in (-\frac{\pi}{2}, 0)$, the series move in phase, but variable $u(t)$ leads $o(t)$.

A phase difference of π or $-\pi$ denotes a negative relationship between the variables, namely,

When $\theta_{\varepsilon\tau}(o,u) \in (\frac{\pi}{2}, \pi)$, the series move in antiphase and variable $u(t)$ leads $o(t)$. The opposite holds when $\theta_{\varepsilon\tau}(o,u) \in (-\pi, -\frac{\pi}{2})$.

2.7 The most common wavelet functions

It is useful to have the most frequently used wavelet functions gathered in these guide and reference pages. Thus the most common wavelet function types in literature are the following (Bilgili, 2015):

(i) Morlet wavelet function:

$$\psi_M = \pi^{\frac{-1}{4}} e^{iw_0 n} e^{\frac{-n^2}{2}} \tag{11}$$

(ii) Paul wavelet function:

$$\psi_\rho = \frac{2^m i^m m!}{\sqrt{\pi(2m)!}} (1 - in)^{-(m+1)} \tag{12}$$

(iii) Derivative of Gaussian function:

$$\psi_{DOD} = \frac{-1(m+1)}{\sqrt{\Gamma(m+{}^1/_2)}} \frac{d^m}{dn^m} \left(e^{-n^2/2}\right) \tag{13}$$

The following additional notation applies for Eqs. (12), (13):

π = pi number
e = exponential
i = imaginary complex number
w_0 = frequency parameter
n = time parameter
γ = parameter gamma
d = derivative

$m = \text{order}$

$m! = 1*2*\ldots*m$

2.8 The maximal overlap discrete wavelet transform

The maximal overlap discrete wavelet transform (MODWT) can be found in literature mainly as the time-invariant version of the wavelet analysis. Among many other abilities, it can handle any type of series, not only the dyadic ones, offers higher resolution at condensed scales, and offers asymptotically efficient variance estimators. This transform adds new qualities to the standard discrete wavelet analysis. Conversely to up-to-date literature where the decomposition of time occurs in a subjective way, in this version, the decomposition occurs via the minimization of Shannon entropy criterion (Uddin et al., 2018). Also the MODWT can be applied to any sample size, while the conventional discrete wavelet transform (DWT) can be applied only to samples that are multiples of 2^j. Last the MODWT is invariant to time shifts, and thus a time shift does not cause any changes to the coefficients of the function. The MODWT is written as shown in Eqs. (14), (15) (Ha et al., 2018):

$$w_{j,t} = \sum_{l=0}^{L=1} \omega_{j,i} X_{t-l \bmod N} \tag{14}$$

and

$$v_{j,t} = \sum_{l=0}^{L=1} \delta_{j,l} X_{t-l \bmod N} \tag{15}$$

The following additional notation applies for Eqs. (14), (15):

$v_{j,\,t} =$ the scaling coefficient.
$w_{j,\,t} =$ the detail coefficient.
$\omega_l =$ rescaled father wavelet filter obtained by scaling its DWT respective parameter with $1/_{2^{j/2}}$.
$\delta_l =$ rescaled mother wavelet filter obtained by scaling its DWT respective parameter with $1/_{2^{j/2}}$
$\chi_t =$ the original time series

At this point the reader has been acquainted with the basic roles played by different tools and functions in wavelet analysis. The presentation is extensive, but other tool variations also exist. Readers should not be frustrated by this, because the reported base is sufficient enough to facilitate the understanding of any additional variations that the creativity and imagination of field researchers might generate. Section 3 will continue with recent indicative literature examples.

3 The employment of the wavelet approach in indicative energy-growth nexus case studies

Case study 1: The energy-growth nexus in Saudi Arabia with a wavelet approach

This study employs the wavelet approach (they call it a wavelet windowed correlation function) to study the information on the fluctuation of the cross-correlation intensity across time and frequency, something that the conventional Granger causality framework cannot offer.

Therefore, they employ a 1980–2013 dataset on six Persian Gulf countries, namely, Saudi Arabia, United Arab Emirates, Oman, Bahrain, Qatar, and Kuwait. Their data have been sourced from the International Energy Agency, the Bloomberg database, and the World Development Indicators of the World Bank. They estimate a maximum level of decomposition equal to 3: thus the first level of variation occurs between 1 and 2 years, the second at 4 and 8 years, and the third at 8 and 16 years. They find that GDP is stable in the long run (8–16 years horizon), less stable in the mid run (4–8 years), and instable in the short run (1–2 years horizon). The authors, in their window cross correlation version, have first analyzed the interactions between energy consumption and carbon dioxide emissions and then the interactions of GDP with energy consumption with a 5-year reference length time and a 10-year lag (front lag or back lag).

One advantage of the method is that no time is spent on unit root analysis. Researchers usually engage into tedious work with different competing unit root tests. This is avoided in wavelet analysis because this method can handle all types of data irregularities: policy shifts, shocks, asymmetries, nonlinearities, heavy tailness, extreme values, roughness, drifts, spikes, and other noise types.

One drawback in this method is that one has to visually observe the correlations in every detail and decide which variable leads the other in each of the time horizons that have been decided at the beginning of the study. This is very cumbersome and can lead to mistakes and objective judgments. The study results can be summarized as follows:

(1) Technologies in the gulf countries have reached a maximum point of performance, and the same technologies can no longer reduce the carbon emissions.

(2) Nevertheless, in the short run, the gulf countries seem to have adopted cleaner technologies, because the economic activity is not correlated with the carbon emissions. This is attributed to reuse and recycling procedures that have been adopted by those countries.

(3) A bidirectional and rather homogeneous relationship is observed between energy consumption and economic growth for all gulf countries.
(4) Evidence of the Environmental Kuznets curve hypothesis is also strongly supported for these countries.

Policy implication and recommendation in this study: The gulf countries are intense energy consumers and emission producers. They need to engage in air pollution control and energy efficiency actions. Awake environmental consciousness to citizens so that their increased income can be directed on best practice energy consumption, also in the transport sector. Industries should invest on research and development and transform their infrastructures and functioning to a more environmental friendly one.

Reproduced from Jammazi, R., Aloui, C., 2015. Environmental degradation, economic growth and energy consumption nexus: a wavelet-windowed cross correlation approach. Physica A 436, 110–125.

Case study 2: Electricity generation and industrial production in Singapore
Sharif et al. (2017) study the electricity-growth nexus in Singapore with the wavelet approach: They employ the continuous wavelet transform, the cross-wavelet transform, and the wavelet coherence ratio transform. They employ monthly data from January 1983 to January 2016 of electricity generation and the industrial production index (both sourced from the Department of Statistics of Singapore). The authors first use the ARDL approach as well as the Johansen-Juselius approach for corroboration of their findings, and they find significant long-run relationships. Also, they perform unit root test analysis, because they employ first the latter two methods, whereby unit root investigation is essential and necessary. Thus, this study performs the cointegration analysis with conventional methods but continues with both a long-run and short-run investigation of the causality with the wavelet procedure (wavelet coherence).

The variables were decomposed into six scale domains ranging low to high frequencies, namely, short-run to the long-run horizon. Those scale domains are 2–4 months, 4–8 months, 8–16 months, 16–32 months, 32–64 months, and 64–128 months.

Their results can be summarized as follows:

(1) Both energy generation and the industrial production are characterized by drifts and spikes. The most abrupt changes occur between 2 and 4 months for the industrial production and 2 and 8 months for the energy generation.
(2) The short lived sudden changes between 1987 and 1999 may imply strong positive comovements for the electricity and industry in Singapore. Similar comovements occurred between 1999 and 2003 and 2011 and 2015.

(3) A middle-run horizon unidirectional causality appears to have taken place with the rising electricity demand having caused economic growth. This phenomenon has repeated itself in 2003–07 and 2011–15.

(4) This middle run horizon situation is interrupted by two short intervals between 1999–2003 and 2007–11, which coincide with the dot com crisis and the global financial crisis. Such detailed information is useful to know for investors, since this gives the opportunity for the generation of abnormal gains.

(5) Strong positive comovement is observed starting from 1999, which can be attributed to global market alignment.

Policy implication and recommendation in this study: According to the authors of this study, electricity is a main driver of economic growth in Singapore. Government of Singapore should enhance investment in the electricity generation technologies and strengthen partnerships between the public and the private sector. Also the government might also start microfinance proposals for hydroenergy and bioenergy production.

Reproduced from Sharif, A., Jammazi, R., Raza, S.A., Shahzad, S.J.H., 2017. Electricity and growth nexus dynamics in Singapore: fresh insights based on wavelet approach. Energy Policy 110, 686–692.

Case study 3: A sectoral energy-growth nexus in the United States

Ben-Salha et al. (2018) use aggregate and disaggregate quarterly data from the first quarter of 2005 to the third quarter of 2015 to study the sectoral energy growth nexus by energy source in the United States. The energy sources are coal, natural gas, petroleum, nonrenewable, nuclear (expressed in trillion Btu), and electricity (expressed in million Kilowatt-hours). These data have been sourced from US Energy Information Administration. The sectors are industry, transport, commercial, and residential. They employ three variants of the wavelet approach, namely, the continuous wavelet methodology, the wavelet power spectrum, and the wavelet coherence. The authors state that it is important to study and compare aggregate and disaggregate results (among other reasons) due to the Simpson's paradox, according to which coevolutions may be hidden at the aggregate level, while they may become evident in the disaggregate level. However, one cannot oversee the fact that there are great disparities between energy sources and sectors.

The aggregate analysis results:

(1) The consumption of all energy types has comovements with real output.

(2) The growth period is supported for both the renewable energy consumption and the nonrenewable energy consumption.

(3) When investigating disaggregated forms of energy, the study finds that only natural gas has comovements with real output.

(4) In the existence of comovement between nuclear energy and electricity consumption and real output, no clear result is reached about the direction. This can be considered a drawback of the method that despite the clear indication of comovement, direction cannot necessarily be decided.

The disaggregate analysis results:

(1) The relationship between energy sources and the added value of the sectors (which is a proxy for the respective part of real output they produce) is not stable.

(2) Between 2011 and 2014, there is high comovement for natural gas, electricity, and transport-added value, and the latter is found to lead the energy use.

(3) In the industrial sector, the value added is generally lagging energy consumption.

(4) In the commercial sector, there is moderate comovement between coal consumption, natural gas consumption, and the added value of the sector. Higher coherence is identified for electricity consumption in the long run.

(5) In the residential sector, similar patterns are found with the commercial sector. Stronger patterns are found in the long run between 2007 and 2011.

Policy implication and recommendation in this study: Given the variety of results among the different sectors, policy makers should design policies for each sector separately and not at an economy wide level. The economy of the United States relies heavily on fossil energy and hence contributes significantly to greenhouse emission generation. Thus energy conservation will withhold the economy in general.

Reproduced from Ben-Salha O., Hkiri, B., Aloui, C., 2018. Sectoral energy consumption by source and output in the US: new evidence from wavelet-based approach. Energy Econ. 72, 75–96.

Case study 4: The energy-growth nexus in China with linear and nonlinear causality

This study is an example of those papers that do not use the wavelet analysis throughout. Instead, they use it for a very short part of their research, as a means to a very specific end: In this case to produce a different set of series, the wavelet decomposed version appeared to be more informative. This usage of the wavelet approach shows the vast variety of combinations that are possible, depending on what the study framework requires and the creative imagination of researchers unfolds.

The authors in this study use data from 1953 to 2013 to investigate the energy-growth nexus in China. The variables are energy consumption per capita and real GDP per capita. They first perform the Toda-Yamamoto test with bootstrapped critical values and a nonlinear causality test, which reveals no causal relationship between energy and economic growth. Then, they applied the wavelet approach, only to receive the decomposition of the initial series into six new decomposition levels (series): Level 1 corresponds to 2–5 years horizon, level 5 corresponds to a 32–64 years horizon. The 6th series is the s5, which represents the trend of the original series. The produced series are not necessary to be studied individually. Sometimes they can be grouped and studied in neighboring dyads without any loss of information. The authors performed again the Toda-Yamamoto test on the new series and found different causality results, which would remain hidden if the decomposition of the series had not taken place. Their results can be summarized as follows:

(1) In the short run, there is support for the growth hypothesis; the estimated parameter is −0.679. According to this finding, 1% increase in energy consumption will cause a decrease in real GDP.

Authors explain that the negative causality implies a shift of production to less energy-intensive sectors. This is reflected in recent plans of the National Development and Reform Commission of China.

(2) In the medium run the estimated parameter is −0.046 with a similar interpretation as in the short run.

(3) In the long run, there is bidirectional causality (support for the feedback hypothesis) and the estimated parameter is 0.212. This means that 1% in energy consumption will cause GDP increase by 0.212% and vice-versa.

Policy implication and recommendation in this study: The energy-growth nexus in China is rather complex and time horizon dependent. Thus, if policy makers aim to act prudently with respect to their development goals, they should take into consideration these elaborate results. The authors advise that developing less energy intensive industries should pertain in the long run too and it is not something that can fully materialize in the short run. The reduction of energy consumption should be continually supervised and particularly at the state owned businesses. For the long-run situation, the study advises the attention to be focused on the development of green energies and energy efficiency mechanisms rather than the pure reduction of energy consumption.

Reproduced from Ha, J., Tan, P.-P., Goh, K.-L., 2018. Linear and nonlinear causal relationship between energy consumption and economic growth in China: new evidence based on wavelet analysis. PLoS One 13(5), 1–21, e0197785.

Case study 5: The nexus between geopolitics and crude oil markets

This study investigates the relationship between crude oil markets and various types of uncertainty such as financial, economic, speculation, and sentiment for different business cycles. The study employs monthly data from April 1990 to December 2015 and a new version of the wavelet approach, called entropy-based wavelet approach, and concerns the introduction of a mixed discrete-continuous multiresolution analysis. It is called this way, because authors use the entropic criterion for the selection of the optimal decomposition level of a maximal overlap discrete wavelet transform. Besides the novel approach the study also contributes to the first identification of nonlinear and nonparametric attributes of the aforementioned relationship.

The variables have been sourced from Thomson Datastream International database, the Federal Reserve Bank of St Louis, the University of Michigan Database, and the following:

(1) EPU-US: the economic policy uncertainty for the United States
(2) EPU-EU: the economic policy uncertainty for EU
(3) MOVE: the financial uncertainty index measured by the implied US bond volatility index
(4) VIX: the implied volatility uncertainty index of the US stock markets
(5) SENTIMENT: the market sentiment based on the Michigan consumer confidence index
(6) Working-T: the speculation index

According to Table 1 the optimal level of decomposition is 8, with the entropic criterion being 83.690. The correlation wavelet transform reveals that both variables are on phase at business cycle and higher frequencies (viz., short-term horizon) throughout time. At low frequencies uncertainty appears to lead oil (e.g., for the US and the speculation index). In some other cases, there is a high degree of comovement but negative correlation. An example of this result is traced in the 4.5–8 bands for the speculation index and oil. Furthermore, high coherence between oil and EPU-US occurs between 1995 and 2002 in the scale of 3–5.5 frequency band and 2.25–3 band accordingly. Low coherence is shown between 1996 and 2006 for the bands 4–5.8 and between 2007 and 2010 for the bands of 2–3. As far as oil and uncertainty are concerned, the interaction of oil and uncertainty occurs between 1995 and 2002 at the 2–4 frequency band, while for oil and the volatility

Table 1 Optimum minimum-entropy decomposition for the crude oil price series.

Wavelet scale	1	2	3	4	5	6	7	8
Entropy	2.481	4.408	8.070	9.860	16.459	22.123	59.056	83.690

From Uddin, G.S., Bekiros, S., Ahmed, A., 2018. The nexus between geopolitical uncertainty and crude oil markets: an entropy-based wavelet analysis. Physica A 495, 30–39.

index occurs between 1995 and 1996 and 2002 and 2003 at 0.25–2 bands. Furthermore, the authors use the FIU index by Jurado et al., (2015) to estimate the synchronization and the phase or their opposites in pairs with oil. Thus they find high interaction of the FIU with oil in various year spans and mostly at lower bands. Finally the authors observe comovements between oil prices and sentiment or speculation indices. For oil and speculation, they observe a strong relationship between 1997 and 2010 at the 2–3.5 bands, while for speculation the impact is revealed for the period 2002–12 for generally low bands.

4 Discussion

The wavelet approach is a statistical method that has recently started being explored by researchers in the energy-growth nexus. The comparison of Figs. 2–4 in the second part of this paper is sufficient for somebody to understand the richness of the results this method can give compared with the standard Granger-causality analysis. However, even in this method, researchers act differently and report results in a different way, and this makes understanding difficult and comparisons obscure. The fact that several papers rely on visual observations of the behavior of wavelet construct functions is not very good on reliability terms.

I think readers would be tremendously benefited from a wavelet result report comparison. This comparison clearly shows three different writing styles in reporting and how much they can affect understanding depending on the identity of the reader, namely, depending on whether he is a technically proficient wavelet specialist, whether he is a casual energy-growth researcher, or a policy maker (the naive reader).

4.1 Result discussion model from Case study 1

Jammazi and Aloui (2015) write in page 119 of their paper while they present their findings:

In the long run (D3), the co-existence of red (the highest level of positive CCF between EG and CO_2 emissions) and blue colors (the negative CCF) reveals that the CCF reaches its zenith then it follows the opposite tendency.

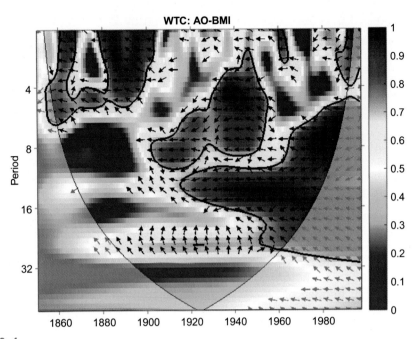

FIG. 4

Example of wavelet coherence graph.

Source: Grinsted, A., Moore, J.C., Jevrejeva, S., 2004. Application of the cross wavelet transform and wavelet coherence to geophysical time series. Nonlinear Process. Geophys. 11, 561–566.

This is a statement that concerns the description of a visual finding. Immediately afterward follows an explanation of this finding in policy making terms with practical examples from reality:

> *This may be explained by the fact that technologies in GCC countries may have reached their maximum performance and an improvement in the manufacturing process is required in order to reduce CO_2 emissions.*

They continue this pattern for every visual finding they describe. An explanation follows every statement of findings.

> *The wavelet functions are presented in spectral figures with various colors and the evolution of every color has a different meaning. With the presentation in this paper, the reader learns how each color is interpreted and what each formation means for policy making.*

This is a quite eloquent and extrovert presentation that can be understood with reasonable effort even from researchers with little background.

Visual Finding 1, Explanation 1; Visual Finding 2, Explanation 2; etc.

4.2 Result discussion model from Case study 2

The aforementioned pattern is even better followed in Sharif et al. (2017) in page 691. Here follows an example of the presentation of their results:

A long lasting red vortex is detected between 8 and 16 months persistent over 200 months indicating strong middle term co-movements when the EG index lead the IPI index....

An explanation follows every statement of findings:

In other words, a growing electricity demand occurred between 1987 and 2003 as the electricity generation also increased continuously to satisfy the industry needs.

As aforementioned, this offers the reader the possibility to deeply understand the meaning of the results and also he gets the opportunity of training in the interpretation of spectral graphs.

4.3 Result discussion model from Case study 3

Conversely to the previous two models of result discussion, a more technical one is the one by Ben-Salha et al. (2018). This paper cannot be read by wavelet freshmen without first having to take a lesson on the basics. To make this point more clear, an extract from the result presentation is provided in page 85:

This couple displays high power coherence at both high and low frequency bands during the period 2007-2011. The wavelet coherence plots undeniably allows depicting the co-movement behavior between the demand for energy sources and the transportation value added....

The text here is seething with technical descriptions, which are not directly discussed, probably they have no correspondence with real facts from the economy, or the authors follow a different writing style. However, this writing style is much heavier, loaded with technicalities, which cannot be retained by readers unless they are accompanied by strong real facts.

4.4 Results presentation recommendation in the wavelet approach energy-growth studies

Next in Table 2 follows a suggestion of how the results presentation should be organized. It starts with the strict presentation of the technical results (this is a presentation of a first level); it is followed with a presentation of a second level, namely, the one that explains the interpretation of the technical statement, namely, what each color and each shape in the spectral graph means with respect to the time horizon that characterizes an effect or a causal relationship between variables; and lastly followed with the third level of presentation, which describes the policy recommendation or a fact confirmation. If authors of new papers follow this rule, journal reviewers will have fewer

Table 2 Suggested writing style as ideal for the understanding of all groups of readers' experience.

Result level	Result description
(1) Statistical fact/technical description	"…Red vortices pertain (in the spectral graph) from year t_1 to year t_2…"
(2) Interpretation of the statistical: What does the statistical fact mean in the wavelet approach method?	"…This translates into a long run effect running from energy to growth"
(3) What is the relevant policy conclusion from this?	"This is true for the country, because it went through a period of enormous industrial revolution which was fueled with great amounts of energy…"

Source: Author's conception.

comments to make with respect to result discussion and clarifications about them. An example of a wavelet coherence graph is shown in Fig. 4.

4.5 Result presentation and discussion model from Case study 5

The study by Uddin et al. (2018) is very important because it is among the very few ones that are so extrovert and explain the way the visual findings from a cross-wavelet coherence and phase diagram are explained. In page 36, they note useful technical interpretations:

- Arrows indicate the direction of comovement between variables.
- Arrows pointing to the right indicate perfectly phased variables.
- The direction right-up indicates lagging of the variable (e.g., uncertainty).
- The direction right-down indicates leading of the variable.
- Arrows pointing to the left indicate out of phase variables.
- The direction left-up indicates leading of the variable.
- The direction left-down indicates lagging of the variable.
- In phase variables indicate cyclicality.
- Out of phase indicate anticyclicality.
- The thick black contour line is the 5% significance level.

More about the interpretation of a wavelet coherence graph and the axis and color representations are provided by Uddin et al. (2018) in page 36.

Note: An example of a wavelet coherence graph is provided in Fig. 4.

5 Conclusion

This chapter dealt with one of the new econometric methods applied in the energy-growth nexus field. After many years of research and the still controversial results received from many studies applying different econometric methods, some scholars believe that the nexus should start incorporating new methods and techniques, which are supposed to generate more sophisticated results. One such methodology is the wavelet approach.

However, the introduction of new methodologies can find inexperienced researchers unprepared in reading and interpreting the results of those new papers, compare them with other literature, and become able to appreciate their value. The value of the energy-growth papers lies in the replicability of results, their corroboration, and their ability to recommend something useful for policy making. However, energy-growth researchers usually concentrate on one methodology, which they know well and they prefer making improvements and alterations around them, but they rarely expand easily on new methodologies.

However, when it comes to read about the actuality in the energy-growth nexus, one must be able to read a wide variety of texts to estimate whether the method one is useful or other methods exist, which can do the job in a more effective way. This underlines the need for energy-growth nexus researchers to be in shape and be able to read and understand various methodologies. Herein lies the contribution and usefulness of this chapter: to equip new readers or rare readers in the wavelet approach with the basic paraphernalia that one would need to understand quickly the meaning and the way of thought in this methodology.

The chapter also provides case studies that reveal the variety of cases where the methodology can be applied and the vast opportunities that are inherent in the method, which can be applied in papers as the only method throughout or as a secondary method for result corroboration or as a method that transforms data for other conventional energy-growth nexus methodologies to use.

One advantage of the method is that no time is spent on unit root analysis. Researchers usually engage into tedious work with different competing unit root tests. This is avoided in wavelet analysis because this method can handle all types of data irregularities: policy shifts, shocks, asymmetries, nonlinearities, heavy tailness, extreme values, roughness, drifts, spikes, and other noise types. However, there are papers that employ both the wavelet approach and other conventional methods, and hence, they cannot avoid unit roots testing.

A drawback in the wavelet analysis is that in some cases researchers have to visually observe the correlations and decide which variable leads the other in each of the time horizons that have been decided at the beginning of the study. This is very cumbersome and can lead to mistakes and objective judgments.

Also the method, as used in economics papers, makes a qualitative rather than a quantitative representation of the connection between the variables of interest. Thus, when there results are reported, the stakeholder is not aware of how strong is the comovement and correlation of variables. The wavelet approach identifies causality with the observation of the lead–lag relationships. The identification of comovement is not an adequate condition for the identification of the causality direction.

Last, most wavelet energy-growth papers do not explain in detail the way they interpret the visual results of their wavelet analysis. To the best of my knowledge, Uddin et al. (2018) does explain this in his paper (p. 36) on the nexus between geopolitical uncertainty and crude oil markets. It is very useful and instructive for readers to present the results as in the aforementioned paper. Moreover, it is very important to start from the technical observation in detail and then expand on what that means in practical terms and policy recommendation terms. This chapter also recommends best-practice methods in result presentation of this type of papers.

References

Ben-Salha, O., Hkiri, B., Aloui, C., 2018. Sectoral energy consumption by source and output in the US: new evidence from wavelet-based approach. Energy Econ. 72, 75–96.

Bilgili, F., 2015. Business cycle co-movement between renewables' consumption and industrial production: a continuous wavelet coherence approach. Renew. Sust. Energ. Rev. 52, 325–332.

Graps, A., 1995. An Introduction to Wavelets. Available from: https://www.eecis.udel.edu/~amer/CISC651/IEEEwavelet.pdf. (Accessed 18 August 2019).

Ha, J., Tan, P.-P., Goh, K.-L., 2018. Linear and nonlinear causal relationship between energy consumption and economic growth in China: new evidence based on wavelet analysis. PLoS One 13 (5), 1–21. e0197785.

Jammazi, R., Aloui, C., 2015. Environmental degradation, economic growth and energy consumption nexus: a wavelet-windowed cross correlation approach. Physica A 436, 110–125.

Jurado, K., Ludvigson, S.V., Ng, S., 2015. Measuring uncertainty. Am. Econ. Rev. 105 (3), 1177–1216.

MathWorks, 2019. What is a Wavelet? Available from: https://www.mathworks.com/help/wavelet/gs/what-is-a-wavelet.html. (Accessed 18 August 2019).

Ryan, M., 2019. What is Wavelet and How We Use It for Data Science. Available from: https://towardsdatascience.com/what-is-wavelet-and-how-we-use-it-for-data-science-d19427699cef. (Accessed 18 August 2019).

Sharif, A., Jammazi, R., Raza, S.A., Shahzad, S.J.H., 2017. Electricity and growth nexus dynamics in Singapore: fresh insights based on wavelet approach. Energy Policy 110, 686–692.

Tangborn, A., 2019. Wavelet Transforms in Time Series Analysis, Global Modeling and Assimilation Office. Goddard Space Flight Center. Available from: https://www.atmos.umd.edu/~ekalnay/syllabi/AOSC630/Wavelets_2010.pdf. (Accessed 18 August 2019).

Uddin, G.S., Bekiros, S., Ahmed, A., 2018. The nexus between geopolitical uncertainty and crude oil markets: an entropy-based wavelet analysis. Physica A 495, 30–39.

Variance decomposition approaches and impulse response functions in the energy-growth nexus

1 Introduction

Given the wide selection of methodologies and approaches, a new researcher in the energy-growth field will be encountered, one may feel frustrated not only when one is writing his first own paper but also when one is reading the wide energy-growth literature and is trying to compare his/her perused methodology with another. As the purpose of this book is, the new researcher needs to feel assured that he can find resource to a quick reference book that will give him the necessary background and remind him the essentials of the methodology in a concise matter that would be necessary for the understanding and comparison of one's results with an existent paper. It is almost impossible to compare results and to understand the gaps that a piece of research leaves behind and the scope for further research unless you have a sufficient grasp of the methodology. This is the purpose of the chapter with respect to variance decomposition and the impulse response function.

A similar need must be addressed when one is serving as a reviewer for a paper that employs the variance decomposition or the impulse response function. One needs a quick brush up of the approach and the things that one must observe in the reviewed paper and ascertain their fulfillment. Again this is achieved in this chapter.

Another aspect that should by no means be overseen is the crucial points that need to be discussed as results of a certain approach, the way the presentation or tabulation or graphing of results is customized and presented in the papers, and having some best examples and practices handy to find resource to when necessary. Of course, these aims are also served in the X-variable-growth nexus, a term that has been coined by Menegaki (2018).

The rest of this chapter is structured as follows: after the brief introduction, Section 2 provides the primer or background material for the variance decomposition approach and the impulse response function. Section 3 typically provides a selection of two indicative case studies, and Section 4 concludes the chapter.

A Guide to Econometric Methods for the Energy-Growth Nexus. https://doi.org/10.1016/B978-0-12-819039-5.00018-5

---

2 Background and "first-aid" stylized material

This section provides some primer material that serves as a quick reminder of the methodology approach or a quick help to grasp its basics (if a researcher is not familiar with it).

(i) The variance decomposition approach

To recall from the notion of variance, the variance of a variable Y (in a relationship between Y and X) is the sum of its expected value plus the variance of its expected value, namely, the sum of the expected variation due to X plus the unexplained variation with origin different to X. The decomposition of variance is used when we handle a dynamic stochastic system.

As described very accurately in Lütkepohl (2010), the term variance decomposition or better "variance decomposition of forecast errors" is used in macroeconomics more narrowly to describe an interpretation tool on the relationships pertaining to vector autoregressive (VAR) models. This method supported by Sims (1980) has been alternatively used to simultaneous equations models and has been criticized for this usage. Variance decomposition has been employed by many researchers in the energy-growth nexus since this field too falls under the broader macroeconomic scope of studies. Since in a VAR model framework, all variables are considered to be endogenous, we need the variance decomposition tool to throw light to the underlying relationships in the variables and to do that directly from the coefficient matrices. In essence the method contributes to the knowledge of how much of the forecast error variance of each of the variables can be explained by exogenous shocks to other variables. Thus suppose we have the following three variable models in Eqs. (1)–(3):

$$lny_t = a_1 + \sum_{i=1}^{k} a_{1i} \, ln \, y_{t-i} + \sum_{i=1}^{k} b_{1i} \, ln \, x_{t-1} + \sum_{i=1}^{k} d_{1i} \, lnz_{t-i} + e_{1t} \tag{1}$$

$$lnx_t = a_2 + \sum_{i=1}^{k} a_{2i} \, ln \, x_{t-i} + \sum_{i=1}^{k} b_{2i} \, ln \, y_{t-1} + \sum_{i=1}^{k} d_{2i} \, lnz_{t-i} + e_{2t} \tag{2}$$

$$lnz_t = a_3 + \sum_{i=1}^{k} a_{3i} \, ln \, z_{t-i} + \sum_{i=1}^{k} b_{3i} \, ln \, y_{t-1} + \sum_{i=1}^{k} d_{3i} \, lnx_{t-i} + e_{3t} \tag{3}$$

The main problem with simple Granger causality is that it shows the relative strength of causality and does not provide any information about the time period, nor does it capture the exact causal effect of one variable to or from the other. According to Shan (2005) the variance decomposition method reveals the exact amount of feedback in a variable due to innovative shocks in another variable over various time horizons (Kyophilavong et al., 2015). One advantage of this method is that it is not sensitive to the orderings of the variables. The variance decomposition method and the IRF are regarded by the aforementioned literature as substitutes, but in my opinion, they rather act as complements, and it should not be considered a mistake to use both. The explanation can be found in subsection (ii).

(ii) The impulse response function (IRF); a substitute or complement to the variance decomposition approach

The term impulse is derived from signal processing. A brief signal is called impulse. The impulse response of a dynamic system is its output after a brief signal. The IRF is an important tool in the energy-growth nexus, because it can inform about the effectiveness of the policy it suggests. Due to the difficulty in the interpretation of the estimated VAR model, we also estimate the IRFs. Although not all VAR energy-growth papers use them, they do provide essential information, and they should not be omitted. At least they could be added in an appendix.

The IRF is a function that describes a shock to the VAR system. It answers what the response of the dependent variable to a shock is. The dependent variable is an endogenous variable. The IRF applies a unit shock (through the standard deviation of the error term) on the VAR system. The IRF also describes the evolution of the variable along a specified time horizon, starting from a base year or time period. Most importantly it underlines the effects on present and future values of the dependent variable of one standard deviation shock to one of the innovations.

For the calculation of the IRF, it is important to order the variables such as with Cholesky degree of freedom adjusted in Eviews. The IRF can be applied to both the VAR (unrestricted VAR and the restricted VAR) (VECM). The interested reader is advised to consult Marques et al. (2014) on this matter as well.

For the implementation of the IRF, the VAR must be specified in levels. The u term is the shock or impulse. It is important to comment what happens after the shock. Does the dependent variable stay stable for some period? Does it always have a positive response? Does this response ever become negative? Is the response symmetric or asymmetric? The responses need to be intuitively correct or to be consistent with economic theory and a priori expectations. Typically, reviewers seek this information and ask for revisions unless it is correctly and sufficiently provided. Next, we provide a graphical example of the IRF and the necessary discussion that should accompany their visual inspection. Typically, IRFS come to the end of the analysis in a VAR paper. After model specification, stationarity, decision about the lag length, the estimation of the basic VAR and its diagnostics, last but not least, comes the IRF.

As promised, next, we provide a visual representation of the IRFs from a study by Marques et al. (2014). The study deals with the electricity-growth nexus in Greece for the period 2004:m8 to 2013:m10 and uses a wide spectrum of all the different energy sources that contribute to the production of electricity in this country. The following nomenclature applies for the variables in that study: LORP, electricity generated from lignite, oil, and gas (MWh); LRES, electricity generated from the renewable energy sources (without hydropower) in MWh; HYDRO, electricity generated from hydropower in MWh; LIPI, seasonality adjusted industrial production index (manufacturing); LRXM, rate of coverage of imports by exports; and LRUMP, electricity consumption in water pumping systems in MWh. The IRFs of these variables are shown in Fig. 1A and B. The authors of this study state that they employ the IRFs to study in detail the behavior of each variable after an increase in another specific variable. This also enables the observation of the duration of the effect Fig. 1B.

Based on the visual representation of the IRFs of the aforementioned variables, the study by Marques et al. (2014) discusses the results as follows:

- "The variable LHYDRO after a one standard deviation shock on LORP has a negative response and this result is persistent." Why is this happening? It is important to provide explanations for what we describe in these results. The authors in this study attribute this specific finding to the base load role played by hydropower.

- "The variable LRXM after a one standard deviation shock on LORP has a positive response and this takes place abruptly. For LRES applies the other way round."

- "The variable LRXM after a one standard deviation shock on LRES has a positive response and then this turns to negative." Why is this so? The study suggests that the increase in the employment of intermittent renewable needs a larger backup."

- "The variable LRES after a one standard deviation shock on LORP shows no response with the exception of a shock on LHYDRO in which the response is negative and strong."

Unless similar statements as previous ones are made, it is not adequate to present the plain graphical representation of IRFs or their description without providing some rationale as well.

(iii) A historical decomposition (bootstrap) vs a variance decomposition

In 2018, Balcilar et al. (2018) have inaugurated in an energy-growth type paper, the historical decomposition method for the investigation of the renewable energy-growth nexus. This approach throws light to the time-varying effects of the relationship and employs a bootstrap. More specifically, they employ a moving average VAR(p) process, which can be decomposed as of Eq. (4):

$$y_{t+j} = \sum_{i=0}^{j-1} \Theta_i w_{T+j-i} + \sum_{i=j}^{\infty} \Theta_i w_{T+j-i} \tag{4}$$

The following notation applies for the previous equation:

$\sum_{i=0}^{j-1} \Theta_i w_{T+j-i}$ represents the shocks after time T. Therefore, this part determines the effect of a shock on a particular variable up to T.

$\sum_{i=j}^{\infty} \Theta_i w_{T+j-i}$ is the base projection.

Balcilar et al. (2018) state the typical IRF is not sufficient to explain business cycles, because the former are based on single positive shocks. A negative shock that will possibly take place right afterward will destroy the impact of a positive shock. The historical variance decomposition can solve this problem, because it allows for a depiction of the cumulative shocks on business cycles. For a more detailed discussion and presentation of this method variant, the interested reader should refer directly to the original article by Balcilar et al. (2018).

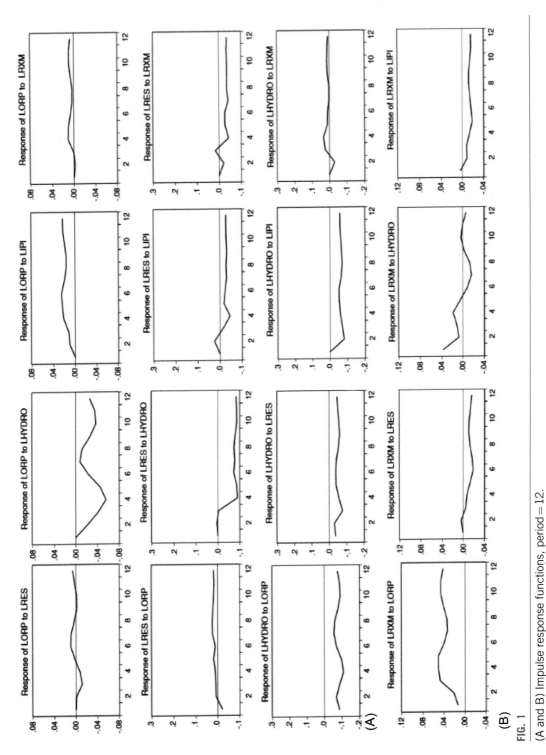

FIG. 1

(A and B) Impulse response functions, period = 12.

From Marques, A.C., Fuinhas, J.A., Menegaki, A.N., 2014. Interactions between electricity generation sources and economic activity in Greece: a VECM approach. Appl. Energy 132, 34–46, pg. 43.

3 An indicative selection of case studies in the energy-growth nexus that use the variance decomposition approach

This part contains two case studies with simplified extracts from the relevant papers by Kyophilavong et al. (2015) and Shahbaz et al. (2015). We provide the tabulated results with focus on their interpretation and the statements that are expected to be made in such a paper.

Case study 1: Trade openness and the energy-growth nexus in Thailand

Country/ies: Thailand

Data-span: 1971–2012

Variables: Real output (real GDP), energy, capital, labor, trade openness (real exports +real imports), and energy consumption (kg of oil equivalent). Total population has been employed to produce the per capita magnitudes.

Methodology: Bayer and Hanck combined cointegration analysis, VECM Granger causality, Variance decomposition approach, and IRF.

The motivation for this study is the limitations Thailand is facing with respect to fossil energy resources, the financial crises, which had hit the country and the fact that the Thai economy exports led growing. The financial crisis of Asia in 1997, the political instability in 2006, and the global financial crisis in 2008 have changed the economic and energy landscape in the country and drive the need for this study.

The authors find cointegration among the involve variables with the Bayer and Hanck combined cointegration analysis and then they investigate the causality with a VECM approach. According to causality results, they find support for the feedback hypothesis between energy consumption and economic growth. This is also supported for the relationship between trade openness and economic activity. This implies that energy consumption curtailment will retard economic growth. However, these results provide only relative causal accountability and not absolute or a time horizon informed one. This is pursued through the variance decomposition analysis and the IRF. The latter is not reported here due to space considerations. The interested reader is advised to refer directly to Kyophilavong et al. (2015), pg. 272.

The following statements apply for the results:

- **Based on evidence from Table 1, we observe in the last raw of the first panel that:**
  "85.92% of economic growth is explained by its own innovative shocks,"
  "11.13% of economic growth is explained by innovative shocks in energy consumption,"
  "2.94% of economic growth is explained by innovative shocks in trade openness."

Table 1 Variance decomposition for trade openness and the energy-growth nexus.

Period	Standard error	Ln (economic growth)	ΔLn (energy consumption)	Ln (trade openness)
Variance decomposition of Ln (economic growth)				
1	0.0158	100.0000	0.0000	0.0000
2	0.0268	97.6050	2.3920	0.0028
3	0.0354	96.4162	3.1850	0.3987
4	0.0413	95.1537	4.4924	0.3538
5	0.0451	93.1168	6.5610	0.3221
6	0.0474	91.1658	8.2542	0.5799
7	0.0491	89.3401	9.5036	1.1561
8	0.0504	87.8475	10.3101	1.8423
9	0.0515	86.7323	10.8044	2.4632
10	0.0525	85.9252	11.1303	2.9443
Variance decomposition of the ΔLn (energy consumption)				
1	0.0160	65.4711	34.5289	0.0000
2	0.0281	70.5301	28.8904	0.5793
3	0.0387	75.8130	23.8711	0.3157
4	0.0473	78.0197	21.7408	0.2394
5	0.0538	77.6319	22.0739	0.2940
6	0.0585	76.5080	22.9019	0.5810
7	0.0621	75.1549	23.7258	1.1192
8	0.0650	73.9715	24.2464	1.7820
9	0.0675	73.1019	24.4683	2.4297
10	0.0697	72.5309	24.4918	2.9772
Variance decomposition of the Ln (trade openness)				
1	0.0276	25.9019	2.8525	71.2455
2	0.0354	35.0462	10.5194	54.4342
3	0.0415	30.1727	25.5903	44.2369
4	0.0441	28.9381	31.2702	39.7915
5	0.0459	27.6416	35.5917	36.7665
6	0.0470	26.8504	37.9840	35.1655
7	0.0477	26.4550	39.2942	34.2506
8	0.0483	26.3073	40.0805	33.6121
9	0.0488	26.4116	40.5025	33.0857
10	0.0493	26.7349	40.6846	32.5804

Source: Kyophilavong, P., Shahbaz, M., Anwar, S., Masood, S., 2015. The energy-growth nexus in Thailand: does trade openness boost up energy consumption? Renew. Sust. Energy Rev. 46, 265–274.

Continued

- **To continue the description of results from** Table 1, **we observe in the last raw of the second panel that:**

  "72.53% of energy consumption is explained by innovative shocks in economic growth,"

  "24.49% of energy consumption is explained by its own innovative shocks,"

  "2.97% of energy consumption is explained by innovative shocks in trade openness."

- **To continue the description of results from** Table 1, **we observe in the last raw of the third panel that:**

  "26.73% of trade openness is explained by innovative shocks in economic growth,"

  "40.68% of trade openness is explained by innovative shocks in energy consumption,"

  "32.58% of trade openness is explained by its own innovative shocks."

  – All the previous statements lead to the conclusion that economic growth causes energy consumption and trade openness and vice-versa.

Albeit stated as substitutes in Shan (2005), I would say that the variance decomposition method and the IRF should be rather regarded as complements in the energy-growth nexus field. This is so, because the latter reveals the time length of the causal effect, while this piece of information may be rather obscure in the variance decomposition approach.

The benefits of different perspective information generated by the variance decomposition analysis can be also better perceived when it becomes juxtaposed to the marginal analysis offered in the elasticity terms in the typical short and long-run analysis. The result statements are produced as follows:

- **Long run analysis:**

  "1% increase in energy consumption leads economic growth by 0.5283%."

  "1% increase in trade openness leads economic growth by 0.1422%."

- **Short run analysis:**

  "1% increase in energy consumption causes a 0.7409% increase in economic growth."

  "The speed of adjustment is −0.2415 from the short-run deviations to the long-run equilibrium path."

Modified from Kyophilavong, P., Shahbaz, M., Anwar, S., Masood, S., 2015. The energy-growth nexus in Thailand: does trade openness boost up energy consumption? Renew. Sustain. Energy Rev. 46, 265–274.

Case study 2: The renewable energy-growth nexus in Pakistan
Country/ies: Pakistan
    Data-span: 1972q1–2011q4
    Variables: Domestic output in real terms, renewable energy consumption, and real capital and labor.
    Methodology: ARDL and rolling window approach for cointegration, VECM Granger causality, and Variance decomposition.
    The study has found that all variables were cointegrated. Causality analysis has provided support of the feedback hypothesis. The rolling window approach has confirmed that renewable energy consumption explained economic growth except for few time quarters (Shahbaz et al., 2015). The rolling regression is used for corroboration of the stability of the coefficients in ARDL. Then the variance decomposition approach is used to reveal the magnitude of the predicted error variance for a series accounted for by innovations from each of the independent variable over different time-horizons beyond the selected time period. The results from the variance decomposition approach are shown in Table 2.
    Based on results from Table 2, the following statements can be made:

- **The variance decomposition of economic growth reveals that:**
  "40.61% of economic growth can be explained by innovative shocks in renewable energy consumption,"
  "0.799% of economic growth can be explained by innovative shocks in capital,"
  "4.902% of economic growth can be explained by innovative shocks in labor,"
  "53.68% of economic growth can be attributed to other factors outside the model such as technological advancements."
- **The variance decomposition of renewable energy reveals that:**
  "70.98% of renewable energy consumption can be explained by its own innovative shocks,"
  "18.948% of renewable energy consumption can be explained by innovative shocks in economic growth,"
  "9.480% of renewable energy consumption can be explained by innovative shocks in capital,"
  "0.590% of renewable energy consumption can be explained by innovative shocks in labor."
- **The variance decomposition of capital reveals that:**
  "10.146% of capital can be explained by innovative shocks in economic growth,"
  "23.643% of capital can be explained by innovative shocks in renewable energy consumption,"
  "61.678% of capital can be explained by its own innovative shocks,"
  "4.531% of capital can be explained by innovative shocks in labor."

Continued

Table 2 The variance decomposition approach for the renewable energy-growth nexus in Pakistan.

Period	Variance decomposition of LN (economic growth)				Variance decomposition of LN (renewable energy)				Variance decomposition of LN (capital)				Variance decomposition of LN (labor)			
	Ln Yt	Ln Rt	Ln Kt	Ln Lt	Ln Yt	Ln Rt	Ln Kt	Ln Lt	Ln Yt	Ln Rt	Ln Kt	Ln Lt	Ln Yt	Ln Rt	Ln Kt	Ln Lt
1	100.000	0.000	0.000	0.000	13.244	86.755	0.000	0.000	4.348	1.212	94.439	0.000	1.151	0.992	0.739	97.116
2	98.868	0.931	0.001	0.199	13.863	85.972	0.017	0.146	5.314	1.301	93.105	0.279	1.710	2.208	1.426	94.653
3	96.950	2.374	0.001	0.674	14.324	85.217	0.065	0.393	5.320	1.763	92.296	0.619	1.661	3.096	2.086	93.155
4	96.782	4.945	0.002	1.269	15.113	84.038	0.099	0.748	5.575	2.234	90.983	1.205	1.527	3.929	2.824	91.717
5	88.797	8.082	0.005	3.115	15.736	82.361	1.224	0.677	6.380	1.967	90.503	1.148	3.154	2.203	3.041	91.601
6	85.626	11.539	0.153	2.680	16.118	80.746	2.449	0.685	7.021	2.197	89.267	1.513	3.706	2.023	3.943	90.326
7	81.871	15.505	0.392	2.230	16.240	79.291	3.739	0.729	7.314	2.844	87.790	2.050	3.670	2.296	4.878	89.154
8	77.774	19.549	0.648	2.027	16.308	77.947	4.942	0.801	7.564	3.784	85.882	2.768	3.513	2.815	5.881	87.789
9	72.732	23.181	0.755	3.330	16.671	76.220	6.373	0.734	8.318	4.929	83.895	2.857	3.912	2.249	5.691	88.147
10	69.819	25.951	0.988	3.240	16.982	74.804	7.505	0.707	8.913	6.420	81.450	3.215	4.090	2.473	6.278	87.157
11	67.293	28.640	1.161	2.903	17.171	73.711	8.402	0.714	9.225	8.224	78.850	3.699	3.987	2.984	6.987	86.040
12	64.960	31.195	1.263	2.580	17.306	72.893	9.056	0.743	9.371	10.164	76.205	4.258	3.833	3.660	7.769	84.736
13	62.002	32.962	1.219	3.816	17.606	72.106	9.585	0.702	9.754	12.290	73.715	4.239	4.023	3.346	7.529	85.101
14	60.337	34.471	1.214	3.976	17.875	71.575	9.978	0.671	9.954	14.308	71.407	4.329	4.113	3.674	7.932	84.278
15	58.964	36.036	1.175	3.823	18.064	71.264	10.016	0.656	9.980	16.228	69.312	4.481	4.025	4.233	8.473	83.268
16	57.751	37.557	1.114	3.576	18.205	71.110	10.034	0.649	9.928	17.972	67.420	4.678	3.902	4.911	9.089	82.096
17	55.999	38.231	1.001	4.767	18.452	70.946	9.956	0.644	10.056	19.735	65.653	4.554	4.040	4.682	8.864	82.412
18	55.086	38.918	0.922	5.072	18.671	70.885	9.817	0.626	10.129	21.214	64.163	4.491	4.113	4.999	9.172	81.714
19	54.341	39.748	0.854	5.055	18.828	70.910	9.653	0.607	10.146	22.514	62.852	4.486	4.050	5.505	9.615	80.828
20	53.683	40.614	0.799	4.902	18.948	70.981	9.480	0.590	10.146	23.643	61.678	4.531	3.957	6.101	10.132	79.808

From Shahbaz, M., Loganathan, N., Zeshan, M., Zaman, K., 2015. Does renewable energy consumption add in economic growth? An application of auto-regressive distributed lag model in Pakistan. Renew. Sustain. Energy Rev. 44, 576–585, pg. 584.

Continued

- **The variance decomposition of labor reveals that:**
  "3.957% of labor can be explained by innovative shocks in economic growth,"
  "6.101% of labor can be explained by innovative shocks in economic growth,"
  "10.132% of labor can be explained by innovative shocks in capital,"
  "79.808% of labor can be explained by its own innovative shocks."

Modified from Shahbaz, M., Loganathan, N., Zeshan, M., Zaman, K., 2015. Does renewable energy consumption add in economic growth? An application of auto-regressive distributed lag model in Pakistan. Renew. Sustain. Energy Rev. 44, 576–585.

4 Conclusion

As what the general aim of this book is, so complies that current chapter. It constitutes a quick reference to the general implementation of the variance decomposition and the impulse response function in the energy-growth nexus research field. Consistent to the requirements of a first aid guide, this chapter summarizes the essentials for understanding, remembering, or applying the variance decomposition approach or and the impulse response function in their papers. This chapter provides valuable primer and background material and relevant reminders, it addresses practitioners with best practices and case studies that aim to be treasured by potential new authors, young researchers and responsible article reviewers.

The chapter wishes to help new energy-growth researchers to put all the existent methodologies into perspective. Most of the times, researchers and research students start their journey to the energy-growth field with a focus on a certain methodology, which they also master during their studies. But as they start reading the existent literature more critically, they realize that there is a vast array of methodologies with which one is encountered when reading energy-growth nexus papers written by other researchers. Unless otherwise specified by circumstances, researchers wish they had a quick reference guide to find resource to for quick understanding, which will enable easier reading and comparisons with results from peer papers or review tasks.

References

Balcilar, M., Ozdemir, Z.A., Ozdemir, H., Shahbaz, M., 2018. The renewable energy consumption and growth in the G-7 countries: evidence from historical decomposition method. Renew. Energy 126, 594–604.

Kyophilavong, P., Shahbaz, M., Anwar, S., Masood, S., 2015. The energy-growth nexus in Thailand: does trade openness boost up energy consumption? Renew. Sust. Energ. Rev. 46, 265–274.

Lütkepohl, H., 2010. Variance decomposition. In: Durlauf, S.N., Blume, L.E. (Eds.), Macro-econometrics and Time Series Analysis. The New Palgrave Economics Collection. Palgrave Macmillan, London.

Marques, A.C., Fuinhas, J.A., Menegaki, A.N., 2014. Interactions between electricity generation sources and economic activity in Greece: a VECM approach. Appl. Energy 132, 34–46.

Menegaki, A.N., 2018. The Economics and Econometrics of the Energy-Growth Nexus. Elsevier.

Shahbaz, M., Loganathan, N., Zeshan, M., Zaman, K., 2015. Does renewable energy consumption add in economic growth? An application of auto-regressive distributed lag model in Pakistan. Renew. Sustain. Energy Rev. 44, 576–585.

Shan, J., 2005. Does financial development 'lead' economic growth? A vector auto-regression appraisal. Appl. Econ. 37, 1353–1367.

Sims, C.A., 1980. Macroeconomics and reality. Econometrica 48, 1–48.

A note on nonparametric and semiparametric strategies in the energy-growth nexus

1 Introduction

Given the controversy and conflict in the energy-growth results so far, it is reasonable to experiment with different methods and assumptions. After more than 40 years of empirical modeling in the energy-growth nexus, it is reasonable to wonder who these studies can be made comparable and how they can provide the most useful and reliable information for policy making. The empirical implementation of this important field of energy-economics and economics in general (through the so-called X-variable-growth nexus) seems a bit chaotic in its implementation, the same applying for peer review. For example, the descriptive statistics that is one of the most important starting bases in any statistical analysis is not given the solemn importance that it should be attributed, and this may mislead new researchers for its importance altogether. Some reviewers require the descriptive statistics as very basic information, and they require that it is removed from the paper; others require that it is moved to an appendix, or others require making only a recommendation that information about this will be available upon readers' request. However, this way, researchers are not accustomed to the considerations of researchers about normality or nonnormality. Sometimes, normality is imposed, or nonnormality is blinded and neglected.

Overall, before embarking on any statistical analysis and modeling, it is a typical process to examine the descriptive statistics that give researchers initial useful information about the modeling strategies that should be followed based on the structural and inherent characteristics of the data. Understandably the observation of skewness and kurtosis can provide useful information and combined with the treatment that different authors decide to apply can constitute fruitful exercise for the solutions given and the result sensitivity for cointegration and causality at different levels of deviation from normality.

It should be agreed that the production of the descriptive table should be a necessary starting point that should not be omitted evidence in any study. Nonparametric analysis offers many advantages among which are the greater statistical power of the tests, capability to work with smaller samples that may be the case for more rare and sophisticated energy data, and the acceptability of all data types such as nominal. Of course, since this path of analysis is not very often followed, computer software has

253

not been developed at a very high level, and thus critical values for various tests are not an easy task, and they need manual calculation or programming skills.

The rest of the chapter consists of some background information with useful definitions and reminders (Section 2), an indicative selection of case studies in the energy-growth nexus field (Section 3), and a conclusion (Section 4).

2 Background information for a reminder

This section provides some background information on useful definitions and statistics that a researcher needs to be reminded of when working on the energy-growth nexus. The terms parametric, nonparametric, and semiparametric; a few rules of thumb; and critical statistics are briefly noted in this section with the aim to constitute a first aid-type reference for new energy-growth researchers that encounter the dilemma on whether to work under the assumptions of a parametric, nonparametric, and semiparametric environment.

a. The parametric context

Parametric modeling assumes that the variables of interest follow mainly a normal distribution whose density function is provided as follows in Eq. (1):

$$f_X(x) = \frac{1}{\sqrt{2\pi\sigma^2}} \exp\left[\frac{1}{2\sigma^2}(x-\mu)^2\right], x \in R \tag{1}$$

b. The nonparametric context

Nonparametric refers to the methodology wherein the normal distribution is not assumed to be followed by the data. The term nonparametric implies that the number and nature of the parameters are flexible and not fixed in advance. Rather the shape of the distribution is assumed after the shape of the distribution is estimated.

Nonparametric statistics don't necessarily rely on specified distributions of the mean and the variance. So, they may be distribution-free statistics, or they may be relied on specific distributions but with the parameters of the distribution being unspecified. Nonparametric analysis may be more useful in small samples with outliers. In the energy-growth nexus, rarely are used other data than continuous. Discrete data occur mostly in covariates with social, environmental, or institutional data. So far, these studies are very rare and can be encountered mostly in metaanalyses applied in the energy-growth nexus. Also, microdata may contain these variables such as nominal or interval, but it is more rare for macroeconomic data.

c. The semiparametric context

The semiparametric analysis combines both parametric and nonparametric elements. This strategy is followed when the fully nonparametric modeling does not perform well. Another occasion that semiparametric modeling may be deemed necessary is when for a subset of regressors, the functional form cannot be known with reasonable certainty. Thus, while parametric modeling makes some convenient simplifications that render it comfortable to work with, it is sometimes far from realistic and cannot offer information for the real world. However, a combination of both parametric and nonparametric modeling allows one to get the best from the two worlds (Statisticshowto.com, 2020). One example of semiparametric model is the Cox proportional hazards model that describes the time remaining before the occurrence of failure or another ending event. It is used in medicine to reveal the remaining time before the death of a patient.

Overall a good rule-of-thumb advice is to observe the mean and median, and depending on which resembles the center of one's data distribution, one is advised to use parametric and nonparametric analysis, respectively (The Minitab Blog, 2015).

d. A reminder on skewness and kurtosis

A normal distribution has a bell shape. Normal distribution is symmetric, and we take this as reference point to assess the normality or the deviation of normality of others, based on the descriptive measures called skewness and kurtosis. Skewness refers to tailedness (either from the left or the right), while the kurtosis refers to the mass accumulation of the distribution. These both measures describe the lack of asymmetry and the deviation from normality.

Based on Fig. 1, positive skewness is there when the distribution has a longer tail on the right and the main mass of the distribution is accumulated o the left. In this case the mean is larger than the median. On the other hand, negative skewness is there when the distribution has left tailedness and its main mass is concentrated on the right. In this case the median is larger than the mean.

In essence, kurtosis describes how peaked the distribution is in relation to the peakedness of the normal distribution. In Fig. 2, we observe five examples of kurtosis of distribution. The more peaked the distribution, the more leptokyrtic is the regarded the distribution with positive kurtosis. When kurtosis is negative, this denotes a platikyrtic distribution, namely, a wide distribution. An intermediate case is neither very peaked nor wide; thus this is a mesokyrtic distribution.

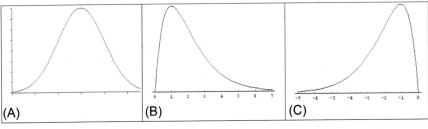

(A)   (B)   (C)

FIG. 1

Example of normal distribution (A), positive skewness (B), and negative skewness (C).

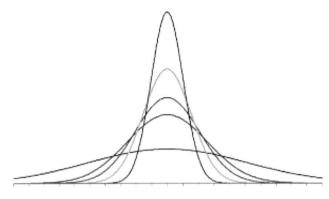

FIG. 2

Examples of kurtosis (leptokyrtic, mesokyrtic, and platikyrtic distributions).

3 An indicative selection of case studies that juxtapose parametric with nonparametric results in the energy-growth nexus

Section 2 contains brief summaries and information about three studies in the energy-growth nexus field that have employed nonparametric analysis together with parametric and have shown the benefits from using both types of strategies in their results. These studies are by Wesseh Jr and Zoumara (2012), Abdallh and Abugamos (2017), and Dergiades et al. (2013). These studies are among the few that have appeared in the Scopus database (which is the main search base) with keywords such as "energy-growth nexus" and "nonparametric."

Case study 1: Energy consumption and economic growth in Liberia
  Countries: Liberia
    Data span: 1980–2008
    Variables: Primary energy consumption per capita, real gross domestic product per capita, total employment (Source: World Development Indicators, US Energy Information Administration).
    Methodology: Bootstrap methodology. Next follows Table 1 which describes causality results from nonparametric causality.

Table 1 Results from a nonparametric bootstrapped causality test.

	P-value	
Null hypothesis	**Asymptotic test**	**Bootstrap test**
Short run Energy consumption does not granger cause economic growth	.835	.000*

Table 1 Results from a nonparametric bootstrapped causality test—cont'd

	P-value	
Null hypothesis	**Asymptotic test**	**Bootstrap test**
Economic growth does not granger cause energy consumption	.000*	.000*
Energy consumption does not granger cause employment	.041*	.185
Employment does not Granger cause energy consumption	.000*	.201
Economic growth does not granger cause employment	.004*	.663
Employment does not Granger cause economic growth	.001*	.061*
Long run		
Energy consumption	.017*	.001*
Economic growth	.144	.020*
Employment	.086*	.121

Note: Significance entails rejection of the null hypothesis that "x does not Granger cause y." Asterisk denotes significance at 10%.

3.1 Examples and Case studies

Case study 2: The urbanization and environment nexus in MENA countries
Countries: 20 MENA countries (Algeria, Bahrain, Egypt, Iraq, Israel, Jordan, Kuwait, Lebanon, Libya, Morocco, Oman, Qatar, Saudi Arabia, Syria, Sudan, Tunisia, West Bank and Gaza, United Arab Emirates, Iran, and Yemen).
   Data span: 1980–2014.
   Variables: Carbon dioxide emissions measures in metric tons per capita, GDP per capita, energy use (kilogram of oil equivalent) per $1000 GDP (constant 2011 PPP), total population, urban population (percent of total). All variables except for urbanization have been transformed into logarithms.
   Methodology: Parametric and semiparametric panel-fixed effect regression.
   High subsidies on oil products entail the increased use of energy and the consequent generation of greenhouse emissions. In conjunction with energy use, the increasing urbanization also contributes to the pollution increase in MENA countries.

The authors of the study find the semiparametric modeling as useful because it provides consistent estimation for a dynamic partially linear panel data model, it is more flexible, and it is tolerant to model misspecification, also avoiding dimensionality problems through the combination of both parametric and nonparametric elements. The study employs a stochastic version of the IPAT model as follows in Eq. (2):

$$I_i = a p_i^b A_i^c T_i^d \epsilon_i \tag{2}$$

And then, it investigates evidence for the EKC. The model is estimated as follows in Eq. 3 (Table 2):

$$\ln CO_2 = a_i + \beta_1 \ln (\text{Population})_{it} + \beta_2 (\ln \text{GDP per capita})_{it}$$
$$+ \beta_3 \ln (\text{Energy use})_{it} + \beta_4 \ln (\text{Urbanization})_{it}$$
$$+ \beta_5 \ln (\text{Urbanization})_{it}^2 + T_t + \varepsilon_{it} \tag{3}$$

Table 2 Result comparison between parametric and nonparametric results in the urbanization-environment nexus.

Variables	Parametric approach	Nonparametric approach
Constant	−7.78 (1.80)	–
GDP per capita	0.85* (0.073)	0.68* (0.13)
Energy use	0.58* (0.05)	0.50* (0.11)
Population	0.03 (0.07)	0.19** (0.09)
Urbanization	0.001 (0.10)	–
Urbanization^2	−0.00003 (0.000051)	–
Adjusted R^2	0.85	

Notes: *One and two asterisks stand for significance at 1% and 5% level accordingly. Cluster-robust standard errors are in parentheses, N = 481.*

Based on Table 1, there is a partial fit for the urbanization-environment nexus under the semiparametric framework. Also, under the parametric approach, urbanization is not significant. When urbanization is low and thus the rural concentration is higher, rural poverty leads to a mistreatment of the environment. The study has also calculated the turning point of urbanization to be 17%. Policy recommendations from this study suggest that MENA countries with high emissions should concentrate on energy use and the pattern of economic growth rather than the urbanization rate. They also suggest that attention should be made to the policies that aim at rural development by restraining population in rural regions rather than letting them move to big cities. They suggest that this may have opposite results for the quality of the environment in rural regions due to rural poverty and the need to exploit natural resources quite heavily to cope with that.

Case study 3: Energy consumption and economic growth in Greece
Countries: Greece
    Data span: 1960–2008
    Variables: Real gross domestic product (2000 = 100), energy consumption (in tons of oil equivalent) has been adjusted for qualitative differences among its building components through the thermodynamics of energy conversion. Data have been sourced from World Bank Development Indicators.
    Methodology: Parametric and nonparametric causality tests.

This study is presented here for its novelty for its combination of nonlinear techniques and the quality-weighted energy consumption series that was first initiated by Cleveland et al. (2000) and Zachariadis (2007). Since in each sector, energy is characterized by a different efficiency that depends on the type of energy and the perused technology; total energy is described in this study (Dergiades et al., 2013) as follows in Eq. (4):

$$E = \sum_{i=1}^{k} \sum_{j=1}^{l} \sum_{\lambda=1}^{\pi} F_{i,j,\lambda} Q_{j,\lambda} \tag{4}$$

The following notation applies for the earlier equation:

E = useful energy
i = sector (e.g., industrial, agricultural, commercial, residential, and transportation)
λ = transformation technology
F = final energy
Q = quality factor.

Based on Table 3, energy consumption Granger causes economic growth, while the opposite causality direction cannot be supported. Afterward the study employs two parametric tests and investigates the causal relationships in a nonlinear context. These tests are the Hiemstra and Jones (1994) and the Diks and Panchenko (2006). The latter boasts an advantage over the former, which is the correction of overrejection of the null hypothesis (when true). Thus the study uses the two tests for corroboration reasons. Testing with these tests involves a two-step sequential procedure. First the test is applied on raw differenced series (results are shown in Panel A of Table 4). Second, causality testing is applied on the delinearized raw differenced series (results are shown in Panel B of Table 4). Based on results from the two tests, it is observed that the null hypothesis of no causality from economic growth to energy consumption is only rarely rejected (Panel A). Combined with the results from Panel B, it is generally concluded that the causal relationship from economic growth to energy consumption cannot be supported. The opposite causal relationship is supported though. For more details on the findings of this study, the interested reader should refer to Dergiades et al. (2013) for the full study.

Table 3 The standard causality test.

The null hypothesis	F-statistic	P-value
Economic growth does not Granger cause energy consumption	0.654	.422
Economic consumption does not Granger cause economic growth	6.480**	.014

Note: Two asterisks denote significance at 5%. The VAR lag order was 1 and was decided based on the Akaike Information Criterion.

Table 4 The nonparametric causality test.

	GDP causes energy consumption		Energy consumption causes GDP	
lx = ly	$\varepsilon = 1,5$		$\varepsilon = 1,5$	
	Hiemstra and Jones test (P-value)	Diks and Panchenko test (P-value)	Hiemstra and Jones test (P-value)	Diks and Panchenko test (P-value)
Panel A: without filtering				
1	1.42* (.07)	1.46* (.07)	1.46* (.07)	1.49* (.07)
2	1.17 (.12)	1.16 (.12)	1.65** (.04)	1.38* (.08)
3	0.03 (.48)	0.19 (.42)	1.99** (.02)	1.81** (.03)
4	0.25 (.40)	0.33 (.37)	1.97** (.02)	1.41* (.08)
5	1.29*(.09)	1.33* (.09)	1.90** (.02)	1.71** (.04)
Panel B: with VAR filtering				
1	1.43 (.08)	1.50* (.06)	1.54* (.06)	1.72** (.04)
2	1.01 (.16)	0.23 (.11)	1.29* (.09)	1.04 (.15)
3	−0.73 (.77)	−0.25 (.60)	1.62* (.05)	1.39* (.08)
4	−0.03 (.51)	0.18 (.42)	1.61* (.05)	1.22 (.11)
5	0.77 (.22)	1.16 (.12)	1.74** (.03)	1.67** (.05)

Note: One and two asterisks stand for 10%, 5%, and 1% significance, respectively. The VAR lag order was 1 and was decided based on the Akaike information criterion.

4 Conclusion

After four decades of research in the energy-growth nexus, it is high time that the field adopts and imposes some strict protocols in the implementation of the econometric analysis in the relevant papers. Unless this is done, the various pieces of research with the different methodologies will never be comparable across countries, data spans, and methodologies, and there is a long way to cover before the field becomes able to provide continuous information for policy making. One such dilemma is borne when researchers are between following parametric and nonparametric analyses and strategies.

The knowledge that a statistical population does not have a normal distribution drives researchers to the usage of nonparametric analysis. This is why it is very important to observe the descriptive statistics of the employed variables in the energy-growth nexus. This is sometimes a step that is omitted in its presentation or even in its implementation. Foremost, there is no cutting point beyond which researchers are compelled to use a nonparametric analysis even side by side with the parametric in an attempt to provide support for final modeling strategies in a study. This is an additional point that should be decided in the future after careful empirical analysis or metaanalysis and could constitute a point of further research. Sensitivity analysis is also interesting from the point of view of deciding at which point is it safe to assume or worse impose normality to the employed variables in the energy-growth nexus modeling. This chapter clearly shows (from three case studies) that there are differences between the results produced in the causality results when between parametric and nonparametric strategies. Thus this aspect should not be ignored and should be more carefully investigated in the future. Not least the chapter reminds of basic definitions, concepts, and statistics that a new researcher may feel that is in need of, while one is reading the relevant energy-growth literature.

References

Abdallh, A.A., Abugamos, H., 2017. A semi-parametric panel data analysis on the urbanisation-carbon emissions nexus for the MENA countries. Renew. Sust. Energ. Rev. 78, 1350–1356.

Cleveland, C.J., Kaufmann, R.K., Stern, D.I., 2000. Aggregation and the role of energy in the economy. Ecol. Econ. 32, 301–317.

Dergiades, T., Martinopoulos, G., Tsoulfidis, L., 2013. Energy consumption and economic growth: parametric and non-parametric causality testing for the case of Greece. Energy Econ. 36, 686–697.

Diks, C., Panchenko, V., 2006. A new statistic and practical guidelines for nonparametric Granger causality testing. J. Econ. Dyn. Control. 30, 1647–1669.

Hiemstra, C., Jones, J.D., 1994. Testing for linear and non-linear Granger causality in the stock price-volume relationship. J. Financ. 49 (5), 1639–1664.

Statisticshowto.com, 2020. Semiparametric Models: Simple Definition and examples. Available from: https://www.statisticshowto.com/semiparametric. (Accessed 24 May 2020).

The Minitab Blog, 2015. Choosing Between a Nonparametric Test and a Parametric Test. Available from: https://blog.minitab.com/blog/adventures-in-statistics-2/choosing-between-a-nonparametric-test-and-a-parametric-test. (Accessed 26 May 2020).

Wesseh Jr., P.K., Zoumara, B., 2012. Causal independence between energy consumption and economic growth in Liberia: evidence from a non-parametric bootstrapped causality test. Energy Policy 50, 518–527.

Zachariadis, T., 2007. Exploring the relationship between energy use and economic growth with bivariate models: new evidence from G-7 countries. Energy Econ. 29, 1233–1253.

Making the energy-growth nexus useful through a metaanalysis

14

1 Introduction

The energy-growth nexus is a topic with contradictory results that vary depending on the country, group of countries, period in which it is applied, and the employed method. Thus studies with similar characteristics such as countries and data spans are found with different hypotheses applicable. A metaanalysis could contribute to making these studies more helpful and reliable as far as policy making is concerned. According to Hajko (2017), metaanalysis is mostly used in biomedical research whereby the studies rely on controlled experiments. This is easily confirmed if one types the term metaanalysis in the Scopus database, one will receive 239,921 papers (accessed on April 15, 2019) most of them on medicine, psychology, and other relevant sciences, while the number of the relevant papers in the energy-growth nexus will be limited to hardly a handful of them.

The term of metaanalysis was coined in 1976 by the statistician Gene V. Glass (2000). To perform a metaanalysis a homogeneous body of literature must be available Russo (2007). The main advantage of the metaanalysis is that it can combine small individual studies that cannot be generalized for larger samples and groups of countries and render these individual studies combinable.

The metaanalysis is regarded as "a study of studies" on a certain topic. A researcher, who applies a metaanalysis, collects all possible studies on a topic and then uses these studies as observations in a new study, which is the metaanalysis that aims to develop a single conclusion with great statistical power. Metaanalyses are important because, in a sense, they recapitulate results in a certain scientific topic and build robust global relationships. Metaanalyses are different from literature reviews, because while the former can be of quantitative nature as well, the latter is only a qualitative presentation and discussion of past literature, which aims to reveal and prove the existence of a gap in literature. This gap is claimed to be covered by a new study. Thus the literature review aims to create a framework of the past knowledge and explain how a new proposed study will add to fill a gap. The usual problem with the literature review is that they are a bit subjective and arbitrary and they have to reconcile many different results. The new study will probably agree or disagree with some of them or propose something completely different.

263

A Guide to Econometric Methods for the Energy-Growth Nexus. https://doi.org/10.1016/B978-0-12-819039-5.00011-2

The metaanalysis however is an objective macroscopic recapitulation of the past studies and can merge all of the past studies in a single relationship. Noteworthy is that many studies describe the metaanalysis as a systematic review. Caution should be placed at this point, because it is not literally a systematic review, but it could be benefited from one, or it could contribute to one. This is explained by the fact that to collect the metasample, one has to make a systematic review, in the sense that it will be a thorough, comprehensive, and exhaustive review of literature that will enable the selection of the most suitable papers. On the other hand, after the metaanalysis is finalized, this can contribute to a better understanding of the literature, and this can also lend to the term "systematic." Last, if the term systematic carries the element of repetition, this is not done in a static review but in a dynamic one. The metaanalysis is static by nature, but if it is continuously updated with new studies and the regression is reestimated, then it can be dynamic as well.

Metaanalysis is an active area of inquiry in environmental economics, and this has been particularly realized after the 17 environmental and resource economics topics that have been measured by Nelson and Kennedy (2009). Metaanalyses are important, because they enable a general, multifaceted picture of a subject. To admire the view, often one has to climb to a higher spot, which will enable him or her to see more and better. The same is done with a metaanalysis, and it is done in an accurate and quantitative way.

Hence, metaanalyses should take place at regular periods of time to update previous metaanalytic relationships. Both the literature review and the metaanalysis follow distinctive procedures, but sometimes, they have to adapt to the needs of the study. While students and researchers are more accustomed to the concept of the literature review in the energy-growth nexus, there is less guiding literature and reference on the details of the metaanalysis tailor made for the energy-growth nexus. Thus the purpose of this paper is to give guidelines on how to construct an energy-growth nexus metaanalysis project and revisit the concept of literature review and all that is tailor made for the energy-growth nexus and the "X-variable"-growth nexus. The latter refers to other nexuses such as the environment-growth nexus and the tourism-growth nexus. This chapter is structured as follows: After this introduction, Section 2 deals with general background information and guidelines about the metaanalysis, Section 3 deals with guidelines and steps, Section 4 contains four case studies of metaanalysis in the energy-growth nexus, Section 5 handles the new trend of metaanalytic review, and Section 6 offers the conclusion.

2 The essential advantages of metaanalysis

Studies on the energy-growth nexus focus on the same question and try to answer it using samples from different countries and data spans. They all pursue to reveal the effect of energy conservation in various economies and sectors. Despite their similar conceptual context, they end up producing contradicting results and cannot be transferred to similar environments and contexts without a reasonable error. Pooling estimates of elasticities of energy consumption with respect to economic growth, and other production parameters such as labor and capital can provide a kind of a weighted average from the results of all the previous studies. Thus the estimated metaanalytic relationship can provide a basis of comparison and benchmarking for the corresponding relationships in individual studies. Of course, to achieve that, one must be very careful with the selection criteria of the individual studies feeding with new observations the metaanalysis, and this will be explained further in the sections that follow.

(i) Results are generated from pooling from a larger population

Each individual study contributes observations to the metasample. Depending on how the sample is specified, if the study is a single country, it can produce a single observation. If the study is a multicountry one, it can produce as many observations as the countries. The total sample is created from pooling these observations into one metasample.

(ii) The statistical power of the estimated results is improved

As a result of the larger sample, the statistical power of the metaregression estimated coefficients is improved. Each individual study can generate many variables because it has many characteristics (please see next section). The higher the number of variables, the lesser the degrees of freedom. Therefore increasing the sample size rectifies this problem and gives more statistical power to the estimated results and hence of increased validity. This is why a metaanalysis can contribute to the generation of global theoretical assumptions about the energy-growth nexus relationship, something which is currently missing from the field.

(iii) Disagreement across individual studies can be highlighted and its sources be sought

This advantage can be regarded under a double perspective: The first is in accordance with the aforementioned point, namely, after a global relationship is established, and this will become a benchmark for the rest of the studies to come and to be added in an update of the metasample. The second perspective can occur during the phase of building the metasample. Researchers seek to fill in information about each study that is not evident on first sight. Since methods, data, and countries are heterogeneous, the presentation of each paper is different in its details. Reviewers most of the time try to make comments that bring these deficiencies on the surface so that authors handle them and papers can answer all possible questions of a reader. Thus metaanalyses will lead authors to better and more transparent writing of their energy-growth nexus papers.

(iv) Reliable hypothesis testing can be implemented

This benefit should be seen in conjunction with point number (ii) because the higher statistical power of the estimated metacoefficients entails reliable hypothesis testing. The most important coefficient is the one of energy that is the gist of the energy-growth nexus research. It is crucial for policy makers to be able to make reliable forecasting about the consequences of energy conservation with respect to income.

(v) Research on publication bias should be investigated

Publication bias occurs when not all studies get an equal chance of being published. Publishing negative results is not very appealing to editors, and this may produce a wrong picture of reality. This is difficult to be handled, and it relies on the good ethics shown by editors. Justifiably or not, published papers acquire a validity status because they have been examined by peers and approved. There are papers and reports on the net that have not been published in journals.

Nowadays, there are numerous journals present, as publication outlets that one would normally expect to find very few unpublished papers in this field (Sebri, 2015). Therefore this type of bias is not very worrying in this particular research field, as it would have been in biomedical research where metaanalysis has originated from.

The use of a funnel plot in the investigation of publication bias

The funnel plot is a good means for testing whether small studies have an unjustifiably favorable result to the examined hypothesis. In essence the funnel plot is a scatter plot of the standard error versus the effect size (precision). Typically, larger studies have less scatter compared with the small studies, which have a higher scatter and larger standard errors. The idea is that if many negative studies have not been published, the remaining studies form a skew to one side of the funnel plot. However, if the plot is symmetrical, this means that no publication bias is present.

(vi) They can play a key role in planning new studies. Some funding bodies require metaanalyses to take place before any funding takes place for new projects (Biostat Inc (2019))

A metaanalysis is more sophisticated to traditional literature review and can highlight correlations and links between studies that may not be readily available when one sees only the individual studies (Shuttleworth and Wilson 2019). Thus it can be an essential part of a new research proposal, because it summarizes the past. Although this is most important for biomedical research, it is equally important for the energy-growth nexus field because scrutinizing energy-growth papers needs expert reading, and hence, this can be a topic for future research. Besides the fundamental question of what happens to growth when an economy or sector lowers its energy consumption through energy conservation initiatives is a question that many societies would be keen to know with enough certainty and detail. A metaanalysis can give rise to funding more sophisticated research projects but can also be itself a topic of research.

3 Guidelines and steps for a metaanalysis in the energy-growth nexus

Guidelines and steps in metaanalysis can be found in not only many biomedical texts but also lately in environmental and resource sciences texts. Up to date, these guidelines and steps have not been provided anywhere else in the energy-growth nexus research texts, except for (and partly) in the four identified pieces of metaanalysis that have been identified and briefly presented and commented in Section 4 of the current paper. Next, follow 13 steps for a proper and all-inclusive implementation of a metaanalysis in the energy-growth nexus:

(1) Formulation of research question (the primary question is the elasticity of energy with respect to income, and the secondary question is to gather information on other elasticities calculated, such as capital and labor).

Typically the energy-growth nexus studies are of two types: One is the production function orientation, and the other is the demand function orientation. There are other variants too such as the environmental Kuznets curve, but these should be examined separately, although some studies place a dummy to retain this information, if it generally contains the variables sought in the metaanalysis. However, it is advisable that the metaanalysis remains focused on one type of energy-growth nexus study, for example, the production function type. As will be seen in the next section, which contains the four pieces of metaanalysis in the energy-growth nexus that have been implemented so far, the study by Sebri (2014) appears as the most verbose and conclusive one, probably because it focuses on one type of energy too. But this need further research to be confirmed.

In most cases the energy-growth studies employ GDP per capita (in logarithmic form) in the left-hand side of the equation to be estimated, and in the right-hand side of the equation, they employ capital, labor, energy (separated in renewable and nonrenewable terms), and many other variables that vary depending on the context of the particular problem or topic the study focuses on. Inglesi-Lotz (2018) provides a rich account of all the variables and covariates that the energy-growth nexus studies have employed so far and the vast margin for more variables to be used in the future. The interested reader should refer to that text.

For the educative purposes of this chapter, we will assume that the energy-growth studies contain in their production function setup only capital, labor, and energy consumption (in logarithmic form). These variables are also transformed in the per capita version after they become divided with population. This means that the sampled studies produce results for the elasticity of capital to GDP, the elasticity of labor to GDP, and the elasticity of energy (RES and non-RES) to GDP. So, these are the results that are kept from each study as well as the research data span, data type, data frequency age of the study (this is year of publication), econometric methods for cointegration and causality, the investigation of breaks, the geographic characteristics of the study, and main results (through the hypothesis that is supported: growth, conservation, feedback, and neutrality). It is up to observant and inventive energy-growth nexus researchers to identify more characteristics in these studies, for example, the type of unit root tests employed could be a novel characteristic to retain in a metaanalysis study.

(2) Literature search (keywords; databases; language limitations, e.g., English; and inclusion and exclusion criteria for a study)

All scientific studies should be transparent and reproducible and describe their search protocol in sufficient detail as well as the inclusion or exclusion criteria of relevant variables or studies. This means that the reader must be aware of the channels the researcher/author has gone through to collect the data—in this case the studies participating in the energy-growth nexus. It is advisable to use major, international, academic databases such as the Scopus or ScienceDirect. Other smaller databases also exist (most of the times they are hosted in the Scopus), but for this topic, namely, the energy-growth nexus, the Scopus database is sufficient. For search keywords is employed the phrase "energy-growth nexus." Hajko (2017) in his metaanalysis is very detailed in his selection of studies, and he reproduces this information within his paper from Scopus database search routines. This is presented in Box 1.

In addition to the earlier, Hajko (2017) clearly states that he sourced papers in his metaanalysis originated from journals indexed in Scopus in the subject area of economics, written in English after 2000 that had at least 10 citations using the keywords, energy, economy, growth, relationship, causal, nexus, causality, and cointegration.

(3) Set the yardstick of the selection of studies (keywords, phrases, etc.). The yardstick must be an explicit and objective criterion, and the selected study is assigned a quality score. Later in the sensitivity analysis, low score studies can be dropped, and the metaanalytic regression can be recalculated.

The number of papers in this field is vast, and this means that several hundreds of papers will be there for the metaanalyst to read and decide to keep or not. A quick reading of the abstract will give a serious indication whether the paper should be fully downloaded and further read in detail. On the one hand, such voluminous fields become easier when the work, namely, the number of papers to be read for result extraction, is vast, because one can acquire a sufficient metasample. On the other hand, voluminous fields require many researchers to be involved or much time to be devoted for a thorough studying

---

BOX 1 The search code in Scopus for the metaanalysis sample papers in Hajko (2017).

```
(TITLE-ABS-KEY(energy economy OR growth relationship OR causal OR
   nexus) AND PUBYEAR>1999) AND
(causality OR cointegration) AND
(LIMIT-TO (SUBJAREA, "ECON")) AND
(LIMIT-TO (LANGUAGE, "English")) AND
(LIMIT-TO (SRCTYPE,"j"))
```

From Hajko, V., 2017. The failure of energy-economy nexus: a meta-analysis of 104 studies. Energy 125, 771–787.

of the papers and the isolation of the proper data. If the metaanalyst is lucky enough to have several research assistants, this mission becomes less tiresome and complicated. Otherwise a single metaanalyst and researcher should define a daily exercise for oneself that of reading 5–10 papers daily depending on time availability and deadlines. Each relevant paper that fulfills some initial prerequisites should be downloaded, and the salient points to be used in the metadataset should be marked or underlined for future reference and validation. It is true that the deeper one digs for older papers in the field, the more one realizes that they are not comparable with the more recent ones. The methods are simpler, results are sparser, and the variables are richer now than in the past. Therefore, if a researcher decides to include an older paper in the metasample, he may be confronted with the dilemma of having to leave out many variables that the more recent studies can fill in. Two of the metaanalyses presented in Section 4 of the present paper clearly state that the sampled papers came from 2000 and afterward, while the metaanalysis by Menegaki (2014) states that it is a metaanalysis of the last two decades. Apparently, this occurs for the reason of noncomparability of the studies of the distant past and the origins of the energy-growth nexus research.

Furthermore, besides the possible exclusion of the very old papers, the exclusion of poorly written papers is also advisable. Since the metaanalysis cannot correct for poorly implemented individual studies, these should be excluded from the metaanalysis, because they will alienate metaanalytic results. The metaanalysis study must be reproducible, transparent, and objective and is thus designed, so that to eliminate all possible sources of bias, only if the participant studies are individually correctly performed.

(4) Data abstraction: Which dependent and independent variables are to be selected for inclusion in the metaanalytic regression? The selection entails a highly structured format.

The following characteristics are only indicative. The energy-growth researcher can trace more of them and be inventive with new ones. Next follow 10 of them.

The name of the study

The name of the study is defined by the author or authors in the way we use references in a text.

Year of publication

The year of publication is provided both in raw form, for example, 1998, and with a form that can be used in the analysis to account directly for the publication age. Thus publication age is calculated as today's year, let's say 2020 minus the year of publication plus one. Thus the age of the aforementioned publication can be calculated as $(2020 - 1998) + 1 = 22 + 1 = 23$ years old. The year of publication may reveal important patterns in research results, because it may have a correlation with other parameters such as statistical methods and data spans.

Another form of presentation of the publication age is reporting the decade of publication as a categorical variable. For example, denote with 1 the papers that have been published in the 1980 with 2 the papers that have been published in the 1990 etc. This is how Kalimeris et al. (2014) denote paper publication dates in their metaanalysis.

The data span

In a way analogous to the treatment of the publication year, the data span should be expressed as the years away from today, both for the starting year and the end year. Thus, if the data span is, for example, 1975–2018, this should be converted into 46 and 3 as the starting and end years, respectively. Categorical variables could also be invented as explained in the previous paragraph.

Number of countries in the study

In the energy-growth nexus, there are both single country studies and groups of countries. Sometimes, results are different for each country or group of countries. Therefore one study may emit various lines of different results, which must be reflected in the metaanalysis. Therefore, when this happens, we should devote one separate line of data for each different country or group of countries. Understandably, such studies have more weight in the metaanalysis, and there are ways to handle this. For example, the original sample size of each study has been used as a weight in Sebri (2015). The interested reader is advised to read the whole paper for details.

Geographical location the study handles

It is interesting to investigate whether some energy-growth hypotheses are validated more frequently in specific continents or other geographical or economic regions. Therefore we assign a code for each different continent or geographical or economic location presented in these studies, namely, 1, for Europe; 2, for North America; and 3, for South America. Other studies have used terms such as OECD, non-OECD, low-income countries, and high-income countries.

Number of covariates

Although we may be interested in three variables, namely, capital, labor, and energy consumption (RES and non-RES), the number of variables may be bigger, and we may construct variables for all of them. It could be three of them, four or five. Rarely do we see more variables in an energy-growth nexus function. Many variables are not advisable due to a loss in the degrees of freedom.

Types of covariates

It is useful to use different letters or codes to represent each variable. Usually, it is used L for labor, K for capital, E for energy, and RES for renewable energy. When one starts the reading of the relevant papers and the construction of the dataset, one cannot be aware of the multitude and the variant of the variables that will be encountered. This means that we keep adding names and codes for the new variables we meet, as we proceed with our searching and reading of the sampled papers. Another point that needs special attention is the unit of measurement in variables that must be homogeneous. Particularly, this applies in the energy consumption variable. Hajko (2017) has identified several measurement units in energy, and this is the only metaanalysis that takes into account this matter.

Econometric methods

There are various econometric methods applicable, and as years go by, new methods appear. Although they should be reaching the same results, it is interesting to investigate whether the produced results are correlated with the employed method. Each method should be assigned a different name or code in the same way it has been done for the variables. All metaanalyses conclude that the energy-growth results are not independent of the methodology in a paper; thus the econometric method is responsible to some degree for the produced result. Sebri (2015) has explained in his metaanalysis of renewable energy-growth nexus, which methods are most likely to support a certain hypothesis.

Results

The results should be reported with respect to the four hypotheses. Thus the growth hypothesis could be assigned as 1, the conservation hypothesis could be assigned as 2, the feedback hypothesis could be assigned as 3, and the neutrality hypothesis could be assigned as 4. Depending on the method, results on the four hypotheses may have to be reported separately for the long-run and short-run relationships. This categorical representation of the hypothesis confirmed leads the way to using the multinomial regression modeling.

Other qualitative characteristics of the study

It is advisable to collect data on as many variables as possible. The energy-growth nexus field must be observed in detail, and various pieces of evidence can then appear and be collected. For example, keeping a record of the unit root tests employed by each study is also a good idea.

(5) Select means to standardize the collected data

One example of standardization is the one aforementioned for the years of publication and the data span. Another example of standardization is the number of observations in studies or the number of observations each study contributes to the metasample.

(6) Detailed declaration of data manipulation

This must be reported with much care and detail so that the metaanalysis can be replicated. For example, data exclusion or inclusion and data imputation must be reported for readers.

(7) Select the metaanalysis regression model

There is no specific model that should necessarily be used in the metaanalysis. The metaregression can take any form the data dictate. Thus panel data can be analyzed with fixed effect or random effect models, time series data with cointegration, and causality analysis and the cross-sectional data with a linear regression. In the case of the energy-growth nexus regression, we should use the latter. Data do not contain time, while the publication data or data spans are used mostly as qualitative characteristics. Another suitable modeling technique is the multivariate regression, which is used in two out of the four case studies that are presented in Section 4. Also, nonparametric techniques that contribute to group or cluster formation that is permeated by special rules are also useful.

(8) Heterogeneity between studies. This test investigates whether studies have been similar to combine.

In a metaregression, data are examined for all the reasons they are examined in the conventional regression, and the residuals are used for these reasons. The significance of the model as a whole is examined together with the significance of individual coefficients. One way to measure metadata heterogeneity is with the usage of Cochran's Q test, which is calculated as the weighted sum of squared differences between individual studies and the pooled sample of studies. This statistic is distributed as χ^2 with $k-1$ degrees of freedom. When the number of studies is small, the test has a small power.

(9) Study the robustness of the estimated model

Investigating the stability of the model is required in the metaanalysis. This is one way to investigate its robustness. Robustness is also checked through the investigation of heteroskedasticity and heterogeneity.

(10) Design a systematic review with continuous updates of new data

As soon as the metadata table is compiled and the metaregression is estimated, then the metadata table should be continuously updated with the new studies and the reregression reestimated. This is a procedure that should continue eternally. This can be also implemented through a type of cumulative metaanalysis that entails plotting the result of the first study; then it pools it with a second study, and then it pools it with the third and so on. As a result of that, the data shift in time as the metasample is enriched with new energy-growth nexus studies that take place in time.

(11) Sensitivity analysis

Sensitivity analysis can be performed in several ways. It can be an ad hoc piece of exercise or one based on statistical randomness. The ad hoc refers to investigating the effect on the estimated regression when leaving out specific studies, for example, some studies that contribute a large number of observations or studies that contribute extraordinary values that seem to be outliers. On the other hand the statistical randomness sensitivity is based on a Chow-type test, which examines the stability of the estimated metaregression. Sensitivity analysis can also be implemented by using different estimation methods. For example, the Box-Cox transformation (Box and Cox, 1964) as an alternative model for the metaregression estimation is a good idea, when the requirements are fulfilled, namely, when the dependent variable is all positive. This method makes residuals less heteroskedastic. This method is applied in Sebri (2016) for a metaanalysis in water demand. However, irrespective of the exact data field where these methods have been originally applied, it is useful to note them as good practice examples.

(12) Applicability of results

Results from a metaanalysis study in the energy-growth nexus can generate a global relationship for this relationship and thus strengthen the theory. A sound metaanalysis can form the foundation for a new research program and strengthen the application for research funds.

4 Case studies of metaanalysis in the energy-growth nexus

Case study 1: The metaanalysis on the energy-growth nexus by Menegaki (2014)

The first metaanalysis in the energy-growth nexus field was produced by Menegaki (2014). It contained 51 studies of the two decades previous the publication of the study, and she found that results were not independent of the statistical method employed, the data type, and the inclusion of certain variables such as capital.

She had not made separate metaanalyses for production function and demand function types, but she had included dummy variables for the demand function-type elements, which however did not contribute sufficient observations for a separate model estimation. The same applied for environmental Kuznets curve modeling. Namely, she introduced a dummy for those studies, but the observations were insufficient to produce a separate metaregression. Therefore the perspective of this first study stayed rather limited.

Table 1 shows the included studies in the first metaanalysis by Menegaki (2014). It contains the year of publication and the number of metaanalytic observations each study contributed to the metaanalysis. Note that the number of observations is generated by the different models applicable in different countries and groups of countries as well as their results.

Table 2 offers the variables selected in the first metaanalysis and their basic descriptive statistics. The selection of variables is only indicative but not exclusive, because it depends on what the surveyed studies can offer in a collective way. Namely, a metaanalytic list of variables could not contain a variable encountered only once in a study. This cannot generate any information, only in exceptional cases where one individual study contributes many observations.

As observed, Table 2 is divided in five parts. One is the general study characteristics with elements such as year of publication, whether stability examination with breaks is present and the type of the data, the time span, and the start year of the time span. Second is the method of analysis that contains the most frequently met method. If some methods appear only once or in another rare frequency, researchers could create another category termed as "other." Third in this table appears the geographical allocation of the studies. It would be advisable to separate them based on the continent or some major countries such as the United States could be placed alone in separate categories. Another division could be made based on the economic development performance of the country as provided by World Bank. In this part is also included another variable that contains the number of countries in the study,

Continued

so that the reader can be aware not only of the geographical location of the study but also of the number of countries studies in each continent or geographical location.

The third part of variables contains the variables selected in the long-run relationship, while the fourth part deals with the description of causality. The variable inclusion can be as rich as the studies allow and as imaginative as the researcher can reach.

Table 3 contains the metaanalytic results of the first study. Apparently the researcher has provided several model estimations to show that heteroskedasticity was not a problem and support the robustness of the estimated model. The weighted least squares (WLS) is generally estimated using the weights from the inverse standard errors of effect sizes or a monotonic transformation of the primary study sample size.

Table 1 Author, publication year, and number of observations.

Authors	Year of publication	Observations
Acaravci and Ozturk	2010	12
Akinlo	2008	7
Al-Iriani	2006	6
Altinay and Karagol	2004	1
Altinay and Karagol	(Altinay and Karagol, 2005)	1
Ang	2007	1
Ang	2008	1
Apergis and Payne	2009a	4
Apergis and Payne	2009b	6
Apergis and Payne	2010	9
Asafu-Adjaye	2000	4
Balcilar et al.	2010	7
Bartleet and Gounder	2010	2
Belloumi	2009	1
Bowden and Payne	2009	5
Chiou-Wei et al.	2008	9
Eggoh, Bangake, and Rault	2011	10
Erdal et al.	2008	1
Esso	2010	7
Friedl and Getzner	2003	1
Fuinhas and Marques	2012	5
Ghali and El-Sakka	2004	1

Table 1 Author, publication year, and number of observations—cont'd

Authors	Year of publication	Observations
Glasure and Lee	1998	2
Gosh	2002	1
Halicioglou	2009	1
Hamit-Hagar	2012	1
Ho and Siu	2007	1
Hondroyiannis et al.	2002	2
Jalil and Mahmud	2009	1
Lean and Smyth	2010	5
Lee	2005	17
Lee and Chang	2008	16
Lee and Chien	2010	7
Lise and Van Montford	2007	1
Mahadevan and Asafu-Adjaye	2007	20
Masih and Masih	1996	6
Mozumder and Marathe	2007	1
Narayan and Prasad	2008	30
Odhiambo	2010	3
Odhiambo	2009	1
Oh and Lee	2004	2
Ozturk and Acaravci	2010	1
Ozturk et al.	2010	3
Paul and Bhattacharya	2004	1
Shiu and Lam	2004	1
Squalli	2007	11
Tsani	2010	4
Wang et al.	2011	1
Yuan et al.	2008	4
Zhang and Cheng	2009	1
Zhixin and Xin	2011	1

From Menegaki, A., 2014. On energy consumption and GDP studies; a meta-analysis of the last two decades. Renew. Sust. Energ. Rev. 29, 31–36.

Table 2 Description of variables.

Variable name	Explanation	Mean	St. deviation
i. General study characteristics			
YEAR	Year of publication	2007.67	2.364
STAB	Stability examined with breaks: 1, yes; 0, no	0.07	0.259
TIPA	Type of data: 1, time series; 0, panel data	0.54	0.498
NYEA	Number of years (time span) in each study	34.50	8.49
STYEA	Start year of the time span	1967.92	8.09
ii. Method of analysis			
ARDL	Method for cointegration: 1, ARDL bounds test; 0, otherwise	0.88	0.28
PEDR	Method for cointegration: 1, Pedroni; 0, otherwise	0.21	0.41
JOHA	Method for cointegration: 1, Johansen; 0, otherwise	0.05	0.22
TODA	Method for cointegration: 1, Toda-Yamamoto; 0, otherwise	0.07	0.25
COIN	Method for cointegration: 1, general analysis; 0, otherwise	0.52	0.49
iii. Countries in the study			
EURO	1, Europe; 0, otherwise	0.36	0.48
AMER	1, America; 0, otherwise	0.14	0.35
AFRI	1, Africa; 0, otherwise	0.12	0.33
ASIA	1, Asia; 0, otherwise	0.31	0.46
AUST	1, Australia; 0, otherwise	0.03	0.16
NCOU	Number of initial countries included in the analysis	18.04	9.66
iv. Variables included in the long-run relationship			
ELEC	Electricity included in total energy consumption: 1, if electricity is included; 0, not included	0.34	0.47
ECEL	Energy consumption elasticity	0.54	0.39
PRDU	Prices of goods: 1, if P exists in the equation; 0, if it doesn't	0.06	0.23
EKCD	1, if EKC is examined in the equation; 0, if it doesn't	0.06	0.23
CAPI	Elasticity of capital	0.27	0.20
CO2D	CO_2 emissions: 1, if CO_2 exists in the equation; 0, if it doesn't	0.01	0.10
LABD	1, if labor exists in the equation; 0, if it doesn't	0.20	0.39
v. Causality			
BIDI	Bidirectional causality between EC and GDP: 1, yes; 0, no	0.22	0.41

Modified from: Menegaki, A., 2014. On energy consumption and GDP studies; a meta-analysis of the last two decades. Renew. Sust. Energ. Rev. 29, 31–36.

Table 3 Metaregression results (Models 1, 2, 3, and 4).

	Model 1: OLS		Model 2: heteroskedasticity robust covariance model		Model 3: heterogeneity robust model		Model 4: weighted heteroskedasticity robust model	
	Coefficient (St. error)	P	Coefficient (St. error)	P	Coefficient (St. error)	P	Coefficient (St. error)	P
Constant	−2949.95 (10,916.06)	.787	−2949.95 (10,051.60)	.769	−2949.95 (12,045.49)	.806	−4679.77 (6818.90)	.493
Type of data	138.97 (71.30)	.052*	138.97 (74.36)	.062**	138.97 (95.24)	.145	72.98 (73.22)	.319
Electricity	−211.91 (67.98)	.002*	−211.91 (72.90)	.004*	−211.91 (93.15)	.023*	−72.17 (69.17)	.297
ARDL method	457.07 (64.30)	<.001*	457.07 (110.58)	<.001*	457.07 (103.23)	<.001*	383.97 (171.46)	.026*
Pedroni cointegration	308.33 (91.49)	<.001*	308.33 (138.36)	.026*	308.33 (108.88)	.005*	414.63 (204.41)	.043*
Other cointegration	18.62 (65.78)	.777	18.62 (68.58)	.786	18.62 (63.12)	.768	38.11 (59.57)	.523
Number of countries	4.44 (2.79)	.113	4.44 (4.83)	.358	4.44 (5.59)	.427	−0.88 (4.05)	.826
Number of years	−2.94 (5.29)	.578	−2.94 (4.57)	.520	−2.94 (6.47)	.649	2.00 (3.16)	.527
Start year of the time span	1.40 (5.45)	.796	1.40 (5.01)	.778	1.40 (5.96)	.813	2.17 (3.40)	.524
Prices of goods	−290.60 (79.18)	<.001*	−290.60 (64.38)	<.001*	−290.60 (71.15)	<.001*	−163.53 (69.53)	.019*
Environmental Kuznets curve	436.89 (81.67)	<.001*	436.89 (137.18)	.001*	436.89 (134.51)	.001*	400.39 (159.39)	.012*

Continued

Table 3 Metaregression results (Models 1, 2, 3, and 4)—cont'd

	Model 1: OLS		Model 2: heteroskedasticity robust covariance model		Model 3: heterogeneity robust model		Model 4: weighted heteroskedasticity robust model	
	Coefficient (St. error)	P	Coefficient (St. error)	P	Coefficient (St. error)	P	Coefficient (St. error)	P
Capital formation	0.72 (0.12)	<.001*	0.72 (0.18)	<.001*	0.72 (0.13)	<.001*	0.66 (0.21)	.001*
Carbon emissions	−180.48 (97.86)	.066**	−180.48 (126.52)	.155	−180.48 (88.21)	.041*	−293.94 (131.58)	.026*
Labor	135.55 (117.66)	.250	135.55 (168.51)	.422	135.55 (137.76)	.326	298.80 (197.98)	.132
Bidirectional causality	0.07 (0.05)	.152	0.07 (0.04)	.101	0.07 (0.04)	.099**	0.014 (0.02)	.615
Stability	−130.64 (89.02)	.143	−130.64 (117.62)	.267	−130.64 (99.15)	.188	−227.27 (205.14)	.269
Adjusted R^2	0.68		0.68		0.70		0.79	
F	37.08		37.08		37.08		63.39	
Br./Pagan LM χ^2(15)			311.27				718.99	
VIF	<10							
CUSUM	40%							
Number of clusters					17			
Observations	247		247		247		247	

Note: * 5% significance, ** 10% significance.
From Menegaki, A., 2014. On energy consumption and GDP studies; a meta-analysis of the last two decades. Renew. Sust. Energ. Rev. 29, 31–36.

Case study 2: The metaanalysis on energy-growth nexus by Kalimeris et al. (2014)

In the same year, Kalimeris et al. (2014) have published the second metaanalysis, which is based on a much larger sample of 158 studies and a very comprehensive analysis. Nevertheless, they could support neither a macrodimension nor a neutrality hypothesis between the energy and growth relationship. This study used a different classification of variables, which reveals that the spectrum of variable representation is vast. Thus, for example, the year of publication is a dummy variable with groups termed based on the decade the publication was issued, for example, 1970s and 1980s. While Menegaki (2014) uses a continuous variable to count the year of publication from the present time, this study offers a different idea on how to represent the publication year, and this reveals the vast horizons open to variable definition and codification.

Therefore the study by Kalimeris et al. (2014) uses a dummy for the data size, between the groups of 10–19, 20–29, 30–39, etc. Furthermore, instead of a pure geographical description of the countries in the sample, the authors use a description of their economic development and status, for example, G7 countries and OECD countries. They also use seven econometric methodologies and nine energy types. They also underline the importance of the energy measurement. Many studies are not clear of this definition, but Kalimeris et al. (2014) note nine distinct types of energy measurement such as Btu's and oil equivalent. Instead of generating many observations from one study, they have used a dummy variable to separate their sample into single countries and more than one country studies. Causality was represented with one variable for every hypothesis: conservation, growth, neutrality, and feedback (Table 4).

Kalimeris et al. (2014) performed their analysis with a rough set data analysis method to create rules inserted in functional relationships for the whole dataset. However, the method failed to provide concrete and effective results about the direction of causality, and this entailed that the direction of causality could not be described by a theoretically testable argument. The authors in this study continued with a multinomial logistic regression with dependent variables being the causality categories identified minus one. They concluded that the direction of causality is probably sensitive to the econometric method, and there is no general macrorule among the attributes of the study that leads to a certain hypothesis. Thus, for example, the only weak indication that the Johansen-Juselius methodology with oil equivalent energy measurement leads to the support of the conservation hypothesis could not be of much use, since it is not based on robust findings (Table 5).

Continued

Table 4 Variables and frequencies in the metaanalysis by Kalimeris et al. (2014).

Variable	Description	Frequency (N = 686)
Length of study period in years	<10	5
	10–19	8
	20–29	191
	30–39	353
	40+	127
Economic development of the country	G7	121
	Other OECD	163
	Non-OECD high development	148
	Other non-OECD	245
	Region of country	9
One or more countries	Single country	637
	Group of countries	49
Econometric methodology	Sims, Engle, and Granger	207
	Johansen-Juselius	189
	Toda-Yamamoto	116
	Pedroni	52
	ARDL bounds test	52
	Other	70
Energy input source	Energy per capita	272
	Total energy	214
	Electricity	139
	Coal	22
	Oil	14
	Gas	13
	Other (nuclear, renewables, and total fossil fuels)	12
Energy measurement method	Oil equivalent	357
	Electricity	168
	Btu	49
	Coal equivalent	25
	Crude quantity	12
	Other (Devisia index, joule, exergy)	8
	Undefined	67

Modified from Kalimeris, P., Richardson, C., Bithas, K., 2014. A meta-analysis investigation of the direction of the energy-GDP causal relationship: implications for the growth-degrowth dialogue. J. Clean. Prod. 67, 1–13.

Table 5 Multinomial logistic results: rate ratios with 95% confidence intervals.

Attribute	Categories	Rate ratio and 95% CI versus E ≠ GDP		
		E → GDP	**GDP → E**	**E ↔ GDP**
Econometric methodology	Sims and Engle-Granger	1.14 (0.53–2.43)	1.12 (0.51–2.44)	2.46 (1.01–5.98)
	Johansen-Juselius	4.34 (1.90–9.94)	2.39 (1.00–5.72)	8.80 (6.40–22.8)
	Toda-Yamamoto	0.99 (0.44–2.22)	1.55 (0.70–3.43)	0.53 (0.17–1.60)
	Pedroni	35.5 (4.29–293)	14.0 (1.60–123)	33.0 (3.69–295)
	ARDL	1.95 (0.66–5.78)	3.14 (1.13–8.75)	4.70 (1.46–15.1)
	Others (this is the reference category)	1	1	1
Energy measurement	Btu	0.18 (0.06–0.58)	1.28 (0.45–3.61)	0.13 (0.04–0.47)
	Oil equivalent	0.96 (0.45–2.05)	1.74 (0.73–4.16)	1.00 (0.46–0.47)
	Electricity	0.87 (0.38–2.00)	1.60 (0.63–4.03)	0.52 (0.21–1.27)
	Others	0.39 (0.12–1.27)	1.16 (0.34–4.01)	0.47 (0.15–1.49)
	Undefined	1	1	1

From Kalimeris, P., Richardson, C., Bithas, K., 2014. A meta-analysis investigation of the direction of the energy-GDP causal relationship: implications for the growth-degrowth dialogue. J. Clean. Prod. 67, 1–13.

Case study 3: The metaanalysis on the energy-growth nexus by Hajko (2017)

Hajko (2017) initially identified 277 studies, and he retained only 105 of them as qualifying for participation in his sample. He employed a multitude (about 31) of continuous (integer), dummy (two categories), and other qualitative (categorical) variables, as shown in Table 6.

Continued

Table 6 Variable description in the metaanalysis of Hajko (2017).

Variable	Description
Number of cross sections	Integer
Number of observations	Integer
Length of study in years	Integer
Sample size	Integer
Publication year	Integer
Number of citations	Integer
Number of separate individual estimates	Integer
United States only	Dummy, Yes, 1; No, 0
China only	Dummy, Yes, 1; No, 0
EU only	Dummy, Yes, 1; No, 0
Panel data	Dummy, Yes, 1; No, 0
Single region	Dummy, Yes,1; No, 0
Multiple Energy Types	Dummy, Yes, 1; No, 0
Cointegration testing performed	Dummy, Yes, 1; No, 0
Correction for multiple testing	Dummy, Yes, 1; No, 0
Multivariate	Dummy, Yes, 1; No, 0
Price as control variable	Qualitative, Yes, 1; No, 0; Mixed, 2
EKC link	Qualitative, Yes 1; No, 0; Mixed, 2
Structural breaks considered	Qualitative, Yes, 1; No, 0; Mixed, 2
Significance level	Qualitative, 1 = 5%; 2 = 1%; 3 = not specified
Sectoral	Qualitative,1, aggregate; 2, sectoral; 3, both
Variables per capita	Qualitative,1, total; 2, per capita; 3, both/mixed
Sign of causality considered	Qualitative,1, no; 2, in cointegration equation only partially; 3, yes; 4, inconclusive/unclear
Frequency	Qualitative,1, annual; 2, quarterly; 3, monthly; 4, other
Overall economic level	Qualitative,1, low- and lower-income economies; 2, middle-income economies; 3, high-income economies; 4, mixed
Basic causality direction concluded	Qualitative,1, neutrality; 2, growth; 3, conservation; feedback; 5, mixed
Production control variables	Qualitative,1, none; 2, capital; 3, labor; 4, both; 5, mixed
Estimation method for causality	Qualitative,1,standard granger causality (Engle-Granger, Sims); 2, modified Granger causality (Hsiao, Toda-Yamamoto); 3, ARDL; 4, panel causality analysis; 5, other

Table 6 Variable description in the metaanalysis of Hajko (2017)—cont'd

Variable	Description
Geographic area	Qualitative,1, mixed; 2, Asia (with Australia); 3, Europe; 4, Latin America and Caribbean, 5: Middle East and Africa; 6, North America
Cointegration method	Qualitative,1, none; 2, Engle-Granger; 3, Johansen; 4, panel-Pedroni/Larsson; 5, other; 6, mixed
Energy types	Qualitative,1, aggregate/all; 2, fossil fuels (oil, gas, and coal); 3, electricity; 4, renewables; 5, nuclear heat; 6, exergy; 7, mixed

Modified from Hajko, V., 2017. The failure of energy-economy nexus: a meta-analysis of 104 studies. Energy 125, 771–787.

Hajko (2017) used the nonparametric method of classification trees and forests as alternative to the multinomial regression model. The pursuit was to divide the sample into more similar subgroups that could possibly be described by a set of rules. Hajko in this article is critical of the energy-growth nexus field and claims that it is not useful for policy making due to all the theoretical gaps and empirical manipulations that can be subject to. He numbered a series of handicaps such as the publication bias, the omitted variable bias, the incomplete multivariate specifications, the lack of correctly specified energy data with lower frequencies, the heterogeneous cross sections, and the insufficient incorporation of the sign of the causality. This metaanalysis carries the most pessimistic message for the usefulness of the energy-growth nexus, but at the same time, it establishes the foundation for a correction of its research framework. Therefore, in this respect, this study is very fruitful.

Case study 4: The metaanalysis on the renewable energy-growth nexus by Sebri (2015)

Sebri's collection of studies was mainly based on three following keywords: "renewable energy" AND "economic growth," "renewable energy" AND "GDP," "causality" AND "renewable energy" AND "economic growth," "cointegration" AND "renewable energy" AND "economic growth," and "energy-growth nexus." Reporting these keywords provides readers with a good idea of how one can search through academic bases and select the appropriate sample of papers for a metaanalysis. Sebri (the author) states that since the renewable energy-growth nexus field is more recent than the general energy-growth nexus field, this justifies the fact that studies in this analysis are more recent in this case. Thus the search period ranges from 2009 to 2013. Besides the standard databases, this study has also searched in Google Scholar. Overall the study ended with an inclusion of 40 papers and 153 observations. The codification of variables in this study is shown in Table 7.

Continued

Table 7 Variable description in the metaanalysis by Sebri (2015).

Variable	Description
Dependent variable	
Hypothesis	1, Feedback; 2, conservation; 3, growth; 4, neutrality
General study characteristics	
Short run	1, Short-run causality; 0, long-run causality
Published	1, Published study; 0, unpublished study
Model specification	
Bivariate	1, If the study is based on a bivariate model; 0, if it is based on a multivariate model
CO_2	1, If emissions are controlled for; 0, if otherwise
Structural break	1, If structural break is investigated; 0, otherwise
Aggregate	1, Aggregate data are used; 0, otherwise
Panel data	1, Panel data are used; 0, otherwise
Cointegration approach	
Johansen	1, If the Johansen approach is applied; 0, otherwise
ARDL	1, If the ARDL approach is applied; 0, otherwise
Pedroni	1, If the Pedroni approach is applied; 0, otherwise
Another cointegration	1, If another cointegration approach is applied; 0, otherwise
Causality test	
Granger	1, If the error correction model is applied; 0, otherwise
Toda	1, If the Toda-Yamamoto model is applied; 0, otherwise
Hatemi	1, If the Hatemi model is applied; 0, otherwise
Another causality	1, If another causality model is applied; 0, otherwise
Development level	
Developed	1, If the study is conducted on a developed country; 0, otherwise
Developing	1, If the study is conducted on a developing country; 0, otherwise
Mixture	1, If the study is conducted on a panel of developed and developing countries; 0, otherwise

From Sebri, M., 2015. Use renewables to be cleaner: meta-analysis of the renewable energy consumption-economic growth nexus. Renew. Sust. Energ. Rev. 42, 657–665.

The author has identified 19 variables and has separated them in six categories: (1) the dependent variable, (2) the general study characteristics, (3) model specification, (4) the cointegration approach, (5) the causality test, and (6) the development level of the country.

Then the study employed the multinomial logit model since the dependent variable is a categorical variable (the four hypotheses in the energy-growth nexus). The interested reader can read about the merits of the multinomial model in Horowitz (1981), Long and Freese (2001), and Hausman and McFadden (1984). Since heteroskedasticity may arise due to the adoption of different sample sizes and estimation approaches and heterogeneity may also appear due to different study designs and methods, results have been cross examined for robustness through the implementation of the weighted with cluster robust standard errors version (the natural logarithm of primary studies sample sizes are used as weights) and the classic weighted version of multinomial logit regression.

The study finds that the direction of causality significantly differed between the long-run and the short-run horizon. The probability of obtaining the result of the neutrality hypothesis is more likely to be greater in the short run. Only the conservation hypothesis is likely to be found in equal occurrence in the short and the long run. The study also found that the method, the type of the data frequency, or the aggregation type does have an effect on the supported hypothesis. Also the consideration of breaks has had an effect. The author also suggests that grouping developed with developing countries in the same panel may produce inaccurate results. This study has also found that there was no publication bias in the renewable energy growth literature, since so systematic differences were observed between the relevant published and unpublished papers. The study also finds that in the bivariate model it is more likely to have the outcome of growth and neutrality (Table 8).

Table 8 Factors that increase the occurrence of a hypothesis.

Feedback	Neutrality	Growth	Conservation
Bivariate	Bivariate Short run	Bivariate	
Breaks	Breaks		Breaks
Per capita, aggregate data		Per capita, aggregate data	
	Decreases with panel data		
ARDL		ARDL	
	Pedroni		Pedroni
	Toda-Yamamoto, Hatemi	Toda-Yamamoto, Hatemi	
			Developing countries

Author's compilation from Sebri, M., 2015. Use renewables to be cleaner: meta-analysis of the renewable energy consumption-economic growth nexus. Renew. Sust. Energ. Rev. 42: 657–665.

Continued

Sebri's metaanalysis was more proliferate in positive results, and this could possibly be attributed to its pooling of more recent studies and more homogeneous with respect to the energy type it focuses on (renewable energy). Nevertheless, it provides a clear indication that the energy-growth nexus research results are not independent of most of the characteristics of the study.

5 A new trend; metaanalytic literature reviews instead of ordinary literature reviews

Literature reviews in the energy-growth nexus are quite various. Each author has a different style, and writing may partly be an art, but technical writing, as a literature review requires, should comply with some prerequisites. Researchers find the literature review quite a painful task, because it requires reading a lot of material and then position one's new paper among them, proving its originality and usefulness in gauging a gap in literature.

Sometimes one gets the feeling that this part in a paper is arbitrary, and the researcher writes about some landmarks in literature, and some papers considers to be important. However, a researcher should not think like this about literature review. This should be at some degree transparent and reproducible. Therefore it is good to begin one's literature review with the search criteria and search details. Researchers may feel bewildered and distressed when they are confronted with a search result of thousands of entries after a search attempt. A high number of results do not mean that the researcher needs to review all those papers in one's literature review. Typically, one starts with the most recent ones always paying attention to the most high-impact factored journals.

The more respected the journal is, the better literature reviews it contains, and researchers can be referred to seminal literature even without originally digging so deep in literature and searching those papers in a blind way. When the most useful papers are identified, be it around 20–30, an author must start compiling one's literature review. The literature review must show the evolution of research in time, how the topic started being studied for the first time, and how this studying evolved, for example, in the energy-growth nexus, researchers started using different types of data and variables. The review should also show the evolution of methods. How did researchers begin studying the question 20 years ago and how they gradually enriched this way of studying with new methods and methodological setups. When one assumes an outline answering these questions, one turns out with a literature review, a narrative that eventually shows that the new paper is going to say something different and add to literature.

Particularly for the energy-growth nexus field, researchers should be careful when they construct their literature reviews and not placing all literature in one basket. For example, literature based on single countries should be presented separately from literature based on multiple country studies. Literature with aggregate data should also be presented separately from literature with disaggregate data. A good literature review enables a good discussion of the results to be produced by a new paper.

Since literature in the energy-growth nexus field is abundant and controversial and contradictory in its results, a tabulation of literature is necessary because the reader can get with one glimpse an update and understanding of the novelty of the new paper. Thus it is customary in to tabulate the literature with the following column titles: study (author name and year), data span of the study, country, dependent variable, covariates, energy variable type, econometric method, and results (based on which hypothesis is supported by the results of the paper). When the literature review has been based on a sufficiently large number of papers, one can also produce insightful statistics such as percentages of study classifications based on geographical location, energy type, and the confirmed result. This generates what we term as metaanalytical review and has also been presented in detail in Menegaki and Tsani (2018) in Tsani and Menegaki (2018).

6 Conclusion

Robust metaanalysis is one way out the deadlock, wherein the energy-growth nexus literature has led itself into. The deadlock has been gradually built due to the huge development of contradicting literature, huge variety of data, and the continuous improvement of econometric methods, which can overcome data hindrances and deficiencies of the past.

This chapter has provided the main steps in a metaanalysis with guidelines that answer to some of the main criticisms against metaanalyses. The main part of the chapter had dealt with the presentation of the most important points and the results of four metaanalyses that have taken place in the energy-growth nexus field. All four of them have found that the different econometric methods used are one of the reasons for the contradictory results. Two of them have employed the multinomial regression analysis, one of them a nonparametric method and one of them a traditional regression analysis. Two of them are inconclusive and one pessimistic, and they somehow confirm the dead-end this research field has ended into. The fourth one (in the turn they are discussed in this chapter) provides clear results on what appears to affect the results in the nexus, but this is a narrower study because it contains only renewable energy-growth studies. One reason that this occurs is that renewable energy growth studies are more recent, and this may render them more homogeneous both in the methods employed and their data.

The fact that all four metaanalyses underline much the importance of the econometric method opens the way to the rest of this book, which is a presentation and explanation of all the econometric methods employed in the nexus and equips researchers with a necessary handbook that will acquaint them with all the methodologies with the aim to connect them and enable researchers to compare and transfer results from one study to the other.

Last, but not least, this chapter highlights the new trend in reviewing literature in the energy-growth nexus field. Since the nexus is seething with papers, one must be able to show the novelty of one's new paper in a quick and comprehensive way, which will cause no doubt to readers and reviewers about its novelty. The metaanalytical review is one way to achieve that.

References

Acaravci, A., Öztürk, I., 2010. On the relationship between energy consumption, CO_2 emissions and economic growth in Europe. Energy 35 (12), 5412–5420.

Akinlo, E.A., 2008. Energy consumption and economic growth: evidence from 11 sub-Sahara African countries. Energy Econ. 30 (5), 2391–2400.

Al-Iriani, M.A., 2006. Energy–GDP relationship revisited: an example from GCC countries using panel causality. Energy Policy 34 (17), 3342–3350.

Altinay, G., Karagol, E., 2004. Structural break, unit root, and the causality between energy consumption and GDP in Turkey. Energy Econ. 26 (6), 985–994.

Altinay, G., Karagol, E., 2005. Electricity consumption and economic growth: evidence from Turkey. Energy Econ. 27, 849–856.

Ang, J.B., 2007. CO_2 emissions, energy consumption, and output in France. Energy Policy 35 (10), 4772–4778.

Ang, J.B., 2008. Economic development, pollutant emissions and energy consumption in Malaysia. J. Policy Model 30 (2), 271–278.

Apergis, N., Payne, J.E., 2009a. Energy consumption and economic growth: evidence from the commonwealth of independent states. Energy Econ. 31 (5), 641–647.

Apergis, N., Payne, J.E., 2009b. Energy consumption and economic growth in Central America: evidence from a panel cointegration and error correction model. Energy Econ. 31 (2), 211–216.

Apergis, N., Payne, J.E., 2010. Energy consumption and growth in South America: evidence from a panel error correction model. Energy Econ. 32 (6), 1421–1426.

Asafu-Adjaye, J., 2000. The relationship between energy consumption, energy prices and economic growth: time series evidence from Asian developing countries. Energy Econ. 22 (6), 615–625.

Balcilar, M., Ozdemir, Z.A., Arslanturk, Y., 2010. Economic growth and energy consumption causal nexus viewed through a bootstrap rolling window. Energy Econ. 32 (6), 1398–1410.

Bartleet, M., Gounder, R., 2010. Energy consumption and economic growth in New Zealand: results of trivariate and multivariate models. Energy Policy 38 (7), 3508–3517.

Belloumi, M., 2009. Energy consumption and GDP in Tunisia: cointegration and causality analysis. Energy Policy 37 (7), 2745–2753.

Biostat Inc, 2019. Why Perform a Meta-Analysis? Available from: www.Meta-analysis.Com/pages/why_do.Php?Cart=. (Accessed 16 April 2019).

Bowden, N., Payne, J.E., 2009. The causal relationship between U.S. energy consumption and real output: a disaggregated analysis. J. Policy Model 31 (2), 180–188.

Box, G.E.P., Cox, D.R., 1964. An analysis of transformation. J. R. Stat. Soc. Series B 26, 211–252.

Chiou-Wei, S.Z., Chen, C.-F., Zhu, Z., 2008. Economic growth and energy consumption revisited—evidence from linear and nonlinear granger causality. Energy Econ. 30 (6), 3063–3076.

Eggoh, J.C., Bangake, C., Rault, C., 2011. Energy consumption and economic growth revisited in African countries. Energy Policy 39 (11), 7408–7421.

Erdal, G., Erdal, H., Esengün, K., 2008. The causality between energy consumption and economic growth in Turkey. Energy Policy 36 (10), 3838–3842.

Esso, L.J., 2010. Threshold cointegration and causality relationship between energy use and growth in seven African countries. Energy Econ. 32 (6), 1383–1391.

Friedl, B., Getzner, M., 2003. Determinants of CO_2 emissions in a small open economy. Ecol. Econ. 45 (1), 133–148.

Fuinhas, J.A., Marques, A.C., 2012. Energy consumption and economic growth nexus in Portugal, Italy, Greece, Spain and Turkey: an ARDL bounds test approach (1965–2009). Energy Econ. 34 (2), 511–517.

Ghali, K.H., El-Sakka, M.I.T., 2004. Energy use and output growth in Canada: a multivariate cointegration analysis. Energy Econ. 26 (2), 225–238.

Glass, G.V., 2000. Meta-Analysis at 25. Available from: https://www.gvglass.info/papers/meta25.html. (Accessed 14 August 2019).

Glasure, Y.U., Lee, A.-R., 1998. Cointegration, error-correction, and the relationship between GDP and energy: the case of South Korea and Singapore. Resour. Energy Econ. 20 (1), 17–25.

Gosh, S., 2002. Electricity consumption and economic growth in India. Energy Policy 30 (2), 125–129.

Hajko, V., 2017. The failure of energy-economy nexus: a meta-analysis of 104 studies. Energy 125, 771–787.

Halicioglou, F., 2009. An econometric study of CO_2 emissions, energy consumption, income and foreign trade in Turkey. Energy Policy 37 (3), 1156–1164.

Hamit-Hagar, M., 2012. Greenhouse gas emissions, energy consumption and economic growth: a panel cointegration analysis from Canadian industrial sector perspective. Energy Econ. 34 (1), 358–364.

Hausman, J., McFadden, D., 1984. Specification tests for the multinomial logit model. Econometrica 52, 1219–1240.

Ho, C.-Y., Siu, K.W., 2007. A dynamic equilibrium of electricity consumption and GDP in Hong Kong: an empirical investigation. Energy Policy 35 (4), 2507–2513.

Hondroyiannis, G., Lolos, S., Papapetrou, E., 2002. Energy consumption and economic growth: assessing the evidence from Greece. Energy Econ. 24 (4), 319–336.

Horowitz, J., 1981. Identification and diagnosis of specification errors in the multinomial logit model. Transp. Res. B Methodol. 15, 345–360.

Inglesi-Lotz, R., 2018. The role of potential factors/actors and regime switching modeling. In: Menegaki, A. (Ed.), The Economics and Econometrics of the Energy-Growth Nexus. Academic Publishing.

Jalil, A., Mahmud, S.F., 2009. Environment Kuznets curve for CO_2 emissions: a cointegration analysis for China. Energy Policy 37 (12), 5167–5172.

Kalimeris, P., Richardson, C., Bithas, K., 2014. A meta-analysis investigation of the direction of the energy-GDP causal relationship: implications for the growth-degrowth dialogue. J. Clean. Prod. 67, 1–13.

Lean, H.H., Smyth, R., 2010. CO_2 emissions, electricity consumption and output in ASEAN. Appl. Energy 87 (6), 1858–1864.

Lee, C.-C., 2005. Energy consumption and GDP in developing countries: a cointegrated panel analysis. Energy Econ. 27 (3), 415–427.

Lee, C.-C., Chang, C.-P., 2008. Energy consumption and economic growth in Asian economies: a more comprehensive analysis using panel data. Resour. Energy Econ. 30 (1), 50–65.

Lee, C.-C., Chien, M.-S., 2010. Dynamic modelling of energy consumption, capital stock, and real income in G-7 countries. Energy Econ. 32 (3), 564–581.

Lise, W., Van Montfort, K., 2007. Energy consumption and GDP in Turkey: is there a cointegration relationship? Energy Econ. 29 (6), 1166–1178.

Long, J.S., Freese, J., 2001. Regression Models for Categorical Dependent Variables Using Stata. Stata Press, College Station, TX.

Mahadevan, R., Asafu-Adjaye, J., 2007. Energy consumption, economic growth and prices: a reassessment using panel VECM for developed and developing countries. Energy Policy 35 (4), 2481–2490.

Masih, A.M.M., Masih, R., 1996. Energy consumption, real income and temporal causality: results from a multi-country study based on cointegration and error-correction modelling techniques. Energy Econ. 18 (3), 165–183.

Menegaki, A., 2014. On energy consumption and GDP studies; a meta-analysis of the last two decades. Renew. Sust. Energ. Rev. 29, 31–36.

Menegaki, A.N., Tsani, S., 2018. Critical issues to be answered in the energy-growth nexus (EGN) research field. In: The Economics and Econometrics of the Energy-Growth Nexus. Elsevier, pp. 141–184.

Mozumder, P., Marathe, A., 2007. Causality relationship between electricity consumption and GDP in Bangladesh. Energy Policy 35 (1), 395–402.

Narayan, P.K., Prasad, A., 2008. Electricity consumption–real GDP causality nexus: evidence from a bootstrapped causality test for 30 OECD countries. Energy Policy 36 (2), 910–918.

Nelson, J.P., Kennedy, P.E., 2009. The use and abuse of meta-analysis in environmental and natural resource economics: an assessment. Environ. Resour. Econ. 42, 345–377.

Odhiambo, N.M., 2009. Energy consumption and economic growth nexus in Tanzania: an ARDL bounds testing approach. Energy Policy 37 (2), 617–622.

Odhiambo, N.M., 2010. Energy consumption, prices and economic growth in three SSA countries: a comparative study. Energy Policy 38 (5), 2463–2469.

Oh, W., Lee, K., 2004. Energy consumption and economic growth in Korea: testing the causality relation. J. Policy Model 26 (8–9), 973–981.

Özturk, I., Acaravci, A., 2010. CO_2 emissions, energy consumption and economic growth in Turkey. Renew. Sust. Energ. Rev. 14 (9), 3220–3225.

Özturk, I., Aslan, A., Kalyoncu, H., 2010. Energy consumption and economic growth relationship: evidence from panel data for low and middle income countries. Energy Policy 38 (8), 4422–4428.

Paul, S., Bhattacharya, R.N., 2004. Causality between energy consumption and economic growth in India: a note on conflicting results. Energy Econ. 26 (6), 977–983.

Russo, M.W., 2007. How to review a meta-analysis. Gastroenterol. Hepatol. 3 (8), 637–642.

Sebri, M., 2015. Use renewables to be cleaner: meta-analysis of the renewable energy consumption-economic growth nexus. Renew. Sust. Energ. Rev. 42, 657–665.

Sebri, M., 2015. Use renewables to be cleaner: meta-analysis of the renewable energy consumption-economic growth nexus. Renew. Sustain. Energy Rev. 42, 657–665.

Sebri, M., 2016. Forecasting urban water demand: a meta-regression analysis. J. Environ. Manag. 183, 777–785.

Shiu, A., Lam, P.-L., 2004. Electricity consumption and economic growth in China. Energy Policy 32 (1), 47–54.

Shuttleworth, M., Wilson, L.T.W., 2019. Meta-Analysis. Available from: explorable.Com/meta-analysis, Accessed 16 April 2019.

Squalli, J., 2007. Electricity consumption and economic growth: bounds and causality analyses of OPEC members. Energy Econ. 29 (6), 1192–1205.

Tsani, S.Z., 2010. Energy consumption and economic growth: a causality analysis for Greece. Energy Econ. 32 (3), 582–590.

Tsani, S., Menegaki, A.N., 2018. The energy-growth nexus (EGN) checklist for authors. In: The Economics and Econometrics of the Energy-Growth Nexus. Elsevier, pp. 347–376.

Wang, S.S., Zhou, D.Q., Zhou, P., Wang, Q.W., 2011. CO_2 emissions, energy consumption and economic growth in China: a panel data analysis. Energy Policy 39 (9), 4870–4875.

Yuan, J.-H., Kang, J.-G., Zhao, C.-H., Hu, Z.-G., 2008. Energy consumption and economic growth: evidence from China at both aggregated and disaggregated levels. Energy Econ. 30 (6), 3077–3094.

Zhang, X.-P., Cheng, X.-M., 2009. Energy consumption, carbon emissions, and economic growth in China. Ecol. Econ. 68 (10), 2706–2712.

Zhixin, Z., Xin, R., 2011. Causal relationships between energy consumption and economic growth. Energy Procedia 5 (0), 2065–2071.

An A-Z guide for the energy-growth nexus studies

1 Introduction

A new researcher always feels insecure about the best steps one has to take for the implementation of his/her energy-growth project. Also, at the beginning, it takes much time to understand the literature that one reads. This is a very hectic period that can be reduced in the psychological burden it causes when the steps are structured. This saves much time for the researcher and renders him/her directly functional in the research field. Otherwise, he will have to spend a significant part of his time to address this need. Therefore this chapter is very important and necessary to be read by every junior researcher in the energy-growth nexus. The steps that are described below do not necessarily follow the order they have been enumerated.

This chapter is structured in a very simple and straightforward way. After this brief introduction, 26 pieces of advice follow for the energy-growth researchers. Section 3 offers some closing remarks.

2 The A-Z catalogue of advice for energy-growth nexus researchers

A

The new researcher must spend adequate time to search the databases with keywords that are necessary. Each researcher wants to study a brand new topic or resume a topic that has been initiated by somebody else or try an existent topic with new data or a new methodology. Thus to find out what is going on in the field, one must spend some time reading major journals in the field such as energy economics, renewable and sustainable energy reviews, applied energy, and many others for the last 5 years. Reading what the most important journals are publishing on this field will generate ideas and implicit recommendations about the keywords. For example, if there is a focus in the study of the energy-growth nexus with a focus to the contribution of the financial sector. Only by reading recent literature in crucial journals does it become evident what keywords one should peruse. In this way the idea crystallized what relationship to investigate.

293

A Guide to Econometric Methods for the Energy-Growth Nexus. https://doi.org/10.1016/B978-0-12-819039-5.00013-6

B

After the topic is decided with its keywords, the researcher is advised to start the search in major platforms, for example, Scopus and ScienceDirect. Most of the time the literature review looks like a black box, as far as the selection of the reviewed papers is concerned. The latter takes place in a rather arbitrary way, which cannot be reproduced or assessed for its quality. Articles related to a particular topic can be searched in many available databases such as Web of Science (WoS), Scopus (SC), ScienceDirect (SD), ProQuest (PQ), and Business Sources (EBSCO). Each of these databases has its pros and cons. For instance the advantage of SC and WoS is that they not only provide the title, abstract, and bibliographic information but also provide citation information, funding institutions, and reference list. This information is necessary to carry out citation analysis. The disadvantage of SC and Wob is that they do not allow to search in the full body text of the article database. On the other hand, SD, PQ, and EBSCO allow the user to search the full body text of the articles included in their respective databases. However, they do not provide the citation information, and their web interface does not allow the reference list of each article to be exported for analysis. Citation analysis can still be carried out though, by manually adding the citation information from Google Scholar, SC, and WoS. The citation information from Google citations has some issues related to the quality of the citations, as pointed out in some studies (Harzing and Alakangas, 2016; Harzing and Van Der Wal, 2009). On the contrary, citations' counts in SCOPUS and WoS are only coming from the publications within the respective databases. Unlike Google citations, the citations from WoS are considered the highest quality. The citation information from SC is considered a good compromise between the two extremes (Google citations and WoS citations), and it appears to be more accurate than WoS.

Overall and for the aforementioned reasons, it is important that the search database is exactly specified and the keywords are also defined in detail. This gives transparency to the search process and the freedom to reproduce at a certain degree. The reason I am saying "at a certain degree" is because the generation of new papers is continuous and thus the database in continually enriched and updated. Also the date of search should be reported to be able to judge how updated the literature review is. The selected papers should be kept at a separate file. Not all of them are going to be used necessarily in our literature review, because not all of them will be saying something noteworthy for our route of research. Sometimes the titles of the papers are misleading, and they do not refer to what their title might suggest.

C

Third: There is an initial scan of literature to trace the papers that are important for our topic and will be finally included in the literature review. We read and underline the important lines in the papers. There is a specific trend in the literature review of the energy-growth nexus papers. Irrespective of the particular type of literature review that one follows, it is almost tacitly "compulsory" to include a tabulation of the literature that has been included in the review. The tabulation enables a quick overview at all dimensions (name of the study, data span, type of data, number and names of covariates, econometric methodology, and results, basically which of the four main hypotheses are supported). Depending on the focus of the research, the results may also include the estimated elasticities. At this point, I would recommend that the type of the unit root analysis is also included in another column of the table. Needless to say that the table can be enriched with any additional elements pertain to all studies and the researcher can trace them. The presentation of a literature to a table provides a quick overview, which facilitates tremendously a metaanalytic overview of the literature. One can calculate what percentage of papers have confirmed each type of hypotheses, what percentage of studies have used time series data or panel data, what type of studies uses yearly data or monthly or quarterly data, etc. Moreover a reader can make a quick calculation on the percentage of studies using each type of methodology. Of course the literature review table is not the only constituent part of the literature review. It must be supplemented with a text, and this is what I explain in the following step.

D

Fourth: This step explains young researchers what their text in the literature review should contain, besides the table described in the third step. Sometimes studies provide a summary of a few lines for each reviewed paper. This is wrong or at least not useful, because it offers no more than one would get by reading the abstracts of the papers alone. That way the review reads like a blunt text, which does not give readers an idea of the trend in the reviewed literature. Thus the literature review should never read like this. The author of the literature review should prove that he has read and digested the content of the literature. Only that way can he reproduce the gist of every paper and do that comparatively in a way that shows the gaps existent in the literature and the roads through which these can be gauged. At the same time, this way of literature presentation will show the necessity of the paper the new researcher is trying to write.

E

Fifth: The literature review must be commented on all its dimensions. Usually, I provide a narrative with the literature in a chronological order because there is an evolution of science with time. Of course sometimes we see new studies that have used old methods. That's true, but that is an exception. Therefore the presentation of the evolution of a scientific field in a chronological order is the most natural presentation of the literature. For example, readers are interested to know how the methodology has evolved from past up to date, how the usage of variables and covariates has been enriched with time, and whether results present any significant and systematic pattern with respect to the most important constituent parameters of the studies.

However, one may wonder where to start from and where to finish since the number of involved papers may be vast. To address the problem the answer may lie in a citation-based literature review. Over the past two decades, the development in data collection techniques, computing speed, and new academic journal have made the literature in every field to grow exponentially. It is difficult to comprehend the overwhelming literature using traditional literature survey tools. Citation or bibliometric analysis has become a very handy tool to provide a systematic analysis to a large body of literature and to infer trends over time and compare the relative impact of most prolific authors, top journals, and highly cited papers. Moreover, it presents an overall big picture of the literature, which is very useful to the new researcher planning to start their research in that research area. Ahmad and Menegaki (2020) have published a paper entitled "Systematic Literature Review of Tourism Growth Nexus: An overview of the literature and a content analysis of 100 most influential papers" published in the Journal of Economic surveys. This paper contains some good advice on how to conduct a citation-based literature review and with this manner how not to escape one the most influential papers in a certain field. The advantage is the existence of substantial effective statistical algorithms, access to high-quality numerical routines, and integrated data visualization tools (Aria and Cuccurullo, 2017). Several other software packages have been developed to carry out a bibliometric analysis. Generally, these tools can be divided into two main categories, one functioning on the R language platform (used in this study) and other using java applications and various others. Available software tools that consist of the second group are CitNetExplorer, VOSviewer, SciMAT, BibExcel, Science of Science (Sci2) Tool, CiteSpace, and VantagePoint. The main advantage of this group of software packages is that almost all of them are open and freeware source applications except for Vantagepoint, which functions on a commercial basis. Moreover the majority of the aforementioned tools, except for BibExcel software, offer a function of data visualization and mapping.

F

Sixth: In the previous step, I have said that the literature review section must not only make obvious the novel contribution of the paper but also should most importantly prove that novelty by highlighting the gaps existent in literature, either through the new relationship that is going to study or through the new and more sophisticated methodology or through an updated dataset or all of them. The gap that the new paper is going to gauge should be "advertised" in the abstract and the introduction. The latter must make a good opening scene for the paper, which will motivate the existence and the foundation of the paper. A new energy-growth nexus paper contains both new variables in the model, a new dataset is possibly with a higher frequency, and a new methodology is invincible in the review process (of course on the condition that it was adopted a good writing style and the appropriate academic language).

Some other papers, before or after the literature review, they also enclose a conceptual framework. This is not very customary in typical energy-growth nexus papers. The conceptual framework is an established methodology in the energy-growth nexus, nowadays, so it is not much of use.

G

Seventh: One crucial factor, maybe the most important, is the selection of the dataset to be used for analysis. Tiwari et al. (2018) provide many suggestions about possible databases. Those that are free of charge usually become the object of analysis by many researchers, and thus the chances that you have a unique paper are reduced. For this reason, it would be ideal to acquire a rare dataset, possibly with a high frequency and highly disaggregated. This will increase the value of your paper and the likelihood of being published in a highly esteemed journal with a high impact factor. Unfortunately such datasets are not free of charge, so one must pay to buy them. Unless you have proper funds available, you will have to pay out of pocket for that dataset. The dataset must be adequately referenced and described. The measurement units must also be properly reported and justified. It is common practice to use per capita magnitudes. These take into account population adjustments and give a fair idea of what is going on with the variables in the model.

H

Eighth: The selection of the methodology presupposes that a good literature review will have taken place first, which will enable the new researcher with sufficient knowledge of what methodologies the latest and the best papers have used so far. The researcher must always use a method that is at least as novel and good as the most recently applied in the field and at the same time try to improve it. If the researcher is an econometrician or a researcher with a good grasp of econometrics has high probability of improving a methodology, advance it and get the credit for that. It is also a good practice to use more than a single methodology for corroboration reasons. Of course researchers should not engage in practices of using redundant methodologies just for the sake of impressions. Each process and each method should be adequately justified.

It is true that one never knows what background reviewers will have that will review the paper. Sometimes reviews are so unfair and unexpected, but it is a better strategy to provide more in the first submitted version of the paper and then start cutting depending on the instructions of the reviewers and the editor. It is advisable not to leave anything unexplained under the assumption that is basic knowledge and everybody has it. It is better to assume that our readership will have average knowledge and thus explain everything in the paper, given that there is no word restriction. Some journals are very strict on the word limit, others are more flexible, and they make different acceptance arrangements when they see merit in a promising paper.

I

Ninth: Best research practices dictate that one's estimated results are reproducible. It becomes a growing practice that journals require uploading the dataset and estimation codes for a paper together with the whole submission. Furthermore, it is advisable that researchers make clear and transparent statements about the software they have employed for their estimations. Energy-growth researchers work on various software with a lot of readymade convenient estimation routines that render estimation work a quite friendly process even for researchers who are less experienced in econometric estimation. Nowadays, some new free software (e.g., R) is gaining ground and maybe this is the best knowledge investment a new researcher could make forever. This will free you from the worries of buying licenses and updates of certain software. If you invest enough time to learn well a programming language such as R, this will pay you off in the future and will give you the opportunity to become the single author in your papers. Note: Single authorship of a paper is a proof that a researcher can implement all stages in paper writing by himself. This is high recognition and one must do it sometime in one's career. I am not saying it is the best strategy to follow if you want to publish a lot. Publishing a lot presupposes high work division and specialization. Remember the comparative advantage in the theory of international trade and apply it in your research lives too. It is good that you can work completely independently and be self-sufficient, but it is not productive. It is advisable to specialize practicing the aspect of paper writing at which you are the best. If you are the best in econometric estimation, then concentrate on that. If you have a good writing style, practice writing introductions, literature reviews or discussions, or conclusions or one of these.

J

Tenth: After you make your estimations, it is crucial to decide what you keep and what you decide to include in the paper's result section. Many energy-growth nexus studies consider the presentation of descriptive statistics as a very important part of their results and I agree. However, although indispensable because it gives one an indication of whether to use parametric or nonparametric or semiparametric estimation, one should save space in the main paper and provide the descriptive statistics as an appendix. It is useful to make a comment of one line in your paper about the data normality. Also to avoid presentation within the paper (always with the aim to save space), one can state that the required table is available upon request. By the way, this should be the case for every other point in your paper that you have omitted or you have spent little text explaining that. Everything should be available upon request when your peers kindly ask for it or have a query to be answered. Personally, although I do not always have research assistants or a secretary and my timetable is full with obligations, I always try to enlighten my peers when they ask me little things about my papers (at least the recent ones, because about the older ones, I tend to forget some tiny details of implementation).

K

Eleventh: As you already have gone through many energy-growth papers, you will have observed that the sequence in the presentation of results, most of the times, goes like this: unit root investigation with many alternative tests, cointegration analysis, and last causality analysis. Depending on particular methodologies, one of these steps may be omitted in some papers. Many papers devote too much space presenting unit root analysis, while in my opinion, they should devote the least space. By no means, does this mean that they should not devote much effort on that. On the contrary, this analysis requires much effort, but it should be presented as briefly as possible, and this allow the allocation of more space for cointegration and causality analysis. The study of unit roots is really a major component of any analysis, and it has become quite sophisticated in the recent years. However, still researchers do employ first generation unit root tests with second generation unit root tests for reasons of corroborations. It is quite important to pay attention to structural breaks, and for this reason, we should have studied the economic history and actuality of the country whose energy-growth nexus we are investigating. Unless we have some ex-ante knowledge and expectation of the breaks, we will not be able to recognize them or discuss them when they appear. Thus this is a challenging point. Finding the breaks entails corroborating them. Have any major economic, politic, or social changes taken place? Have any energy transformations taken place in that country or group of countries? This is a hard topic to answer unless you are quite familiar and close to the country you are studying. This is one of the many reasons that writing a paper is not an easy task. There are many people having estimated results at hand, but they never make it to the writing of the full paper, because this requires a lot of long, tedious, and systematic work.

L

Twelfth: One of the initial parts of the analysis together with unit root analysis is the investigation of cross-sectional analysis. I will spare the details here, because I have devoted a whole chapter in this book that deals with the topic. However, this is a step that should not be avoided because it will undermine the quality of your estimated results and it may turn out that false regression results will appear. Needless to say that cross-sectional analysis evidence needs to be justified and adequately discussed. We need to particularly "suspicious" in cases with countries that belong to the same economic union or other form of union. This situation entails by definition that there is a type of connection and simultaneous pursuit of certain economic, environmental, energy, and development goals that lead to similar evidence, coevolution, and interdependence across the sampled countries.

M

Thirteenth: Cointegration is a very important part of the energy-growth analysis, and this book devotes several chapters on distinctive methods. This is most of the times recognized as the long-run relationship of variables across the variables. The confirmation of cointegration is not necessary to proceed to the next step, which is the causality analysis. Energy-growth researchers are trying to employ continuously improved methods, but there also some older methods, which are regarded as benchmark methods, and they continue to appear even in new papers, sometimes with additional caveats, sometimes not. For example recently Menegaki and Tiwari (2020) have employed a Fourier approximated Toda-Yamamoto estimation. The Toda-Yamamoto is an older method, but the additional twist of the Fourier approximation lends the paper a fresh perspective and renders as a very important contribution. Quite often, researchers trust old methods, and they employ them under the veil of the very important results that are generated or under a "sexy" title. But the title is another topic I deal in another point, toward the end of the paper. Although the latter read first in a paper, it should be decided in the last minute.

Fourteenth: Causality analysis is the most important part of the energy-growth analysis and the most controversial one. But the latter is another point I will return later. Causality is the gist of the research. It generated the information we seek from the beginning. It is true we make a long journey toward it, but that long work should also be presented for educative reasons and most importantly for corroboration reasons. The causality analysis should be presented as much detail as possible. The causality analysis takes much care in the presentation, the explanation, and the discussion of causality directions among the involved variables. This is often termed as the short-run relationships among variables. Another important information that is generated at this stage by several studies is the estimation of the adjustment speed (from the short run to long run equilibrium after the deviations that take place in the short run).

N

Fifteenth: Some papers choose to present separately the results and their discussion. So they devote one section with results and their technical description, and in the other section, they discuss their practical meaning, their interpretation, and most importantly their comparison with previous relevant literature. Attention should be provided at this point. It is very crucial and should be discussed sufficiently and with special care. It is not only good to have results conforming to previous literature but also good to have results opposing to previous literature. Both outcomes are desired. I guess the latter is even more challenging because it will make your piece of research as breakthrough and not as mainstream. Understandably enough, you must be ready to defend the extraordinary outcome. Find well-documented reasons and why they have occurred, and if this remains a puzzle, then you definitely need to shape your directions for further future research.

O

Sixteenth: Connect to policy interpretations and suggestions. The quintessential need for the energy-growth studies is the information of energy policy makers. Given that many governments have signed binding agreements on carbon dioxide emission cuts or they have set energy conservation goals, policy makers are keen to learn how they are going to implement those goals without putting at stake the so longed for economic growth (as expressed by GDP growth). Namely, achieve the goals at the lowest cost.

P

Seventeenth: Previously, I claimed that it is of vital importance the researcher of the energy-growth nexus be highly informed of the economic history and actuality of the country or group of countries he is studying. Here, I come to another reason why that is so. An uninformed researcher will not be able to connect one's results with policy interpretations and recommendations unless he is informed of them. Almost all journals that publish energy-growth nexus papers place high emphasis on the connection of empirical results with policy making insights and suggestions, and it becomes a permanent legitimate comment of reviewers. Without policy making connections, I think that energy-growth nexus papers are mere, educative econometric applications, but they tell very few about real-life and energy policy, which has been placed so high in the agendas of every economy and society.

Q

Eighteenth: The tables and figures that one is using in his paper must be comprehensive and all inclusive. Generally, we should avoid congesting the paper with tables and graphs that have been sparsely compiled. One should challenge oneself by compiling highly convertible and versatile graphs and tables that contain as much information as possible, without confusing or overwhelming the reader, but they make the most of publication space. Foremost, make sure that all tables and figures are legible and comprehensible and they are discussed sufficiently. This book has presented various core methodologies in every chapter and presents the necessary least statements that should be made and no researcher should forget to unveil those perspectives. Needless to say that all tables and figures should be referred to in the text with their numbers. It is not uncustomary that the editing office of a journal sends the final proofs to authors with comments of the type "Fig. 3 is nowhere reported in the text" or "You refer to Table 5, but this does not exist in your manuscript." Of course, all tables and figures should contain their source of origin, and if they have been compiled by the author himself/herself, then one should write: "Source: Author's compilation" or "The authors." It is not big deal if you omit this statement, but it is politically correct.

R

Nineteenth: The conclusion of the paper is another fundamental part of the energy-growth nexus and for this matter for every paper in academia. In some papers, it appears as concluding remarks. In both cases, it is a section that concludes or better say finishes the paper. In my opinion, this part, together with the abstract, is the most crucial parts of the paper. Personally, I always read papers in this unorthodox turn of sections. I read the abstract and then the conclusion. Afterward, if they still interest me, I move on to the methodology and results and then the rest of the paper. I usually read literature reviews in the end, and to be honest, I almost do that when I am writing my own paper's literature review to make sure that I don't leave out some important piece of literature. So the conclusion is a very important part and should be given analogous attention. Be careful! This is the last part of your research and you may feel exhausted and impatient. You may be pressed by different deadlines and obligations, and you want to submit your paper as soon as possible. Well, do not do that. Devote enough time to your conclusion so that you make it serve well its purpose. The conclusion should always recapitulate your study in its main parts and then emphasize on the innovations of the paper and the major findings. Thus, while the abstract announces what will be done and read in the paper, the conclusion confirms what you have read and seen, also highlighting it in a way that if you read the conclusion first (as I do), you will be enticed to read the main paper. Lastly, the conclusion quite often contains statements about future research whereby also the author admits what he/she could have done in a better way in the paper.

Since I mentioned previously the concept of Concluding remarks, I would like to return to that point now. The Concluding remarks are a bit different from a typical conclusion. They are brief, shorter than the conclusion, and they are some final remarks that one could make before closing the paper, or with the aim not to close the paper so abruptly. Sometimes, when papers are too long, or they are reviews or short commentaries, then a Concluding remarks section may be more appropriate. I believe that in the energy-growth nexus papers, this title should be avoided. I strongly recommend the compilation of a proper and full conclusion part.

S

Twentieth: I do not regard as necessary to talk about references, because journals have their own strict guidelines about them. The editing office after the acceptance of a paper is very helpful in this too. It is good to work with software that accommodates and transforms all your references from one style to the other. This will save time and energy, and you will devote your attention to actually reading and rereading your manuscript. However, I must admit that I love journals that have a system of "Your paper, your way," which allows one the freedom to submit the paper at the initial stage without conforming strictly to the protocols. I think it is so inappropriate asking an author (after first submission) to change the reference style of his paper and then just desk-reject the paper. It is so much waste of scarce research resources. Just think about it.

T

Twenty-first: The writing of appendices is another point; I will stop for a while. Appendices are useful when one needs more space within the main manuscript but he/she does not have it. Therefore appendices contain material that the reader finds resource to when he needs to. The descriptive statistics or the extra unit root analysis or any type of additional analysis can be accommodated here instead of the main paper. It is of secondary importance, but it is always referred to in the main manuscript. Some journals have prepared additional publication sectors, which are called supplementary material. This happens when the paper is loaded with mathematical formulae and proofs, which may not be of interest to the average academic reader who may be more interested in policy conclusions. Appendices are convenient and reduce the obscurity of a paper particularly for the new researcher. It depends on the editor and reviewers whether they accept them or not.

U

Twenty-second: I promised somewhere in the above points that I would return to one of the most important elements of the paper, which is the title. Here I am. The title is extremely important and difficult to build. The energy-growth nexus typically involved titles that describe (i) the main variables of interest, namely, energy and economic growth or other crucial covariates, (ii) the involved countries, and (iii) the employed methodology. This is an exact mirror of the paper and can help readers trace your paper when they seek papers in this field. However, the tendency nowadays is to use "sexy" titles. Titles that include a promise, a mystery, an intriguing question that the paper attempts to answer, and it does answer it or does not eventually. Sometimes, good papers are doomed just because their title is not promising enough. So, be aware of that and observe what your paper eventually concludes and pose that as a title. However, those papers, albeit promising, they cannot help readers discern them from some distance. When one is looking for papers in a certain field and he does that with a sole criterion being the title, then he such an entitled paper may escape him/her.

V

Twenty-third: Writing not only is a talent but also can be skill that can be cultivated. Unless you are proficient in English language and its technical writing, it is advisable to ask a professional to read your paper and make language corrections. This is not too expensive and will save you from redundant paper rejections or major revisions. The best choice of a technical editor is a person not only with an excellent command of English but also with a sound background at energy economics.

When I write a paper, I hate interruptions. I am a mother of two children, and I also have two dogs. Interruptions are my daily main dish! However, when I start writing a paper, I put this task above all, and I do not assume new ones, unless I finish this. Most of the times, I try to write on a daily basis until I finish. The first weeks are really difficult, and I am slow because I read a lot. Then, as weeks go by, research results are articulated in a text form, and the story takes a full body that gradually needs only format and embellishment. It is almost impossible that you stay uninterrupted in your writing process. However, even if interruption are there, try to write a little bit every day. Even if that bit is only a short paragraph, this is net benefit at the end of the day.

W

Finding a journal where you can submit is a tiring process. Usually the references you have used in your paper are a good indicator of where to submit. There are plenty of journals in the energy-growth field, but there is also voluminous ongoing research; thus the journals are seething with new submissions. Sometimes, papers are directly rejected by an editor (desk rejected) either because they are not good papers or because they are good papers but the field no longer interests the journal. Since each paper may have different submission guidelines, which may require a restructure of the paper and references, I have a preference for submission with the same publishing house. For example, it is highly convenient to submit at Elsevier journals, which have adopted the "Your paper, Your way." This gives author the ability to change references only at the final stage when the paper is finally accepted for publication.

X

Some journals require that the author gives names of potential reviewers for his submitted paper. Some authors recommend those names based on their own circle of colleagues, experts, and peers, while others do that on the basis of the references they have used on their paper. Namely, the find the details of the authors whom they have cited in their paper and recommend them. Some journals use the suggestions made by the author. Others do not, but they keep collecting this information to enlarge their reviewer database. The energy-growth nexus is a huge field, and reviewers are plenty. Other rare research topics with only a handful or researchers worldwide may find the strategy of reviewer suggestion by the author very functioning for the fulfillment of the review process. So, it is highly improbable that the editor (assigned with your submission) will follow your own reviewer name suggestions. But do not worry about that. Trust the merit of your work.

Y

Various journals have various submission specificities. One very common requirement, however, is the compilation and submission of a cover letter. The cover letter can be directly written within an indicated space in the submission platform or it can be uploaded in a separate file. Although most of the times the cover letter says nothing more than your notification of submission and the expectation of a review, you can also add some short detail that will catch the attention of the editor in a positive way. The editor is a very busy person, he can also make mistakes. Thus, if you have something to say that will help him/her discern your paper from the bulk of the other submissions, say it. Nicely and politely.

Z

After the paper has returned from review (this can take quite some time in some of the journals that host energy-growth papers), you will receive a verdict. You will feel lucky if your paper has not be rejected. You may be assigned a lot of corrections or few of them. Irrespective of their number and implementation difficulty, I suggest that you follow them one by one and address them seriously with much respect and gratitude for the time the reviewer spent reading and correcting your work. It is not guaranteed that your paper will be accepted after the submission of the revised paper, even if you feel you have answered everything. With my experience as an energy-growth researcher and author, my papers have been reviewed by experts and sometimes by nonexperts. Sometimes, I found funny and absolutely straightforward the comments I received. Sometimes, I felt the reviewer had less knowledge than me and could not understand my answers. Therefore, you need to develop your answers to reviewers' comments in a very detailed way, either to show the reviewer that you know what you are doing or to teach him/her in a kind way about what you are doing. There is not such good news as "Your paper has been accepted" email. This is heaven. Soon afterward you will be sent the proofs of your paper for inspection, and within some time you will receive notification about its final publication in the journal with details about the volume and page numbers. Also, we you will be able to find your paper in international databases. Do not forget to gain as much publicity as you can for your paper through academic social media and various other sources you will gradually discover.

3 Closing remarks

Instead of a conclusion or even concluding remarks, I opt to close my list of advice in this chapter with the following few lines: I hope these 26 pieces of advice will help you tremendously to pave the way toward your personalized research and writing style. I wish they save you valuable time to be spend to crucial issues in the energy-growth nexus such as the comparability of results among studies and their connection to policy making, which as the two main thorns.

References

Ahmad, N., Menegaki, A.N., 2020. Systematic literature review of tourism growth nexus: an overview of the literature and a content analysis of 100 most influential papers. J. Econ. Surv. (forthcoming).

Aria, M., Cuccurullo, C., 2017. Bibliometrix: an R-tool for comprehensive science mapping analysis. J. Informetr. 11 (4), 959–975.

Harzing, A.-W., Alakangas, S., 2016. Google scholar, scopus and the web of science: a longitudinal and cross-disciplinary comparison. Scientometrics 106 (2), 787–804.

Harzing, A.W., Van Der Wal, R., 2009. A Google scholar h-index for journals: an alternative metric to measure journal impact in economics and business. J. Am. Soc. Inf. Sci. Technol. 60 (1), 41–46.

Menegaki, A.N., Tiwari, A.K., 2020. The Stability of Interaction Channels Between Tourism and Financial Development in Selected Top Tourism Destinations. Evidence From a Fourier Toda Yamamoto Estimator (April 2, 2020).

Tiwari, A.K., Forte, A., Garcia-Donato, G., Menegaki, A.N., 2018. Practical issues on energy-growth nexus data and variable selection with Bayesian analysis. In: The Economics and Econometrics of the Energy-Growth Nexus. Elsevier, Academic Publishing, UK and USA, pp. 187–227.

Further reading

Menegaki, A.N., Tsani, S., 2018. Critical issues to be answered in the energy-growth nexus (EGN) research field. In: The Economics and Econometrics of the Energy-Growth Nexus. Elsevier, Academic Publishing, UK and USA, pp. 141–184.

Tsani, S., Menegaki, A.N., 2018. The energy-growth nexus (EGN) checklist for authors. In: The Economics and Econometrics of the Energy-Growth Nexus. Elsevier, Academic Publishing, UK and USA, pp. 347–376.

A conclusion to the guide in energy-growth nexus

16

The energy-growth nexus is a research field that has been at the forefront of energy economics in the last 20 years, but its origins were placed by Kraft and Kraft almost 40 years ago with a simple but neat paper entitled: Kraft, J., Kraft, A. (1978), On the relationship between energy and GNP. *The Journal of Energy and Development*, 3 (2), 401–403. Since that seminal paper and due to the oil crises and ascending energy prices together with the worries about climate change and the progress in environmental economics, the energy-growth nexus field has gained the academic attention of many researchers, because it gives answers to what if scenarios about economic growth when energy consumption is reduced.

The increasing environmental awareness after the realization that humanity had reached a dead end from fueling its economic growth through increasing energy consumption led to the stipulation of various international agreements and deadlines about the introduction of measures and behaviors that aim to reduce fossil energy consumption and increase energy efficiency, also replacing fossil energy with renewable energy wherever possible.

The research on the energy-growth nexus aims to generate answers about the economic impact of energy consumption, and through this research, we have identified (i) economies that will not experience an impact in their economic growth through the reduction of energy consumption (this constitutes evidence for the conservation hypothesis); (ii) economies whose economic growth will be at serious stake if energy consumption is reduced, because they can fuel their growth only through more and more energy consumption (this constitutes evidence for the growth hypothesis); (iii) economies whose economic growth is heavily dependent on energy consumption and the latter is mutually dependent on economic growth; and last (iv) economies that exhibit no relationship whatsoever between energy consumption and economic growth (this constitutes evidence for the feedback hypothesis). The situations described from (i) to (iv) are the so-called four hypotheses whose investigation belongs to the typical results reported in an energy-growth nexus research paper.

While the inauguration of the energy-growth nexus research field took place through the investigation of a bivariate relationship between energy and economic growth, through the years, this nexus followed the evolution of time series data and panel data modeling and has been investigated with numerous methods, approaches, and tests. The number of variables inserted as covariates or the variety

307

A Guide to Econometric Methods for the Energy-Growth Nexus. https://doi.org/10.1016/B978-0-12-819039-5.00012-4

of variables used as proxies for economic growth in the energy-growth relationship has also increased, and the nature of variables has given new and endless food for thought.

At the same time, researchers become continuously more meticulous and disaggregate energy consumption either by fuel and source or by sector. All these thoughts and experimentation have generated a vast research body that has happened to produce contradictive results in some occasions and thus cannot lead policy decisions unequivocally and safely. Thus future research is required and maybe in a more coordinated way so that researchers reach an understanding on how much their results are due to the substance (viz., the underlying relationship) and how much is due to the econometric methodology and data choices. Therefore literature reviews and metaanalyses or systematic reviews have been produced to give the general pulse, sketch the trends, and show the ways out. In my humble opinion the energy-growth nexus field is at crossroads and must be led to its new directions through some kind of central planning. Let's assume that the world academia had 10 research groups that worked on the energy-growth nexus. These 10 groups meet with each other every year at an annual conference. With the help of a central planner, they are allocated datasets and are asked to work with a specific methodology. Or they are asked to work on the same dataset with a variety of methodologies. Then the research groups work for a year and meet again the following year and compare results across datasets and methodologies. This process should be repeated for several years until some reliable results are reached about the comparability of results that originate from different methods and data sources. Unless this does not happen, policy makers will not be able to benefit from this research field in full and in a reliable way.

Similar to the energy-growth nexus research field are the tourism-growth nexus, the environment-growth nexus, or other fields that I have termed as "X-variable-growth nexus," and they keep pace with the energy-growth nexus on ambiguity and controversy of results.

When a new researcher enters the energy-growth nexus field or the "X-growth nexus field," he or she becomes overwhelmed with the volume of research and methodologies. After so many years of research in the field, still there were no books that could give new researchers a yardstick, a reference point, or a boat to start navigation. My book entitled "The Economics and the Econometrics of the Energy-Growth Nexus" was the first book in the field that was published in 2018 by Elsevier (Academic Publishing) and then gave the impetus for additional books in the field or other subfields of the broad energy-growth nexus.

However, all these books have been collected volumes with the latest work been done by established scholars in the field. Personally, I wanted to write a book that would be always by the desktop of each new energy-growth researcher and would help him or her quickly to get on track of mature research. Instead of spending much time learning and gathering material or taking helpful notes for various aspects that one must have in mind while working in the energy-growth nexus field, this book would serve as a first aid kit, as a book of first reference that equips researchers with the fundamental tools and thus empowers then to go out for the most difficult aspects of further research and continue drive the field forward.

Thus this book is destined for graduate students, people who are doing their masters or writing a masters' thesis, or they are already new ambitious PhD students who have been fascinated by the energy-growth nexus field and dream of making their contribution therein. It is written in a very simple form ad contains many examples and applications. It has been divided into 16 chapters with this conclusion counting as one of them.

The structure of this book has been the following:

Chapter 1. Introduction to the econometrics of the energy-growth nexus: An overview of new challenges
This chapter was an introductive chapter that has updated new energy-growth researchers with what energy economics is concerned with today. This chapter will equip new researchers with all the up-to-date knowledge in energy economics, and this in turn will cause new questions whose answer will be pursued.

Chapter 2. Stationarity and an alphabetical directory of the unit roots often used in the energy-growth nexus
As the title suggests, this chapter highlights the importance of stationarity and reviews the vast variety of unit root tests employed in the energy-growth nexus literature. Although there are several tests that are used by most studies in the field, there are a vast number of them, each addressing a specialized feature of the energy-growth nexus dataset.

Chapter 3. The ARDL approach: An all-inclusive method for the X-growth nexus
Numerous studies in the energy-growth nexus and other X-variable nexus studies such as the tourism-growth nexus, the environment-growth nexus, or the food-growth nexus have used the ARDL bounds test approach for cointegration. However, these papers rarely include all the ARDL procedure steps in a detailed way, and thus they leave junior researchers puzzled with the series of steps that must be followed and the best-practice examples that need to be followed to receive the least possible number of negative comments by journal reviewers due to the obscure aspects they leave. This chapter also suggests the steps that need to be taken before the ARDL procedure takes place and the steps that should be taken afterward with respect to causality investigation and robust analysis.

Chapter 4. The VECM approach in the variable X-growth nexus analysis
A lot of papers in the energy-growth nexus have been entitled with this approach and claim to be using the vector error correction method approach. This approach is not used alone, and although it is mostly centered on short-term causality discussions, it gives the impression that it can be used alone in the energy-growth

nexus literature. However, the truth is not as such, and the method is used in complementarity with VAR formulations and other cointegration analyses. Since this is a first aid chapter on the implementation of the VECM approach on the energy-growth nexus, various important points are summarized to enable junior energy-growth researchers on what to expect to read and find in such an entitled paper and for reviewers to recapitulate quickly the discussion on the results from such a method so that they can become quickly ready for the evaluation of such papers.

Chapter 5. Adjustment speeds, elasticities, and semielasticities: Their importance in the variable X-growth nexus

A lot of papers in the energy-growth nexus have been entitled with this approach and claim to be using the vector error correction method approach. This approach is not used alone, and although it is mostly centered on short-term causality discussions, it gives the impression that it can be used alone in the energy-growth nexus literature. However, the truth is not as such, and the method is used in complementarity with VAR formulations and other cointegration analyses. Since this is a first aid chapter on the implementation of the VECM approach on the energy-growth nexus, various important points are summarized to enable junior energy-growth researchers on what to expect to read and find in such an entitled paper and for reviewers to recapitulate quickly the discussion on the results from such a method so that they can become quickly ready for the evaluation of such papers.

Chapter 6. Quantile regression approach: A new approach in the variable X-growth nexus with substantial benefits for asymmetric accounting

Aberrant behaviors in energy consumption are to be expected due to the institutional, economic, and geographical differences across countries and the different degree of resilience of the countries to extreme events in climate change. For this reason the energy-growth nexus modeling may be confronted with more complex data and may require more sophisticated techniques to cope with this new realization and era. Besides the involuntary changes in energy patterns that may happen to unforeseen circumstances stemming from global warming and climate change, there are also desired and intentional changes implied by energy conservation targets that appear and require our complying with them, due to an energy transition required to cope with environmental damages and resource scarcity. However, not all countries or sectors will be free of economic growth setbacks if they embark on this route. The quantile regression is claimed to reveal more information regarding extreme events or outliers in data and therefore could contribute to the provision of more solid policy information, something which we are far from in the energy-growth nexus, particularly due to the controversy and the contradicting results encountered in many energy-growth nexus studies. This chapter is going to explain for new researchers in the energy-growth nexus and what the nature of the quantile regression is and will provide an overview of the way it has been used up to date. The chapter will focus on the particular aspects the method has addressed so far and the challenges that the method poses for this particular field.

Chapter 7. Time-varying Fourier analysis in the variable X-growth nexus
The inconclusive evidence and contradictive results in the field of the energy-growth economics, despite the vast amount of studies, lead researchers to the employment of more sophisticated methods that may throw additional light or may provide a renewed perspective from which to study the energy-growth relationship. The Fourier analysis regards the relationship as a bunch of sine and cosine waves with various frequencies and phases. Therefore Fourier analysis allows researchers identify the frequencies of the relationship together with their magnitude and phase. This intrinsic characteristic of the Fourier series may enlighten cases of series with structural breaks, cross-sectional dependence, or autocorrelation that make the series and the energy-growth relationship move in oscillations.

Chapter 8 The cross-sectional dependence in the variable X-growth nexus data and its remedies
This chapter explains the problem of cross-sectional dependence in the energy-growth nexus, the ways with which it is examined and solved, and the reasons why this problem occurs in the energy-growth nexus. Notwithstanding that cross-sectional dependence is an inevitable situation as globalization grows, it should not be taken for granted either. The chapter encloses four case studies and shows the seriousness of the problem and how it has been handled by various researchers. It also adds a case study from the tourism-growth nexus and shows how the older energy-growth nexus can inform the tourism-growth nexus and the more general X-variable-growth nexus.

Chapter 9. Simultaneous equation modeling in the variable X-growth nexus
This chapter reveals the low usage of simultaneous equation modeling (SEM) in the energy-growth nexus literature with a few hints on the basic econometric tools used in this framework. Despite the high potential and theoretical justifications of the SEM, this framework remains underutilized in the energy-growth nexus field, and this fact may be attributed to the lack of sufficient theoretical underpinnings in the energy-growth nexus that fail to safely characterize the involved variables as purely endogenous or clearly exogenous. Foremost the chapter will serve as a guide and encouragement for future usage by energy-growth nexus researchers and academics, because this framework is convenient to the dual nature of the energy-growth nexus that can be set up both in a production function orientation and a demand function orientation or/and an emission Kuznets curve orientation. Continuous experimentation in the econometrics of the energy-growth nexus may eventually enrich the relevant theory and start bringing results and researchers in unison.

Chapter 10. The Johansen cointegration method in the variable X-growth nexus
Numerous studies in the energy-growth nexus and other "X-variable" nexus studies such as the tourism-growth nexus, the environment-growth nexus, or the food-growth nexus have used various approaches to test cointegration. While the ARDL remains the flagship of cointegration methods, other methods had evolved

before the ARDL method and some after it, and they too grasp different aspects of cointegration. This chapter presents the essentials of the Johansen-Juselius method of cointegration together with other methods and variants. The chapter does not only aim to show the evolution of these methods in time, but most importantly, it equips new researchers with the whole array of methods, because older methods have not been abandoned from researchers and they are still in use alone or together with other methods in the same piece of research, for reasons of corroboration.

Chapter 11. The wavelet transformation approach in the "variable X-growth nexus" analysis

New methodologies enter the energy-growth nexus field in an attempt to make its results more accurate and elaborate. One such methodology is the wavelet approach counting already a few examples in the energy-growth nexus. However, the energy-growth empirical works seem to use the method in a fragmented and piecemeal way, and thus energy-growth researchers do not yet have a complete picture of the method as used nowadays in the field. This chapter aims to explain the basic theory of the wavelet approach, the reasons that led to the advent of this method in the nexus, and how it addresses the claimed problems. The chapter does not involve complicated mathematical formulae, but explains the method in down to earth words. For researchers who are lured by the method but would like to refrain from tedious and intimidating mathematics, this chapter equips them with the background knowledge that is necessary to survive everyday readings, when one comes across such papers in the energy-growth nexus. The chapter also presents various case studies and discusses the virtues and drawbacks of the method vis-à-vis the required deliverables of the studies in this field.

Chapter 12. Variance decomposition approaches in the "variable X-growth nexus" analysis

New methodologies enter the energy-growth nexus field in an attempt to make its results more accurate and elaborate. One such methodology is the wavelet approach counting already a few examples in the energy-growth nexus. However, the energy-growth empirical works seem to use the method in a fragmented and piecemeal way, and thus energy-growth researchers do not yet have a complete picture of the method as used nowadays in the field. This chapter aims to explain the basic theory of the wavelet approach, the reasons that led to the advent of this method in the nexus, and how it addresses the claimed problems. The chapter does not involve complicated mathematical formulae, but explains the method in down to earth words. For researchers who are lured by the method but would like to refrain from tedious and intimidating mathematics, this chapter equips them with the background knowledge that is necessary to survive everyday readings, when one comes across such papers in the energy-growth nexus. The chapter also presents various case studies and discusses the virtues and drawbacks of the method vis-à-vis the required deliverables of the studies in this field.

Chapter 13. Parametric versus nonparametric analysis in the "variable X-growth" nexus

The knowledge that a statistical population does not have a normal distribution drives researchers to the usage of nonparametric analysis. Sometimes, normality is assumed or imposed, and it is not allocated a proper slot for investigation in the energy-growth nexus studies. Foremost, there is not a consensus on reviewers in the field, come require it as a very important starting point in the analysis—as it should be—and some do not. This chapter summarizes the main points that the energy-growth nexus new researcher should have in mind for this serious but a bit neglected topic. Conforming to the aims and objectives of this book, the chapter will serve as a first aid kit for new researchers who need to be reminded the essentials of their topic together with some quick reference examples from energy-growth nexus studies that have employed nonparametric analysis or semiparametric analysis vis-à-vis the parametric ones.

Chapter 14. Guidelines for a metaanalysis: A very important tool in the "variable X-growth nexus

This chapter deals with the importance of metaanalysis in the energy-growth nexus and provides useful guidelines that must be followed for the metaanalysis to become verbose and successful. It analyzes the four identified pieces of energy-growth nexus research that have implemented a metaanalysis so far and suggests useful variables and methods and recapitulates the lessons from them. Given that the energy-growth nexus field is quite controversial, the implementation of a comprehensive metaanalysis will generate a global theoretical relationships, which will start be examined in the future by energy-growth academicians. Therefore this chapter recommends a continuously updated metaanalytical relationship, which will keep stakeholders steadily informed.

Chapter 15. An A-Z guide for the new entrant in the "variable X-growth" nexus field

This chapter aims to help new energy-growth researchers to develop order in their research by following golden research rules by peers. These rules are a product of ongoing experience, and the reason they are shared in this chapter is for the quick establishment of basic research and writing skill background that will lead new researchers to a direct and huge leap onward toward the net evolution of the energy-growth nexus field. The chapter is articulated in exactly 26 steps or pieces of advice (A-Z) that will boost the confidence of new energy-growth researchers a lot. The advice concerns all implementation stages of a new paper in the energy-growth nexus from the conception of the initial idea up to the publication of the relevant paper. Foremost, this chapter is an indispensable tool for postgraduate students writing a relevant master thesis, or they are starting a PhD degree.

Chapter 16. The conclusion

This chapter recapitulates the book structure and stresses once again the importance and utility of such a book and the reason it was generated.

As the book was being written, more ideas and questions on the implementation of research in the energy-growth nexus have sprung. This means that there is a huge scope of books on this area of support of young researchers and new entrants in such a prolific research field such as the energy-growth nexus or the "X-variable-growth nexus" and while these fields evolve. I genuinely believe that such books will be highly valued by students who specialize in this field.

Acknowledgment

I would like to thank all authors and sources, and particularly Elsevier, who granted me the permissions to use certain graphs and Figures, which enabled myself to build educative case studies necessary for the support of my advice and arguments.

Disclaimer

All errors in the book are of my own.

Index

Note: Page numbers followed by *f* indicate figures, *t* indicate tables and *b* indicate boxes.

Printed in the United States
By Bookmasters